Child and
Youth Security
SOURCEBOOK

Security Reference Series

Child and Youth Security SOURCEBOOK

Basic Information for General Readers about Protecting Children and Youth from Drug and Substance Abuse, Sexual and Violent Crime, Family Offenses, Peer Conflict, Mental Health Risks, Juvenile Delinquency, and School and Campus Unrest, including Information for Students, Resources for Parents, and Strategies for Educators

Along with Statistics, Recovery Programs for Young Victims of Violence, a Glossary of Related Terms, and Resources for Further Information

Edited by Chad T. Kimball

615 Griswold Street • Detroit, MI 48226

Bibliographic Note

Because this page cannot legibly accommodate all the copyright notices, the Bibliographic Note portion of the Preface constitutes an extension of the copyright notice.

Edited by Chad T. Kimball

Security Reference Series

Chad T. Kimball, *Series Editor*
Peter D. Dresser, *Managing Editor*
Elizabeth Barbour, *Permissions Associate*
Dawn Matthews, *Verification Assistant*
Laura Pleva Nielsen, *Index Editor*
EdIndex, Services for Publishers, *Indexers*

* * *

Omnigraphics, Inc.

Matthew P. Barbour, *Senior Vice President*
Kay Gill, *Vice President—Directories*
Kevin Hayes, *Operations Manager*
Leif Gruenberg, *Development Manager*
David P. Bianco, *Marketing Consultant*

* * *

Peter E. Ruffner, *Publisher*

Frederick G. Ruffner, Jr., *Chairman*

Copyright © 2003 Omnigraphics, Inc.

ISBN 0-7808-0613-1

Library of Congress Cataloging-in-Publication Data

Child and youth security sourcebook : basic information for general readers about protecting children and youth from drug and substance abuse, sexual and violent crime, family offenses, peer conflict, mental health risks, juvenile delinquency, and school and campus unrest, including information for students, resources for parents, and strategies for educators, along with statistics, recovery programs for young victims of violence, a glossary of related terms, and resources for further information / edited by Chad T. Kimball.-- 1st ed.
    p.cm. -- (Security reference series)
    Includes bibliographical references and index.
    ISBN 0-7808-0613-8
    1. Children--Crimes against--United States--Prevention. 2. Youth--Crimes against--United States--Prevention. I. Kimball, Chad T. II. Series

HV6250.4.C48C43 2003
362.7--dc21

                                                                    2002045010

Table of Contents

v

Part III: Protection from Child Abuse and Neglect

Part IV: Protection from Sexual Abuse

Part V: Missing and Abducted Children

Part VI: Protection from Youth Substance Abuse

Part VII: Protection from Social Harm

Part VIII: Protection from Youth Mental and Emotional Health Risks

Part IX: Additional Help and Information

Preface

About This Book

Recent reports show that one in five young people are afraid of attending school because of the threat of various crimes. Seven out of ten crimes committed against young people occur at school, in their home neighborhood, or at a nearby park or playground. In addition to these dangers, many children face threats of abuse and other offenses at home.

The Child and Youth Security Sourcebook provides important information for students, parents, and educators about protecting children and youth from substance abuse, crime and violence in school and in the community, juvenile delinquency, gangs, school and campus unrest, and peer conflict. This *Sourcebook* also presents information regarding offenses and dangers in the home, including abuse and neglect, child care maltreatment, and child witnesses of sexual and violent crimes. Special sections include statistics, recovery programs for young victims of violence, a glossary of related terms, and resources for further information.

Other books produced by Omnigraphics provide additional information about health, safety, and security concerns in children and youth. They include the following:

- *Adolescent Health Sourcebook* discusses health issues related specifically to adolescent children;

- *Childhood Diseases and Disorders Sourcebook* offers information regarding various health problems that occur primarily in pre-adolescent children;

- *Domestic Violence and Child Abuse Sourcebook* gives the reader in-depth information about violence and abuse in the home, including various forms of child abuse;

- *Drug Information for Teens* provides students with facts about drug use, abuse, and addiction;

- *Healthy Children Sourcebook* includes helpful information about the physical and mental development of children between the ages of 3 and 12, focusing on prevention of childhood diseases and disorders;

- *Infant and Toddler Health Sourcebook* contains detailed information about the physical and mental development of newborns, infants, and toddlers;

- *Pediatric Cancer Sourcebook* describes cancers that occur most commonly in children.

How to Use This Book

This book is divided into parts and chapters. Parts focus on broad areas of interest. Chapters are devoted to single topics within a part.

Part I: Introduction to Violent Crime and Youth outlines statistics and general background information on child victims and witnesses of violent crime and gun violence. It also offers general tips for protecting children and youth from crime.

Part II: Protection from School Crime and Violence discusses ways to prevent and protect children from school crime and violence. It also addresses concerns about bullies, fear based truancy, school shootings, and getting to and from school safely.

Part III: Protection from Child Abuse and Neglect defines various forms of child abuse and neglect and discusses how to report and respond to a disclosure of abuse. Information on child fatalities from abuse, shaken baby syndrome, proper discipline techniques, and choosing safe child care are also presented.

Part IV: Protection from Sexual Abuse explores ways to teach children to avoid sexual abuse, offers advice regarding parenting a sexually abused child, and discusses youth sex offenders, dating violence, and date rape drugs.

Part V: Missing and Abducted Children presents statistics on missing children and provides advice on what to do if your child is missing. It also offers information on preventing domestic and international child and infant abduction as well as parental abduction.

Part VI: Protection from Youth Substance Abuse describes ways to teach children to avoid drugs and discusses how to detect and address suspected youth drug abuse. Information about alcohol, tobacco, marijuana, and other drugs are also provided.

Part VII: Protection from Social Harm gives an overview of conflict resolution and delinquency prevention techniques, including mentoring, peer mediation, and diversity training. Tips are presented for preventing harm from Internet sex offenders, media violence, gangs, and witnessing violence or natural disasters.

Part VIII: Protection from Youth Mental and Emotional Health Risks discusses the management of youth mental disorders, depression, suicide, and childhood aggression.

Part IX: Additional Help and Information includes a glossary of child and youth security-related terms, a list of recovery programs for young victims of violence, a directory of resources, and a list of references for additional reading.

Bibliographic Note

This volume contains documents and excerpts from publications issued by the following U.S. government agencies: Administration on Children, Youth and Families; ArmyLINK News; Bi-Partisan Working Group on Youth Violence; Centers for Disease Control and Prevention (CDC); Consumer Product Safety Commission; Federal Bureau of Investigation (FBI); National Clearinghouse on Child Abuse and Neglect Information; National Highway Traffic Safety Administration; National Institute of Child Health and Human Development; National Institute of Mental Health (NIMH); National Institute on Alcohol Abuse and Alcoholism (NIAAA); National Institute on Drug Abuse; National Institutes of Health (NIH); National Women's Health Information Center; Office of Justice Programs, Office for Victims of Crime; Office of Juvenile Justice and Delinquency Prevention; Office of Juvenile Justice and Delinquency Prevention; U.S. Department of Education; U.S. Department of Justice; U.S. Department of State; and the U.S. Drug Enforcement Administration.

In addition, this volume contains copyrighted documents from the following organizations, individuals, and publications: A.D.A.M., Inc.; American Academy of Child and Adolescent Psychiatry; American Humane Association; Anti-Defamation League; California Governor's Office of Criminal Justice Planning; Canadian Hockey Association; Coalition for Children, Inc.; Health Canada; Jackie Reilly. M.S.; James Chandler, M.D., FRCPC; Karen DeBord, PhD; Minister of Public Works and Government Services Canada; Myria Media, Inc.; National Association of Child Care Resource and Referral Agencies; National Crime Prevention Council (NCPC); National Institute on Media and Family; National Parent Teacher Association (National PTA); Nemours Foundation; Richard Niolon, Ph.D.; Sally S. Martin, Ph.D.; University of Nevada Cooperative Extension; VAWnet (National Electronic Network on Violence against Women).

Full citation information is provided on the first page of each chapter. Every effort has been made to secure all necessary rights to reprint the copyrighted material. If any omissions have been made, please contact Omnigraphics to make corrections for future editions.

Acknowledgements

In addition to the organizations, agencies, and individuals listed above, special thanks go to many others who worked behind the scenes to help bring this book to fruition. The editor wants to give special thanks to Karen Bellenir for her production support and editorial consultation and to Jacki Bustos for her editorial assistance.

Part One

Introduction to
Violent Crime and Youth

Chapter 1

Child Victims of Violent Crime

Introduction

When we hear the term "juvenile crime" or "youth violence," we tend to think of juveniles primarily as offenders, not victims. This chapter, derived from *Juvenile Offenders and Victims: 1999 National Report*, documents the impact of crime on society's most vulnerable victims—children.

Juveniles are twice as likely as adults to be victims of serious violent crime and three times as likely to be victims of assault. Many of these victims are quite young. Law enforcement data indicate that 1 in 18 victims of violent crime is under age 12. In one-third of the sexual assaults reported to law enforcement, the victim is under age 12. In most cases involving serious violent crime, juvenile victims know the perpetrator, who is not the stereotypical "stranger," but a family member or acquaintance.

Children with a history of maltreatment experience increased risk factors for delinquency. In addition, maltreatment and victimization can damage self-esteem, demolish families, and destroy futures. The statistics highlighted in this chapter should act as an urgent call to communities, schools, juvenile justice agencies, courts, families, and others to make combating crimes against children a priority.

Excerpted from "Children as Victims," Office of Juvenile Justice and Delinquency Prevention, Office of Justice Programs, U.S. Department of Justice, http://www.ncjrs.org/html/ojjdp/2000_5_2/contents.html, May 2000.

Between 1980 and 1997, Nearly 38,000 Juveniles Were Murdered in the U.S.

The Federal Bureau of Investigation (FBI) Maintains Detailed Records on Murders in the U.S.

The FBI's Uniform Crime Reporting Program asks local law enforcement agencies to provide detailed information on all homicides. These Supplementary Homicide Reports (SHR's) capture information on victim and offender demographics, the victim-offender relationship, the weapon used, and the circumstances surrounding the crime. The FBI estimates that 91% of all homicides committed in the U.S. between 1980 and 1997 were reported to the FBI.

The Number of Murders in 1997 Was the Lowest Since 1971

Estimates from the SHR data show that murders peaked in 1991 with 24,700 victims, or a rate of nearly 10 murders for every 100,000 persons living in the U.S. While the number of murders was high, rates similar to the 1991 rate were experienced in other years since 1970 (e.g., 1974, 1979, 1980, 1981).

Between 1991 and 1997, the number of murders dropped 26%, to 18,200, or about 7 murders for every 100,000 persons living in the U.S. The number of murders had not been this low since 1971, and the murder rate had not been this low since 1968.

Murders of Juveniles Remain High

In the U.S., one of the leading causes of death for juveniles is homicide. In 1997, the National Center for Health Statistics listed homicide as the fourth leading cause of death for children ages 1 to 4, third for youth ages 5 to 14, and second for persons ages 15 to 24.

The number of juveniles murdered peaked in 1993 at 2,900, about 4 murders for every 100,000 persons under age 18 living in the U.S. By 1997, this figure had dropped to 2,100, or about 3 murders per 100,000 juveniles. Unlike the pattern of all murders, however, the number of juvenile murders in 1997 was still substantially above the levels of the mid-1980's, when about 1,600 juveniles were murdered annually.

In 1997, about Six Juveniles Were Murdered Daily

Of all persons murdered in 1997, 11% were under the age of 18. Of these 2,100 juvenile murder victims in 1997:

- 33% were under age 6 and 50% were ages 15 through 17

- 30% were female

- 47% were black

- 56% were killed with a firearm

- 40% (among those whose murderers were identified) were killed by family members, 45% by acquaintances, and 15% by strangers

The murders of younger and older juveniles had different characteristics. Compared with youth under age 12, older juvenile victims in 1997 were more likely to be male (81% vs. 55%) and black (53% vs. 39%). Family members killed a greater proportion of younger rather than older juvenile victims (70% vs. 10%). Offenders with firearms killed a larger proportion of older rather than younger juveniles (83% vs. 16%).

Juveniles Ages 12–17 Are as Likely to Be Victims of Serious Violence as Are Young Adults Ages 18–24

Juveniles and Young Adults Have the Greatest Risk of Victimization

The National Crime Victimization Survey (NCVS) asks individuals whether they have been the victim of a crime, and from their responses generates victimization rates for various demographic groups. These rates reflect the number of victimizations reported per equivalent-size population units (e.g., aggravated assault victimizations per 1,000 persons ages 12–17).

In 1995 and 1996, victimization rates for serious violent crimes (i.e., rape, robbery, aggravated assault) varied substantially across age groups. Senior citizens had much lower victimization rates than young adults ages 18–24. In fact, within the adult population, these young adults had the highest victimization rates for rape, robbery, and aggravated assault.

The serious violent crime victimization rates for juveniles were roughly equivalent to those for young adults, while the simple assault victimization rate for juveniles was triple that for young adults. Overall, juveniles were at greater risk of violent victimizations in 1995 and 1996 than even the most victimized age group of adults.

5

Juvenile Victims Are Likely to Know Their Offender

In 1996, juveniles ages 12–17 who were the victims of a serious violent crime knew their offenders in 64% of these victimizations: 18% of victimizations involved an acquaintance, 34% a friend, and 11% a relative. In the other 36% of victimizations, the offender was a stranger. The offender was more likely to be known to the juvenile victim in simple and aggravated assaults (73% and 70%, respectively) than in robberies (45%).

Most serious violent juvenile victimizations (60%) involved only a single offender. Multiple offenders were more likely in juvenile robberies (46%) and aggravated assaults (41%) than in simple assaults (22%). Juveniles were injured in 74% of serious violent victimizations. Juveniles were more likely to be injured as the result of a robbery (61%) or aggravated assault (80%) than a simple assault (45%).

Most Victimizations of Juveniles Are Not Reported to Police

In 1996, about half (48%) of the serious violent victimizations of juveniles were not reported to police or any other authority (e.g., teachers, school principals). Victims reported 33% of serious violent victimizations directly to police; victims reported 19% to some other authority, and about one-third of these incidents were subsequently reported to law enforcement. Therefore, law enforcement eventually learned of about 4 of every 10 serious violent juvenile victimizations, including about 25% of simple assaults, 40% of aggravated assaults, and 44% of robberies. Juvenile victims in 36% of robberies, 50% of aggravated assaults, and 52% of simple assaults never reported the incident to either police or other officials.

In One-Third of All Sexual Assaults Reported to Law Enforcement, the Victim Was Younger than Age 12

1 in 18 Victims of a Violent Crime Known to Police Is under Age 12

The FBI's National Incident-Based Reporting System (NIBRS) data indicate that between 1991 and 1996, young juveniles (persons under the age of 12) were the victim in 5.5% of all violent crime incidents reported to a law enforcement agency. Young juvenile victims were more common in some types of crimes than others: kidnaping (21%), sexual assault (32%), robbery (2%), aggravated assault (4%), and simple assault (4%). More than one-third (37%) of these young victims were younger than age 7. About half (47%) of these young victims were female.

1 in 3 Victims of Sexual Assault Is under Age 12

NIBRS is an important source of information on the sexual assaults of young children, a crime that is hard to assess through victim surveys. These data point to large differences between the younger and older victims of sexual assault. For example, while just 4% of adult sexual assault victims were male, as were 8% of victims ages 12 to 17, 26% of sexual assault victims under age 12 were male. Younger sexual assault victims were also far more likely to have juvenile offenders.

Crime locations also differed by victim age. For adult victims, 57% of sexual assaults occurred in a residence or home, compared with 71% of the sexual assaults against older juveniles and 84% of the sexual assaults of children under age 12.

The relationship of victim to offender also differed by victim age. In sexual assaults of adults, the offender was a stranger in 25% of incidents, a family member in 12%, and an acquaintance in 63%. In contrast, for victims under age 12, the offender was a family member in 47% of incidents, an acquaintance in 49%, and a stranger in just 4%.

The Likelihood of Victims Reporting Crime to Police Varies by Victim Age and the Nature of the Incident

Juveniles Are Less Likely to Report Violent Crimes than Adults Are

Finkelhor and Ormrod's analysis of the National Crime Victimization Survey for 1995 and 1996 studied the variations in the proportion of crime victims reporting to police or other authorities (e.g., guards, school principals). The study revealed that adults were more likely than juveniles to report both completed and attempted violent crime to some authority regardless of the:

- location of the incident

- presence of a weapon

- degree of injury

- age of the perpetrator
- relationship between the victim and perpetrator

Their analysis also revealed that adults and juveniles generally report completed theft offenses to some authority in equal proportions. Juveniles, however, were more likely than adults to report thefts that took place in school and thefts of less valuable items (i.e., items worth less than $250).

Juveniles Are More Likely to Report Some Crimes than Others

Certain factors increase the likelihood that juveniles will report a crime to some official:

- Violent crimes were more likely to be reported when the incident took place at school rather than away from school (49% vs. 41%), resulted in injury rather than did not result in injury (57% vs. 40%), or involved an adult rather than a juvenile perpetrator (51% vs. 42%).

- The relationship between the victim and perpetrator or the presence of a weapon did not influence the probability of a violent incident being reported.

- Theft offenses were more likely to be reported by juveniles when the incident took place at school than away from school (51% vs. 22%) or involved a stranger rather than someone known to the victim (42% vs. 20%). In addition, thefts of items worth more than $250 were more likely to be reported than thefts of items worth less than $250 (49% vs. 38%).

- The proportion of theft offenses reported did not vary by the victim's sex or by whether the perpetrator was an adult or juvenile.

The Proportion of Violent Crimes Reported by Juveniles to the Police Increased with Victim Age

Overall, the proportion of violent crimes reported to any authority ranged between 42% and 48% for each age group between 12 and 17, but the authority to whom the incident was reported varied with the victim's age.

The youngest victims of violence (youth ages 12 and 13) were more likely to report to authorities other than the police. By age 14, a greater proportion of violent crimes were reported to the police (26%) than to other officials (17%). The increasing use of police and the corresponding reduction in use of other authorities continued through age 17.

Regardless of Age, Juveniles Are More Likely to Report Thefts to Authorities Other than Police

Reporting of theft offenses peaked at 44% for 14-year-old victims and declined to 31% for 17-year-old victims. While thefts are more likely to be reported to officials other than police, the proportion reported to the police increased with age, from 7% for 12-year-olds to 14% for youth age 17.

The Number of Children Abused, Neglected, or Endangered Almost Doubled from 1986 to 1993

In 1993, Nearly 3 Million Children Were Maltreated or Endangered

The third National Incidence Study of Child Abuse and Neglect (NIS-3) reported information on children harmed or believed to be harmed by maltreatment in 1993. Child maltreatment includes physical, sexual, and emotional abuse, and physical, emotional, and educational neglect by a caretaker. Victims of maltreatment may die as the result of abuse or neglect or may experience serious or moderate harm. A child may also be in danger of harm as the result of maltreatment, or harm may be inferred when maltreatment is sufficiently severe.

NIS-3 included maltreatment reported to researchers not only by child protective service agencies, but by other investigatory agencies (e.g., police, courts, public health departments) and community institutions (e.g., hospitals, schools, daycare centers, and social service agencies). It did not include cases known only to family members or neighbors.

Most Maltreated Children Were Neglected in 1993

NIS-3 counts each incident of abuse or neglect that occurs. A single child may experience many types of abuse or neglect. In 1993, 70% of maltreated children were victims of neglect, and 43% were victims of abuse. More specifically:

- 47% were physically neglected.

- Almost equal proportions of maltreated children were physically abused (22%), emotionally neglected (21%), and emotionally abused (19%).

- 11% were sexually abused; 14% were educationally neglected.

Types of Maltreatment Were Related to the Characteristics of the Child

The incidence of maltreatment varied by sex and age but not by race or ethnicity:

- The incidence of sexual abuse was almost three times greater among females than males in 1993. In contrast, emotional neglect was more common among males than females.

- The incidence of maltreatment increased more among males than among females between 1986 and 1993 (102% vs. 68%).

- Between 1986 and 1993, the incidence of maltreatment grew among all children except those ages 15–17.

- Moderate injuries were more frequent among older than younger children. Age differences were not found for other levels of injury.

- The incidence of endangerment was greater for younger children (ages 0–11) than older children (ages 15–17) in 1993.

- Children ages 0–2 and 15–17 had the lowest incidence of maltreatment in 1993.

More Maltreatment Was Reported among Lower-Income Families

Children from families with an annual income of less than $15,000 had substantially more maltreatment of all types in 1993 than children from families in other income groups. The abuse rate in these lowest-income families was two times the rate in other families, and the neglect rate was more than three times higher. Children in lowest-income families had higher injury rates in every injury category except fatalities.

Children of Single Parents Were at Higher Risk of Maltreatment

The overall risk of maltreatment in 1993 was twice as great for children living with single parents as for children living with both parents. Compared with children living with both parents, children living with single parents were twice as likely to be neglected and were marginally more likely to be abused. Children living with a single parent of either sex experienced a higher incidence of physical and educational neglect than those living with both parents and were marginally more likely to experience emotional neglect. Children from single-parent homes were at greater risk of injury and of being endangered by maltreatment than those living with both parents.

Maltreatment Was Related to Family Size

Children living in larger families (with four or more children) were physically neglected almost three times more often than those living in one-child families and more than twice as often as those living in families with two or three children.

The Majority of Maltreated Children Were Victimized by Their Birth Parents

Birth parents were responsible for the largest proportion of maltreatment victimizations in 1993 (78%), followed by other categories of parents (14%) and other perpetrators (9%). Children victimized by their birth parents were twice as likely to experience neglect as abuse. More specifically, among children victimized by their birth parents:

- The most common forms of maltreatment involved educational neglect (29%), physical neglect (27%), and physical abuse (23%).

- 16% were victims of emotional neglect, 14% were victims of emotional abuse, and 5% were victims of sexual abuse.

In contrast to children victimized by their birth parents, those maltreated by other categories of parents were almost twice as likely to be abused as to be neglected. For example:

- Physical abuse was the most common form of maltreatment (37%).

- One-quarter of these children were victims of sexual abuse.

11

- One-fifth were victims of educational neglect.

- The least common forms of maltreatment involved physical neglect (9%) and emotional abuse (13%).

Most Maltreatment Cases Were Identified by Schools

Because of the large volume of children attending schools, more maltreated children were identified by schools in 1993 than by all other community agencies and institutions combined.

1 in 3 Alleged Maltreatment Cases Was Investigated by Child Protective Service Agencies

Child protective service agencies investigated 33% of the cases known to community agencies and institutions in 1993. The remaining cases either were not reported to child protective service agencies or were reported but not investigated. The highest investigation rates occurred among cases identified by police and sheriff departments (52%), hospitals (46%), and mental health agencies (42%). In contrast, the lowest investigation rates occurred among cases identified by daycare centers (3%) and public health agencies (4%).

Investigations Were More Likely in Cases Involving Abuse than Neglect

Cases in which children were alleged to be physically or sexually abused were investigated by child protective services more frequently than other maltreated children.

Child Protective Service Agencies Received Reports on More than 3 Million Maltreated Children in 1996

About 1.6 Million Child Abuse and Neglect Investigations Were Conducted in 1996

Child protective service agencies conducted investigations on 80% of the estimated 2 million reports of child abuse and neglect in 1996. In 35% of these investigations, the allegation was either substantiated (i.e., the allegation of maltreatment or risk of maltreatment was supported or founded) or indicated (i.e., the allegation could not be substantiated, but there was reason to suspect the child was maltreated or was at risk of maltreatment). More than half (58%) of all investigations were not substantiated or indicated. The remaining 7% were closed without a finding or resulted in another disposition. Detailed data from 11 States indicated that reports from professionals were more likely than those from nonprofessionals to be substantiated or indicated (51% vs. 35%).

Most Perpetrators Were Related to the Victim

The 1996 national summary data on substantiated or indicated maltreatment found the following:

- 52% of victims were female.

- 55% of victims were white, 28% were black, 12% were Hispanic, and 5% were other races.

- 19% of victims were age 2 or younger, 52% were age 7 or younger, and 7% were age 16 or older.

- 80% of perpetrators were parents of the victim.

- An estimated 1,077 children died as the result of maltreatment in 1996.

- About 16% of victims in substantiated or indicated cases were removed from their homes.

Case-Level Data from States Provide a Profile of Victims

Detailed information from States reporting case-level data on victims of substantiated or indicated maltreatment in 1996 found the following:

- Neglect was the most common form of maltreatment found among all age groups (58%).

- Younger children (under age 8) were more likely than older children (age 8 and older) to have been neglected (65% vs. 49%).

- Older victims were more likely than younger victims to have been physically abused (29% vs. 19%) or sexually abused (15% vs. 7%).

- Female victims were three times more likely than males to have experienced sexual abuse (16% vs. 5%) and less likely to have experienced neglect (54% vs. 62%).

- More than half (56%) of fatalities were male.

- White youth were more likely than black youth to be victims of sexual abuse (13% vs. 7%) and less likely to be victims of some form of neglect (58% vs. 70%).

- Death due to child abuse and neglect was found mostly among very young children. Three in four deaths (76%) involved children under age 4.

Chapter 2

Child Witnesses of Violent Crime

Breaking the Cycle of Violence

Invisible Victims: Children Who Witness Violence

In this country, children witness violent crimes on a daily basis, including homicide, rape, assault, and domestic violence. Even when child witnesses do not suffer physical injury, the emotional consequences of viewing or hearing violent acts are severe and long-lasting. In fact, children who witness violence often experience many of the same symptoms and lasting effects as children who are victims of violence themselves, including post-traumatic stress disorder (PTSD).

Although child witnesses to violent crimes are often on the scene when police respond, investigators may overlook both the child's ability to provide information and the child's trauma from witnessing the violence. Adults often minimize or deny the presence of children at the scene while crimes are occurring. However, when children are questioned later about events they witnessed or heard, they are able

This chapter contains text from "Breaking the Cycle of Violence: Recommendations to Improve the Criminal Justice Response to Child Victims and Witnesses," U.S. Department of Justice, Office of Justice Programs, Office for Victims of Crime, http://www.ojp.usdoj.gov/ovc/publications/factshts/monograph.htm, June 1999, and "Safe from the Start, Taking Action on Children Exposed to Violence," U.S. Department of Justice, Office of Justice Programs, Office of Juvenile Justice and Delinquency Prevention, http://www.ncjrs.org/pdffiles1/ojjdp/182789.pdf, November 2000.

to provide, depending on their stage of development, a detailed description of the events. It is not uncommon for adults—even some mental health professionals—to minimize the impact on children of witnessing violence and fail to provide appropriate intervention. Caretakers may mistakenly believe that young children will forget about the violent event if they are left alone and not reminded of it. On the contrary, children need to talk about what they saw and their perceptions of the consequences. Further, child victims and witnesses need to be free from intimidation and persuasion aimed at pressuring them to change their description of events.

While exact numbers are not available, it is clear that each year hundreds of thousands, if not millions, of children witness domestic violence and are present in many domestic violence incidents to which police agencies respond. It is estimated that physical abuse of children occurs in between a third and half of domestic violence situations involving abuse of the mother. Children who are present during domestic violence are at an increased risk for being murdered or physically injured. Children who are exposed to domestic violence experience feelings of terror, isolation, guilt, helplessness, and grief. Many children exhibit psychosomatic complaints such as headaches, stomach problems, and other medical problems. Children can experience problems with depression, anxiety, embarrassment, and, if exposed to violence for an extended period of time, ambivalence. Children act out what they see; their demonstration of violent behavior can be a manifestation of their exposure to domestic violence.

Approximately 34 percent of rapes are estimated to occur in the victim's home where children are likely to be present to see or hear the sexual assault of their mothers or caretakers. Depending on the age of the children and their knowledge of sexual activity, their perceptions of the assault and their reactions will vary significantly. Children who are present during a sexual assault are at significant risk for developing post-traumatic stress disorder. Children may have recurrent and intrusive thoughts about the sexual assault and may reenact the event in repetitive play. Feeling a loss of control and the inability to protect their mothers may leave children feeling anxious, depressed, vulnerable, and angry. After witnessing a sexual assault, children may become more concerned with their own safety and may exhibit more anger and irritability than prior to the assault.

Children witness many different types of homicide. They may witness the death of a sibling, parent, another relative, a friend, or a stranger. When a child witnesses the fatal abuse of a sibling or parent, it is highly probable that the child knows the perpetrator intimately as a parent or other family member. A child who witnesses a homicide is likely to be traumatized and may experience a range of grief responses. The child may have recurrent and intrusive thoughts about the homicide, traumatic or anxiety-provoking dreams, other sleep disturbances, and a diminished interest in activities.

Long-Term Impact of Victimization and Witnessing Violence

Exposure to violence as a victim or witness poses a serious threat to American children. In "The Cycle of Violence," by Cathy Spatz Widom, University of Albany, New York, the study revealed a significant link between victimization in childhood and later involvement in violent crimes, revealing a cycle of violence. Those who had been abused or neglected as children were more likely to be arrested as juveniles and as adults for violent crimes. On average, abused and neglected children begin committing crimes at younger ages, they commit nearly twice as many offenses as non-abused children, and they are arrested more frequently. Widom also interviewed a large number of people 20 years after their childhood victimization. Findings from this follow-up study suggest that the long-term consequences of childhood victimization may also include mental health problems, educational difficulties, alcohol and drug abuse, and employment problems.

Saunders and Kilpatrick found that approximately 2 million adolescents, ages 12–17, appear to have suffered from post-traumatic stress disorder (PTSD)—a long-term mental health condition characterized by depression, anxiety, flashbacks, nightmares, and other behavioral and physiological symptoms. A significant number of these adolescents abuse alcohol and drugs as a method of coping with PTSD. Estimates are that 25 percent of disabled adults were disabled as a result of physical or sexual victimization. In younger children, victimization and PTSD can derail normal mental, emotional, and physical development.

Since trauma in children may not be revealed for months or years, caretakers, service providers, and support persons should not postpone reporting abuse or providing assistance in the form of support or therapy because they feel the child is too young to understand, appears to be unaffected, or suffered the victimization years ago. While a child's traumatic reaction to victimization cannot be prevented, it can be minimized when assistance is provided quickly.

Children who are victims of or witnesses to violence need to be identified quickly and their continued safety ensured. They need to be able to communicate what happened and to have the reality of their experience validated. Child victims and witnesses need emotional support from non-offending family members, their caretakers, the school, and the professionals involved in any investigation or civil or criminal case. Child victims need age-appropriate therapeutic services from mental health professionals who have training and experience working with violent victimization and traumatized children.

Not all children who are exposed to violence develop symptoms associated with the trauma. Many children, supported by non-offending family members and other support systems, can be very resilient. The criminal justice response can be a critical turning point in defining how experiencing violence will impact a child's life.

Child Victims and Witnesses in the Criminal Justice System

Child victims and witnesses face some difficult issues that may impact their ability to participate effectively in the criminal justice process. First, children are just that—children. The way they understand, communicate, and participate is determined by their developmental status. The adult professionals working with children must be able and willing to adjust their approach to the child's developmental level. Since most law enforcement officers and prosecutors are not child development specialists, it becomes critical to do two things— to involve other professionals who can provide advice and assistance in dealing with children and to give police and prosecutors enough training to provide them a basic understanding of child development.

If the perpetrator is a family member, child protective services and the dependency court are likely to become involved. Disclosure of abuse or violence can result in total upheaval of the child's life. Care givers and parents often initially disbelieve the child, minimize the acts, or withdraw affection. The suspected abuser may be arrested, causing havoc in the family, including loss of financial support and recriminations from family members. The child may be removed from the home and placed in foster care. Social service and legal system responses may feel like punishment to the child, prompting the child to recant the disclosure. A child victim may have tried to report previously but the report was not documented. The child may have been threatened with personal harm, harm to a loved one, or public embarrassment.

Children are more likely than adult victims to blame themselves, particularly when they have a close bond with the abuser. Perpetrators often tell their child victims that the abuse or violence was the child's fault. Since adults are powerful authority figures, the child is likely to accept that explanation. In a child's mind, it is easier for the child to believe he or she was somehow to blame for the abuse than to recognize and accept that an adult who was supposed to protect the child instead intentionally harmed the child.

Like adults, children find it upsetting to talk about traumatic events. As they talk about it, children may re-live the abuse and feel the associated emotions again. This is particularly true of younger children. Professionals should be sensitive to the potential impact of this re-emergence into the details of the crime. This re-living of the abuse may intensify the victim's trauma and generate behavior that poses additional barriers to successful investigation and prosecution.

Most children do not make up stories of abuse. False allegations are the exception. Professionals should not let the possibility of a false report prevent a thorough investigation. They should know that it is far more likely a child will lie to conceal abuse to protect the abuser.

Children disclose abuse and facts regarding traumatic events over time. The more comfortable a child becomes with an adult, the more likely he or she is to provide additional information. This dynamic can present particular problems for police and prosecutors who may face challenges to the child's credibility because the child did not present complete information at the initial interview.

A System Designed for Adults

The criminal justice system is not designed to accommodate the special developmental needs of children. Many police officers, attorneys, judges, and other criminal justice professionals find it difficult to work with children. Many children find the criminal justice system intimidating, particularly the courtroom experience. Under these circumstances, the child can be a poor witness, providing weak testimony and contributing less information than needed to make or win the case. Also, the lengthy process of navigating the formal and adversarial criminal and civil justice systems can affect the child's psychological development in significant and long-lasting ways. Listed below are a number of court-related factors that have been identified as stressful for child victims and witnesses:

- multiple interviews and not using developmentally appropriate language
- delays and continuances
- testifying more than once

- lack of communication between professionals
- fear of public exposure
- lack of understanding of complex legal procedures
- face-to-face contact with the defendant
- practices that are insensitive to developmental needs
- harsh cross-examination
- lack of adequate support and victims services
- sequestration of witnesses who may be supportive to the child
- placement that exposes the child to intimidation, pressure, or continued abuse
- inadequate preparation for testifying
- lack of evidence other than the testimony of the child

It is clearly in the best interest of the child and criminal justice system to handle child victims and witnesses in the most effective and sensitive manner possible. A number of studies have found the following: reducing the number of interviews of children can minimize psychological harm to child victims; testifying is not necessarily harmful to children if adequate preparation is conducted; and, having a trusted person help the child prepare for court and be with the child when he or she testified reduced the anxiety of the child.

To ensure children receive special assistance, all professionals working with child victims and witnesses must be willing to learn the basics of child development, to tailor their methods of practice to children, and to take advantage of the skills and services of allied professionals such as victim-witness advocates and child interview specialists. Studies indicate that the participation of victim-witness advocates in child sexual abuse cases appears to increase the percentage of guilty verdicts. One study found the conviction rate for child sexual abuse cases almost doubled (38 percent to 72 percent) after offices implemented child victim-witness advocacy programs. The proportion of offenders receiving prison sentences also almost doubled, from 25 percent to 48 percent. Over the same period, prison sentences increased from 9.24 years to 16.48 years. Research consistently suggests that prepared and relaxed child victims and witnesses are more credible, enabling prosecutors to present stronger cases and win more convictions.

Working effectively with child victims is emotionally demanding. While some adults have a natural ability to relate comfortably to children, many do not, especially to children whose lives and experiences are different from their own. With training and guidance, however, all professionals can develop skills that improve their ability to work with young victims and witnesses.

Safe from the Start, Taking Action on Children Exposed to Violence

In some respects, the notion of collaboration among diverse professionals has come to feel like a flavor of the month. It sounds good and it makes sense, but too often what results is collaboration for its own sake. Yet when it comes to responding to the tragedy of violence, coordination among professionals is absolutely crucial. Children exposed to violence encounter a dizzying array of professionals (e.g., police, child protection workers, school counselors, domestic violence advocates, physicians, lawyers, therapists, judges), and whereas families must coordinate their interactions with these multiple practitioners, the agencies themselves are not required to coordinate their activities. Without coordination among this virtual crowd of helpers, children and their family members can be seriously re-traumatized and may remain unprotected while perpetrators of violence go unpunished. Coordination is also critical to prevention. It creates a web of supports and protections that can provide a buffer against risks and can even eliminate (or at least postpone) the need for intervention.

In the final analysis, no one program has the resources or the expertise to develop a truly comprehensive response to children and families experiencing violence. Programs must work together. In fact, experience shows that coordinated responses to children exposed to violence can accomplish the following:

- reduce the number of interviews and other agency procedures a child undergoes

- minimize the number of individuals involved in a case

- enhance the quality of evidence discovered

- provide essential information to family and child protection services agencies

- help build comprehensive safety plans for battered women and their children

- prevent the system from holding battered women accountable for the actions of the abuser (thereby increasing the danger to mothers and children)

- generally minimize the likelihood of conflicts and finger-pointing among agencies with different philosophies and mandates

In addition to collaborative practice, there is an equally pressing need for collaborative leadership. Interdisciplinary leadership bodies such as a state or community board, coordinating council, or task force can monitor program availability, effectiveness, and inclusiveness; publicly articulate needs; and help secure resources for joint use. At the agency and intergovernmental level, collaborative leadership stimulates the development of supportive systems, offers front line staff a vehicle for solving problems that may arise from collaboration, and raises the level of accountability for collective effectiveness.

Finally, collaboration must go beyond service agencies, community-based organizations, and individual professionals. It must include affected families, youth, and other community members while recognizing their differing levels of experience in, and readiness for, engaging in collaborative work. Too often, these voices are missing or are inadequately supported. As a result, agencies lose important information about how to design social support systems and services that are age-appropriate, culturally meaningful, and effective within local neighborhoods. Safety planning for battered women and their children is an excellent example of a multi disciplinary effort that actively involves the affected family members in the collaboration.

Take Action!

Collaboration can range from taking steps to coordinate the activities of various disciplines to constructing a new and mutual helping system. It can mean joint training, consultation, or actual joint practice. Many states have laws requiring joint investigations and cooperation between law enforcement and child protection agencies in child abuse cases. Other states have laws authorizing creation of multi disciplinary teams that bring together law enforcement professionals, child protective services professionals, domestic violence advocates and service providers, healthcare professionals, and other practitioners.

The following are examples of specific collaboration action steps that can be taken:

Child protective services professionals. Professionals providing child protective services can work with law enforcement professionals on integrated approaches to prosecution. For example, by seeking guidance from law enforcement about investigation and evidentiary issues, child protective services workers can enhance their contribution to prosecuting alleged perpetrators and keeping families and children safe.

Child protective services professionals also can work with domestic violence organizations to ensure that assessment and monitoring procedures will identify domestic violence, promote family safety, and support the child's relationship with the non-abusive parent. When domestic violence is an issue, they can work with staff from community-based organizations, battered women and other family members, and others who know the family to assess the child's immediate safety and determine what concrete steps can be taken to make the child safe.

Domestic violence advocates. Those who work as advocates in the area of domestic violence can support and organize regular cross-training activities with agencies and groups that work with families and children. Advocates can teach others why it is important to focus on the safety of mothers to ensure the safety of children. They can suggest strategies to build on the strengths of battered women and reinforce their safety. They also can work with child protective services and the courts to ensure that assessment procedures and advocacy efforts will identify child maltreatment and promote children's safety.

Healthcare professionals. In the healthcare field, professionals can use a team approach to intervening with child victims, taking advantage of the different skills of doctors, nurses (including school nurses), social workers, and other types of practitioners. Because of their leadership role in the healthcare field, doctors have a critical role to play in modeling how to work collaboratively with other healthcare professionals. Cooperation between healthcare professionals and child protection workers and domestic violence advocates should be proactive; i.e., it should take place before a joint intervention is necessary.

Judges. Judges can take a leadership role in knocking down the barriers between different courts (such as delinquency and dependency courts) and restructuring the system to facilitate sharing of information about families. For example, a judge should be aware that a 17-year-old perpetrator standing before him or her is also appearing in another court as a victim of abuse, that the youth's mother has been a victim of domestic violence and has a protection order on file, and that the youth's younger sibling has been picked up for truancy. At a minimum, judges need to collaboratively develop protocols for sharing information and issue orders that foster appropriate communication across agencies where possible.

Law enforcement professionals. Law enforcement professionals can begin by acknowledging that because most officers are not child development specialists or mental health clinicians, it is critical to involve those who can provide expertise in these areas. Law enforcement professionals should have ready access to victim assistance professionals, advocates, and clinicians; involve them in the early stages to help manage cases; and ensure that support and services are provided to child victims and battered women on a continuing basis. In addition, training on child development and on collaboration itself can be incorporated into police academy training, ongoing officer training, and roll call and can be arranged in conjunction with social workers or other professionals.

Attorneys. Attorneys can work through state and local bar associations to identify needed improvements in legislation, financing, and court operations. Some bar associations have created interdisciplinary task forces or commissions through which attorneys can work with a range of other professionals on this issue.

Legislators and policymakers. Elected officials can reassess confidentiality laws and practices that inhibit the sharing of information. In so doing, they need to remain sensitive to and protect the safety concerns of family members.

Researchers. Evaluation is necessary at every step in the process from the initial stages of planning collaborative efforts through joint data collection and the dissemination of findings. Researchers must be consistently and actively involved in collaborative efforts.

School personnel. All school personnel teachers, counselors, administrators, school nurses, secretaries should know their local child protective services workers so that when issues arise, they have ready access and established working relationships.

Chapter 3

Raising Kids to Be Streetwise about Crime

Teens are the age group most vulnerable to crime. But putting into practice some basic crime prevention tips can help you and your friends avoid becoming the victims of crime.

How Streetwise Are You?

Do you...

- stuff your backpack or purse with cash, keys, pager, cell phones, credit cards, checkbooks and then leave it wide open at school or work, near your desk, or on the floor?

- pay attention to your surroundings or do you think about school or your friends when walking, driving, or riding the subway or bus?

- think it's a waste of time to use your locker for valuables or to lock your car when you'll be back in a few minutes?

- walk or jog by yourself early in the morning or late at night when the streets are quiet and deserted?

If you answered "yes" to any of these questions, you need to change a few habits. Even if you answered "no" and made a perfect score, read on. Spend a few minutes now to prevent trouble later.

"Streetwise, the Way to Be," 1999, National Crime Prevention Council. © 1999 National Crime Prevention Council. Reprinted with permission. Original document can be found at http://www.ncpc.org/publications/streetwise.pdf.

Keeping Street Sense in Mind

- Stay alert and tuned in to your surroundings wherever you are—at school or the mall, on the street, waiting for a bus or subway, or driving.

- Send the message that you're calm, confident, and know where you're going.

- Don't accept rides or gifts from someone you don't know well and trust—that includes people you've met on the Internet.

- Trust your instincts. If something or someone makes you uneasy, avoid the person or situation and leave as soon as possible.

- Know the neighborhoods where you live, go to school, and work. Keep in mind locations of fire and police stations and public telephones. Remember which stores and restaurants stay open late.

Strolling Day and Night

- Try to walk places with your friends rather than alone.

- Stick to well-lighted, well-traveled streets. Avoid shortcuts through wooded areas, parking lots, or alleys.

- Take the safest route to and from schools, stores, or your friends' houses. Know where to go for help if you need it.

- Don't display your cash or any other inviting targets like pagers, cell phones, hand-held electronic games, or expensive jewelry and clothing.

- Carry your backpack or purse close to your body and keep it closed. Just carrying a wallet? Put it inside your coat or front pants pocket, not in your back pocket or in your backpack.

- Have your car or house key in your hand before you reach the door.

- If you think someone is following you, switch directions or cross the street. If they're still there, move quickly toward an open store or restaurant or a lighted house. Don't be afraid to yell for help.

- Have to work late? Make sure there are others in the building and that someone—a supervisor or security guard—will wait with you for your ride or walk you to your car or bus or train stop.

- Be alert in the neighborhood. Call police or tell an adult about anything you see that seems suspicious.

Cruising

- Keep your car in good running condition. Make sure there's enough gas to get where you're going and back.

- Turn the ignition off and take your car keys with you, even if you just have to run inside for one minute.

- Roll up the windows and lock car doors, even if you're coming right back. Check inside and out before getting in.

- Avoid parking in isolated areas. If you are uncomfortable, ask a security guard or store staff to watch you or escort you to your car.

- Drive to the nearest gas station, open business, or other well-lighted, crowded area to get help if you think you are being followed. Don't head home.

- Use your cellular phone, if you have one, to call the police if you are being followed or you've seen an accident. Otherwise, stay off your cellular phone while you are driving.

- Don't pick up hitchhikers. Don't hitchhike.

Taking Buses and Subways

- Use well-lighted, busy stops. If you must get off at a little-used stop, try to arrange for a friend or an adult to meet you.

- Stay alert! Don't doze or daydream.

- Say, "leave me alone" loudly if someone hassles you. Don't be embarrassed.

- Watch who gets off your stop with you. If you feel uneasy, walk directly to a place where there are other people.

If Someone Tries to Rob You

- Give up your property don't give up your life.

- Report the crime to the police. Try to describe the attacker accurately. Your actions can help prevent others from becoming victims.

Chapter 4

Kids and Guns: Statistics

Introduction

Guns kill. In many cases, guns kill our children. Sometimes the guns are fired by other juveniles, often by acquaintances or family members. This chapter, drawn from Juvenile Offenders and Victims: 1999 National Report, provides an overview of the national statistics that show the devastating impact that the availability of guns has had on the lives and well being of American youth.

While other types of homicide remained constant, the number of juveniles killed with a firearm increased greatly between 1987 and 1993. A close look at the numbers shows that the rise in murders of juveniles from the mid-1980's through the 1993 peak year was all firearm related, as was the subsequent decline in juvenile murders that occurred between 1993 and 1997.

Guns play a large role in suicides as well. Families, teachers, and friends have virtually no chance to reach out to youth in desperate need of help when that desperation is signaled by the immediate and often fatal impact of a gunshot wound. Statistics show that for every two youth age 19 or younger murdered in 1996, one youth committed suicide. The rate of youth suicides involving a firearm increased 39% between 1980 and 1994, and although firearm-involved suicides declined 19% from 1994 to 1996, these numbers are still much too high.

"1999 National Report Series, Juvenile Justice Bulletin: Kids and Guns," National Center for Juvenile Justice, 2000. http://www.ncjrs.org/html/ojjdp/jjbul2000_03_2/contents.html.

Despite these sobering statistics, it is important to remember that there are steps we can take to make our children and our communities are safer. In fact, a number of communities have made progress in countering the threat of gun-related violence by bringing together law enforcement, elected officials, prosecutors, judges, schools, community organizations, and citizens to develop their own comprehensive, strategic violence prevention plan. The experiences of these communities are described in the Office of Juvenile Justice and Delinquency Prevention (OJJDP) publication, *Promising Strategies to Reduce Gun Violence.* This Office of Juvenile Justice and Delinquency Prevention (OJJDP) Report provides a wealth of practical information and tools that communities can use to develop their own firearm violence reduction programs.

The recent decline in firearm-related juvenile homicides and suicides is encouraging and reinforces the need to remain vigilant in keeping handguns and other weapons out of the hands of children. Rational gun control policies, community involvement in schools, better relationships between law enforcement agencies and communities, support for parents in supervising and disciplining their children, and help for teens in despair are all approaches that we can use in our efforts to reduce the illegal use of firearms by juveniles.

The Rise in Murders of Juveniles between 1984 and 1993 Was All Firearm Related, as Was the Subsequent Decline

The Increase in Juvenile Homicides Is Tied to Firearm Use by Nonfamily Offenders

A study of the 65% increase in juvenile homicides in the 7-year period from 1987 to 1993 shows that increases did not occur proportionately in all types of homicides. Over this period, homicides by family members held constant, while homicides by acquaintances increased substantially. The increase was disproportionate for black victims, with the growth in the number of black victims twice that of white victims. Most significantly, nearly all of the growth in juvenile homicides was in the number of older juveniles killed with firearms.

The decline in juvenile homicides between 1993 and 1997 brought the number to a level just 20% above that of 1987—the last year in which juvenile homicides were within their historic range. Both the decline from 1993 to 1997 and the growth from 1987 to 1993 involved substantial changes in the number of murders by acquaintances and in the number of murders of older youth and black youth. The proportion of homicides committed with a firearm, which had increased dramatically between 1987 and 1993, however, did not decline between 1993 and 1997. Therefore, the major legacy of the growth in juvenile homicides from 1987 through 1993 is that it increased the proportion of juveniles killed by firearms.

Since 1980, 1 in 4 Murders of Juveniles Involved a Juvenile Offender

Nearly 38,000 juveniles were murdered between 1980 and 1997. A juvenile offender was involved in 26% of these crimes when an offender was identified. In murders of juveniles by juveniles, about 1 of every 6 also involved an adult offender. Between 1980 and 1997, the victim and the offender were the same race in 91% of murders of juveniles by juveniles.

The proportion of juvenile murders that involved a juvenile offender increased from 21% in 1980 to 33% in 1994—the peak year for all murders by juveniles. In 1980, an estimated 400 juveniles were killed by other juveniles, growing to nearly 900 in 1994; by 1997, this figure had fallen to about 500, or about 1 of every 4 juveniles murdered that year.

When Juveniles Kill Juveniles, the Victims Are Generally Acquaintances Killed with a Firearm

Of juveniles killed by other juveniles between 1980 and 1997, 13% were under age 6. In nearly half of these murders (47%), the juvenile offender was the parent of the victim. In another 18%, the juvenile offender was another family member. Firearms were rarely used when the victim was under age 6 (10%).

Of juveniles killed by other juveniles, 63% were age 15 or older. Fewer than 5% of these older juvenile victims were killed by family members; 76% were killed by acquaintances and 19% were killed by strangers. Between 1980 and 1997, 77% of these older juveniles were killed with a firearm.

All of the Increase in Homicides by Juveniles between the Mid-1980s and Mid-1990s Was Firearm Related

It Is Difficult to Assess the Exact Number of Murders Committed by Juveniles

Based on the Federal Bureau of Investigation's (FBI's) Supplemental Homicide Report (SHR) data, 18,200 persons were murdered in

31

the U.S. in 1997—the lowest number in more than a generation. Of these murders, about 1,400 were determined by law enforcement to involve a juvenile offender; however, the actual number is greater than this. In 1997, the FBI had no information on the offender(s) for about 6,900 reported murders (38% of the total). These may have been homicides for which no one was arrested or the offender was otherwise not identified, or these may have been cases for which the local agency did not report complete information to the FBI. Regardless, the number of murders committed by juveniles in 1997 was undoubtedly greater than 1,400, but just how much greater is difficult to determine. If it were assumed that the murders without offender information were similar to those with offender information, then about 2,300 murders (or 12% of all murders) in 1997 had at least one offender who was under the age of 18 at the time of the crime.

The 1,400 murders known to involve a juvenile offender in 1997 involved about 1,700 juveniles and 900 adults. Of all murders involving a juvenile, 31% also involved an adult, and 13% involved another juvenile. In all, 44% of all murders involving a juvenile involved more than one person.

Whom Do Juveniles Kill?

Between 1980 and 1997, most victims in homicides involving juveniles were male—83%. Slightly more victims were white (50%) than black (47%). In 27% of homicides by juveniles, the victim was also a juvenile. Victims in 70% of homicides by juveniles were killed with a firearm. Of all victims killed by juveniles, 14% were family members, 55% were acquaintances and 31% were strangers.

Who Are the Juvenile Murderers?

Between 1980 and 1997, the large majority (93%) of known juvenile homicide offenders were male. More than half (56%) were black. Of known juvenile homicide offenders, 42% were age 17, 29% were age 16, and 17% were age 15; 88% of juvenile homicide offenders were age 15 or older.

Murders by the Very Young Are Rare

Annually between 1980 and 1997, fewer than 10 juveniles age 10 or younger were identified as participants in murders—a figure that has remained essentially constant over the time period. The majority of these young homicide offenders were male (88%), and more than half (54%) were black. In these cases, the victim was equally likely to be either a family member or an acquaintance (43%). A firearm was involved in 50% of the murders committed by these young offenders.

Boys and Girls Tend to Kill Different Types of Victims

Between 1980 and 1997, 54% of male juvenile homicide offenders killed an acquaintance, 37% killed a stranger, and 9% killed a family member. In comparison, the victims of females were more likely to be family members (39%) and far less likely to be strangers (15%).

Between 1980 and 1997, about 1% of male offenders killed persons under age 6, while 18% of the female offenders killed young children. Because there were so many more male offenders than female offenders, however, roughly equal numbers of male and female juvenile offenders were involved in the murder of young children. Annually between 1980 and 1997, about 25 male and 25 female juvenile offenders were tied to the death of a child under age 6.

Males were far more likely than females to kill with a firearm. Between 1980 and 1997, 73% of male juvenile homicide offenders used a firearm, while 14% used a knife. In contrast, 41% of female juvenile homicide offenders used a firearm and 32% used a knife. While 27% of females used other means to kill (e.g., hands or feet, strangulation, drowning, or fire), only 13% of males killed by these means.

Black Juveniles Were More Likely to Commit Murders with Firearms than Were Youth of Other Races

In the U.S. in 1997, about 1 of every 16,000 youth between the ages of 10 and 17 was identified as participating in a homicide. This is a rate of 56 known offenders for every 1 million youth in the U.S. population ages 10-17. This rate was greater for black youth than youth of other races: black, Asian/Pacific Islanders, American Indians, and whites.

Between 1980 and 1997, 72% of black juvenile homicide offenders used a firearm in their crimes. This proportion was higher than that for Asian/Pacific Islander (67%), white (59%), or American Indian (48%) youth.

Youth were most likely to kill persons of their own race. Between 1980 and 1997, 81% of juvenile offenders were involved in murders of persons of their own race. Same-race killing was most common for white youth (90%) and less common for blacks (76%), Asian/Pacific Islanders (58%), and American Indians (48%).

A greater proportion of white youth and American Indian youth killed family members than did youth of other races: American Indian (17%), white (16%), black (7%), and Asian/Pacific Islander (7%).

Growth in Murders by Juveniles Is Linked to Weapon Use

Relevant to an understanding of juvenile murder arrest trends is the link between murder rates and weapon use. The relationship of the murder age-arrest curves for 1980 and 1997 is similar to that for weapons law violations. For murders, the rates were lower in 1997 than in 1980 for all persons above age 25, but there were substantial increases in murder rates among juveniles and young adults. The age-specific arrest rate trend profile for weapons violations is comparable to that for murder, showing large increases for juveniles and young adults.

1 in 5 Juvenile Arrestees Carried a Gun All or Most of the Time

Gun Use and Crime among Male Arrestees/Detainees Is Studied

The National Institute of Justice interviewed a sample of arrested and/or detained individuals during the first 6 months of 1995 to learn about gun acquisition and use. Seven of eleven studies site provided data on juvenile males: Denver, District of Columbia, Indianapolis, Los Angeles, Phoenix, St. Louis, and San Diego.

Although sites varied, the juvenile males studied were disproportionately black or Hispanic, and most were age 15 or older. Because 5 of the 7 sites limited the study to juveniles in detention rather than all juveniles arrested, the offense profile for juveniles studied was skewed to more serious offenses (crimes against persons ranged from 15% to 29%). Also, the proportion of juveniles who admitted to current membership in a gang ranged from 2% to 41%.

Juveniles Are More Likely than Arrestees Overall to Commit a Crime with a Gun

The proportion of respondents who were charged with a weapons offense ranged from 1% to 12%. Among the juvenile males interviewed, however, 20% said they carried a gun all or most of the time, compared with 14% of arrestees overall.

Juvenile arrestees were nearly twice as likely as arrestees overall to say they had stolen a gun (25% vs. 13%). Gang members and drug sellers were also more likely than other arrestees to have stolen a gun (each about 30%).

Overall, 23% of arrestees who owned a gun had used one in a crime. The proportion was higher for juveniles (33%) and higher still for drug sellers (42%) and gang members (50%).

Arrestees Were Often the Victims of Gun Violence

Juvenile males and gang members were more likely than arrestees overall to have been shot at. The proportion who said they had been shot at was about 4 in 10 overall, compared with about 5 in 10 for juvenile males and about 8 in 10 for gang members.

Although juveniles were more likely than adults to be shot at, they were not more likely to suffer gun shot injury. Overall, 16% of arrestees reported gunshot injuries.

Arrestees Say They Carry Guns for Protection and Respect

Two-thirds of respondents said they had a gun for protection/self-defense. Almost one-third of arrestees agreed that, "Your crowd respects you if you have a gun." Among drug sellers and gang members, the proportion agreeing was higher (4 in 10). When asked when using a gun was appropriate, 9% of arrestees agreed that, "It is okay to shoot someone who disrespected you." Among juveniles, the proportion agreeing was double (18%). Among drug sellers, 21% agreed; among gang members, 34% agreed.

More than Half of Crime Guns Were Recovered from Adults Ages 25 Years or Older

In 1996, the Bureau of Alcohol, Tobacco and Firearms established the Youth Crime Gun Interdiction Initiative to trace crime guns (i.e., any firearm illegally possessed, used in a crime, or suspected to have been used in a crime) recovered by law enforcement. More than 76,000 crime guns were traced from 27 cities during a 1-year period between 1997 and 1998. Almost one-half (44%) of crime guns were recovered from persons under the age of 25; 11% were recovered from youth age 17 or younger.

4 in 5 Recovered Firearms Were Handguns

A handgun was the most common type of recovered firearm traced by law enforcement. Of these, a semi-automatic pistol was the most frequently possessed handgun among all age groups (52%). Semi-automatic pistols were more common among youth under age 18 (58%) and those ages 18–24 (60%) than among persons age 25 or older (47%).

A New Survey of Youth Shows That Handgun Carrying Is Linked to Other Problem Behavior

A New Survey Will Follow a Cohort of Youth as They Make the Transition from School to Work

The first wave of the 1997 National Longitudinal Survey of Youth (NLSY97) interviewed a nationally representative sample of 9,000 youth who were between the ages of 12 and 16 at year-end 1996. The survey asked youth to report whether they had engaged in a variety of deviant and delinquent behaviors, including carrying a handgun. Plans are to interview members of this cohort every 2 years to track changes in delinquent and criminal activity over the life course.

- Youth who had ever used marijuana were more likely to have sold marijuana (24% vs.<1%), carried a handgun (21% vs. 7%), or been in a gang (14% vs. 2%) at some point than youth who never used marijuana.

- Youth who had ever sold marijuana were more likely to have sold hard drugs (i.e., cocaine, LSD, or heroin) (40% vs. 1%), carried a handgun (35% vs. 8%), or been in a gang (24% vs. 4%) than youth who never sold marijuana.

- Active marijuana users (i.e., youth who used marijuana during the month prior to the survey) were more likely to have consumed alcohol (78% vs. 14%) or carried a handgun (12% vs. 2%) during that period than youth who did not use marijuana.

- Youth who had carried a handgun in the last 12 months were also more likely to have been in a gang than youth who did not carry a handgun during this period (15% vs. 1%).

The survey also found that more than half of all 16-year-olds who had ever committed assault, carried a handgun, or belonged to a gang had done so for the first time by age 12. In contrast, less than one-fifth of all 16-year-olds who had ever used marijuana, sold any drugs, or sold hard drugs (i.e., cocaine, LSD, or heroin) had done so for the first time by age 12.

For Every Two Youth (ages 0-19) Murdered in 1996, One Youth Committed Suicide

7% of All Suicides in 1996 Involved Youth Age 19 or Younger

FBI data indicate that about 3,900 youth age 19 or younger were murdered in the U.S. in 1996. The magnitude of this problem has captured the public's attention, but much less attention has been given to the fact that for every two youth murdered, one youth commits suicide.

The National Center for Health Statistics reported that 30,903 persons committed suicide in the U.S. in 1996. Of these, 7% (2,119) were youth age 19 or younger. Overall, suicides increased 9% between 1980 and 1996. For youth younger than age 15, the increase was 113%. Despite this large increase, these youngest suicide victims accounted for just 1% of all suicides in 1996.

Young Suicide Victims Are Disproportionately Male and White

Males accounted for 8 in 10 youth suicides; white youth also accounted for 8 in 10 suicides.

U.S. Child Homicide and Suicide Rates Exceed Rates for Other Industrialized Countries

Rates of Firearm-Related Homicides and Suicides Are High in the U.S.

A study conducted by the Centers for Disease Control and Prevention compared the homicide and suicide rates for children under age 15 in the U.S. with the rates for several other industrialized countries. Each country reported data for 1 year between 1990 and 1995; U.S. data were reported for 1993. The number of homicides per 100,000 children under age 15 in the U.S. was five times the number in the other countries combined. The rate of child homicides involving a firearm, however, was 16 times greater in the U.S. than in the other countries combined.

A similar pattern was seen in the suicide rates of children under age 15. Overall, the U.S. suicide rate was twice the rate for the other countries combined. For suicides involving firearms, however, the suicide rate in the U.S. was almost 11 times the rate for the other countries combined.

Homicides involving a firearm were about 10% of all homicides among younger children (ages 0–4) in the U.S. in 1993. In contrast, about two-thirds of U.S. homicides among older children (5–14) involved a firearm. In other countries, firearm-related homicides were less than one-quarter of all homicides in either age group.

While nonfirearm-related suicide rates were the same among older children in the U.S. and other countries, firearm-related suicide rates in the U.S. were 10 times greater than those in other countries.

Chapter 5

Kids and Guns:
What Can Parents Do

Too many children in the United States are killed with guns. Families and friends are left to cope with the loss of lives barely lived and to face a future overshadowed by violence. Children who are injured require long-term hospitalization and suffer permanent disabilities.

- A child—between 10 and 19 years old—commits suicide with a handgun every six hours.

- Eighty-eight percent of the children who are injured or killed in unintentional shootings are shot in their own homes or in the homes of relatives or friends. This is even more alarming when you consider the 1.2 million elementary-school-aged latchkey children estimated to have access to guns when they come home from school each day.

You can:

- Teach all of your children—from preschoolers to teenagers— that guns hurt and kill. Tell your children not to touch weapons for any reason unless under the supervision of an adult trained in firearm safety. Repeat the message periodically because children learn gradually and test the rules from time to time.

"Guns and Other Weapons," 1995 National Crime Prevention Council. Copyright © 1995 National Crime Prevention Council. http://www.ncpc.org/10adu6.htm. Reprinted with permission.

Remember that teenagers don't always follow the rules and pre-teens and teens are attracted to guns as symbols of power.

• Encourage your children to tell you or another trusted adult immediately about any weapon he or she knows of.

• Explain to your children that gun violence in TV shows, in the movies, and on video games is not real. Stress that in real-life guns can hurt and kill people.

• Show your children how to settle arguments without resorting to actions or words that can hurt. Set a good example in how you handle anger, disagreements, and sadness.

• Support school staff in their efforts to keep guns, knives, and other weapons out of schools.

• Make sure that any firearms you do choose to keep in your home are unloaded and securely stored. Invest in trigger locks, gun cabinets with locks, or pistol lock-boxes. Lock up ammunition separately. Make sure that your children don't have access to the keys.

Chapter 6

Victims of Gun Violence

Who Are the Victims of Gun Violence?

Durham, North Carolina: April 7, 1998. While walking with his mother, a 5-year-old boy was hit by a stray bullet from a gunfight. The bullet severed his spine, and Taquan Mikell may never walk again. The bullet struck him more than half a block away from the gunfight.

Nashville, Tennessee: July 2, 1999. Nashville teenager Eric Harvey Hazelitt was fatally shot in the chest when gunfire erupted at the John Henry Hale public housing complex in Nashville. Just 14 years old, he was caught in the cross-fire of two groups shooting at each other.

Washington, D.C.: June 21, 1999. Helen Foster-El, a 55-year-old grandmother, was outside her home in the 100 block of 56th Place SE. watching neighborhood children play when gunfire erupted between two groups. On hearing the gunfire, Ms. Foster-El began to shepherd the children into one of the neighborhood homes for their safety. As she was doing so, she was struck in the back by a stray bullet and died instantly.

Harrisburg, Pennsylvania: June 10, 1999. Raphael Rivera, 14, was in the immediate area of an altercation involving several individuals. When the altercation escalated into gunfire, Raphael, who was not involved in the argument, sustained a fatal wound to the chest.

Excerpted from Judith Bonderman, "Working With Victims of Gun Violence," The Office for Victims of Crime, Office of Justice Programs, U.S. Department of Justice, http://www.ojp.usdoj.gov/ovc/publications/bulletins/gun_7_2001/welcome.html, July 2001.

41

The Death Toll

When confronted with the question, "Who are the victims of gun violence?" we usually think first about the fatalities. According to death certificate data compiled by the National Center for Health Statistics, a part of the Centers for Disease Control and Prevention (CDC), a total of 32,436 persons died from firearm injuries in the United States in 1997. The majority of these deaths 54.2 percent were suicides, 41.7 percent were homicides, and the remaining 4.1 percent were unintentional shootings or deaths of an undetermined nature. The effects of gun violence cross all socioeconomic and geographic boundaries from inner cities to remote rural areas to upscale suburbs and in homes, public housing communities, schools, workplaces, recreational areas, bars, and on the street. Gun violence victims are young and old, male and female, African-American and white. In some cases, the shooter and victim are strangers, but in many others, they are intimately related.

In spite of the pervasive nature of gun violence, some demographic groups are disproportionately represented in the gun crime victim population. The 13,252 gun homicide victims recorded in the mortality statistics for 1997 included 5,110 who were 15 to 24 years old. Firearm homicide was the second leading cause of death for the 15- to 24-year-old group. In the 25- to 34-year-old group, there were 3,706 deaths from gun homicide; at younger ages (5 to 14), there were 284 firearm homicides. In fact, firearm homicide was within the top 10 causes of death for all age groups from 5 to 44 years.

Gun homicide victims are disproportionately young and predominantly male. According to CDC, 84 percent were male in 1997. At ages 15 to 19 years, the gun homicide rate for males was 8 times the rate for females in 1997. The Bureau of Justice Statistics (BJS) reports that males of all ages were 3.2 times more likely than females to be murdered in 1998. Moreover, the circumstances of firearm violence differ significantly for men and women. In contrast to men, women are far more likely to be killed by a spouse, intimate acquaintance, or family member than by a stranger.

Firearm homicide also disproportionately affects African-Americans. Approximately 52 percent of gun homicide victims are African-American, even though they represent less than 13 percent of the total population. African-American males between the ages of 15 and 24 have the highest firearm homicide rate of any demographic group. Their firearm homicide rate of 103.4 deaths per 100,000 is 10 times higher than the rate for white males in the same age group (10.5

deaths per 100,000). In 1997, 92 percent of homicides of young African-American men occurred by firearms, compared to 68 percent of homicides by firearms in the general population. Even though violent crime rates, including crimes committed with guns, have declined each year since 1993, according to Federal Bureau of Investigation trend reports, guns remain the leading cause of death for young African-American males.

If all Americans were killed with firearms at the same rate as African-American males between the ages of 15 and 24 (103.4 per 100,000), there would be 276,843 firearm homicide victims annually in the United States. (Based on 1997 CDC numbers and a total population of 267,636,061.)

The Nonfatal Gun Crime Victimization

For every firearm death, there are approximately three nonfatal firearm injuries that show up in hospital emergency rooms. With no mechanism, such as a national registry, to collect uniform national data on nonfatal firearm injuries, this is, at best, an estimate based on a sample of hospitals. There may be many more non-fatal firearm victims who do not go to hospital emergency rooms for treatment. Others have estimated four to six non-fatal injuries for each gun death. In addition, many crime victims may be traumatized by the presence of a gun during a crime, whether or not the gun was fired. According to the National Crime Victimization Survey (NCVS) in 1998, victimizations involving a firearm represented 23 percent of the 2.9 million violent crimes of rape and sexual assault, robbery, and aggravated assault. In 1998, 670,500 crime victims reported facing an assailant with a gun.

Secondary Victims

The number of deaths and injuries is just a crude index of the effects of gun violence in the United States. There is an even greater number of secondary victims, sometimes called co-victims or survivors of homicide. These are the parents, children, siblings, spouses, and others who have lost a loved one or friend to gun homicide. In the aftermath of a homicide, co-victims must deal with law enforcement, the medical examiner, the press, and the court system, among others. They may have to clean up a crime scene, pay the homicide victim's medical bills, and arrange for a funeral and burial. "It is estimated that each homicide victim is survived by an average of three loved ones for whom the violent death produces a painful and traumatic grief." (Deborah Spungen, *Homicide: The Hidden Victims*, Sage Publications, 1998).

Secondary victims also include those who are touched by or witness gun violence in their homes, schools, or workplaces or on the street. In the Nation's largest public housing projects, the damage goes well beyond the lives lost and injuries inflicted. According to a report from the U.S. Department of Housing and Urban Development, public housing residents are more than twice as likely as other members of the population to suffer from firearm victimization, one in five residents reports feeling unsafe in his or her neighborhood, and children show symptoms of posttraumatic stress disorder (PTSD) similar to those seen in children exposed to war or major disasters. This is consistent with numerous studies finding high rates of exposure to violence, particularly among youth in urban communities. In one study, almost two-thirds of high school students had witnessed a shooting, and in another, 70 percent of the youth ages 7 to 18 in a public housing project had witnessed a shooting and 43 percent had seen a murder. Recent data also indicate substantial exposure to gun violence among suburban school-age children.

Multiple-Victim Shootings

While the number of crimes committed with firearms has been falling to levels not seen since the mid-1980s, media coverage and public awareness of gun crime are increasing. "Even those who have never encountered a gun are aware of the widespread presence of guns in our communities, witness news reports of gun-related crime, domestic murders, and high-profile shootings at schools, churches and other public places. The ever-present fear that someone we love might be killed or injured is another form of gun trauma" (From The Bell Campaign's World Wide Web site at www.bellcampaign.org).

In the past few years, a rash of multiple-victim tragedies has erupted in schools, workplaces, churches, nursing homes, fast food restaurants, shopping malls, and transportation. These are very public venues—places that we frequent on a daily basis and where we should feel safe. When a gun massacre interrupts play in a daycare center, prayer in a church, or commuters going home from work, it shatters our most basic sense of security. Consequently, even though the percentage of homicides involving five or more victims was less than 0.05 percent in 1998, these are the ones that receive the overwhelming majority of the media's attention. In addition, the multiple-victim shootings in public places may be ones that create the most secondary victims as whole classrooms of first graders, cafeterias full of teenagers, and hundreds of fellow workers witness a mass shooting. The media coverage alone multiplies the number of persons victimized by the crime.

Needs of Gun Victims

Consider how gun victims may be different from other crime victims and how the differences might affect the services they need or receive. The main themes that emerge are 1) the gun as the weapon of violence, 2) the young age of the victims, 3) the high cost of gun violence, and 4) the extraordinary media attention given to a small subset of gun crimes.

The Gun as the Weapon of Violence

Much has been written on why gun use increases the deadliness of attacks; for example, because guns inflict more damage than other instruments, they can be fired multiple times with little effort, firearms have a greater range, and assailants intending to kill choose the most efficient instrument. Whatever the impact of these different factors, it is clear that the fatality rate from gun assaults is much higher than that from other weapons. This is true regardless of the relationship between the victim and shooter, as the presence of a gun can turn a robbery, an argument, or an abusive relationship into a homicide.

According to a 1996 Bureau of Justice Statistics (BJS) report, 29 percent of firearm homicide victims were killed because of an argument; 21 percent were killed during the commission of another crime, such as a robbery or drug crime; and 6 percent died as a result of a gang-related shooting. Offenders report firing a gun within 15 seconds of brandishing it, even when they had not intended to shoot the victim. Gun victims include those shot during traffic altercations, gambling disputes, and verbal disagreements.

The lethality effect is not lost on the victims. "An important difference is the gun itself. Guns are the only instrument developed to kill; victims facing a gun suffer the trauma of death or the fear of death," says family bereavement counselor Kevin O'Brien. Meanwhile, DeLano Foster, an Office for Victims of Crime (OVC) Program Specialist and survivor of multiple homicides, offers that "the difference between an armed robbery and a homicide could be the time it takes the victim to hand over his wallet." Eyewitness accounts frequently report victims putting their hands in front of them and "holding up articles of all kinds in their last moments in the magical belief that even a sheet of paper might save them."

Gun violence also is frequently more random than other types of criminal victimization. Bullets don't always have a name on them. You can be shot from a great distance even with a bullet meant for someone else. Young men can be casualties of a war they did not partake in when gang members intent on retaliating shoot at random victims when they can't find the rivals they intended to kill. Others talk about small children sleeping in bathtubs to hide from stray bullets penetrating bedroom walls at night.

The bystander victim represents the most impersonal type of crime. But even when the shooter targets a particular victim, the gun crime is somewhat impersonal. The gun, as an instrument of both power and detachment, allows the shooter to remain physically and emotionally distanced from his or her victims. When the victims are shot in the back, as many are, they never even see the shooter's face. This may increase the "Why me?" response of so many gun victims, similar to the feelings of victims of drunk driving.

The ability of mentally disturbed individuals to kill at a distance, together with the enormous firepower of semiautomatic weapons, may have facilitated the gun rampages that have taken so many lives in recent years. Michelle Scully Hobus was shot and her husband killed when a crazed gunman armed with two semiautomatic TEC 9 pistols roamed a San Francisco, California, law firm, shooting 15 people, killing 9 before taking his own life. It was a long time before she could shake the feeling of danger. "Even though I knew that the gun massacre at the law firm was an extremely rare event, I kept having the feeling that it would happen again. I couldn't sit with my back to the door; I thought someone would come in and blow everyone away."

- Just as Larry Gene Ashbrook did on September 15, 1999, when he shot 14 people (7 dead) in the Wedgwood Baptist Church in Fort Worth, Texas.

- Just as Mark Barton did on July 29, 1999, when he shot 22 people (9 dead) at two brokerage firms in Atlanta, Georgia.

- Just as Kip Kinkel did on May 21, 1998, when he shot 24 people (2 dead) at Thurston High School in Springfield, Oregon.

- Just as George Hennard did on October 16, 1991, when he drove his truck into Luby's Cafeteria in Killeen, Texas, and opened fire on the lunchtime crowd, killing 23 people before shooting himself.

Moreover, gun victims face constant reminders of their trauma from the everpresent gun seen on television programs and commercials and in films and videos. Even American slang, for example, "one shot," "take aim," and "set your sights," takes its toll on some victims. Some report that any loud noise, like balloons popping and cars backfiring, could "trigger" a response. The exorbitant media attention paid to each new multiple-victim shooting also is retraumatizing for gun victims of similar tragedies. Security changes, such as metal detectors in schools, hidden cameras, dress codes, and guards in the halls, are constant visual reminders of school shootings.

Like other crime victims, gun victims seek redress against their shooters through the criminal justice and civil justice systems. Many victims, like Scully Hobus and Jaquie Algee, have become activists.

Recommendation: Clinical evidence supports the therapeutic value of victims working as change agents, in grassroots or church activities, informal support groups, and anticrime organizations.

The Young Age of the Victims

As previously noted, gun crime disproportionately affects young people. Their injuries and grief must be understood in this context. Those who work with adolescents speak of the pessimism and despair, particularly in the inner cities, where communities are losing children to gun violence daily. Youngsters whose relatives and friends have been shot automatically think that sooner or later it will happen to them. They plan their funerals, write their obituaries, and specify the clothing in which they want to be buried. A psychological counselor for teenagers in Baltimore, Maryland, Dr. Rosetta Graham, spoke of the need to do much more for this age group: "Around age 14 or 15 they become more private and hold in their grief. They are caught between adults who know how to make their needs known and young children whose caregivers speak for them." Studies of urban youth show a high correlation between exposure to violence and depression and PTSD.

The hopelessness of this population is a recurring theme. One major shooting, or the daily loss of friends and classmates, can have a profound effect on young people just beginning to explore their independence and develop plans for their future. While some hold in their grief, others become suicidal or act out their feelings on the street. Even in suburban settings where violence is rare, a highly publicized school gun massacre can have a significant impact. Counselors working with students at Columbine High School in Littleton, Colorado, worried about kids who were somewhat depressed and doing drugs before the shooting. In the months since the shooting, they have seen an increase in drunk driving, suicide attempts, and fighting. Disaffected students or those who feel alienated or rejected don't trust anyone, don't feel safe, and don't do well in school. Similarly, after the 1998 shooting of 22 students at Thurston High School in Springfield, Oregon, there was a 600-percent increase in referrals to the school nurse and a 400-percent increase in arguments and fights reported to the principal. Many students, even some who were not present at the school but who watched the news coverage, experienced a loss of control, a feeling of being violated, and a sense of guilt that they survived.

For many students, the fear of gun violence is strong enough to interfere with the quality of their lives and their performance in school; they also may suffer from increased absentee, truancy, and dropout rates. Those who work with children explain the importance of getting them to talk about their fears. They are hungry for information and may distort facts and think they could have prevented the shooting. They need to understand that the school shootings on the evening news are rare events and that schools are safe places.

Although exposure to violence will affect all adolescents to some extent, different services are needed when the shooting is an isolated tragedy versus when there is a daily threat of violence in the community. In the high-profile school and workplace shootings, crisis response teams "debrief" the victims and witnesses, often in a group setting. The interventions for schools and communities that witness violence are based on the assumption that the incidents they witnessed are one-time horrific events. Those who had the benefit of this type of crisis response service felt a sense of security while the teams were there and a great void when they left. In the absence of organized training, teachers, school administrators, and guidance counselors are scrambling to get up to speed on crisis response. Many professionals who helped care for the students who were shot or witnessed a massacre of their classmates also became depressed and suicidal. According to school superintendent Jamon Kent, the shooting at Thurston High took place May 21, 1998, and the aftershocks still occupy one-third of his time in the office.

Recommendation: Communities victimized by gun massacres should be offered long-term assistance and training so they can more effectively be involved in the healing process.

Different problems arise and different types of interventions are needed to address chronic gun violence. For the past 10 years at least, young African-American males have experienced violent crime at a rate significantly higher than the rate for other age groups. Sandra DeLeon, Director of the Rise Above It violence prevention program in West Orange, New Jersey, reported that 60 percent of the students they serve know someone who has been shot. In their neighborhoods, gun violence is more predictable than random. They come to school worrying about the gunshots they heard the night before. The students need to hear, preferably from peer counselors, that there is a future to look forward to and they are not destined to be either buried or behind bars in jail. But this is an uphill battle. The strong correlation between poverty and violent crime means that those with the fewest resources are the most vulnerable. In some cases, the parents of homicide victims are very young. An enormous amount of preventive counseling is needed to keep them from exacting retribution while they struggle to get daycare, buy food, and arrange for the burial of a loved one.

The literature on children and adolescent victims reinforces these findings about the vulnerabilities of young gun victims. A Task Force on Adolescent Assault Victim Needs, convened by the American Academy of Pediatrics, recommends addressing the psychosocial needs of young victims along with their physical injuries. To do this effectively, the task force noted that health care providers must acknowledge and address three myths:

1. That all adolescent victims are "bad" kids who probably deserve what they got.

2. That it is dangerous to care for adolescent victims who may be members of a gang.

3. That it is hopeless to help them because of the high risk of reinjury and subsequent acts of violence by the victim.

The myth that all adolescent victims are "bad" kids is particularly harmful for young African-American men growing up in neighborhoods rife with drugs and gun violence. Generalizations about "predator youth" cause added grief for gun victims and stigmatize them and

49

their families unfairly. Future employers may refuse to hire a young man with a bullet in his arm, assuming that he was a gang member or a bad person because he'd been shot. On the other hand, the tendency to use violence is considered a serious potential consequence of being a young victim of gun violence. In fact, "a new study by the National Center on Crime and Delinquency finds that one of the best predictors of whether a teenager will commit a crime is whether he or she has been a victim." Siblings of gunshot victims are frequently preoccupied with revenge fantasies and may be encouraged and assisted by their peers in exacting vigilante justice. Once having resorted to violence, young men engage in more risk-taking behavior. Thus, a cycle of violence continues, and being shot once becomes the greatest predictor for being targeted again. However, the risk factors for this group are often overcome by the resourcefulness and determination of families surviving in the inner city.

Recommendation: Assistance for gun victims, particularly young African-American men, must include programs designed to teach victims to regain their self-respect and status in the community without resorting to more violence. Quick outreach and support to newly bereaved families can help redirect their grief toward positive efforts to honor the memory of their loved ones.

Elementary school-age children also are frequent witnesses to gun violence and often display symptoms of PTSD and other trauma-related disorders. Some children are afraid of school, and many become fatalistic. Some engage in aggressive play and perform poorly in school, while others become desensitized to violence and lose the ability to recognize and avoid dangerous situations. Research studies suggest that witnessing gun violence affects children in many different ways, depending on the type of wound, the proximity to the shooter, the relationship of the shooter and victim, and whether the shooting took place in a context generally considered safe, among other things. Different reactions can be expected from boys and girls. Child witnesses who have been raised in a subculture of violence in the home may have additional risk factors for long-term psychosocial consequences. Effects also can be seen in somatic disturbances. According to Marianne Z. Wamboldt, M.D., a child psychiatrist in Denver, Colorado, clinicians have noted a relationship between the general stress in the community after the shooting at Columbine High and an increase in asthma cases and deaths among preschoolers.

"After my 19-year-old son was shot in Chicago, I went to many support groups, community organizations, and church-affiliated meetings, but I really wasn't getting what I needed. I needed to be more active in the movement to reduce gun trauma. I found comfort in joining The Bell Campaign, a grassroots victim-based organization, modeled after Mothers Against Drunk Driving" (Jaquie Algee, Southeast Regional Director for The Bell Campaign).

The High Cost of Gun Violence

Gunshot injury and death place a burden on the health care system in the United States that far exceeds the toll of other types of criminal victimization. Because of the traumatic nature and extent of their injuries, gunshot victims are more likely than other crime victims to require overnight hospitalization and followup care. BJS reports that gunshot victims represented only 5 percent of the estimated 1.4 million hospital emergency department patients treated in 1994 for violence-related nonfatal injuries. But while the majority of crime victims are treated and released, gunshot victims represent a third of those requiring hospitalization. The average cost of acute care treatment ranges from $14,850 to $32,000 per hospital admission. Because of the young average age of the victims and the frequent need for rehospitalization, the lifetime medical costs are very high, around $35,500 per victim. For all victims of firearm injuries (assaults) and deaths (homicides) in 1994, the lifetime medical costs totaled $1.7 billion. Government programs, primarily Medicaid, are the primary payers for 50 percent of hospitalized gunshot injury cases due to violence.

The growing cost of gun violence can affect the trauma care available for all community members. At King/Drew Medical Center in Los Angeles, California, hospital expenses, not including professional fees, were more than $270.7 million for the 34,893 patients hospitalized for gunshot injuries from 1978 to 1992. Some 96 percent of these costs were paid with public funds. Between 1983 and 1990, the financial strain of treating uninsured patients contributed to the closure of 10 out of 23 trauma centers in Los Angeles County.

In addition to direct health care and related expenditures, gun violence exacts a substantial economic toll on its victims and society in general in terms of lost productivity, use of the criminal justice system, pain and suffering, and diminished quality of life. Economists and public health statisticians estimate an annual bill of more than $100 billion for all of these gun violence costs. An examination of more than 1,000 jury awards in cases involving shooting victims yields an average loss of more than $3 million for a single family of a homicide victim.

The economic loss is even more staggering for victims who sustain spinal cord injuries (SCIs) from gunshot wounds. These relatively rare catastrophic cases account for the lion's share of the medical costs for gun injuries. Each year, approximately 10,000 persons suffer an SCI and require hospitalization. Nearly a quarter of these injuries are caused by acts of violence, primarily gunshot wounds. Violence-related SCIs have increased dramatically since the early 1970s, over-taking falls as the second leading cause of SCIs (after motor vehicle accidents) in past 4 years. The average first-year expenses have been estimated at $217,868 for violence-related SCIs, although the amount varies considerably depending on the extent of neurological damage. With recurring annual charges for violence-related SCIs calculated at $17,275, the lifetime charges are estimated to be more than $600,000 for each victim. This includes charges incurred as a direct result of the injury, such as emergency medical services, hospitalizations, attendant care, equipment, supplies, medications, environmental modifications, physician and outpatient services, nursing homes, household assistance, vocational rehabilitation, and similar miscellaneous items. It does not include indirect costs, such as lost wages, fringe benefits, productivity, pain and suffering, and diminished quality of life, which could be twice as much as the direct costs.

A handful of gunshot SCI victims have fared better than most. For example, the SCI students from the Columbine shootings have had the benefit of a community-wide effort to raise funds for remodeling living areas, paying for medical and living expenses, specially equipped vans, and even college scholarships. But these are atypical cases. The majority of people with violence-related SCIs are young African-Americans with low socioeconomic status. Many in this group have been targets of gun violence and have sustained most of their injuries because of drug- or gang-related activity. Those who return to their communities after surviving months with tubes in their bodies face a daunting challenge in school. Paralyzed for life, they never will be the same active teenagers again. The practical and social problems like calling ahead and waiting hours for transportation, wheelchair access to classrooms, and dealing with colostomy bags are difficult enough without the added fears of testifying in court and being targeted again by the shooter. Those with violence-related SCIs are more likely than other SCI patients to have intractable pain and commit suicide. For others, the cost of acute care and rehabilitation, among other things, can lead to the dim prospect of constant dependence on the Government or family.

The Extraordinary Media Attention to a Small Subset of Gun Crimes

On April 20, 1999, the world watched as two high school students, armed with automatic weapons and shotguns, killed 12 students and a teacher and wounded 23 others before turning the guns on themselves. The tragedy at Columbine High School is considered a defining moment in the public's consciousness about gun violence. The nonstop real-time media coverage of this horrendous massacre, both on the air and in print, was traumatizing to the victims' families and friends, the community, the state of Colorado, the United States, and the world.

Recommendation: The media should be more sensitive to how their coverage of gun violence affects victims and children. OVC should develop training materials and guidelines for media coverage of gun massacres.

School shootings in particular are traumatizing for children because they all go to school. After Columbine, preschoolers in Colorado began talking about where they would be going to school as the place where they would die. School systems around the country saw the phenomenon of school-phobic kids, as both the news media and talk shows exaggerated a child's risk of being shot at school. Although such news coverage should carry a warning caption for parents about the possible adverse effects on young children, older children are hungry to know what has happened and have a great need for information. In all cases, parents and teachers need to help children process the information they see on television, so they can realistically assess their own safety in school.

Unfortunately, the misconceptions about the risk of school shootings are pervasive in all age groups. A recent analysis of opinion polls taken after the shootings in Jonesboro, Arkansas, and Littleton found a 49-percent increase in parents' anxiety about children's safety in the classroom, even though statistical studies by the U.S. Department of Justice (DOJ) and the National School Safety Center showed a 40-percent decrease in school-associated violent deaths in 1998–1999, the school year including the Columbine shooting. These tragic events are truly rare—with 52 million students enrolled in public school, the chance that a school-aged child would die in school in 1998–1999 was 1 in 2 million.

The gap between public fear and reality is not surprising, as media coverage is focused on less than 1 percent of homicides—those with multiple victims. Even within a group of multiple-victim gun homicides, the rarest events get the most media attention. For example:

- December 4, 1999: Sacramento, California. A 31-year-old Asian man shot and killed his daughter and four sons, reportedly after having an argument with his wife. A shotgun and a high-powered rifle were found in the apartment.

- December 5, 1999: Baltimore, Maryland. Five women were found shot to death in their Northeast Baltimore row house. Police said the women, who were not involved in drug activity, were shot to send a message to a relative who was involved in the drug trade.

- December 6, 1999: Fort Gibson, Oklahoma. Five students were injured when a 13-year-old opened fire at a middle school with a 9 mm handgun he took from his home.

The family homicide, an all-too-common occurrence, was reported only by the California press. The Baltimore shooting was prime-time news for a day and then was eclipsed by the middle school shooting in a rural community in Oklahoma.

Even among victims of the same shooting, the media may focus on one or two to represent the face on the story. Perhaps because of their pronounced activism on the gun issue or because of some other special attribute, these chosen victims become the story of the massacre. In *Homicide: The Hidden Victims, A Guide for Professionals*, Deborah Spungen describes how individual victims of multiple-victim shootings "tend to get lost in the scale of the horror," while "co-victims who have had a loved one selected for the [poster victim] may experience feelings of reluctance, exploitation, loss of control, and anger."

Part Two

Protection from
School Crime and Violence

Chapter 7

School Crime and Safety Statistics

The national focus on school crime and safety continues to be of paramount importance. During the past year, overall levels of crime in school decreased, and students seem to feel more safe in school than they did in the last few years. Yet, violence and theft still mar the school experiences of many students and challenge parents, teachers, and school officials to respond.

Continued progress in improving the safety of our children entrusted to schools relies on having accurate information about the nature, extent, and scope of the problem. This text is intended to provide information that will assist in developing policies and/or programs to prevent and cope with violence and crime in schools.

Schools should be safe and secure places for all students, teachers, and staff members. Without a safe learning environment, teachers cannot teach and students cannot learn. In fact, as the data in this chapter show, more victimizations happen away from school than at school. In 1998, students were about two times as likely to be victims of serious violent crime away from school as at school.

Kaufman, P., Chen, X., Choy, S.P., Ruddy, S.A., Miller, A.K., Fleury, J.K., Chandler, K.A., Rand, M.R., Klaus, P., and Planty, M.G. *Indicators of School Crime and Safety*, 2000. U.S. Departments of Education and Justice. NCES 2001 017/NCJ-184176. Washington, D.C.: 2000. This publication can be downloaded from the World Wide Web at http://www.ojp.usdoj.gov/bjs/pub/pdf/iscs00ex.pdf. Single hard copies can be ordered through ED Pubs at 1-877-4ED-PUBS (NCES 2001 017) (TTY/TDD 1-877-576-7734), and the Bureau of Justice Statistics Clearinghouse at 1-800-732-3277 (NCJ-184176).

In 1998, students ages 12 through 18 were victims of more than 2.7 million total crimes at school. In that same year, these students were victims of about 253,000 serious violent crimes at school (that is, rape, sexual assault, robbery, and aggravated assault). There were also 60 school-associated violent deaths in the United States between July 1, 1997 and June 30, 1998 including 47 homicides.

The total nonfatal victimization rate for young people declined between 1993 and 1998. The percentage of students being victimized at school also declined over the last few years. Between 1995 and 1999, the percentage of students who reported being victims of crime at school decreased from 10 percent to 8 percent. This decline was due in part to a decline for students in grades 7 through 9. Between 1995 and 1999, the prevalence of reported victimization dropped from 11 percent to 8 percent for 7th graders, from 11 percent to 8 percent for 8th graders, and from 12 percent to 9 percent for 9th graders.

However, for some types of crimes at school, rates have not changed. For example, between 1993 and 1997, the percentage of students in grades 9 through 12 who were threatened or injured with a weapon on school property in the past 12 months remained constant at about 7 or 8 percent. The percentage of students in grades 9 through 12 who reported being in a physical fight on school property in the past 12 months also remained unchanged between 1993 and 1997 at about 15 percent.

As the rate of victimization in schools has declined or remained constant, students also seem to feel more secure at school now than just a few years ago. The percentage of students ages 12 through 18 who reported avoiding one or more places at school for their own safety decreased between 1995 and 1999 from 9 to 5 percent.

Furthermore, the percentage of students who reported that street gangs were present at their schools decreased. The reader should be cautious in making comparisons between victimization rates on school property and elsewhere. These data do not take into account the number of hours that students spend on school property and the number of hours they spend elsewhere.

In 1999, 17 percent of students ages 12 through 18 reported that they had street gangs at their schools compared with 29 percent in 1995.

There was an increase in the use of marijuana among students between 1993 and 1995, but no change between 1995 and 1997. In 1997, about 26 percent of these students had used marijuana in the last 30 days.

Furthermore, almost one-third of all students in grades 9 through 12 (32 percent) reported that someone had offered, sold, or given them an illegal drug on school property an increase from 24 percent in 1993.

Therefore, the data shown in this chapter present a mixed picture of school safety. While overall school crime rates have declined, violence, gangs, and drugs are still evident in some schools, indicating that more work needs to be done.

Violent Deaths at School

From July 1, 1997 through June 30, 1998, there were 60 school-associated violent deaths in the United States. Forty-seven of these violent deaths were homicides, 12 were suicides, and one was a teen-ager killed by a law enforcement officer in the line of duty. Thirty-five of the 47 school-associated homicides were of school age children. By comparison, a total of 2,752 children ages 5 through 19 were victims of homicide in the United States from July 1, 1997 through June 30, 1998. Seven of the 12 school-associated suicides occurring from July 1, 1997 through June 30, 1998 were of school age children. A total of 2,061 children ages 5 through 19 committed suicide that year.

Student Reports of Nonfatal Student Victimization

Students ages 12 through 18 were more likely to be victims of non-fatal serious violent crime including rape, sexual assault, robbery, and aggravated assault away from school than when they were at school. In 1998, students in this age range were victims of about 550,000 serious violent crimes away from schools, compared with about 253,000 at school.

The percentage of students in grades 9 through 12 who have been threatened or injured with a weapon on school property has not changed significantly in recent years. In 1993, 1995, and 1997, about 7 to 8 percent of students reported being threatened or injured with a weapon such as a gun, knife, or club on school property in the past 12 months.

In 1998, 12- through 18-year-old students living in urban, sub-urban, and rural locales were equally vulnerable to serious violent crime and theft at school. Away from school, however, urban and sub-urban students were more vulnerable to serious violent crime and theft than were rural students.

Younger students (ages 12 through 14) were more likely than older students (ages 15 through 18) to be victims of crime at school. However, older students were more likely than younger students to be victimized away from school.

Principal and Disciplinarian Reports of Violence and Crime at School

In 1996–97, 10 percent of all public schools reported at least one serious violent crime to the police or a law enforcement representative. Principals' reports of serious violent crimes included murder, rape or other type of sexual battery, suicide, physical attack or fight with a weapon, or robbery. Another 47 percent of public schools reported a less serious violent or nonviolent crime (but not a serious violent one). Crimes in this category include physical attack or fight without a weapon, theft/larceny, and vandalism. The remaining 43 percent of public schools did not report any of these crimes to the police.

Elementary schools were much less likely than either middle or high schools to report any type of crime in 1996–97. They were much more likely to report vandalism (31 percent) than any other crime (19 percent or less).

At the middle and high school levels, physical attack or fight without a weapon was generally the most commonly reported crime in 1996–97 (9 and 8 per 1,000 students, respectively). Theft or larceny was more common at the high school than at the middle school level (6 versus 4 per 1,000 students).

Teacher Reports of Nonfatal Teacher Victimization at School

Over the 5-year period from 1994 through 1998, teachers were victims of 1,755,000 nonfatal crimes at school, including 1,087,000 thefts and 668,000 violent crimes (rape or sexual assault, robbery, and aggravated and simple assault). This translates into 83 crimes per 1,000 teachers per year.

In the period from 1994 through 1998, senior high school and middle/junior high school teachers were more likely to be victims of violent crimes (most of which were simple assaults) than elementary school teachers (38 and 60, respectively, versus 18 crimes per 1,000 teachers.

In the 1993–94 school year, 12 percent of all elementary and secondary school teachers were threatened with injury by a student, and 4 percent were physically attacked by a student. This represented about 341,000 teachers who were victims of threats of injury by students that year, and 119,000 teachers who were victims of attacks by students.

School Environment

Between 1995 and 1999, the percentages of students who felt unsafe while they were at school and while they were going to and from school decreased. In 1995, 9 percent of students ages 12 through 18 sometimes or most of the time feared they were going to be attacked or harmed at school. In 1999, this percentage had fallen to 5 percent. During the same period, the percentage of students fearing they would be attacked while traveling to and from school fell from 7 percent to 4 percent.

Between 1993 and 1997, the percentage of students in grades 9 through 12 who reported carrying a weapon on school property within the previous 30 days fell from 12 percent to 9 percent (a 25 percent reduction).

Between 1995 and 1999, the percentage of students ages 12 through 18 who avoided one or more places at school for fear of their own safety decreased, from 9 to 5 percent. In 1999, this percentage represented 1.1 million students.

Between 1995 and 1999, the percentage of students who reported that street gangs were present at their schools decreased. In 1995, 29 percent of students reported gangs being present in their schools. By 1999, this percentage had fallen to 17 percent.

In 1997, about 51 percent of students in grades 9 through 12 had at least one drink of alcohol in the previous 30 days. A much smaller percentage (about 6 percent) had at least one drink on school property during the same period.

There was an increase in the use of marijuana among students between 1993 and 1995, but no change between 1995 and 1997. About one quarter (26 percent) of ninth graders reported using marijuana in the last 30 days in 1997. However, marijuana use on school property did not increase significantly between 1993 and 1995, nor between 1995 and 1997.

In 1995 and 1997, almost one-third of all students in grades 9 through 12 (32 percent) reported that someone had offered, sold, or given them an illegal drug on school property. This was an increase from 1993 when 24 percent of such students reported that illegal drugs were available to them on school property.

In 1999, about 13 percent of students ages 12 through 18 reported that someone at school had used hate related words against them. That is, in the prior 6 months someone at school called them a derogatory word having to do with race/ethnicity, religion, disability, gender, or sexual orientation. In addition, about 36 percent of students saw hate-related graffiti at school.

Chapter 8

Overview:
Preventing School Violence

Preventing Youth Violence

Violence is a learned behavior that can be changed. Parents, students, and school officials can take steps toward reducing violence in schools by responding to children's emotional and psychological needs and by implementing violence prevention programs.

For Parents

- Give your children consistent love and attention. Every child needs a strong, loving relationship with a parent or other adult to feel safe and secure and to develop a sense of trust.

- Children learn by example, so show your children appropriate behavior by the way you act. Settle arguments with calm words, not with yelling, hitting, and slapping.

- Talk with your children about the violence they see on TV, in video games, at school, at home, or in the neighborhood. Discuss

This chapter contains text from "Preventing Youth Violence," from the SAFEusa website, Centers for Disease Control and Prevention (CDC), http://www.cdc.gov/safeusa/youthviolence.htm, page last updated May 24, 2000, and "Stopping School Violence," 1998, National Crime Prevention Council. © 1998 National Crime Prevention Council. Reprinted with permission. Original document can be found at http://www.ncpc.org/teens/stoppingviolence.html.

why violence exists in these contexts and what the consequences of this violence are.

- Try to keep your children from seeing too much violence: limit their TV time, and screen the programs they watch. Seeing a lot of violence can lead children to behave aggressively.

- Make sure your children do not have access to guns. If you own firearms or other weapons, unload them and lock them up separately from the bullets. Never store firearms where children can find them, even if unloaded. Also, talk with your children about how dangerous weapons can be.

- Involve your children in setting rules for appropriate behavior at home; this will help them understand why the rules should be followed. Also ask your children what they think an appropriate punishment would be if a rule were broken.

- Teach your children nonaggressive ways to solve problems by discussing problems with them, asking them to consider what might happen if they use violence to solve problems, and talking about what might happen if they solve problems without violence.

- Listen to your children and respect them. They will be more likely to listen to and respect others if they are listened to and treated with respect.

- Note any disturbing behaviors in your child such as angry outbursts, excessive fighting, cruelty to animals, fire-setting, lack of friends, or alcohol/drug use. These can be signs of serious problems. Don't be afraid to get help for your child if such behaviors exist, and talk with a trusted professional in the community.

For Students

- Be a role model by never physically or verbally harming, bullying, teasing, or intimidating others.

- If your friends tell you about troubling feelings or thoughts, listen well and let them know you care. Encourage them to get help from a trusted adult. If you are very concerned, talk to an adult you trust.

- When you are angry, take a few deep breaths and imagine yourself on a lake or at the beach or anywhere that makes you feel peaceful. After you are more calm, identify what is making you upset. Decide on your options for handling the problem, such as talking the problem out calmly with the people involved, avoiding the problem by staying away from certain people, or diffusing the problem by resolving to take it less seriously. After you decide what to do (or not do) and act on your decision, be sure to look back and decide if what you did helped the situation.

- Work with your school to create a process for students to safely report threats, intimidation, weapon possession, drug selling, gang activity, and vandalism.

- Help develop and participate in activities to promote understanding and respecting differences.

- Volunteer to be a mentor for younger students and/or provide tutoring for your peers.

- If you feel intensely angry, fearful, anxious, or depressed, talk about it with an adult you trust.

- Get involved in your school's violence prevention and response plan. If a plan does not exist, suggest starting one.

For School Officials

- Develop a comprehensive violence prevention plan that does not label or stigmatize children. Involve staff, parents, students, and members of the community in the creation and implementation of this plan.

- Create a school environment that is safe and responsive to all children. Students should be able to share their needs, fears, concerns, and anxieties, and also safely report threats.

- Ensure that opportunities exist for adults to spend quality personal time with children. A positive relationship with an adult who is available to provide support is one of the most critical factors in preventing school violence.

- Discuss safety issues openly. Schools can reduce the risk of violence by teaching children about the dangers of firearms as well as appropriate ways to resolve conflicts and express anger.

- Offer supervised, school-based before- and after-school programs that provide children with support and a range of options, such as counseling, tutoring, clubs, community service, and help with homework.

* Be prepared for a crisis or violent act. Provide in-service training for all faculty and staff to explain what to do in a crisis, including the evacuation procedure, communication plan, and how to contact help.

Who Is Affected?

School-associated violence is a major concern for most Americans. Such violence not only affects the individuals involved, but also has an enormous impact on their families, the entire school population, and the community at large. School-associated violence includes non-fatal events, such as fighting, as well as deaths.

Of high school students nationwide in 1997:

* 15.0% were in one or more physical fights on school property.

* 3.5% were treated by a doctor or a nurse for injuries sustained in a fight.

* 4.0% had missed one or more days of school in the past month because they felt unsafe traveling to or from school.

From an ongoing study of school-associated violent deaths (a school-associated death is one that occurs on school property, at a school-sponsored event, or on the way to or from a school-sponsored event):

* 58 school-associated deaths occurred during the 1997–98 school year.

* The average number of school-associated violent events with multiple victims has increased from one event per school year in 1992 to five events per year in 1998.

Stopping School Violence

The mix has become appallingly predictable: volcanic anger, no skills to vent the anger or ease the pain, no trusted adult to turn to, and accessibility of firearms. Result: dead and wounded students, faculty, and staff at schools in all parts of our nation. We can all help prevent these tragedies in three ways: violence prevention (not reaction) programs in every community; young people taught by all of us how to manage anger and handle conflicts peaceably; and guns kept out of the hands of unsupervised kids and treated as hazardous consumer products.

But the relatively small number of school-site homicides is only the tip of an iceberg that could cost our children their futures and our communities their civic health. Violence in our schools—whether it involves threats, fistfights, knives, or firearms—is unwarranted and intolerable. Children deserve a safe setting to learn in. Teachers and staff deserve a safe place to work in. Communities deserve safe schools that educate kids and help keep neighborhoods safer.

For some schools, violence may be a minor issue; for others, it may be a daily presence. Though the most extreme forms of violence are rare, the threat of all kinds of violence can keep students away from school, prevent them from going to after-school events, and leave them in fear every day.

To make our schools safer, everyone can and must pitch in—teachers, parents, students, policy makers, law enforcement officers, business managers, faith leaders, civic leaders, youth workers, and other concerned community residents. Each of us can do something to help solve the problem. And it's a problem we all must solve.

On your own, with a group, with your child, with a classroom full of children—whatever you do, there's something here you can do. Anything you do will help.

Watch for Signs... Take Action

Know signs that kids are troubled and know how to get them help. Look for such signs as:

- Lack of interest in school.

- Absence of age-appropriate anger control skills.

- Seeing self as always the victim.

- Persistent disregard for or refusal to follow rules.

- Cruelty to pets or other animals.

- Artwork or writing that is bleak or violent or that depicts isolation or anger.

- Talking constantly about weapons or violence.

- Obsessions with things like violent games and TV shows.

- Depression or mood swings.

- Bringing a weapon (any weapon) to school.

- History of bullying.

- Misplaced or unwarranted jealousy.

- Involvement with or interest in gangs.

- Self-isolation from family and friends.

- Talking about bringing weapons to school.

The more of these signs you see, the greater the chance that the child needs help. If it's your child and he or she won't discuss these signs with you, see if a relative, a teacher, a counselor, a religious leader, a coach, or another adult can break the ice.

Get help right away. Talk with a counselor, mental health clinic, family doctor, a psychologist, religious leader, the school's dean of students, or the office of student assistance. The faster you find help, the more likely the problem can be resolved.

Not your child? Recognizing these signs in any child should set off alarm bells for any community member. If you know a child well enough to notice these changes, constructively express concern to the parent(s), who may already be taking action and would welcome your support. If parents appear disinterested, speak to the child's teacher or counselor.

Chapter 9

Integration of Work, Family, and Education

Today, managing work and family obligations more often than not becomes a balancing act for employees. Given economic necessities, it has become increasingly difficult for families to participate in their children's education. In spite of an era of downsizing and scarcer resources, some employers have begun to establish internal and external policies and practices that help employees integrate their work and family lives and their subsequent involvement in children's education.

Researchers at the Families and Work Institute have observed that employers respond in a variety of ways to the family and personal life concerns of their employees, often evolving from one approach to another in stages. Frequently, this evolution is from narrower to broader approaches; for example, moving from focusing on employed mothers in the beginning, to targeting other employee groups, but these stages are not always followed sequentially. Many employers also work on issues of two or more stages at the same time. The five stages of family friendliness are described below.

The Five Stages of Family Friendly Companies

Stage I. Employers focus on addressing women employees' child care needs. Overcoming an initial resistance to address these issues,

Excerpted from an undated pamphlet "Employers, Families, and Education: Integration of Work, Family, and Education," U.S. Department of Education, http://www.ed.gov/pubs/EmpFamEd/integration.html, downloaded July 2002.

the company might offer a child care resource and referral service to help employees find child care, or provide assistance in paying for child care.

Stage II. Employers broaden their scope to include men, as well as women, to address a wider, more coordinated, comprehensive effort relative to family and personal life issues, and thereby expanding the definition of "family." For example, companies might add elder care resource and referral services, parental leave for mothers AND fathers, and beginning and end of day flextime. In communications to employees, they would position this expanded list of policies and programs as an integrated work-family agenda.

Stage III. The focus shifts from work-family to work-life in recognition of the fact that companies are trying to address the needs of all workers throughout the life cycle. Employers realize that their programs and policies will achieve their intended effects only if they exist at the organizational core within a supportive culture. There is an expanded focus on communications: publicizing managers' commitment to work-life issues; finding managers to serve as role models; removing mixed messages within the organization; and trying to align policy with practice. Employers also focus on improving the way front-line supervisors handle employees' work-life experiences and on making the organizational culture more family-friendly, linking work-family issues to business strategies and other human resource issues, such as managing diversity, developing human capital, or improving quality.

Stage IV. Using a work-life lens to focus on work and work processes, employers question how the organization of work affects both business productivity and personal tasks and/or family well-being. The answers become a catalyst for change as companies recognize that they can profit by looking at the whole person. Now companies characteristically look away from the notion of work-life conflict toward work-life synergy looking for ways that work life and family/personal life can enhance, not detract from, each other.

Stage V: Employers' efforts at family friendliness link community with company. Employers build a sense of community in the workplace and align efforts at work with efforts in the community, for example, supporting efforts to increase family involvement in children's education by providing more workplace flexibility and by participating in community efforts to do the same. Now companies also promote and provide training for skills (such as conflict resolution) needed at work, at home, and in community participation.

For employees spending a high proportion of their working hours on the job, the workplace becomes an excellent forum for family support and education. However, employees cannot do it alone; coordinated and cooperative efforts, whether internal to the company or in partnership with other community stakeholders, must be planned and developed to address this important work-life issue.

Successful implementation of internal company policies and practices that support family and employee involvement in education depends on selling top management, gaining widespread organizational support and ownership, and articulating and sharing benefits to the bottom line with managers and employees. Internal policies and practices related to family involvement in education could include flexible time and leave arrangements, job sharing, part-time work arrangements, employer-sponsored seminars and parenting programs, dependent care assistance, resource and referral services (including "hotlines"), on-site day care centers, education assistance benefits, and literacy training for adults.

Internal Policies That Make It Possible for Employees to be Involved in Education

Flextime

In a national survey, many employers reported a "dramatic reduction in both absenteeism and tardiness" when employees were given the option of working flexible hours. The survey also found that after three years of the flextime option, 64 percent of the firms reported turnover reductions.

Some employers offer flextime at the beginning and end of the day. Employees can choose to come in and leave earlier or later than the standard work hours. The band of flexible time at the beginning and end of the day varies from company to company; the wider the window of choice the more employees will be able to take advantage of flextime to be more involved in school activities. At GT Water Products, a small manufacturing company, almost half of the 23 employees work a flexible schedule.

Another version of flextime is sometimes called "lunchtime flex." Employees who work for companies like IBM (which has a formal

71

lunchtime flex policy), work longer days from start to finish, but can take 1 to 2 hours off at lunchtime enabling them to visit a neighborhood school or eat lunch at their child's day care center.

Part-Time Work Options

Employers can offer flexibility by allowing part-time work or job sharing. According to a study by the Families and Work Institute, many employees, including 19 percent of those with young children, say they would willingly trade a full-time income for a part-time one in order to spend more time with their children.

Job sharing is another way to create part-time work. One example can be found in the Jefferson County Public School System in Kentucky where teachers are permitted to job-share; currently, at least 10 elementary and high school classrooms are shared between two teachers.

Telecommuting

Recently there has been much talk of work-at-home, or telecommuting. Allowing employees to work at home on a regular basis (when appropriate to the job) gives them extra flexibility in arranging how and when they get work done, and saves them commuting time. Employers who offer telecommuting opportunities have generally reported that employees continue to perform as well or even better than they had when they worked on-site. Such an arrangement, although no substitute for child care, allows parents to be at home after school, have lunch with their children, or be available to meet with school staff.

Time off for School Meetings and Special Activities

Many employers have taken flextime a step further. Organizations that wish to actively promote family involvement in education have established educational time-off policies which they make available to all employees, whether or not they have dependent children. This encourages all employees—grandparents, aunts and uncles, neighbors and concerned citizens—to become involved in the lives of children in the community.

Some employers allow parents to be absent or late on the first day of school so that they can accompany their children to school, meet classmates, teachers, and other staff, and, in schools that permit it, spend some time with young children to acclimate them to the new setting. RJR Nabisco and NationsBank, among others, have such a policy.

Other employers allow a certain number of hours or days off to participate in school activities. School Specialty, a school supply company, allows each associate 24 hours each year of paid time on educational activities. Those employees who do not have children in school are able to participate in programs with one of the company's local partner schools. On a regular basis, School Specialty associates participate in reading groups, art projects, and special events at the Badger School in the Appleton School District, Wisconsin.

Companies Are Supporting Families through Worksite and Offsite Programs

Child Care through Internal and Community Programs

Our nation will be unable to challenge parents to get involved early in their children's learning unless the quantity and quality of child care is improved. This is of crucial importance, because child care is often children's first learning experience outside the home, and studies reveal that the current quality of early care and education is uneven. Employers' growing awareness of the importance of quality child care and good schools as a matter of public concern has reinforced their own efforts to support working parents who are in their employ relative to child care needs and school improvement. Across three national surveys, employers reported that recruitment and reduced absenteeism were the two most strongly perceived benefits of company child care initiatives.

Consequently, business involvement and efforts have increased. Responding to the need for available, affordable, and quality child care, many businesses are now providing child care for their employees. They are sponsoring child care resource and referral services, collaborating in the training of child care providers and in promoting accreditation, and subsidizing the high costs of child care.

Thirteen percent of large employers provide child care for their employees through on- or near-site centers; such companies include Merck & Company, Inc., SAS Institute, Inc., and Campbell Soup Company. Several organizations that cannot afford to support a center on their own have joined with other employers to form a consortium child care center. One such center, in Randolph, Massachusetts, is co-sponsored by Codman & Schurtleff (a division of Johnson & Johnson), Dunkin' Donuts, and New England Telephone.

Child care resource and referral services, available to 20 percent of employees nationwide, give employees access to trained specialists who can refer them to available child care openings in their communities, and provide educational materials to help them choose quality care. Employers either provide an in-house referral service or contract with an outside service; multisite organizations can contract with one of a number of services that operate nationwide.

Providing quality child care is costly. In turn, it is expensive for parents. To ease this burden, employers such as Levi Strauss & Company have adopted programs that help employees pay for child care, sometimes on a sliding fee scale based on the employee's salary. Other employers arrange discounts for their employees at specific child care centers in the community. Fifty-five percent of large companies take advantage of federal tax law by offering Dependent Care Assistance Plans (DCAP), which allow employees to set aside up to $5,000 of their pretax salaries for child care expenses.

Employers can also work to improve child care in the larger community. For example, the American Business Collaboration for Quality Dependent Care (ABC) consists of over 100 companies and public/ private organizations that have committed more than $127 million to improve the quality and increase the quantity of child and elder care in more than 4 dozen communities around the country. Projects vary widely, because they grow out of regional needs, but some examples are science and technology summer camps (in which school-age children work with professional scientists and engineers); a training program for teachers of infants in child care; and a toy lending library and resource room that provides equipment, materials, toys, and technical assistance to area child care homes and centers.

Designed and initiated by the BankAmerica Foundation and the California Child Care Resource and Referral Network, the "California Child Care Initiative Project" includes 500 corporations, local businesses, and public sector funders that have contributed $7.8 million since its inception in 1985. They have recruited more than 4,400 home-based providers and trained nearly 30,000 new and experienced providers. This project was replicated in Michigan and in Oregon with funding from the states and the Ford Foundation.

Employer-Sponsored Seminars

Employer-sponsored seminars can cover a wide range of topics. Seminars at the workplace are typically run by local parenting experts or through contracts with national or local child care resource and referral services. DuPont has developed lunchtime seminars whose topics range from "What to Expect in Kindergarten" to "How to Connect With Your Teenager."

"Parenting for Education" is a parenting seminar series developed by U.S. West Education Foundation to promote school success. Employers and community groups purchase the 8-hour program, which includes a kit for trainers and materials for parent participants. Interactive exercises and structured discussion groups aim to give parents the understanding, confidence, and skills they need to become positively involved in their children's education.

Parenting and Training Programs

Parenting and training programs for parents are managed both on and off business work sites. A few of these programs are described in the following paragraphs.

Parents as Teachers (PAT) is a home-school-community partnership program designed to support parents of children from birth to age 5 through home visits by parent educators, parent support groups, and a referral network. Established originally by four school districts in Missouri, PAT is now mandated as a service in that state, and has been replicated in hundreds of other school districts around the country. Honeywell and Motorola have each adapted the program for their employees.

Home Instruction Program for Preschool Youngsters (HIPPY) is an early intervention program designed to support parents as a child's first and most influential teacher. The program is delivered by paraprofessionals, themselves former participant teachers in the program. During home visits and group meetings, they role play the educational materials with the parents. This sets up successful learning experiences for the parent and child, who work together with the materials 15–20 minutes each day. Hasbro, Bank of Boston (in Chicago), Primerica (in New York City), and Baltimore Gas and Electric have all contributed substantial funding and in-kind donations to HIPPY.

MegaSkills is a parent education program that trains individuals to run workshops for families. Workshops teach parents how to foster skills that build school success, such as confidence, motivation, responsibility, teamwork, and problem solving. The Fort Wayne, Indiana Chamber of Commerce and Merck are among the many employers to sponsor MegaSkills programs for employees and the community.

Ambassadors for Education is a program disseminated by the National Association of Partners in Education (NAPE). Delivered in the form of a hands-on workshop, it is designed to get adult community members more involved in the schools. Some employers, such as UNUM Life Insurance, BellSouth, and Shell Oil have sponsored workshops for their employees.

Resource and Referral Services

Some employers, such as John Hancock and Southern California Edison, have established family resource libraries from which employers can borrow books or videos. Some employers contract with providers of parent resource hotlines. Employees can call an 800 number for advice and information on education-related issues, such as how to motivate their child, how much to help with homework, or how to help a child who is having trouble with math. Ameritech has a "teenline" a telephone hotline that provides counseling specifically on teen-related issues. Employees of Marriott International call their company's "Associate Resource Line" to consult in one of 17 different languages on issues ranging from child care needs to accessing community services.

Newsletters and Websites

Some employers provide employees with newsletters and other materials or sponsor employee subscriptions to parent newsletters, such as Work & Family Newsletter or Education Today, which is typically customized in some way and distributed free-of-charge to all interested employees. The FamilyEducation Company™, which publishes Education Today, has also developed an information-rich web site, along with a service that helps school districts build their own web sites to connect schools, families, and communities. Through these sites, parents have access to minutes from school board meetings, curriculum information, online discussions with their peers, and more.

Chapter 10

Strong Families: Best Youth Delinquency Prevention

Parents and Families

This text examines the following factors involving the impact of parents and families on the problem of youth violence: strong family relationships; single parent families; welfare dependency; parental responsibility; peer influences; mentoring programs; child care; role models: parents, family, friends.

Strong family relationships. Although there is no single cause for youth violence, the most common factor is family dysfunction. Domestic violence and conflict/tension within the family are often associated with troubled youth. Abuse, neglect and hostility are prevalent in cases of youth violence. Exposure to violence leads to acceptance of violence as a means to solve problems. Research demonstrates that this develops into the cycle of violence.

The importance of strong family relationships to the healthy growth and development cannot be overstated. No one will ever have a more important responsibility than the responsibility to raise their

---

This chapter contains text from "Parents and Families," Bi-Partisan Working Group on Youth Violence, http://www.house.gov/dunn/workinggroup/wkgpf.htm, 1999, and "Family Involvement in Children's Education", U.S. Department of Education, http://www.ed.gov/pubs/FamInvolve/execsumm.html, October 1997. Despite the ages of these documents, readers seeking information on strong families and youth violence prevention will find this information useful.

children in a healthy, secure, nurturing environment. Likewise, the public sector, the private sector and the non-profit community all have a responsibility to help parents obtain the skills and resources they need to meet those obligations.

Single parent families. Research does not reveal any direct, causal link between single parent families and youth violence. However, the lack of parenting skills and knowledge of child development was identified as a serious risk factor for unhealthy youth development.

The teaching of such parenting skills that formerly were taught in such classes as home economics, life sciences/skills, and personal health is recommended. We should also use public health agencies like WIC (Women, Infants, and Children), pre-natal care clinics, and visiting nurses to reach out to mothers in need to help them gain the knowledge they need to raise healthy children. We need to teach parents how to parent. And we need to help all children in the pre-school years. Although ambitious efforts such as Head Start, and Even Start exist, we need to address the gaps in education and health care that fail to reach children's needs.

Welfare dependency. Although welfare itself was not a central focus of the panel's work, Dr. Steinberg stated clearly that poverty is the number one cause of negative parenting. Economic stress raises all other risk factors.

A strong national economy is essential to our progress on the challenge of youth violence. In these times of economic prosperity, we too easily forget that social problems like youth violence are exacerbated dramatically during times of economic hardship. We should use this opportunity to reaffirm our commitment to a national economic policy of providing every family in America the opportunity to succeed economically through hard work.

Parental responsibility. The latchkey factor is not necessarily indicative of a child with a propensity toward violence. Rather, negative parenting is the biggest factor. Statistics indicate that the prevalence of parental disengagement is 25–30 percent, and one-quarter of American adolescents are not sure that their parents love them. Parental engagement is the single most important factor in a child's healthy development.

Character education that involves the parents can help children to develop a healthy sense of self and self-worth. Schools can be a focal point to strengthen the relationship between parents and children through such joint efforts as character education. Character education integrated throughout the curriculum can help children develop and strengthen basic values such as honesty, integrity, courage, respect for self and others, perseverance, kindness, etc. that will help them to become good citizens as well as good students.

Peer influences. With young people, peer relationships are a key factor because youths tend to offend and take offense in groups. All efforts to reach young people must recognize this central fact and work within the reality of the social structure of the youth culture.

Youth-run adjudication and remediation systems can be successful in encouraging youth to take responsibility for their actions and to demand better from their peers.

Mentoring programs. The single most important influence in the healthy development of the child is positive interaction with adults. Mentors can play a key role especially for at-risk youths whose family situations can contribute significantly to the propensity for violence.

Too often today, communities are disconnected from families. Many organizations—such as Boy Scouts, Girl Scouts, Boys and Girls Clubs, boosters, etc.—perform important mentoring functions.

Child care. Study after study have shown the hours of 3–6 PM each day is the key time for youth trouble. Likewise, studies have shown conclusively that the two most dangerous school days of the year are prom night and graduation day. In North Carolina, schools have utilized low levels of federal funds to promote adult-supervised Lock-Ins for students to have an all-night, alcohol- and drug-free event. The results in safety improvement are dramatic.

Families and students need help coordinating the differing schedules of school and work. This could come in the form of support for extended day schools. Studies have shown that teenagers need additional sleep to function optimally. In some areas, high schools are experimenting with school days that start and end later in the day.

Role models. The absence of strong role models inhibits a child's character growth. As mentioned above, Big Brothers/Big Sisters and similar initiatives help at-risk youth develop healthy relationships with adults necessary for healthy growth.

• The importance of strong family relationships to the child's healthy growth and development cannot be overstated.

79

- Parental engagement is the single most important factor in a child's healthy development.

- The single most important influence in the healthy development of the child is positive interaction with adults. Mentors can play a key role, especially for at-risk youths whose family situations can contribute significantly to the propensity for violence.

- Increased support is needed for initiatives that help families and students coordinate the differing schedules of school and work.

Family Involvement in Children's Education

Thirty years of research confirms that family involvement is a powerful influence on children's achievement in school. When families are involved in their children's education, children earn higher grades and receive higher scores on tests, attend school more regularly, complete more homework, demonstrate more positive attitudes and behaviors, graduate from high school at higher rates, and are more likely to enroll in higher education than students with less involved families. For these reasons, increasing family involvement in the education of their children is an important goal for schools, particularly those serving low-income and other students at risk of failure.

Families and Schools as Partners

If families are to work with schools as partners in the education of their children, schools must provide them with the opportunities and support they need to become involved. Too often schools expect families to do it all alone. Developing effective partnerships with families requires that all school staff (administrators, teachers, and support staff) create a school environment that welcomes parents and encourages them to raise questions and voice their concerns as well as to participate appropriately in decision making. Developing partnerships also requires that school staff provide parents with the information and training they need to become involved and that they reach out to parents with invitations to participate in their children's learning.

Schools that are most successful in engaging parents and other family members in support of their children's learning look beyond traditional definitions of parent involvement—participating in a parent teacher organization or signing quarterly report cards—to a broader conception of parents as full partners in the education of their children. Rather than striving only to increase parent participation in school-based activities, successful schools seek to support families in their activities outside of school that can encourage their children's learning. Schools that have developed successful partnerships with parents view student achievement as a shared responsibility, and all stakeholders—including parents, administrators, teachers, and community leaders—play important roles in supporting children's learning.

Successful school-family partnerships require the sustained mutual collaboration, support, and participation of school staffs and families at home and at school in activities that can directly affect the success of children's learning. If families are to work with schools as full partners in the education of their children, schools must provide them with the opportunities and support they need for success.

Strategies for Overcoming Common Barriers to Family Involvement in Schools

Overcoming time and resource constraints. In order to build strong partnerships, families and school staff members need time to get to know one another, plan how they will work together to increase student learning, and carry out their plans. Successful programs find the time and resources for both teachers and parents to develop school-family partnerships.

Providing information and training to parents and school staff. Without the information and skills to communicate with each other, misperceptions and distrust can flourish between parents and school personnel. Through workshops and a variety of outreach activities such as informative newsletters, handbooks, and home visits, parents and school staff in successful programs are learning how to trust each other and work together to help children succeed in school.

Restructuring schools to support family involvement. Developing a successful school-family partnership must be a whole school endeavor, not the work of a single person or program. Traditional school organization and practices, especially in secondary schools, often discourage family members from becoming involved. To create a welcoming environment for parents, one that enlists their support in helping their children succeed, schools can make changes that make them more personal and inviting places. Whatever steps schools take

81

in developing partnerships with families, schools that are most successful are prepared to reconsider all of their established ways of doing business and to restructure in ways that will make them less hierarchical, more personal, and more accessible to parents.

Bridging school-family differences. Language and cultural differences as well as differences in educational attainment separating families and school staff can make communication and family participation in school activities difficult. Strategies to address these differences include reaching out to parents with little formal education, addressing language differences through bilingual services for communicating both orally and in writing with families about school programs and children's progress, and promoting cultural understanding to build trust between home and school.

Tapping external supports for partnerships. Many schools have nourished and strengthened partnerships by tapping the supports available in their local communities and beyond. Collaborative efforts to provide schools and families with the tools they need to support learning can include partnerships with local businesses, health care and other community service agencies, and colleges and universities, as well as supports provided by school districts and states.

Effects on Students and Families

Although it is impossible to attribute student achievement gains or other student outcomes in any of these schools or districts solely to their parent involvement activities, it does appear that many schools that make parent involvement a priority also see student outcomes improve. These positive outcomes may be due to increased parent involvement itself, or, what is more likely, to a whole constellation of factors, including a strong instructional program and a commitment to high standards for all students. Nevertheless, it appears that strong parent involvement is an important feature of many schools that succeed in raising student achievement.

Guidelines for Effective Partnerships

Effective strategies for partnerships differ from community to community, and the most appropriate strategies for a particular community will depend on local interests, needs, and resources. Even so, successful approaches to promoting family involvement in the education of their children share an emphasis on innovation and flexibility. The experiences of current programs suggest the following guidelines for successful partnerships:

There is no "one size fits all" approach to partnerships. Build on what works well. Begin the school-family partnership by identifying, with families, the strengths, interests, and needs of families, students, and school staff, and design strategies that respond to identified strengths, interests, and needs.

Training and staff development is an essential investment. Strengthen the school-family partnership with professional development and training for all school staff as well as parents and other family members. Both school staff and families need the knowledge and skills that enable them to work with one another and with the larger community to support children's learning.

Communication is the foundation of effective partnerships. Plan strategies that accommodate the varied language and cultural needs as well as lifestyles and work schedules of school staff and families. Even the best planned school-family partnerships will fail if the participants cannot communicate effectively.

Flexibility and diversity are key. Recognize that effective parent involvement takes many forms that may not necessarily require parents' presence at a workshop, meeting, or school. The emphasis should be on parents helping children learn, and this can happen in schools, homes, or elsewhere in a community.

Projects need to take advantage of the training, assistance, and funding offered by sources external to schools. These can include school districts, community organizations and public agencies, local colleges and universities, state education agencies, and Education Department-sponsored Comprehensive Regional Assistance Centers.

Change takes time. Recognize that developing a successful school-family partnership requires continued effort over time, and that solving one problem often creates new challenges. Further, a successful partnership requires the involvement of many stakeholders, not just a few.

Projects need to regularly assess the effects of the partnership using multiple indicators. These may include indicators of family, school staff, and community participation in and satisfaction with school-related activities. They may also include measures of the quality of school-family interactions and of student educational progress.

Chapter 11

Benefits of
After-School Programs

Introduction

The Need for After-School Programs

Today, more than 28 million school-age children have parents who
work outside the home. An estimated five to seven million, and up to
as many as 15 million latch-key children return to an empty home
after school. When the school bell rings, the anxiety for parents often
just begins. They worry about whether their children are safe, whether
they are susceptible to drugs and crime.

In response to this pressing concern, many communities have
created after-school programs to keep children and youth out of
trouble and engaged in activities that help them learn. Almost 100
percent of people polled in a recent survey agreed that it is important for children to have an after-school program that helps them
develop academic and social skills in a safe and caring environment.

However, a chronic shortage of quality after-school programs exists. According to parents, the need far exceeds the current supply. One recent study found that twice as many elementary and
middle school parents wanted after-school programs as were currently available.

Excerpted from "After-School Programs: Keeping Children Safe and
Smart," U.S. Department of Education, http://www.ed.gov/pubs/afterschool/
afterschool.pdf, June 2000.

After-school programs provide a wide array of benefits to children, their families, schools, and the whole community. This chapter focuses exclusively on the benefits children receive in terms of increased safety, reduced risk-taking, and improved learning.

Helping Children to Succeed

First and foremost, after-school programs keep children of all ages safe and out of trouble. The after-school hours are the time when juvenile crime hits its peak, but through attentive adult supervision, quality after-school programs can protect our children. As this report shows, in communities with comprehensive programs, children are less likely to commit crimes or to be victimized, and are less likely to engage in risky behavior such as drug, alcohol and tobacco use.

After-school programs also can help to improve the academic performance of participating children. For many children, their reading and math scores have improved, in large part because after-school programs allow them to focus attention on areas in which they are having difficulties. Many programs connect learning to more relaxed and enriching activities, thereby improving academic performance as well.

After-school programs also contribute to raising children's self-confidence as well as academic performance. Both teachers and parents report that children who participate in after-school programs develop better social skills and learn to handle conflicts in more socially acceptable ways. Children indicate that they have higher aspirations for their future, including greater intentions to complete high school and attend college.

Families able to enroll their children in good programs indicate that their children are safer and more successful in school. These families also develop a greater interest in their child's learning. In addition, children develop new interests and skills and improve their school attendance.

In many cases, communities have come together to improve the availability of after-school programs. Partnerships among schools, local governments, law enforcement, youth- and community-based organizations, social and health services, and businesses have resulted in a number of high-quality after-school programs. These partnerships foster a greater volunteer spirit and provide opportunities for parents and other adults to participate in program activities.

86

From school to school, neighborhood to neighborhood, and community to community, every after-school program is different. Successful programs respond to community needs: their creation is the result of a community effort to evaluate the needs of its school-age children when school is not in session.

For many children in neighborhoods across America, after-school programs provide a structured, safe, supervised place to be after school for learning, fun, and friendship with adults and peers alike.

The Potential of After-School Programs

Keeping Children on the Right Track

Preventing Crime, Juvenile Delinquency, and Violent Victimization

The rate for juvenile crime peaks in the after-school hours. About 10 percent of violent juvenile crimes are committed between 3 p.m. and 4 p.m. Children are also at a much greater risk of being the victim of a violent crime (murder, a violent sex offense, robbery, or assault) after the school day, roughly 2 p.m. to 6 p.m. By offering children rewarding, challenging, and age-appropriate activities in safe, structured and positive environments, after-school programs help to reduce and prevent juvenile delinquency and insulate children from violent victimization.

Preventing Drug, Alcohol, and Tobacco Use

Latchkey children are at a substantially higher risk for risk taking behavior, including substance abuse. Youth ages 10–16 who have a relationship with a mentor, an important component of a quality after-school program, are 46 percent less likely to start using drugs and 27 percent less likely to start drinking alcohol. After-school programs can provide youth with positive and healthy alternatives to drug, alcohol, and tobacco use, criminal activity, and other high-risk behaviors during the peak crime hours after school.

Decreasing the Amount of Television Watched

The most common activity for children after school is watching television. After school and in the evenings, children watch, on average, about 23 hours per week of television. Quality after-school programs offer children and youth enjoyable alternatives to television watching during the after-school hours in environments filled with opportunities to learn and grow.

Enhancing Children's Academic Achievement

Improving Children's Grades and Academic Achievement

Young people attending formal after-school programs often spend more time in academic activities and in enrichment lessons than do their peers left unsupervised after school. Children whose out-of-school time includes 20–35 hours of constructive learning activities do better in school.

Studies indicate that students in after-school programs show better achievement in math, reading, and other subjects.

Increasing Children's Interest and Ability in Reading

Quality after-school curricula expose children to an environment rich in language and print. Quality, research-based tutoring programs also produce improvements in reading achievement. Tutoring can also lead to greater self-confidence in reading, increased motivation to read, and improved behavior.

Improving School Attendance, Increasing Engagement in School, and Reducing the Dropout Rate

After-school programs can help children develop greater confidence in their academic abilities and a greater interest in school, both of which have been shown to lead to improved school attendance and completion rates. Students who spent even one to four hours a week in extracurricular activities were 60 percent less likely to have dropped out of school by 12th grade than their peers who did not participate.

Increasing Homework Quality

The structure of an after-school program can make homework part of students' daily routine. This can contribute to children in after-school programs completing more and better-prepared homework because of their participation.

Increasing Aspirations for the Future

By giving children role models and the tools they need to succeed in school, after-school programs can help children realize their full potential.

Supporting Children's Social Development and Their Relationships with Adults and Peers

Improved Behavior in School

Research shows that children who participate in after-school programs behave better in class, handle conflict more effectively, and cooperate more with authority figures and with their peers.

Better Social Skills

The after-school environment allows children to interact socially in a more relaxed atmosphere. Research shows that children with the opportunity to make social connections in after-school hours are better adjusted and happier than those who do not have this opportunity.

Improved Self-Confidence

Youth organizations have indicated that the single most important factor in the success of their programs is the relationship between participants and the adults who work with them. Programs can provide the opportunity for youth to gain self-confidence through development of caring relationships with adults and peers.

Strengthening Schools, Families, and Communities

More Effective Use of Funding

After-school programs can help school districts save money over the long term because of decreased student retention and special education placements. Where there is a decrease in juvenile crime due to a program, communities also save resources.

Greater Family and Community Involvement

Many after-school programs depend on and draw upon parent and community volunteers. Research shows that when families are involved in schools, students do better. Educators can also expect that when family and community members make an investment in an after-school program, they will be more interested and involved in their own children's learning, in the learning of all children in the program, and in the life of the school as a whole.

What Works: Components of Exemplary After-School Programs

Quality after-school programs can provide safe, engaging environments that motivate and inspire learning outside the regular school day. While there is no one single formula for success in after-school programs, both practitioners and researchers have found that effective programs combine academic, enrichment, cultural, and recreational activities to guide learning and engage children and youth in wholesome activities. They also find that the best programs develop activities to meet the particular needs of the communities they serve. Common elements of quality programs include:

Goal Setting, Strong Management, and Sustainability

Community coordination and collaboration are key to running successful programs.

Focus on the goals of the program. After-school programs should be clear about their intended goals. Establish goals through collaborative decision-making. Manage the program to meet those goals.

Solid organizational structure. Successful governance structure combines hands-on, site-based management with regular oversight and accountability.

Effective management and sustainability. Successful programs use annual operating budgets, accurate bookkeeping systems, affordable fee structures, and multiple funding sources, including in-kind support.

Meeting legal requirements. Successful programs meet licensing requirements, address liability issues, carry adequate liability insurance, maintain appropriate records, regularly review health and safety practices, and comply with the Americans with Disabilities Act requirements.

Quality After-School Staff

All programs need staff who are qualified and committed, have appropriate experience and realistic expectations, and can interact productively with regular school staff.

90

Role of the program administrator. The program director helps ensure that the after-school program provides high-quality services that meet the needs of program staff, students, and families. Effective administrators develop strong relationships with schools and community partners.

Hiring and retaining qualified staff. Programs should hire skilled and qualified staff that are experienced in working with school-age children. Programs should also provide attractive compensation and work scheduling packages to retain quality staff.

Professional development for staff. In order to sustain a quality program, staff should be provided with ongoing training and learning opportunities.

Use of volunteers. Volunteers can reduce the price of a program and the staff-to-child ratio. Incorporate volunteers into programs appropriate to their skill levels and interests.

Low staff-to-student ratio. For true student enrichment, the staff to student ratio should be between 1:10 and 1:15 for groups of children age six and older.

Attention to Safety, Health, and Nutrition Issues

Creating safe places with adequate space and materials. Programs should be safe, close to home and accessible to all who want to participate. They should have adequate space for a variety of indoor and outdoor activities and age-appropriate materials for enhancing learning.

Meeting nutritional needs. Good after-school programs provide a nutritious snack and other meals when appropriate, for relaxation and socializing and to promote sound nutrition for participants.

Effective Partnerships

Implementing a quality after-school program requires collaboration among diverse partners: parents, educators, community residents, law enforcement agencies, service providers, community-based and civic organizations, colleges, employers, arts and cultural institutions, museums, park and recreation services, and public officials.

Steps to Building an After-School Partnership

Collaboration often requires changes in traditional roles, responsibilities, expectations, relationships, and schedules.

- Build consensus and partnerships among key stakeholders.

- Assess school/community needs and resources.

- Provide opportunities for both children and families within the school and the community.

- Address logistical issues.

- Obtain qualified staff and clearly define their roles and responsibilities.

Using Community Resources Effectively

Communities can provide a wide range of resources for developing high-quality programs, such as funding, facilities, materials, job shadowing, mentors, tutors, and community service experiences.

Strong Involvement of Families

The success of an after-school program depends on the involvement of both families and the community.

Involving families and youth in program planning. Programs that include families and children in planning draw greater support from participants, families, and the community at large. Activities are more fun and culturally relevant, and capture children and adolescents' interests better.

Attending to the needs of working parents. Good programs are designed with sensitivity to the schedules and requirements of working parents. They also accommodate family schedules, making after-school programs affordable, and provide transportation to and from after-school programs.

Enriching Learning Opportunities

By providing structured enriching learning opportunities, after-school programs can improve children's academic performance and meet their social, emotional, and physical development needs. In addition, enrichment opportunities not available during the regular school day such as art, music, and drama can be offered to complement the regular school-day program.

Providing engaging opportunities to grow and learn. Quality programs allow children to follow their own interests and learn in different ways. Programming reflects the needs, interests, and abilities of children.

Challenging curriculum in an enriching environment. Successful programs make the curriculum challenging, but not overwhelming. A challenging curriculum accommodates individual student needs, coordinates with in-school instruction, and focuses on more than remedial work.

Coordinating learning with the regular school day. Good programs provide a continuity of learning for students through coordination with the regular school day and communication with teachers and staff.

Linking school-day and after-school curriculum. Quality after-school curricula integrate learning and enrichment through clear cycles of assessment, feedback, and evaluation that meet students' needs.

Linkages between School-Day and After-School Personnel

Quality programs support and coordinate their activities with schools in a way that supports true partnering. Quality programs have:

Planning time to maximize children's opportunities. Time is provided for school-day and after-school staff to establish and maintain relationships of mutual respect and understanding.

Coordinated use of facilities and resources. Coordination between school and after-school staff regarding use of facilities and equipment is improved with communication and planning to prevent potential problems and misunderstandings.

Evaluation of Program Progress and Effectiveness

Effective after-school programs have a continuous evaluation component built into the design so that program planners can objectively gauge their success based on the clear goals set for the program.

Using data for improvement. A system of accountability and continuous evaluation supports program improvement. With this data, partners can discuss the progress and success of the program, which will help in decision-making around design and funding. Continuous monitoring and shared understanding of program goals help staff maintain their focus, improve effectiveness and accountability, ensure parent and participant satisfaction, and identify necessary changes.

Designing effective evaluations. Programs should be evaluated regularly in ways that incorporate multiple measures of success that reflect program goals.

Chapter 12

A Guide to Creating and Maintaining Safe Schools

Introduction

Most schools are safe. Although fewer than one percent of all violent deaths of children occur on school grounds—indeed, a child is far
more likely to be killed in the community or at home—no school is
immune.

The violence that occurs in our neighborhoods and communities
has found its way inside the schoolhouse door. And while we can take
some solace in the knowledge that schools are among the safest places
for young people, we must do more. School violence reflects a much
broader problem, one that can only be addressed when everyone—at
school, at home, and in the community—works together.

The 1997–1998 school year served as a dramatic wake-up call to
the fact that guns do come to school, and some students will use them
to kill. One after the other, school communities across the country—
from Oregon to Virginia, from Arkansas to Pennsylvania, from Mississippi to Kentucky—have been forced to face the fact that violence
can happen to them. And while these serious incidents trouble us
deeply, they should not prevent us from acting to prevent school violence of any kind.

There is ample documentation that prevention and early intervention efforts can reduce violence and other troubling behaviors in

Excerpted from "Early Warning, Timely Response: A Guide to Safe
Schools," U.S. Department of Education, http://www.ed.gov/offices/OSERS/
OSEP/Products/earlywrn.html, August 1998.

schools. Research-based practices can help school communities recognize the warning signs early, so children can get the help they need before it is too late. In fact, research suggests that some of the most promising prevention and intervention strategies involve the entire educational community—administrators, teachers, families, students, support staff, and community members—working together to form positive relationships with all children.

If we understand what leads to violence and the types of support that research has shown are effective in preventing violence and other troubling behaviors, we can make our schools safer.

Characteristics of a School That Is Safe and Responsive to All Children

Well functioning schools foster learning, safety, and socially appropriate behaviors. They have a strong academic focus and support students in achieving high standards, foster positive relationships between school staff and students, and promote meaningful parental and community involvement. Most prevention programs in effective schools address multiple factors and recognize that safety and order are related to children's social, emotional, and academic development.

Effective prevention, intervention, and crisis response strategies operate best in school communities that:

Focus on academic achievement. Effective schools convey the attitude that all children can achieve academically and behave appropriately, while at the same time appreciating individual differences. Adequate resources and programs help ensure that expectations are met. Expectations are communicated clearly, with the understanding that meeting such expectations is a responsibility of the student, the school, and the home. Students who do not receive the support they need are less likely to behave in socially desirable ways.

Involve families in meaningful ways. Students whose families are involved in their growth in and outside of school are more likely to experience school success and less likely to become involved in antisocial activities. School communities must make parents feel welcome in school, address barriers to their participation, and keep families positively engaged in their children's education. Effective schools also support families in expressing concerns about their children—and they support families in getting the help they need to address behaviors that cause concern.

Develop links to the community. Everyone must be committed to improving schools. Schools that have close ties to families, support services, community police, the faith-based community, and the community at large can benefit from many valuable resources. When these links are weak, the risk of school violence is heightened and the opportunity to serve children who are at risk for violence or who may be affected by it is decreased.

Emphasize positive relationships among students and staff. Research shows that a positive relationship with an adult who is available to provide support when needed is one of the most critical factors in preventing student violence. Students often look to adults in the school community for guidance, support, and direction. Some children need help overcoming feelings of isolation and support in developing connections to others. Effective schools make sure that opportunities exist for adults to spend quality, personal time with children. Effective schools also foster positive student interpersonal relations—they encourage students to help each other and to feel comfortable assisting others in getting help when needed.

Discuss safety issues openly. Children come to school with many different perceptions—and misconceptions—about death, violence, and the use of weapons. Schools can reduce the risk of violence by teaching children about the dangers of firearms, as well as appropriate strategies for dealing with feelings, expressing anger in appropriate ways, and resolving conflicts. Schools also should teach children that they are responsible for their actions and that the choices they make have consequences for which they will be held accountable.

Treat students with equal respect. A major source of conflict in many schools is the perceived or real problem of bias and unfair treatment of students because of ethnicity, gender, race, social class, religion, disability, nationality, sexual orientation, physical appearance, or some other factor—both by staff and by peers. Students who have been treated unfairly may become scapegoats and/or targets of violence. In some cases, victims may react in aggressive ways. Effective schools communicate to students and the greater community that all children are valued and respected. There is a deliberate and systematic effort—for example, displaying children's artwork, posting academic work prominently throughout the building, respecting students' diversity—to establish a climate that demonstrates care and a sense of community.

Create ways for students to share their concerns. It has been found that peers often are the most likely group to know in advance about potential school violence. Schools must create ways for students to safely report such troubling behaviors that may lead to dangerous situations. And students who report potential school violence must be protected. It is important for schools to support and foster positive relationships between students and adults so students will feel safe providing information about a potentially dangerous situation.

Help children feel safe expressing their feelings. It is very important that children feel safe when expressing their needs, fears, and anxieties to school staff. When they do not have access to caring adults, feelings of isolation, rejection, and disappointment are more likely to occur, increasing the probability of acting-out behaviors.

Have in place a system for referring children who are suspected of being abused or neglected. The referral system must be appropriate and reflect federal and state guidelines.

Offer extended day programs for children. School-based before- and after-school programs can be effective in reducing violence. Effective programs are well supervised and provide children with support and a range of options, such as counseling, tutoring, mentoring, cultural arts, community service, clubs, access to computers, and help with homework.

Promote good citizenship and character. In addition to their academic mission, schools must help students become good citizens. First, schools stand for the civic values set forth in our Constitution and Bill of Rights (patriotism; freedom of religion, speech, and press; equal protection/nondiscrimination; and due process/fairness). Schools also reinforce and promote the shared values of their local communities, such as honesty, kindness, responsibility, and respect for others. Schools should acknowledge that parents are the primary moral educators of their children and work in partnership with them.

Identify problems and assess progress toward solutions. Schools must openly and objectively examine circumstances that are potentially dangerous for students and staff and situations where members of the school community feel threatened or intimidated. Safe schools continually assess progress by identifying problems and collecting information regarding progress toward solutions. Moreover, effective schools share this information with students, families, and the community at large.

Support students in making the transition to adult life and the workplace. Youth need assistance in planning their future and in developing skills that will result in success. For example, schools can provide students with community service opportunities, work-study programs, and apprenticeships that help connect them to caring adults in the community. These relationships, when established early, foster in youth a sense of hope and security for the future.

Research has demonstrated repeatedly that school communities can do a great deal to prevent violence. Having in place a safe and responsive foundation helps all children—and it enables school communities to provide more efficient and effective services to students who need more support. The next step is to learn the early warning signs of a child who is troubled, so that effective interventions can be provided.

Early Warning Signs

Why didn't we see it coming? In the wake of violence, we ask this question not so much to place blame, but to understand better what we can do to prevent such an occurrence from ever happening again. We review over and over in our minds the days leading up to the incident—did the child say or do anything that would have cued us in to the impending crisis? Did we miss an opportunity to help?

There are early warning signs in most cases of violence to self and others—certain behavioral and emotional signs that, when viewed in context, can signal a troubled child. But early warning signs are just that—indicators that a student may need help.

Such signs may or may not indicate a serious problem—they do not necessarily mean that a child is prone to violence toward self or others. Rather, early warning signs provide us with the impetus to check out our concerns and address the child's needs. Early warning signs allow us to act responsibly by getting help for the child before problems escalate.

Early warning signs can help frame concern for a child. However, it is important to avoid inappropriately labeling or stigmatizing individual students because they appear to fit a specific profile or set of early warning indicators. It's okay to be worried about a child, but it's not okay to overreact and jump to conclusions.

Teachers and administrators—and other school support staff—are not professionally trained to analyze children's feelings and motives. But they are on the front line when it comes to observing troublesome behavior and making referrals to appropriate professionals, such as school psychologists, social workers, counselors, and nurses. They also play a significant role in responding to diagnostic information provided by specialists. Thus, it is no surprise that effective schools take special care in training the entire school community to understand and identify early warning signs.

When staff members seek help for a troubled child, when friends report worries about a peer or friend, when parents raise concerns about their child's thoughts or habits, children can get the help they need. By actively sharing information, a school community can provide quick, effective responses.

Principles for Identifying the Early Warning Signs of School Violence

Educators and families can increase their ability to recognize early warning signs by establishing close, caring, and supportive relationships with children and youth—getting to know them well enough to be aware of their needs, feelings, attitudes, and behavior patterns. Educators and parents together can review school records for patterns of behavior or sudden changes in behavior.

Unfortunately, there is a real danger that early warning signs will be misinterpreted. Educators and parents—and in some cases, students—can ensure that the early warning signs are not misinterpreted by using several significant principles to better understand them. These principles include:

- **Do no harm.** There are certain risks associated with using early warning signs to identify children who are troubled. First and foremost, the intent should be to get help for a child early. The early warning signs should not to be used as rationale to exclude, isolate, or punish a child. Nor should they be used as a checklist for formally identifying, mislabeling, or stereotyping children. Formal disability identification under federal law requires individualized evaluation by qualified professionals. In addition, all referrals to outside agencies based on the early warning signs must be kept confidential and must be done with parental consent (except referrals for suspected child abuse or neglect).

- **Understand violence and aggression within a context.** Violence is contextual. Violent and aggressive behavior as an expression of emotion may have many antecedent factors—factors that exist within the school, the home, and the larger social environment. In fact, for those children who are at risk for aggression and violence, certain environments or situations can set it off. Some children may act out if stress becomes too great, if they lack positive coping skills, and if they have learned to react with aggression.

- **Avoid stereotypes.** Stereotypes can interfere with—and even harm—the school community's ability to identify and help children. It is important to be aware of false cues—including race, socio-economic status, cognitive or academic ability, or physical appearance. In fact, such stereotypes can unfairly harm children, especially when the school community acts upon them.

- **View warning signs within a developmental context.** Children and youth at different levels of development have varying social and emotional capabilities. They may express their needs differently in elementary, middle, and high school. The point is to know what is developmentally typical behavior, so that behaviors are not misinterpreted.

- **Understand that children typically exhibit multiple warning signs.** It is common for children who are troubled to exhibit multiple signs. Research confirms that most children who are troubled and at risk for aggression exhibit more than one warning sign, repeatedly, and with increasing intensity over time. Thus, it is important not to overreact to single signs, words, or actions.

Early Warning Signs

It is not always possible to predict behavior that will lead to violence. However, educators and parents—and sometimes students—can recognize certain early warning signs. In some situations and for some youth, different combinations of events, behaviors, and emotions may lead to aggressive rage or violent behavior toward self or others. A good rule of thumb is to assume that these warning signs, especially when they are presented in combination, indicate a need for further analysis to determine an appropriate intervention.

101

We know from research that most children who become violent toward self or others feel rejected and psychologically victimized. In most cases, children exhibit aggressive behavior early in life and, if not provided support, will continue a progressive developmental pattern toward severe aggression or violence. However, research also shows that when children have a positive, meaningful connection to an adult—whether it be at home, in school, or in the community—the potential for violence is reduced significantly.

None of these signs alone is sufficient for predicting aggression and violence. Moreover, it is inappropriate—and potentially harmful—to use the early warning signs as a checklist against which to match individual children. Rather, the early warning signs are offered only as an aid in identifying and referring children who may need help. School communities must ensure that staff and students only use the early warning signs for identification and referral purposes—only trained professionals should make diagnoses in consultation with the child's parents or guardian.

The following early warning signs are presented with the following qualifications: They are not equally significant and they are not presented in order of seriousness. The early warning signs include:

- **Social withdrawal.** In some situations, gradual and eventually complete withdrawal from social contacts can be an important indicator of a troubled child. The withdrawal often stems from feelings of depression, rejection, persecution, unworthiness, and lack of confidence.

- **Excessive feelings of isolation and being alone.** Research has shown that the majority of children who are isolated and appear to be friendless are not violent. In fact, these feelings are sometimes characteristic of children and youth who may be troubled, withdrawn, or have internal issues that hinder development of social affiliations. However, research also has shown that in some cases feelings of isolation and not having friends are associated with children who behave aggressively and violently.

- **Excessive feelings of rejection.** In the process of growing up, and in the course of adolescent development, many young people experience emotionally painful rejection. Children who are troubled often are isolated from their mentally healthy peers. Their responses to rejection will depend on many background factors. Without support, they may be at risk of expressing their emotional distress in negative ways—including violence. Some aggressive children who are rejected by non-aggressive peers seek out aggressive friends who, in turn, reinforce their violent tendencies.

- **Being a victim of violence.** Children who are victims of violence—including physical or sexual abuse—in the community, at school, or at home are sometimes at risk themselves of becoming violent toward themselves or others.

- **Feelings of being picked on and persecuted.** The youth who feels constantly picked on, teased, bullied, singled out for ridicule, and humiliated at home or at school may initially withdraw socially. If not given adequate support in addressing these feelings, some children may vent them in inappropriate ways—including possible aggression or violence.

- **Low school interest and poor academic performance.** Poor school achievement can be the result of many factors. It is important to consider whether there is a drastic change in performance and/or poor performance becomes a chronic condition that limits the child's capacity to learn. In some situations—such as when the low achiever feels frustrated, unworthy, chastised, and denigrated—acting out and aggressive behaviors may occur. It is important to assess the emotional and cognitive reasons for the academic performance change to determine the true nature of the problem.

- **Expression of violence in writings and drawings.** Children and youth often express their thoughts, feelings, desires, and intentions in their drawings and in stories, poetry, and other written expressive forms. Many children produce work about violent themes that for the most part is harmless when taken in context. However, an overrepresentation of violence in writings and drawings that is directed at specific individuals (family members, peers, other adults) consistently over time, may signal emotional problems and the potential for violence. Because there is a real danger in misdiagnosing such a sign, it is important to seek the guidance of a qualified professional—such as a school psychologist, counselor, or other mental health specialist—to determine its meaning.

- **Uncontrolled anger.** Everyone gets angry; anger is a natural emotion. However, anger that is expressed frequently and intensely in response to minor irritants may signal potential violent behavior toward self or others.

- **Patterns of impulsive and chronic hitting, intimidating, and bullying behaviors.** Children often engage in acts of shoving and mild aggression. However, some mildly aggressive behaviors such as constant hitting and bullying of others that occur early in children's lives, if left unattended, might later escalate into more serious behaviors.

- **History of discipline problems.** Chronic behavior and disciplinary problems both in school and at home may suggest that underlying emotional needs are not being met. These unmet needs may be manifested in acting out and aggressive behaviors. These problems may set the stage for the child to violate norms and rules, defy authority, disengage from school, and engage in aggressive behaviors with other children and adults.

- **Past history of violent and aggressive behavior.** Unless provided with support and counseling, a youth who has a history of aggressive or violent behavior is likely to repeat those behaviors. Aggressive and violent acts may be directed toward other individuals, be expressed in cruelty to animals, or include fire setting. Youth who show an early pattern of antisocial behavior frequently and across multiple settings are particularly at risk for future aggressive and antisocial behavior. Similarly, youth who engage in overt behaviors such as bullying, generalized aggression and defiance, and covert behaviors such as stealing, vandalism, lying, cheating, and fire setting also are at risk for more serious aggressive behavior. Research suggests that age of onset may be a key factor in interpreting early warning signs. For example, children who engage in aggression and drug abuse at an early age (before age 12) are more likely to show violence later on than are children who begin such behavior at an older age. In the presence of such signs it is important to review the child's history with behavioral experts and seek parents' observations and insights.

- **Intolerance for differences and prejudicial attitudes.** All children have likes and dislikes. However, an intense prejudice toward others based on racial, ethnic, religious, language, gender, sexual orientation, ability, and physical appearance—when coupled with other factors—may lead to violent assaults against those who are perceived to be different. Membership in hate groups or the willingness to victimize individuals with disabilities or health problems also should be treated as early warning signs.

- **Drug use and alcohol use.** Apart from being unhealthy behaviors, drug use and alcohol use reduces self-control and exposes children and youth to violence, either as perpetrators, as victims, or both.

- **Affiliation with gangs.** Gangs that support anti-social values and behaviors—including extortion, intimidation, and acts of violence toward other students—cause fear and stress among other students. Youth who are influenced by these groups—those who emulate and copy their behavior, as well as those who become affiliated with them—may adopt these values and act in violent or aggressive ways in certain situations. Gang-related violence and turf battles are common occurrences tied to the use of drugs that often result in injury and/or death.

- **Inappropriate access to, possession of, and use of firearms.** Children and youth who inappropriately possess or have access to firearms can have an increased risk for violence. Research shows that such youngsters also have a higher probability of becoming victims. Families can reduce inappropriate access and use by restricting, monitoring, and supervising children's access to firearms and other weapons. Children who have a history of aggression, impulsiveness, or other emotional problems should not have access to firearms and other weapons.

- **Serious threats of violence.** Idle threats are a common response to frustration. Alternatively, one of the most reliable indicators that a youth is likely to commit a dangerous act toward self or others is a detailed and specific threat to use violence. Recent incidents across the country clearly indicate that threats to commit violence against oneself or others should be taken very seriously. Steps must be taken to understand the nature of these threats and to prevent them from being carried out.

105

Identifying and Responding to Imminent Warning Signs

Unlike early warning signs, imminent warning signs indicate that a student is very close to behaving in a way that is potentially dangerous to self and/or to others. Imminent warning signs require an immediate response.

No single warning sign can predict that a dangerous act will occur. Rather, imminent warning signs usually are presented as a sequence of overt, serious, hostile behaviors, or threats directed at peers, staff, or other individuals. Usually, imminent warning signs are evident to more than one staff member—as well as to the child's family.

Imminent warning signs may include:

- Serious physical fighting with peers or family members.

- Severe destruction of property.

- Severe rage for seemingly minor reasons.

- Detailed threats of lethal violence.

- Possession and/or use of firearms and other weapons.

- Other self-injurious behaviors or threats of suicide.

When warning signs indicate that danger is imminent, safety must always be the first and foremost consideration. Action must be taken immediately. Immediate intervention by school authorities and possibly law enforcement officers is needed when a child:

- Has presented a detailed plan (time, place, method) to harm or kill others—particularly if the child has a history of aggression or has attempted to carry out threats in the past.

- Is carrying a weapon, particularly a firearm, and has threatened to use it.

In situations where students present other threatening behaviors, parents should be informed of the concerns immediately. School communities also have the responsibility to seek assistance from appropriate agencies, such as child and family services and community mental health. These responses should reflect school board policies and be consistent with the violence prevention and response plan.

Using the Early Warning Signs to Shape Intervention Practices

An early warning sign is not a predictor that a child or youth will commit a violent act toward self or others. Effective schools recognize the potential in every child to overcome difficult experiences and to control negative emotions. Adults in these school communities use their knowledge of early warning signs to address problems before they escalate into violence.

Effective school communities support staff, students, and families in understanding the early warning signs. Support strategies include having:

- School board policies in place that support training and ongoing consultation. The entire school community knows how to identify early warning signs, and understands the principles that support them.

- School leaders who encourage others to raise concerns about observed early warning signs and to report all observations of imminent warning signs immediately. This is in addition to school district policies that sanction and promote the identification of early warning signs.

- Easy access to a team of specialists trained in evaluating and addressing serious behavioral and academic concerns.

Each school community should develop a procedure that students and staff can follow when reporting their concerns about a child who exhibits early warning signs. For example, in many schools the principal is the first point of contact. In cases that do not pose imminent danger, the principal contacts a school psychologist or other qualified professional, who takes responsibility for addressing the concern immediately. If the concern is determined to be serious—but not to pose a threat of imminent danger—the child's family should be contacted. The family should be consulted before implementing any interventions with the child. In cases where school-based contextual factors are determined to be causing or exacerbating the child's troubling behavior, the school should act quickly to modify them.

It is often difficult to acknowledge that a child is troubled. Everyone—including administrators, families, teachers, school staff, students, and community members—may find it too troubling sometimes to admit that a child close to them needs help. When faced with resistance or denial, school communities must persist to ensure that children get the help they need.

Understanding early and imminent warning signs is an essential step in ensuring a safe school. The next step involves supporting the emotional and behavioral adjustment of children.

Intervention: Getting Help for Troubled Children

Prevention approaches have proved effective in enabling school communities to decrease the frequency and intensity of behavior problems. However, prevention programs alone cannot eliminate the problems of all students. Some 5 to 10 percent of students will need more intensive interventions to decrease their high-risk behaviors, although the percentage can vary among schools and communities.

What happens when we recognize early warning signs in a child?

The message is clear: It's okay to be concerned when you notice warning signs in a child-and it's even more appropriate to do something about those concerns. School communities that encourage staff, families, and students to raise concerns about observed warning signs—and that have in place a process for getting help to troubled children once they are identified—are more likely to have effective schools with reduced disruption, bullying, fighting, and other forms of aggression.

Principles Underlying Intervention

Violence prevention and response plans should consider both prevention and intervention. Plans also should provide all staff with easy access to a team of specialists trained in evaluating serious behavioral and academic concerns. Eligible students should have access to special education services, and classroom teachers should be able to consult school psychologists, other mental health specialists, counselors, reading specialists, and special educators.

Effective practices for improving the behavior of troubled children are well documented in the research literature. Research has shown that effective interventions are culturally appropriate, family-supported, individualized, coordinated, and monitored. Further, interventions are more effective when they are designed and implemented consistently over time with input from the child, the family, and appropriate professionals. Schools also can draw upon the resources of their community to strengthen and enhance intervention planning.

When drafting a violence prevention and response plan, it is helpful to consider certain principles that research or expert-based experience show have a significant impact on success. The principles include:

- **Share responsibility by establishing a partnership with the child, school, home, and community.** Coordinated service systems should be available for children who are at risk for violent behavior. Effective schools reach out to include families and the entire community in the education of children. In addition, effective schools coordinate and collaborate with child and family service agencies, law enforcement and juvenile justice systems, mental health agencies, businesses, faith and ethnic leaders, and other community agencies.

- **Inform parents and listen to them when early warning signs are observed.** Parents should be involved as soon as possible. Effective and safe schools make persistent efforts to involve parents by: informing them routinely about school discipline policies, procedures, and rules, and about their children's behavior (both good and bad); involving them in making decisions concerning school wide disciplinary policies and procedures; and encouraging them to participate in prevention programs, intervention programs, and crisis planning. Parents need to know what school-based interventions are being used with their children and how they can support their success.

- **Maintain confidentiality and parents' rights to privacy.** Parental involvement and consent is required before personally identifiable information is shared with other agencies, except in the case of emergencies or suspicion of abuse. The Family Educational Rights and Privacy Act (FERPA), a federal law that addresses the privacy of education records, must be observed in all referrals to or sharing of information with other community agencies. Furthermore, parent-approved interagency communication must be kept confidential. FERPA does not prevent disclosure of personally identifiable information to appropriate parties—such as law enforcement officials, trained medical personnel, and other emergency personnel—when responsible personnel determine there is an acute emergency (imminent danger).

- **Develop the capacity of staff, students, and families to intervene.** Many school staff members are afraid of saying or doing the wrong thing when faced with a potentially violent student. Effective schools provide the entire school community—teachers, students, parents, support staff—with training and support in responding to imminent warning signs, preventing violence, and intervening safely and effectively. Interventions must be monitored by professionals who are competent in the approach. According to researchers, programs do not succeed without the ongoing support of administrators, parents, and community leaders.

- **Support students in being responsible for their actions.** Effective school communities encourage students to see themselves as responsible for their actions, and actively engage them in planning, implementing, and evaluating violence prevention initiatives.

- **Simplify staff requests for urgent assistance.** Many school systems and community agencies have complex legalistic referral systems with time lines and waiting lists. Children who are at risk of endangering themselves or others cannot be placed on waiting lists.

- **Make interventions available as early as possible.** Too frequently, interventions are not made available until the student becomes violent or is adjudicated as a youthful offender. Interventions for children who have reached this stage are both costly, restrictive, and relatively inefficient. Effective schools build mechanisms into their intervention processes to ensure that referrals are addressed promptly, and that feedback is provided to the referring individual.

- **Use sustained, multiple, coordinated interventions.** It is rare that children are violent or disruptive only in school. Thus, interventions that are most successful are comprehensive, sustained, and properly implemented. They help families and staff work together to help the child. Coordinated efforts draw resources from community agencies that are respectful of and responsive to the needs of families. Isolated, inconsistent, short-term, and fragmented interventions will not be successful—and may actually do harm.

- **Analyze the contexts in which violent behavior occurs.** School communities can enhance their effectiveness by conducting a functional analysis of the factors that set off violence and problem behaviors. In determining an appropriate course of action, consider the child's age, cultural background, and family experiences and values. Decisions about interventions should be measured against a standard of reasonableness to ensure the likelihood that they will be implemented effectively.

- **Build upon and coordinate internal school resources.** In developing and implementing violence prevention and response plans, effective schools draw upon the resources of various school-based programs and staff—such as special education, safe and drug free school programs, and pupil services.

- **Violent behavior is a problem for everyone.** It is a normal response to become angry or even frightened in the presence of a violent child. But, it is essential that these emotional reactions be controlled. The goal must always be to ensure safety and seek help for the child.

Intervening Early with Students Who Are at Risk for Behavioral Problems

The incidence of violent acts against students or staff is low. However, pre-violent behaviors—such as threats, bullying, and classroom disruptions—are common. Thus, early responses to warning signs are most effective in preventing problems from escalating.

Intervention programs that reduce behavior problems and related school violence typically are multifaceted, long-term, and broad reaching. They also are rigorously implemented. Effective early intervention efforts include working with small groups or individual students to provide direct support, as well as linking children and their families to necessary community services and/or providing these services in the school.

Examples of early intervention components that work include:

- Providing training and support to staff, students, and families in understanding factors that can set off and/or exacerbate aggressive outbursts.

- Teaching the child alternative, socially appropriate replacement responses—such as problem solving and anger control skills.

- Providing skill training, therapeutic assistance, and other support to the family through community-based services.

111

- Encouraging the family to make sure that firearms are out of the child's immediate reach. Law enforcement officers can provide families with information about safe firearm storage as well as guidelines for addressing children's access to and possession of firearms.

In some cases, more comprehensive early interventions are called for to address the needs of troubled children. Focused, coordinated, proven interventions reduce violent behavior. Following are several comprehensive approaches that effective schools are using to provide early intervention to students who are at risk of becoming violent toward themselves or others.

Intervention Tactic: Teaching Positive Interaction Skills

Although most schools do teach positive social interaction skills indirectly, some have adopted social skills programs specifically designed to prevent or reduce antisocial behavior in troubled children. In fact, the direct teaching of social problem solving and social decision making is now a standard feature of most effective drug and violence prevention programs. Children who are at risk of becoming violent toward themselves or others need additional support. They often need to learn interpersonal, problem solving, and conflict resolution skills at home and in school. They also may need more intensive assistance in learning how to stop and think before they react, and to listen effectively.

Intervention Tactic: Providing Comprehensive Services

In some cases, the early intervention may involve getting services to families. The violence prevention and response team, together with the child and family, designs a comprehensive intervention plan that focuses on reducing aggressive behaviors and supporting responsible behaviors at school, in the home, and in the community. When multiple services are required there also must be psychological counseling and ongoing consultation with classroom teachers, school staff, and the family to ensure intended results occur. All services—including community services—must be coordinated and progress must be monitored and evaluated carefully.

Intervention Tactic: Referring the Child for Special Education Evaluation

If there is evidence of persistent problem behavior or poor academic achievement, it may be appropriate to conduct a formal assessment to determine if the child is disabled and eligible for special education and related services under the Individuals with Disabilities Education Act (IDEA). If a multidisciplinary team determines that the child is eligible for services under the IDEA, an individualized educational program (IEP) should be developed by a team that includes a parent, a regular educator, a special educator, an evaluator, a representative of the local school district, the child (if appropriate), and others as appropriate. This team will identify the support necessary to enable the child to learn—including the strategies and support systems necessary to address any behavior that may impede the child's learning or the learning of his or her peers.

Providing Intensive, Individualized Interventions for Students with Severe Behavioral Problems

Children who show dangerous patterns and a potential for more serious violence usually require more intensive interventions that involve multiple agencies, community-based service providers, and intense family support. By working with families and community services, schools can comprehensively and effectively intervene.

Effective individualized interventions provide a range of services for students. Multiple, intensive, focused approaches used over time can reduce the chances for continued offenses and the potential for violence. The child, his or her family, and appropriate school staff should be involved in developing and monitoring the interventions.

Nontraditional schooling in an alternative school or therapeutic facility may be required in severe cases where the safety of students and staff remains a concern, or when the complexity of the intervention plan warrants it. Research has shown that effective alternative programs can have long-term positive results by reducing expulsions and court referrals. Effective alternative programs support students in meeting high academic and behavioral standards. They provide anger and impulse control training, psychological counseling, effective academic and remedial instruction, and vocational training as appropriate. Such programs also make provisions for active family involvement. Moreover, they offer guidance and staff support when the child returns to his or her regular school.

Tips for Parents

Parents can help create safe schools. Here are some ideas that parents in other communities have tried:

113

- Discuss the school's discipline policy with your child. Show your support for the rules, and help your child understand the reasons for them.

- Involve your child in setting rules for appropriate behavior at home.

- Talk with your child about the violence he or she sees—on television, in video games, and possibly in the neighborhood. Help your child understand the consequences of violence.

- Teach your child how to solve problems. Praise your child when he or she follows through.

- Help your child find ways to show anger that do not involve verbally or physically hurting others. When you get angry, use it as an opportunity to model these appropriate responses for your child—and talk about it.

- Help your child understand the value of accepting individual differences.

- Note any disturbing behaviors in your child. For example, frequent angry outbursts, excessive fighting and bullying of other children, cruelty to animals, fire setting, frequent behavior problems at school and in the neighborhood, lack of friends, and alcohol or drug use can be signs of serious problems. Get help for your child. Talk with a trusted professional in your child's school or in the community.

- Keep lines of communication open with your child—even when it is tough. Encourage your child always to let you know where and with whom he or she will be. Get to know your child's friends.

- Listen to your child if he or she shares concerns about friends who may be exhibiting troubling behaviors. Share this information with a trusted professional, such as the school psychologist, principal, or teacher.

- Be involved in your child's school life by supporting and reviewing homework, talking with his or her teacher(s), and attending school functions such as parent conferences, class programs and open houses.

- Work with your child's school to make it more responsive to all students and to all families. Share your ideas about how the school can encourage family involvement, welcome all families, and include them in meaningful ways in their children's education.

- Encourage your school to offer before- and after-school programs.

- Volunteer to work with school-based groups concerned with violence prevention. If none exist, offer to form one.

- Find out if there is a violence prevention group in your community. Offer to participate in the group's activities.

- Talk with the parents of your child's friends. Discuss how you can form a team to ensure your children's safety.

- Find out if your employer offers provisions for parents to participate in school activities.

Conclusion

Crises involving sudden violence in schools are traumatic in large measure because they are rare and unexpected. Everyone is touched in some way. In the wake of such a crisis, members of the school community are asked—and ask themselves—what could have been done to prevent it.

We know from the research that schools can meet the challenge of reducing violence. The school community can be supported through:

- School board policies that address both prevention and intervention for troubled children and youth.

- School wide violence prevention and response plans that include the entire school community in their development and implementation.

- Training in recognizing the early warning signs of potential violent behavior.

- Procedures that encourage staff, parents, and students to share their concerns about children who exhibit early warning signs.

- Procedures for responding quickly to concerns about troubled children.

• Adequate support in getting help for troubled children.

Everyone who cares about children cares about ending violence. It is time to break the silence that too often characterizes even the most well-meaning school communities. Research and expert-based information is available for school communities to use in developing and strengthening programs that can prevent crises.

School safety is everyone's job. Teachers, administrators, parents, community members, and students all must commit to meeting the challenge of getting help for children who show signs of being troubled.

Chapter 13

Bullies in Schools

Bullying Widespread in U.S. Schools, Survey Finds

Bullying is widespread in American schools, with more than 16 percent of U.S. school children saying they had been bullied by other students during the current term, according to a survey funded by the National Institute of Child Health and Human Development (NICHD).

The study appears in the April 25, 2001, *Journal of the American Medical Association*. Overall, 10 percent of children said they had been bullied by other students, but had not bullied others. Another 6 percent said that they had both been bullied themselves and had bullied other children. Another 13 percent of students said they had bullied other students, but had not been bullied themselves.

"Being bullied is not just an unpleasant rite of passage through childhood," said Duane Alexander, M.D., director of the NICHD. "It's a public health problem that merits attention. People who were bullied as children are more likely to suffer from depression and low self

This chapter contains text from "Bullying Widespread in U.S. Schools, Survey Finds," National Institutes of Health, National Institute of Child Health and Human Development, http://www.nichd.nih.gov/new/releases/bullying.cfm, April 2001, and "Dealing with Bullies" by Sherryll Kraizer, Ph.D., Executive Director of the Coalition for Children, Inc. © 2000. Reprinted with permission. Dr. Kraizer is also the author of *The Safe Child Book: A Common Sense Approach to Protecting Children and Teaching Children to Protect Themselves* (Simon & Schuster 1996). For more information including the complete text of this material, visit www.safechild.org.

esteem, well into adulthood, and the bullies themselves are more likely to engage in criminal behavior later in life."

The NICHD researchers surveyed 15,686 students in grades six through 10 in public, parochial, and other private schools throughout the U.S. The nationally representative survey was part of the U.S. contribution to the World Health Organization's Health Behavior in School Children survey, an international effort in which many countries surveyed school-age children on a broad spectrum of health-related behaviors.

For this study, researchers defined bullying as a type of behavior intended to harm or disturb the victim, explained the study's first author, Tonja R. Nansel, Ph.D. This behavior occurs repeatedly over time and involves an imbalance of power, with the more powerful person or group attacking the less powerful one, Dr. Nansel added. Bullying may be physical, involving hitting or otherwise attacking the other person; verbal, involving name-calling or threats; or psychological, involving spreading rumors or excluding a person.

The children were asked to complete a questionnaire during a class period that asked how often they either bullied other students, or were the target of bullying behavior. A total of 10.6 percent of the children replied that they had "sometimes" bullied other children, a response category defined as "moderate" bullying. An additional 8.8 percent said they had bullied others once a week or more, defined as "frequent" bullying. Similarly, 8.5 percent said they had been targets of moderate bullying, and 8.4 percent said they were bullied frequently.

Out of all the students, 13 percent said they had engaged in moderate or frequent bullying of others, while 10.6 percent said they had been bullied either moderately or frequently. Some students—6.3 percent—had both bullied others and been bullied themselves. In all, 29 percent of the students who responded to the survey had been involved in some aspect of bullying, either as a bully, as the target of bullying, or both.

Bullying occurred most frequently in sixth through eighth grade, with little variation between urban, suburban, town, and rural areas; suburban youth were 2–3 percent less likely to bully others. Males were both more likely to bully others and more likely to be victims of bullying than were females. In addition, males were more likely to say they had been bullied physically (being hit, slapped, or pushed), while females more frequently said they were bullied verbally and psychologically (through sexual comments or rumors).

Regarding verbal bullying, bullies were less likely to make derogatory statements about other students' religion or race. "There seem to be stronger social norms against making these kinds of statements than against belittling someone about their appearance or behavior," Dr. Nansel said.

Both bullies and those on the receiving end of bullying were more likely to have difficulty adjusting to their environment both socially and psychologically. Students who were bullied reported having greater difficulty making friends and poorer relationships with their classmates. They were also much more likely than other students to report feelings of loneliness.

"It's likely that kids who are socially isolated and have trouble making friends are more likely to be targets of bullying," Dr. Nansel said. "In turn, other kids may avoid children who are bullied, for fear of being bullied themselves."

The study authors also reported that bullies were more likely to be involved in other problem behaviors, such as smoking and drinking alcohol, and to do more poorly academically. However, youth who were both bullies and recipients of bullying tended to fare the most poorly of all, experiencing social isolation, as well as doing poorly in school and engaging in problem behaviors, like smoking and drinking.

"Unfortunately, we don't know much about this group," Dr. Nansel said. "We need to learn more about them to provide them with the help they need." She added that it is not known whether these children are first bullied by others and then imitate the bullying behavior they experienced, or if they are bullies who were later retaliated against.

The study's authors concluded that the prevalence of bullying in U.S. schools suggests a need for more research to understand, and devise ways to intervene against, bullying. The authors noted that researchers in Norway and England have shown that school intervention programs can be successful. These programs focused on increasing awareness of bullying, increasing teacher and parent supervision, establishing clear rules prohibiting bullying, and providing support and protection for those bullied.

Dealing with Bullies

If Your Child Is Being Bullied

If you learn your child is being bullied, you may immediately want to protect your child and confront the aggressor. You may feel embarrassed and want your child to toughen up, to get in there and fight back. You may feel helpless yourself. None of these responses are helpful.

Get as much information as you can about what has happened. Avoid blaming anyone, including the bullying child or children. Look at your own child's behavior and style of interacting. Ask yourself what you know about your child and how you can turn the immediate situation around.

If you are going to get in touch with the parents of a bullying child, remember that they will probably feel defensive. Keep in mind that your goal is to have a safe and nurturing environment for all of the children, not to escalate an already difficult situation.

For your own children, there are several steps you can take.

- Discuss alternatives to responding to bullies.

- Don't react, walk away, get help if pursued.

- Agree with the bully, saying "You're right." and walking away.

- Be assertive.

Role-play—just as in prevention of child abuse, role-play is what makes the skills real. Actually walk through situations and have your child practice different responses. Discuss prevention techniques such as staying with other kids. Do not get involved with bullies in any kind of interchange. Don't take it personally, it's really the bully's problems that are causing the situation, not you.

If Your Child Is the Bully

What every parent doesn't want to hear—your child is behaving like a bully.

Your first response will probably be defensive. Disarm the situation and buy yourself some time to process what's being said. For example, "Instead of labeling my child, please tell me what happened." Make yourself really listen. Remember that this discussion is ultimately about the well-being of your child, regardless of how its being framed.

Even if your child is behaving aggressively or acting like a bully, remember that this behavior is probably coming from your child's feelings of vulnerability. You need to look for what is going on in your child's interactions with others and what is going on internally, causing your child to behave that way.

In talking with your child, do not blame. Do not get into a discussion about the "whys" of what happened. Your discussion should focus on several key points:

- Bullying is not acceptable in our family or in society.

- If you are feeling frustrated or angry or aggressive, here are some things you can do.

- Remember to role-play, act out the new behaviors.

- Ask, how can I help you with this? Who could you go to in school if you see yourself getting into this type of situation again?

- Specify concretely the consequences if the aggression or bullying continue.

- You want to stop the behavior, understand your child's feelings, then teach and reward more appropriate behavior.

Preventing Bullying

As soon as children begin to interact with others, we can begin to teach them not to be bullies and not to be bullied. We can give them words for their feelings, limit and change their behavior, and teach them better ways to express their feelings and wishes. Children do not learn to solve these kinds of problems and get along by themselves. We need to teach them.

When preschoolers begin to call people names or use unkind words, intervene immediately and consistently. In kindergarten, children learn the power of exclusion. We begin to hear things like, "She's not my friend and she can't come to my party." Respond with, "You don't have to be friends with her today, but it's not all right to make her feel bad by telling her she can't come to your party."

In the early elementary grades, cliques and little groups develop which can be quite exclusionary and cruel. Children need to hear clearly from us, "It's not all right to treat other people this way. How do you think she feels being told she can't play with you?" Kids don't have to play with everyone or even like everyone, but they can't be cruel about excluding others.

Boys who are physically small or weak are more prone to victimization. Making fun, picking on, and other forms of bullying need to be identified in their earliest stages. The message needs to be crystal clear: This is not okay. Think about how he must feel. How could you include him and let other kids know its not all right to treat others this way?

Children who are not bullies or victims have a powerful role to play in shaping the behavior of other children. Teach your children to speak up on behalf of children being bullied. "Don't treat her that way, it's not nice." "Hitting is not a good way to solve problems, let's find a teacher and talk about what happened."

Chapter 14

Combating Fear-Based Truancy

Thoreau once wrote in his journal that "nothing is so much to be feared as fear." For many school-age children, however, fear is a realistic response to conditions in and around their schools. The adverse effects of this fear are far reaching and often long lasting. When fear keeps children out of the classroom, it can limit their prospects and their potential contributions to society.

America was founded on the promise of opportunity. Every child in our Nation deserves the chance to live the American dream, and education is the pathway to that dream and to a fulfilling and productive life. We must not allow fears engendered by bullying, gangs, weapons, and substance abuse to disrupt children's journey toward a better tomorrow. This text examines the climate of violence that threatens our schools and describes steps that concerned citizens are taking to restore security and calm.

Public Opinion

Television news programs, daily newspapers, government reports, and results of public polls bombard citizens regularly with accounts

Excerpted from "Combating Fear and Restoring Safety in Schools," U.S. Department of Justice, Office of Juvenile Justice and Delinquency Prevention, April 1998. Despite the age of this document, readers seeking information about combating fear-based truancy will find this information useful. The full document, including references, is available at http://www.ncjrs.org/pdffiles/167888.pdf.

of assaults, sex crimes, robberies, murders, and vandalism, and with the public response to such crime. This bombardment could feed the fear that much of the public already feels. However, in 1996, the juvenile arrest rate for murder was at its lowest level since the beginning of the decade [Editor's note: Recent statistics show a continued decrease in juvenile arrest rates for murder]. A 1996 analysis of juvenile homicides examined where such crimes occurred and found that 56 percent of the country's juvenile homicide arrests were made in six States and that four large metropolitan centers (containing only 5.3 percent of the Nation's juvenile population) accounted for 30 percent of such arrests. Nonetheless, the media have helped engender widespread fear that violent acts are taking an unacceptable toll on the lives, education, and opportunities of many young people in this country.

A national school-based survey that polled a representative sample of high school students showed that students' fear for their personal safety at school or traveling to or from school compelled as many as 4.4 percent of responding students to miss a day of school each month. Of the respondents to a national random telephone survey of more than 1,300 high school students, nearly half of those in public high schools reported drugs and violence as serious problems in their schools. Data from a fall 1993 national survey polling 1,000 teachers and 1,180 students in grades 3 through 12 revealed that 23 percent of the responding students and 11 percent of the responding teachers had been victims of violence in and around schools.

In addition to fearing personal victimization, many students also feel fear in response to violence experienced by other students. For example, *USA Weekend*, published an unscientific survey, the results of which were based on the written answers of 65,193 students (6th through 12th graders) who responded individually or as class members. Sixty-three percent reported that they would learn more at school if they felt safer; 43 percent avoided restrooms; 20 percent avoided hallways; and 45 percent avoided the school grounds. In a recent survey sponsored by Metropolitan Life Insurance Company, nearly one-fourth of students in grades 7 through 12 reported that their schools had very serious problems regarding social tension and violence.

These problems were measured by students reporting the occurrence on their campuses of specific behaviors, such as hostile or threatening remarks between groups of students, threats or destructive acts other than physical fights, turf battles between groups of students, physical fights among groups of friends, and gang violence.

Invasive Violence

A community's manifestations of street violence, bullying, gangs, the possession and use of weapons, substance abuse, and violence in the community could be a direct cause of the decline in educational opportunity. These manifestations cause students to be fearful of going to school.

Bullying

The acts of violence featured in headlines are not the only concerns on today's school grounds. Age-old "lesser" forms of violence are also widespread in and near schools. Among the problems confronting students and schools is bullying—more insidious and fear inducing because of its commonplace occurrence at school and away from the notice of adults.

In this country, bullying has traditionally been viewed as some perverse sort of child's play, its occurrence usually eliciting the common phrase, "Kids will be kids." Today, bullying is rightfully being recognized for what it is: an abusive behavior that often leads to greater and prolonged violent behavior. This phenomenon is more accurately termed "peer child abuse." Schoolyard bullying, which occurs in kindergarten through 12th grade, spans many different behaviors from what some may call minor offenses to the more serious criminal acts. Name calling, fistfights, purposeful ostracism, extortion, character assassination, libel, repeated physical attacks, and sexual harassment all are bullying tactics.

In May 1987, international authorities on schoolyard bullies and victims gathered at Harvard University for a Schoolyard Bully Practicum, which was sponsored by NSSC (National School Safety Center) in conjunction with OJJDP (Office of Juvenile Justice and Delinquency Prevention). The practicum was one of the first meetings of prominent researchers, psychologists, school and law enforcement authorities, and public relations practitioners for the purpose of developing an awareness and prevention program to address bullying in the United States.

The following list of services, strategies, and suggested training classes were identified by practicum participants as ways to mediate bullying:

- Rules against bullying that are publicized, posted school wide, and accompanied by consistent sanctions.

125

- Student and adult mentors who assist victims and bullies to build self-esteem and to foster mutual understanding of and appreciation for differences in others.

- A buddy system that pairs students with a particular friend or older buddy with whom they share class schedule information and plans for the school day and on whom they can depend for help.

- An on-campus parents' center that recruits, coordinates, and encourages parents to take part in the educational process, volunteer, and assist in school activities and projects.

- Classes for adults in parenting skills and for students in anger management, assertiveness training, and behavior modification training.

- Behavior contracts signed by students and parents and written behavior codes for students, teachers, and staff members that are circulated to all parents and students.

- Emphasis on discipline that stresses right behavior instead of reprimands that focus on punishing wrong behavior.

- Friendship groups that support children who are regularly bullied by peers.

- Peer mediation programs and teen courts that train students to mediate problems among themselves.

- Conflict and dispute resolution curriculums available in all grades.

- Close monitoring of cafeterias, playgrounds, and "hot spots" where bullying is likely to occur away from direct adult supervision.

- Cooperative classroom activities and learning tasks, with care taken to vary the grouping of participants and to monitor groups for balanced reception and treatment of participants.

- Classroom and school wide activities designed to build self-esteem by spotlighting special talents, hobbies, interests, and abilities of all students.

- Publicity about organizations and groups that build children's social skills and self-discipline, such as the Boys & Girls Clubs, scouting, and junior cadet programs, and various disciplines such as yoga, tai chi chuan, jujitsu, karate, kung fu, and tae kwon do.

Gangs

A significant factor contributing to a climate of fear and intimidation in schools is the presence of youth gangs in the community and at school. The U.S. Department of Justice estimates that there are as many as 23,000 youth gangs in the United States with more than 660,000 members. The existence of youth gangs has been reported in all 50 States.

The fear associated with gangs is related to such student-expressed concerns as the following:

- Fearing gang disruptions at school or in the neighborhood.

- Encountering gang members on the way to and from school.

- Anticipating violence from known gang members enrolled at school.

- Receiving specific threats or being harassed by gang members who stake out territory on school campuses or in neighborhoods.

- Facing peer pressure to join a gang.

- Being mistaken as a gang member during school or in neighborhood skirmishes between rival gangs.

- Feeling threatened by school/neighborhood graffiti displaying gang territorial claims.

- Perceiving an increased presence at school of firearms and other weapons related to gang activity.

- Experiencing alarm due to escalating interracial/ethnic tensions between gangs at school and in the community.

Public opinion supports the belief that gangs on school campuses are a major problem in communities across America. For example, in a survey of 700 communities nationwide, 40 percent of the suburban communities and nonmetropolitan towns and cities responding said gangs were a factor in the violence in their schools. In addition, the Gallup Organization, in conjunction with the Phi Delta Kappan, annually polls the public regarding its perception toward public schools.

In the 1997 survey of persons 18 years and older, respondents reported that the four biggest problems for the public schools in their communities were lack of discipline; lack of financial support; use of drugs; and fighting, violence, and gangs. The 1996 Twenty-Seventh Annual Survey of High Achievers sampled behavior trends, opinions, and attitudes of 16- to 18-year-old high school students who had A or B averages. Of the teenagers surveyed, 19 percent knew of the presence of gangs in their schools.

Beginning with gang initiation, intimidation and a new kind of fear that feeds on violent exploitation of others lead youth away from the mainstream and into byways and back alleys where weapons, drugs, delinquency, and crime replace schooling and responsible citizenship.

In any case, if educators are to deal effectively with gang members on campus, they must remain vigilant yet innovative in exploring ways to advance school purposes and policies. The following list represents strategies that schools currently use to that end:

- Establishing ongoing professional development and inservice training programs for all school employees, including training techniques in classroom management and in dealing with cultural diversity, disruptive students and parents, and campus intruders.

- Conducting leadership training classes to assist students in developing insight and skills that enable them to work harmoniously with diverse individuals and groups.

- Offering classes incorporating curriculums on life skills and resistance to peer pressure, values clarification, and cultural sensitivity.

- Implementing dress codes designed to eliminate gang colors and clothing, publicizing the codes at school, and distributing them to all students and parents.

- Adopting school uniforms—particularly for elementary and middle school students—sometimes optional and sometimes mandated. Financial assistance should be available to parents who cannot afford uniforms.

- Reducing the length of time between classes to discourage loitering.

- Establishing partnership academies, schools-within-schools, alternative schools, beacon schools, in-school suspension programs, and school-to-work programs in collaboration with colleges and businesses in order to relocate and continue educating students with histories of classroom disruption, lack of motivation, and gang membership.

- Implementing victim/offender programs requiring juvenile offenders to make restitution to victims for damage or loss incurred or to perform community service.

- Creating a climate of ownership and school pride by including students, parents, teachers, and community leaders in the safe-school planning process.

- Staging regular campus wide graffiti and vandalism cleanup campaigns and cleanup rallies in response to specific incidents of defacement and destruction.

- Organizing crisis intervention teams to counsel students coping with troubling violence in and near school.

- Offering students, especially juvenile gang members, special outreach and after-school programs as an alternative to gang membership.

Weapons

Carrying weapons to school has become an acceptable risk for many students, both those who are fearful and those who intend to exploit others. Underlying the reasons students bring weapons to school may be the societal attitude that violence is an effective way to deal with problems. Television and movies depict violence as an effective problem-solving technique used by "good guys" and "bad guys" alike. Regardless of whether weapons are used in an act of aggression or as a defense against another's aggression, the reason weapons are brought to school often is related to the proliferation of gangs and drug activity on or near many school campuses.

A weapon is any instrument used with intent to inflict physical or mental harm on another person. Although school officials are concerned with all weapons, knives, guns, and explosive devices present the greatest threat to school safety. Weapons have been found and used on school campuses nationwide. Of the 3,370 high school students surveyed in the Twenty-Seventh Annual Survey of High Achievers, 29 percent reported that they knew someone who had brought a weapon to school, and 17 percent claimed it was not very difficult to obtain weapons at school.

Examples of strategies being implemented to prevent or intervene in the use of weapons in schools include:

- Passage of state and local gun-free school zones legislation.

- Public awareness campaigns, such as a Boston billboard nearly the length of a football field depicting the faces of children and other victims of gun violence, "the largest of 200 signs erected in the state to remind people of the costs of handgun violence."

- Public service gifts and donations, such as the 350 free *In a Flash* videos and teaching aids designed to show the "lethal and injurious effects of gun violence" donated by the nonprofit National Emergency Medicine Association to public, private, and special education schools in the Baltimore area.

- Hotlines, such as the one at George Washington High School in San Francisco, used for the anonymous reporting of weapons, drug use and possession, bullying, harassment, and other school associated violence and crime.

- Emphasis on "telling is not tattling" word-of-mouth campaigns to encourage students to break their informal code of silence and to report weapons and other instances of campus crime and violence that threaten safety.

- Use of handheld or permanent weapons detectors.

- Use of see-through book bags to prevent weapons concealment.

- Removal or permanent locking of hall lockers to prevent weapons concealment and to discourage loitering in hallways.

- Standardized incident-reporting forms for documenting all instances of school violence and crime, and requirement that schools report to police when a weapon is found in school.

- Implementation of a school resource officer program, such as Community Policing within Schools in the Robeson County School Outreach Program, which places sworn officers in targeted high schools.

- Partnerships with community agencies that enhance school resources and activities, such as coordinating campus security with local law enforcement agencies; orchestrating presentations from local fire and police departments regarding ways students and school personnel can assist in responding to school safety crises; and involving county mental health, child protective services, and juvenile probation agencies in identifying and monitoring potentially dangerous or law-violating students.

Substance Abuse

A fourth problem area that concerns educators, parents, law enforcement officials, legislators, and the public at large is the use and trafficking of drugs and alcohol in America's schools.

Recent survey by the U.S. Department of Health and Human Services. A recent, comprehensive national survey of drug abuse in America was released August 6, 1997, by the U.S. Department of Health and Human Services. Based on a 1996 representative sample of the U.S. population ages 12 and older, including people who live in households and group quarters such as dormitories and homeless shelters, the report pictured "the bright and the dark side of drug use by adolescents."

For the first time since 1992, illicit drug use by U.S. adolescents declined. The survey includes information on drug use, specifically revealing information on use of heroin, hallucinogens, alcohol, tobacco, marijuana, and cocaine and offering population breakdowns featuring youth ages 12 to 17 and 18 to 26.

While the rate of drug use among youth ages 12 to 17 fell from 10.9 percent in 1995 to 9.0 percent in 1996, the survey indicated that in this age bracket, there was more first-time heroin use, increased use of hallucinogens, fewer teens who believed cocaine is harmful, and little change in cigarette smoking. An estimated 62 million Americans were found to smoke, including 4.1 million adolescents ages 12 to 17. Smokers in this age bracket were found to be about 9 times as likely to use illicit drugs and 16 times as likely to drink heavily as nonsmoking youth.

Not only are adults disturbed by this national epidemic, but students are also concerned. Regarding factors that contribute to violence against teens, three in five teens blamed drugs, according to a study sponsored by the National Crime Prevention Council (NCPC), the National Institute for Citizen Education in the Law (NICEL), and OJJDP. Why do students regard alcohol and other drug use as one of the leading causes of violence on their campuses, and why does substance abuse trigger fear? Many students fear for the lives of their friends who have turned to alcohol and other drugs to cope with the problems, stress, or boredom they experience in their daily lives. Often it is violence—including extortion, theft, prostitution, or drug dealing—that supports their habitual substance abuse.

Gangs who fight over their territorial rights to sell drugs on the street or on campus also engender fear. With the encroachment of the drug subculture onto school campuses, many young people fear that they may succumb to peer pressure and end up addicted to drugs, thereby subjecting themselves to physical, mental, and emotional harm; risking the loss of opportunities to succeed; and compromising their long-held goals. Strategies used to counter the influence of drugs and drug users among students include the following:

- Declaring specified areas surrounding schools to be Drug-Free School Zones.

- Instituting educational programs at all school levels that teach students to resist drugs.

- Developing a critical thinking curriculum, such as AdSmarts, designed to teach students to examine and analyze the media's influence on consumption.

- Establishing cooperative programs such as the Adolescent Social Action Program (ASAP), in which trained college students team with middle and high school student volunteers; they visit hospitals and detention centers to learn about individuals' life experiences that led to substance abuse.

- Involving parents in learning about substance abuse through organizations such as the Parents Association to Neutralize Drug and Alcohol Abuse, Inc. (PANDAA).

- Introducing TREND, a national student-led organization begun at the 1987 National Council on Alcoholism and Drug Abuse, which encourages youth to become involved in their communities and schools and take a leadership role in advocating a drug free lifestyle.

Violence in the Community

While bullies, gangs, weapons, and substance abuse all contribute to the fear experienced by many of today's students, violence in America's neighborhoods and communities cannot be overlooked. Notwithstanding the sometimes unfounded and overgeneralized fear and apprehension about violence among children and adults, often fueled by the media, violence in America is a legitimate concern for everyone.

Likewise, research and statistics regarding juvenile victimization cannot be entirely discounted as mere media sensationalism.

Many young people, aware of the dangers that exist within their communities and schools, feel compelled to make changes in their lifestyles. Louis Harris and Associates, Inc., conducted a survey, "Between Hope and Fear: Teens Speak Out on Crime and the Community." Survey results were obtained from interviews of a nationally representative sample of more than 2,000 students in grades 7 through 12. The purpose of this survey was to focus on "the effect of the awareness and fear of violence and crime on young people and the loss of freedom that results."

Of the students interviewed, 29 percent said that they worried about being victimized in a drive-by shooting, and 46 percent had made at least one change in daily routines because of concerns about personal safety and crime and violence in their communities. Following is a list of changes made in daily routines:

- Changed friends (22 percent).

- Avoided particular parks or playgrounds (20 percent).

- Changed the way they went to or from school (13 percent).

- Carried a weapon (e.g., bat, club, knife, gun) to protect themselves (12 percent).

- Got lower grades in school than they think they otherwise would have (12 percent).

- Stayed home from school or cut class (11 percent).

- Found someone to protect them (10 percent).

- Stopped attending a particular activity or sport (10 percent).

Approximately 1 in 8 students changed the way they went to and from school and more than 1 in 10 stayed home from school or cut class because of concerns about crime and violence in their communities. Such behavior reveals that many students fear for their personal safety while merely attempting to attend school.

The roots of violence reach deep into society, tapping into such complex conditions as poverty, racism, joblessness, and hopelessness. Each epidemic of violence triggers "knee-jerk" calls for legislation and quick fixes. Often, however, little is done in the long run to change conditions that give rise to violent behaviors. It should be apparent that educators by themselves cannot carry out their mandate of educating children while trying to rid their schools and surrounding communities of violence. The National Association of School Boards of Education has pointed out, "A community problem necessitates community-wide solutions. What has been coined 'school violence' is nothing more than societal violence that has penetrated the schoolhouse walls."

Community violence gives rise to subsets of associated violence that impact schools. The effects of campus violence can be devastating to both individual students and specific learning environments. Schools that lack effective discipline, respect for academic standards, and basic humanitarian values falter in their mission to provide safe and effective learning environments. Students who live in fear of violence, witness violent acts, or actually become victims of violence suffer an array of consequences ranging from personal injury and debilitating anxiety that interrupt the learning process to a pattern of absence and truancy that can lead to dropping out of school and delinquency. Such disassociation restricts individual options and limits the development of academic and life skills.

Listed below are some of the types of legislation and collaborative programs undertaken by national, state, and local agencies working in partnership that are producing positive results in reestablishing schools as safe havens for learning:

- Nearly all states have developed some sort of crime-free, weapon-free, or safe-school zone statute. Most states have defined the zones also to include school transportation and locations of school-sponsored functions.

- The above statutes have given rise to zero-tolerance policies for such things as weapons and drugs. These policies are enforced by school districts and individual schools, often with support from local police forces or school-based resource officers.

- Federal regulations established in 1994 mandate that all school districts set up programs to test school bus drivers for drug and alcohol use.

- Schools are forging partnerships with court officials, probation officers, and other youth-serving professionals to share information on and monitor students who have criminal records or who are in aftercare programs following their terms of incarceration in juvenile justice facilities.

- School districts are formulating crisis prevention/intervention policies and are directing individual schools to develop such policies and individual safe school plans.

- School districts, in response to local needs, have stepped up efforts to improve school security by installing security aids or devices and providing services such as:

  - Completing criminal background checks on teachers and school staff members before a work assignment is made.

  - Establishing Neighborhood Watch programs in areas near schools.

  - Recruiting parents to provide safe houses along school routes and to monitor "safe corridors" or walkways to and from school.

  - Enlisting parent volunteers to monitor hallways, cafeterias, playgrounds, and school walkways in order to increase visibility of responsible adults.

  - Creating block safety watch programs carried out by area residents at school bus stops as a crime deterrent for school children and area residents.

  - Fencing school grounds to secure campus perimeters.

  - Replacing bathroom doors with zigzag entrances, to make it easier to monitor sounds, and installing roll down doors to secure bathrooms after hours.

  - Designating one main door entry to school, equipping exits with push bars, and locking all other doors to outside entry.

  - Installing bulletproof windows.

  - Equipping the school with closed circuit video surveillance systems to reduce property crime such as break-ins, theft, vandalism, and assaults.

  - Designing landscaping to create an inviting appearance without offering a hiding place for trespassers or criminals.

  - Installing motion-sensitive lights to illuminate dark corners in hallways or on campus.

- Mounting convex mirrors to monitor blind spots in school hallways.

- Equipping classrooms with intercom systems connected to the central school office.

- Issuing two-way radios to security patrols or campus staff members.

- Purchasing cellular phones for use in crises or emergency situations.

- Requiring photo identification badges for students, teachers, and staff and identification cards for visitors on campus.

Creating Safer Schools

During the past decade in America, educational opportunity has gradually eroded in the Nation's schools. That opportunity has been undermined by violence and the fear of violence. Yet the Nation's basic precepts are intact: to provide educational opportunity, foster individual accomplishment in a diverse society, and preserve guaranteed rights and freedoms for all citizens.

Numerous prevention and intervention strategies have been outlined here, each developed to ensure that the Nation's schools are able to educate children in safe environments and that all youth have the opportunity to learn, grow, and mature as socially responsible citizens.

Although these strategies are a good starting point, more such interventions are needed. Through the efforts of educators, law enforcement officials, and parents working in concert to implement these strategies and continuing to test new ones it is possible to reduce the violence found in today's schools and create safe schools in every community.

Chapter 15

A School Shooter: A Threat Assessment Perspective

Introduction

Why would a student bring a weapon to school and without any explicable reason open fire on fellow students and teachers? Are school shooters angry? Are they crazy? Is their motive revenge? Hatred for the victims? A hunger for attention?

The origins of human violence are complex. Thinkers, historians, and scientists have explored the issue for centuries, but answers remain elusive. The roots of a violent act are multiple, intricate, and intertwined. The mix of factors varies according to the individual and the circumstances. Understanding violence after it has occurred is difficult enough. Trying to assess a threat and keep it from being carried out is even more of a challenge.

This text presents a systematic procedure for threat assessment and intervention. The model is designed to be used by educators, mental health professionals and law enforcement agencies.

This model is not a "profile" of the school shooter or a checklist of danger signs pointing to the next adolescent who will bring lethal violence to a school. Those things do not exist. Although the risk of an actual shooting incident in any one school is very low, threats of violence are potentially a problem in any school. Once a threat is

Excerpted from "The School Shooter: A Threat Assessment Perspective," U.S. Department of Justice, Federal Bureau of Investigation (FBI), http://www.fbi.gov/publications/school/school2.pdf, 2000.

made, having a fair, rational, and standardized method of evaluating and responding to threats is critically important.

Assessing Threats

All threats are *not* created equal. However, all threats should be accessed in a timely manner and decisions regarding how they are handled must be done quickly. In today's climate, some schools tend to adopt a one-size-fits-all approach to any mention of violence. The response to every threat is the same, regardless of its credibility or the likelihood that it will be carried out. In the shock-wave of recent school shootings, this reaction may be understandable, but it is exaggerated — and perhaps dangerous, leading to potential underestimation of serious threats, overreaction to less serious ones, and unfairly punishing or stigmatizing students who are in fact not dangerous. A school that treats all threats as equal falls into the fallacy formulated by Abraham Maslow: "If the only tool you have is a hammer, you tend to see every problem as a nail." Every problem is not a nail, of course, and schools must recognize that every threat does not represent the same danger or require the same level of response.

Some threats can herald a clear and present danger of a tragedy on the scale of Columbine High School. Others represent little or no real threat to anyone's safety. Neither should be ignored, but reacting to both in the same manner is ineffective and self-defeating. In every school, an established threat assessment procedure managed by properly trained staff can help school administrators and other school staff distinguish between different levels of threats and choose different appropriate responses.

Threat assessment seeks to make an informed judgment on two questions: how credible and serious is the threat itself? And to what extent does the threatener appear to have the resources, intent, and motivation to carry out the threat?

What Is a Threat?

A threat is an expression of intent to do harm or act out violently against someone or something. A threat can be spoken, written, or symbolic — for example, motioning with one's hands as though shooting at another person.

Threat assessment rests on two critical principles: first, that all threats and all threateners are not equal; second, that most threateners are unlikely to carry out their threat. However, all threats must be taken seriously and evaluated.

In NCAVC's (National Center for the Analysis of Violent Crime) experience, most threats are made anonymously or under a false name. Because threat assessment relies heavily on evaluating the threatener's background, personality, lifestyle, and resources, identifying the threatener is necessary for an informed assessment to be made—and also so criminal charges can be brought if the threat is serious enough to warrant prosecution. If the threatener's identity cannot be determined, the response will have to be based on an assessment of the threat alone. That assessment may change if the threatener is eventually identified: a threat that was considered low risk may be rated as more serious if new information suggests the threatener is dangerous, or conversely, an assessment of high risk may be scaled down if the threatener is identified and found not to have the intent, ability, means, or motive to carry out the threat.

Motivation

Threats are made for a variety of reasons. A threat may be a warning signal, a reaction to fear of punishment or some other anxiety, or a demand for attention. It may be intended to taunt; to intimidate; to assert power or control; to punish; to manipulate or coerce; to frighten; to terrorize; to compel someone to do something; to strike back for an injury, injustice or slight; to disrupt someone's or some institution's life; to test authority, or to protect oneself. The emotions that underlie a threat can be love; hate; fear; rage; or desire for attention, revenge, excitement, or recognition.

Motivation can never be known with complete certainty, but to the extent possible, understanding motive is a key element in evaluating a threat. A threat will reflect the threatener's mental and emotional state at the time the threat was made, but it is important to remember that a state of mind can be temporarily but strongly influenced by alcohol or drugs, or a precipitating incident such as a romantic breakup, failing grades, or conflict with a parent. After a person has absorbed an emotional setback and calmed down, or when the effects of alcohol or drugs have worn off, his motivation to act on a violent threat may also have diminished.

Signposts

In general, people do not switch instantly from nonviolence to violence. Nonviolent people do not "snap" or decide on the spur of the moment to meet a problem by using violence. Instead, the path toward violence is an evolutionary one, with signposts along the way. A threat is one observable behavior; others may be brooding about frustration or disappointment, fantasies of destruction or revenge in conversations, writings, drawings, and other actions.

Types of Threats

Threats can be classed in four categories: direct, indirect, veiled, or conditional.

A direct threat identifies a specific act against a specific target and is delivered in a straightforward, clear, and explicit manner: "I am going to place a bomb in the school's gym."

An indirect threat tends to be vague, unclear, and ambiguous. The plan, the intended victim, the motivation, and other aspects of the threat are masked or equivocal: "If I wanted to, I could kill everyone at this school!" While violence is implied, the threat is phrased tentatively—"If I wanted to"—and suggests that a violent act COULD occur, not that it WILL occur.

A veiled threat is one that strongly implies but does not explicitly threaten violence. "We would be better off without you around anymore" clearly hints at a possible violent act, but leaves it to the potential victim to interpret the message and give a definite meaning to the threat.

A conditional threat is the type of threat often seen in extortion cases. It warns that a violent act will happen unless certain demands or terms are met: "If you don't pay me one million dollars, I will place a bomb in the school."

Factors in Threat Assessment

Specific, plausible details are a critical factor in evaluating a threat. Details can include the identity of the victim or victims; the reason for making the threat; the means, weapon, and method by which it is to be carried out; the date, time, and place where the threatened act will occur; and concrete information about plans or preparations that have already been made.

Specific details can indicate that substantial thought, planning, and preparatory steps have already been taken, suggesting a higher risk that the threatener will follow through on his threat. Similarly, a lack of detail suggests the threatener may not have thought through all of the contingencies, has not actually taken steps to carry out the threat, and may not seriously intend violence but is "blowing off steam" over some frustration or seeking to frighten or intimidate a particular victim or disrupt a school's events or routine.

Details that are specific but not logical or plausible may indicate a less serious threat. For example, a high school student writes that he intends to detonate hundreds of pounds of plutonium in the school's auditorium the following day at lunch time. The threat is detailed, stating a specific time, place, and weapon. But the details are unpersuasive. Plutonium is almost impossible to obtain, legally or on the black market. It is expensive, hard to transport, and very dangerous to handle, and a complex high explosive detonation is required to set off a nuclear reaction. No high school student is likely to have any plutonium at all, much less hundreds of pounds, nor would he have the knowledge or complex equipment to detonate it. A threat this unrealistic is obviously unlikely to be carried out.

The emotional content of a threat can be an important clue to the threatener's mental state. Emotions are conveyed by melodramatic words and unusual punctuation—"I hate you!!!!!" "You have ruined my life!!!!" "May God have mercy on your soul!!!!"—or in excited, incoherent passages that may refer to God or other religious beings or deliver an ultimatum. Though emotionally charged threats can tell the assessor something about the temperament of the threatener, they are not a measure of danger. They may sound frightening, but no correlation has been established between the emotional intensity in a threat and the risk that it will be carried out.

Precipitating stressors are incidents, circumstances, reactions, or situations which can trigger a threat. The precipitating event may seem insignificant and have no direct relevance to the threat, but nonetheless becomes a catalyst. For example, a student has a fight with his mother before going to school. The argument may have been a minor one over an issue that had nothing to do with school, but it sets off an emotional chain reaction leading the student to threaten another student at school that day—possibly something he has thought about in the past.

The impact of a precipitating event will obviously depend on predisposing factors: underlying personality traits, characteristics, and temperament that predispose an adolescent to fantasize about violence

141

or act violently. Accordingly, information about a temporary "trigger" must be considered together with broader information about these underlying factors, such as a student's vulnerability to loss and depression.

Levels of Risk

Low level of threat. A threat which poses a minimal risk to the victim and public safety.

- Threat is vague and indirect.

- Information contained within the threat is inconsistent, implausible or lacks detail.

- Threat lacks realism.

- Content of the threat suggests person is unlikely to carry it out.

Medium level of threat. A threat which could be carried out, although it may not appear entirely realistic.

- Threat is more direct and more concrete than a low level threat.

- Wording in the threat suggests that the threatener has given some thought to how the act will be carried out.

- There may be a general indication of a possible place and time (though these signs still fall well short of a detailed plan).

- There is no strong indication that the threatener has taken preparatory steps, although there may be some veiled reference or ambiguous or inconclusive evidence pointing to that possibility— an allusion to a book or movie that shows the planning of a violent act, or a vague, general statement about the availability of weapons.

- There may be a specific statement seeking to convey that the threat is not empty: "I'm serious!" or "I really mean this!"

High level of threat. A threat that appears to pose an imminent and serious danger to the safety of others.

- Threat is direct, specific, and plausible.

- Threat suggests concrete steps have been taken toward carrying it out, for example, statements indicating that the threatener has acquired or practiced with a weapon or has had the victim under surveillance.

Example: "At eight o'clock tomorrow morning, I intend to shoot the principal. That's when he is in the office by himself. I have a 9mm. Believe me, I know what I am doing. I am sick and tired of the way he runs this school." This threat is direct, specific as to the victim, motivation, weapon, place, and time, and indicates that the threatener knows his target's schedule and has made preparations to act on the threat.

NCAVC's experience in analyzing a wide range of threatening communications suggests that in general, the more direct and detailed a threat is, the more serious the risk of its being acted on. A threat that is assessed as high level will almost always require immediate law enforcement intervention.

In some cases, the distinction between the levels of threat may not be as obvious, and there will be overlap between the categories. Generally, obtaining additional information about, either the threat or the threatener will help in clarifying any confusion. What is important is that schools be able to recognize and act on the most serious threats, and then address all other threats appropriately and in a standardized and timely fashion.

The Four-Pronged Assessment Model

This innovative model is designed to assess someone who has made a threat and evaluate the likelihood that the threat will actually be carried out. Anyone can deliver a spoken or written message that sounds foreboding or sinister, but evaluating the threat alone will not establish if the person making it has the intention, the ability, or the means to act on the threat. To make that determination, assessing the threatener is critical.

Educators, law enforcement, mental health professionals, and others must realize they cannot handle threats in the same old way. Those tasked with assessing threats must be trained in the basic concepts of threat assessment, personality assessment and risk assessment as presented in this monograph, and realize the importance of assessing all threats in a timely manner.

What information about students can help us tell which threateners are likely to carry out their threats? Their age? Their grades in chemistry class? Their socioeconomic level? The experience of the NCAVC is that frequently, only limited information is known about someone being evaluated for threat assessment, or information may be available only in certain areas—a student's academic record, or family life, or health. All aspects of a threatener's life must be considered when evaluating whether a threat is likely to be carried out. This model provides a framework for evaluating a student in order to determine if he or she has the motivation, means, and intent to carry out a proclaimed threat. The assessment is based on the "totality of the circumstances" known about the student in four major areas:

- Prong One: Personality of the student
- Prong Two: Family dynamics
- Prong Three: School dynamics and the student's role in those dynamics
- Prong Four: Social dynamics

Here is how the Four-Pronged Assessment Model can be used when a threat is received at a school: A preliminary assessment is done on the threat itself, as outlined above. If the threatener's identity is known, a threat assessor quickly collects as much information as is available in the four categories. The assessor may be a school psychologist, counselor, or other staff member or specialist who has been designated and trained for this task. Information can come from the assessor's personal knowledge of the student or can be sought from teachers, staff, other students (when appropriate), parents, and other appropriate sources such as law enforcement agencies or mental health specialists.

If the student appears to have serious problems in the majority of the four prongs or areas and if the threat is assessed as high or medium level, the threat should be taken more seriously and appropriate intervention by school authorities and/or law enforcement should be initiated as quickly as possible.

In order to effect a rapid assessment, it may not be possible to evaluate a student thoroughly in each of the four prongs. Nonetheless, having as much information as possible about a student and his or her life is important in order to determine if that student is capable and under enough stressors to carry out a threat.

The following section outlines factors to be considered in each of the four prongs:

Personality of the Student: Behavior Characteristics and Traits

According to *Webster's*, personality is "the pattern of collective character, behavioral, temperamental, emotional, and mental traits of an individual." This pattern is a product of both inherited temperament and environmental influences. Personality shapes how people consistently view the world and themselves and how they interact with others. Forming an accurate impression of someone's personality requires observing his or her behavior over a period of time and in a wide variety of situations.

Understanding adolescent personality development is extremely important in assessing any threat made by someone in that age group. An adolescent's personality is not yet crystallized. It is still developing. During adolescence, young people are likely to explore or engage in what others perceive as strange behavior. Adolescents struggle with vulnerability and acceptance ("Am I lovable and able to love?"), with questions of independence and dependence, and with how to deal with authority, among other difficult issues.

Clues to a student's personality can come from observing behavior when the student is:

- Coping with conflicts, disappointments, failures, insults, or other stresses encountered in everyday life.

- Expressing anger or rage, frustration, disappointment, humiliation, sadness, or similar feelings.

- Demonstrating or failing to demonstrate resiliency after a setback, a failure, real or perceived criticism, disappointment, or other negative experiences.

- Demonstrating how the student feels about himself, what kind of person the student imagines himself or herself to be, and how the student believes he or she appears to others.

- Responding to rules, instruction, or authority figures.

- Demonstrating and expressing a desire or need for control, attention, respect, admiration, confrontation, or other needs.

- Demonstrating or failing to demonstrate empathy with the feelings and experiences of others.

- Demonstrating his or her attitude toward others. (For example, does the student view others as inferior or with disrespect?)

Assessors who have not been able to observe a student first-hand should seek information from those who knew the student before he or she made a threat.

Family Dynamics

Family dynamics are patterns of behavior, thinking, beliefs, traditions, roles, customs and values that exist in a family. When a student has made a threat, knowledge of the dynamics within the student's family—and how those dynamics are perceived by both the student and the parents—is a key factor in understanding circumstances and stresses in the student's life that could play a role in any decision to carry out the threat.

School Dynamics

The relationship between school dynamics and threat assessment has not been empirically established and therefore its level of significance can either increase or decrease depending on additional research into these cases. While it may be difficult for educators/assessors to "critique" their own school, it is necessary to have some level of understanding of the particular dynamics in their school because their school can ultimately become the scene of the crime.

School dynamics are patterns of behavior, thinking, beliefs, customs, traditions, roles, and values that exist in a school's culture. Some of these patterns can be obvious, and others subtle. Identifying those behaviors which are formally or informally valued and rewarded in a school helps explain why some students get more approval and attention from school authorities and have more prestige among their fellow students. It can also explain the "role" a particular student is given by the school's culture, and how the student may see himself or herself fitting in, or failing to fit in, with the school's value system.

Students and staff may have very different perceptions of the culture, customs, and values in their school. Assessors need to be aware of how a school's dynamics are seen by students. A big discrepancy between students' perceptions and the administration's can itself be a significant piece of information for the assessor.

Social Dynamics

Social dynamics are patterns of behavior, thinking, beliefs, customs, traditions, and roles that exist in the larger community where students live. These patterns also have an impact on students' behavior, their feelings about themselves, their outlook on life, attitudes, perceived options, and lifestyle practices. An adolescent's beliefs and opinions, his choices of friends, activities, entertainment, and reading material, and his attitudes toward such things as drugs, alcohol, and weapons will all reflect in some fashion the social dynamics of the community where he lives and goes to school.

Within the larger community, an adolescent's peer group plays an especially crucial role in influencing attitudes and behavior. Information about a student's choice of friends and relations with his peers can provide valuable clues to his attitudes, sense of identity, and possible decisions about acting or not acting on a threat.

Findings

This section lists certain types of behavior, personality traits, and circumstances in the family, school, and community environment that should be regarded as warning signs if all or most of them—in all four categories—seem to fit a student who has made a threat. It should be strongly emphasized that this list is not intended as a checklist to predict future violent behavior by a student who has not acted violently or threatened violence. Rather, the list should be considered only after a student has made some type of threat and an assessment has been developed using the four-pronged model. If the assessment shows evidence of these characteristics, behaviors, and consistent problems in all four areas or prongs, it can indicate that the student may be fantasizing about acting on the threat, has the motivation to carry out the violent act, or has actually taken steps to carry out a threat.

The following cautions should also be emphasized:

1. No one or two traits or characteristics should be considered in isolation or given more weight than the others. Any of these traits, or several, can be seen in students who are not contemplating a school shooting or other act of violence. The key to identifying a potentially dangerous threatener under this four-pronged assessment model is that there is evidence of problems on a majority of the items in each of the four areas. However, there is no "magical" number of traits or constellation of traits which will determine what students may present a problem. Hopefully, subsequent empirical research in this area will determine which are the significant traits and how they should be weighted. However, a practical and common sense application of this model indicates that the more problems which are identified in each of the four prongs, the greater the level of concern for the assessor.

147

2. Behavior is an expression of personality, but one bad day may not reflect a student's real personality or usual behavior pattern. Accurately evaluating someone's behavior requires establishing a baseline—how he or she typically behaves most of the time. Those responsible for assessing a student should seek information from people who have known the student over a period of time and have been able to observe him in varying situations and with a variety of people.

3. Many of the behaviors and traits listed below are seen in depressed adolescents with narcissistic personality characteristics and other possible mental health problems. Despite the overlap between this list and diagnostic symptoms, evaluation under the four-pronged threat assessment model cannot be a substitute for a clinical diagnosis of mental illness. Signs of serious mental illness and/or substance abuse disorders can significantly elevate the risk for violence and should be evaluated by a mental health professional.

Prong One: Personality Traits and Behavior

Leakage

Leakage occurs when a student intentionally or unintentionally reveals clues to feelings, thoughts, fantasies, attitudes, or intentions that may signal an impending violent act. These clues can take the form of subtle threats, boasts, innuendos, predictions, or ultimatums. They may be spoken or conveyed in stories, diary entries, essays, poems, letters, songs, drawings, doodles, tattoos, or videos.

Another form of leakage involves efforts to get unwitting friends or classmates to help with preparations for a violent act, at times through deception (for example, the student asks a friend to obtain ammunition for him because he is going hunting).

Leakage can be a cry for help, a sign of inner conflict, or boasts that may look empty but actually express a serious threat. Leakage is considered to be one of the most important clues that may precede an adolescent's violent act.

An example of leakage could be a student who shows a recurring preoccupation with themes of violence, hopelessness, despair, hatred, isolation, loneliness, nihilism, or an "end-of-the-world" philosophy. Those themes may be expressed in conversation or in jokes or in seemingly offhand comments to friends, teachers, other school employees, parents, or siblings. Statements may be subtle, or immediately minimized by comments such as, "I was just joking," or "I didn't really mean that."

Another example of leakage could be recurrent themes of destruction or violence appearing in a student's writing or artwork. The themes may involve hatred, prejudice, death, dismemberment, mutilation of self or others, bleeding, use of excessively destructive weapons, homicide, or suicide. Many adolescents are fascinated with violence and the macabre, and writings and drawings on these themes can be a reflection of a harmless but rich and creative fantasy life. Some adolescents, however, seem so obsessed with these themes that they emerge no matter what the subject matter, the conversation, the assignment, or the joke. In an actual case, a student was taking a home economics class and was assigned to bake something. He baked a cake in the shape of a gun. His school writings and other work also contained recurrent themes of violence.

Low Tolerance for Frustration

The student is easily bruised, insulted, angered, and hurt by real or perceived injustices done to him by others and has great difficulty tolerating frustration.

Poor Coping Skills

The student consistently shows little if any ability to deal with frustration, criticism, disappointment, failure, rejection, or humiliation. His or her response is typically inappropriate, exaggerated, immature, or disproportionate.

Lack of Resiliency

The student lacks resiliency and is unable to bounce back even when some time has elapsed since a frustrating or disappointing experience, a setback, or putdown.

Failed Love Relationship

The student may feel rejected or humiliated after the end of a love relationship, and cannot accept or come to terms with the rejection.

Injustice Collector

The student nurses resentment over real or perceived injustices. No matter how much time has passed, the injustice collector will not forget or forgive those wrongs or the people he or she believes are responsible. The student may keep a hit list with the names of people he feels have wronged him.

Signs of Depression

The student shows features of depression such as lethargy, physical fatigue, a morose or dark outlook on life, a sense of malaise, and loss of interest in activities that he once enjoyed. Adolescents may show different signs than those normally associated with depression.

Some depressed adolescents may display unpredictable and uncontrolled outbursts of anger, a generalized and excessive hatred toward everyone else, and feelings of hopelessness about the future. Other behaviors might include psychomotor agitation, restlessness, inattention, sleep and eating disorders, and a markedly diminished interest in almost all activities that previously occupied and interested him. The student may have difficulty articulating these extreme feelings.

Narcissism

The student is self-centered, lacks insight into others' needs and/or feelings, and blames others for failures and disappointments. The narcissistic student may embrace the role of a victim to elicit sympathy and to feel temporarily superior to others. He or she displays signs of paranoia, and assumes an attitude of self-importance or grandiosity that masks feelings of unworthiness. A narcissistic student may be either very thin-skinned or very thick-skinned in responding to criticism.

Alienation

The student consistently behaves as though he feels different or estranged from others. This sense of separateness is more than just being a loner. It can involve feelings of isolation, sadness, loneliness, not belonging, and not fitting in.

Dehumanizes Others

The student consistently fails to see others as fellow humans. He characteristically views other people as "nonpersons" or objects to be thwarted. This attitude may appear in the student's writings and artwork, in interactions with others, or in comments during conversation.

Lack of Empathy

The student shows an inability to understand the feelings of others, and appears unconcerned about anyone else's feelings. When others show emotion, the student may ridicule them as weak or stupid.

Exaggerated Sense of Entitlement

The student constantly expects special treatment and consideration, and reacts negatively if he doesn't get the treatment he feels entitled to.

Attitude of Superiority

The student has a sense of being superior and presents himself as smarter, more creative, more talented, more experienced, and more worldly than others.

Exaggerated or Pathological Need for Attention

The student shows an exaggerated, even pathological need for attention, whether positive or negative, no matter what the circumstances.

Externalizes Blame

The student consistently refuses to take responsibility for his or her own actions and typically faults other people, events or situations for any failings or shortcomings. In placing blame, the student frequently seems impervious to rational argument and common sense.

Masks Low Self-Esteem

Though he may display an arrogant, self-glorifying attitude, the student's conduct often appears to veil an underlying low self-esteem. He avoids high visibility or involvement in school activities, and other students may consider him a nonentity.

Anger Management Problems

Rather than expressing anger in appropriate ways and in appropriate circumstances, the student consistently tends to burst out in temper tantrums or melodramatic displays, or to brood in sulky, seething silence. The anger may be noticeably out of proportion to the cause, or may be redirected toward people who had nothing to do with the

151

original incident. His anger may come in unpredictable and uncontrollable outbursts, and may be accompanied by expressions of unfounded prejudice, dislike, or even hatred toward individuals or groups.

Intolerance

The student often expresses racial or religious prejudice or intolerant attitudes toward minorities, or displays slogans or symbols of intolerance in such things as tattoos, jewelry, clothing, bumper stickers, or book covers.

Inappropriate Humor

The student's humor is consistently inappropriate. Jokes or humorous comments tend to be macabre, insulting, belittling, or mean.

Seeks to Manipulate Others

The student consistently attempts to con and manipulate others and win their trust so they will rationalize any signs of aberrant or threatening behavior.

Lack of Trust

The student is untrusting and chronically suspicious of others' motives and intentions. This lack of trust may approach a clinically paranoid state. He may express the belief that society has no trustworthy institution or mechanism for achieving justice or resolving conflict, and that if something bothers him, he has to settle it in his own way.

Closed Social Group

The student appears introverted, with acquaintances rather than friends, or associates only with a single small group that seems to exclude everyone else. Students who threaten or carry out violent acts are not necessarily loners in the classic sense, and the composition and qualities of peer groups can be important pieces of information in assessing the danger that a threat will be acted on.

Change of Behavior

The student's behavior changes dramatically. His academic performance may decline, or he may show a reckless disregard for school rules, schedules, dress codes, and other regulations.

Rigid and Opinionated

The student appears rigid, judgmental, and cynical, and voices strong opinions on subjects about which he has little knowledge. He disregards facts, logic, and reasoning that might challenge these opinions.

Unusual Interest in Sensational Violence

The student demonstrates an unusual interest in school shootings and other heavily publicized acts of violence. He may declare his admiration for those who committed the acts, or may criticize them for "incompetence" or failing to kill enough people. He may explicitly express a desire to carry out a similar act in his own school, possibly as an act of "justice."

Fascination with Violence-Filled Entertainment

The student demonstrates an unusual fascination with movies, TV shows, computer games, music videos or printed material that focus intensively on themes of violence, hatred, control, power, death, and destruction. He may incessantly watch one movie or read and reread one book with violent content, perhaps involving school violence. Themes of hatred, violence, weapons, and mass destruction recur in virtually all his activities, hobbies, and pastimes. The student spends inordinate amounts of time playing video games with violent themes, and seems more interested in the violent images than in the game itself.

On the Internet, the student regularly searches for web sites involving violence, weapons, and other disturbing subjects. There is evidence the student has downloaded and kept material from these sites.

Negative Role Models

The student may be drawn to negative, inappropriate role models such as Hitler, Satan, or others associated with violence and destruction.

Behavior Appears Relevant to Carrying out a Threat

The student appears to be increasingly occupied in activities that could be related to carrying out a threat—for example, spending unusual amounts of time practicing with firearms or on various violent websites. The time spent in these activities has noticeably begun to exclude normal everyday pursuits such as homework, attending classes, going to work, and spending time with friends.

Prong Two: Family Dynamics

Turbulent Parent-Child Relationship

The student's relationship with his parents is particularly difficult or turbulent. This difficulty or turbulence can be uniquely evident following a variety of factors, including recent or multiple moves, loss of a parent, addition of a step parent, etc. He expresses contempt for his parents and dismisses or rejects their role in his life. There is evidence of violence occurring within the student's home.

Acceptance of Pathological Behavior

Parents do not react to behavior that most parents would find very disturbing or abnormal. They appear unable to recognize or acknowledge problems in their children and respond quite defensively to any real or perceived criticism of their child. If contacted by school officials or staff about the child's troubling behavior, the parents appear unconcerned, minimize the problem, or reject the reports altogether even if the child's misconduct is obvious and significant.

Access to Weapons

The family keeps guns or other weapons or explosive materials in the home, accessible to the student. More important, weapons are treated carelessly, without normal safety precautions; for example, guns are not locked away and are left loaded. Parents or a significant role model may handle weapons casually or recklessly and in doing so may convey to children that a weapon can be a useful and normal means of intimidating someone else or settling a dispute.

Lack of Intimacy

The family appears to lack intimacy and closeness. The family has moved frequently and/or recently.

Student "Rules the Roost"

The parents set few or no limits on the child's conduct, and regularly give in to his demands. The student insists on an inordinate degree of privacy, and parents have little information about his activities, school life, friends, or other relationships. The parents seem intimidated by their child. They may fear he will attack them physically if they confront or frustrate him, or they may be unwilling to face an emotional outburst, or they may be afraid that upsetting the child will spark an emotional crisis. Traditional family roles are reversed: for example, the child acts as if he were the authority figure, while parents act as if they were the children.

No Limits or Monitoring of TV and Internet

Parents do not supervise, limit or monitor the student's television watching or his use of the Internet. The student may have a TV in his own room or is otherwise free without any limits to spend as much time as he likes watching violent or otherwise inappropriate shows. The student spends a great deal of time watching television rather than in activities with family or friends. Similarly, parents do not monitor computer use or Internet access. The student may know much more about computers than the parents do, and the computer may be considered off limits to the parents while the student is secretive about his computer use, which may involve violent games or Internet research on violence, weapons, or other disturbing subjects.

Prong Three: School Dynamics

If an act of violence occurs at a school, the school becomes the scene of the crime. As in any violent crime, it is necessary to understand what it is about the school which might have influenced the student's decision to offend there rather than someplace else. While it may be difficult for educators/assessors to "critique" or evaluate their own school, one must have some degree of awareness of these unique dynamics—prior to a threat—in order to assess a student's role in the school culture and to develop a better understanding—from the student's perspective—of why he would target his own school.

Student's Attachment to School

Student appears to be "detached" from school, including other students, teachers, and school activities.

Tolerance for Disrespectful Behavior

The school does little to prevent or punish disrespectful behavior between individual students or groups of students. Bullying is part of the school culture and school authorities seem oblivious to it, seldom or never intervening or doing so only selectively. Students frequently act in the roles of bully, victim, or bystander (sometimes, the same student plays different roles in different circumstances). The school atmosphere promotes racial or class divisions or allows them to remain unchallenged.

Inequitable Discipline

The use of discipline is inequitably applied—or has the perception of being inequitably applied by students and/or staff.

Inflexible Culture

The school's culture—official and unofficial patterns of behavior, values, and relationships among students, teachers, staff, and administrators—is static, unyielding, and insensitive to changes in society and the changing needs of newer students and staff.

Pecking Order among Students

Certain groups of students are officially or unofficially given more prestige and respect than others. Both school officials and the student body treat those in the high-prestige groups as though they are more important or more valuable to the school than other students.

Code of Silence

A "code of silence" prevails among students. Few feel they can safely tell teachers or administrators if they are concerned about another student's behavior or attitudes. Little trust exists between students and staff.

Unsupervised Computer Access

Access to computers and the Internet is unsupervised and unmonitored. Students are able to use the school's computers to play violent computer games or to explore inappropriate web sites such as those that promote violent hate groups or give instructions for bomb-making. Schools should maintain documentation of all prior incidents or problems involving students so it can be considered in future threat assessments.

Prong Four: Social Dynamics

Media, Entertainment, Technology

The student has easy and unmonitored access to movies, television shows, computer games, and Internet sites with themes and images of extreme violence.

Peer Groups

The student is intensely and exclusively involved with a group who share a fascination with violence or extremist beliefs. The group excludes others who do not share its interests or ideas. As a result, the student spends little or no time with anyone who thinks differently and is shielded from the "reality check" that might come from hearing other views or perceptions.

Drugs and Alcohol

Knowledge of a student's use of drugs and alcohol and his attitude toward these substances can be important. Any changes in his behavior involving these substances can also be important.

Outside Interests

A student's interests outside of school are important to note, as they can mitigate the school's concern when evaluating a threat or increase the level of concern.

The Copycat Effect

School shootings and other violent incidents that receive intense media attention can generate threats or copycat violence elsewhere. Copycat behavior is very common, in fact. Anecdotal evidence strongly indicates that threats increase in schools nationwide after a shooting has occurred anywhere in the United States. Students, teachers, school administrators, and law enforcement officials should be more vigilant in noting disturbing student behavior in the days and weeks or even several months following a heavily publicized incident elsewhere in the country.

Chapter 16

Getting to and from School Safely

Help Your Kids Get Back to School Safely

As summer days grow shorter, communities across America will soon be observing that timeless annual ritual: the first day of school. It's a time when parents breathe a sigh of relief and students and teachers anticipate new beginnings and new challenges. Unfortunately, the beginning of school is also a time when children are at increased risk of transportation related injuries from pedestrian, bicycle, school bus, and motor vehicle crashes because there are many more children on the road each morning and afternoon and many drivers' patterns change. Shorter daylight hours make it especially difficult to see young pedestrians and bicyclists. So as schools open their doors, it's time for everyone—motorists, parents, educators, and students— to improve their traffic safety practices. The following tips can help make this a safe and happy school year for the whole community.

Tips for Motorists

• Slow down and obey all traffic laws and speed limits.

Excerpted from "Help Your Kids Get Back to School Safely," http://www.nhtsa. gov/people/injury/buses/GTSS/newsback2school.html, "Safety Tips for Traveling to School on Public Transit," http://www.nhtsa.gov/people/injury/buses/ GTSS/newspublictransit.html, and "School Bus Safety," http://www.nhtsa.gov/ people/injury/buses/GTSS/newsbus_safety.html, National Highway Traffic Safety Administration, Getting to School Safely Community Action Kit, 2001– 2002 edition.

- Always stop for a school bus that has stopped to load or unload passengers. Red flashing lights and an extended stop arm tell you the school bus is stopped to load or unload children. State law requires you to stop.

- Be alert and ready to stop. Watch for children walking in the street, especially where there are no sidewalks. Watch for children playing and gathering near bus stops. Watch for children arriving late for the bus, who may dart into the street without looking for traffic. When backing out of a driveway or leaving a garage, watch for children walking or biking to school.

- When driving in neighborhoods or school zones, watch for young people who may be in a hurry to get to school and may not be thinking about getting there safely.

Tips for Parents

- Help your children learn and practice the safety rules for walking, bicycling, or riding in a passenger car, school bus, or transit bus.

- Supervise young children as they are walking or biking to school or as they wait at the school bus stop.

- Be a good role model, especially when you are with your kids. Always buckle up in the car, always wear a helmet when biking, and always follow pedestrian safety rules.

Tips for Educators

- Teach young children the safety rules for traveling to school, whether it be walking, bicycling, or riding in a motor vehicle or on a school bus.

- Be a good role model. Always use your seat belt, wear a helmet when bicycling or riding a motorcycle and practice pedestrian safety rules.

Tips for Students

- Always buckle up when you're riding in a car.

- Always ride in the back seat. It's the safest place for young people.

- Always wear a helmet and follow traffic safety rules when riding your bike.

- If you ride a school bus, learn and practice the safety rules for waiting at the bus stop, getting on and off the bus, and riding the bus.

- If you walk to school, learn and practice the safety rules for pedestrians. Always cross at cross walks, obey all traffic signs, traffic lights and safety patrol instructions.

- Be a good role model for your younger brothers and sisters and friends, and help them learn and practice the safety rules.

Safety Tips for Traveling to School on Public Transit

When we think of school transportation, most of us think of students riding a school bus, walking, riding a bike, or perhaps by car. But in some locations, many students use public mass transit. In fact, a study conducted by the American Public Transportation Association found that students traveling to or from school accounted for fifteen percent of all transit trips (mass transit carried over 8.1 billion passengers in 1999, according to the National Transit Database).

Mass transit is one of the safest forms of transportation, but it is not without risks, particularly for school-age children. Students need to learn to recognize and avoid these risks so they can get to and from school safely.

Safety on a Public Bus

There are a number of critical differences between riding a public transit bus and riding a school bus. Motorists do not have to stop when a public transit bus stops to pick up and drop off school children. Public buses move away from the bus stop as soon as passengers have gotten on or off. The drivers do not supervise children as they cross the street like school bus drivers do. And most public bus stops are at intersections, many of which do not have a traffic light or crossing signal. For these reasons, students who travel to school on a public bus need to observe the following precautions:

- Stay seated until the bus comes to a complete stop.

- Be alert as you get off the bus.

- Never cross the street in front of a public bus.

- Wait for the bus to pull away so you have a clear view of the street.

- Cross at the cross walk or street corner, and wait for the light to turn green or for the WALK signal.

Safety on the Subway or Train

Students who travel by subway or commuter train need to learn and observe the following safety rules:

- Stand at least two feet away from the edge of the platform.

- Step carefully over the gap between the train door and the platform.

- For safety and courtesy, let others leave the train before you enter.

- Report any unattended packages to a transit police officer, station manager, or train operator.

- Do not touch the train doors when they are opening or closing.

- Do not lean against the train doors.

- Do not run or play in the station—it would be easy to fall off the platform onto the tracks.

- Do not sit on the edge of the platform.

- If a seat is not available, hold tightly onto a hand rail at all times.

- Do not use rear exit doors to travel from car to car unless directed to do so by a subway or train system employee.

Safety on the Escalator

The escalators found in many subway, train, and bus stations pose a danger to passengers who do not use them correctly. When riding an escalator, students should know and observe the following rules for safety and courtesy:

- Step on and off quickly and carefully.

- Hold the handrail.

- Don't touch the sides of the escalator below the handrail.

- For courtesy, stand to the right and walk on the left.

- Always stand and face forward—never sit on the steps.

- Keep hands, feet, and clothing clear of moving parts—loose shoe laces, bulky sweaters or coats, rubber boots, and baggy clothes can get caught and cause injury.

- Always wear shoes on an escalator.

- Check the direction of the escalator before taking the first step—never walk up the down escalator, or vice versa.

- Never stop, stand, or play at an escalator landing—it can cause a dangerous pileup.

School Bus Safety

Twenty-three million students nationwide ride a school bus to and from school each day. Wherever you live, the familiar yellow school bus is one of the most common motor vehicles on the road. It is also the safest. School buses manufactured after January 1, 1977 must meet more federal motor vehicle safety standards than any other type of motor vehicle. In fact, during normal school transportation hours over the past 10 years, school buses are 87 times safer than passenger cars, light trucks, and vans, according to the Fatality Analysis Reporting System at the U.S. Department of Transportation. But school bus transportation is not without its hazards. Between 1989 and 1999, an average of 30 school age children (ages 5 through 18) were fatally injured each year in school bus-related crashes. Pedestrian fatalities while loading and unloading school buses accounted for nearly three out of every four of those fatalities; more than half of the pedestrian fatalities were young children between 5 and 7 years old.

Getting on and off the Bus Safely

Because getting on and off the bus is the most dangerous part of the school bus ride, the loading and unloading area is called the *Danger Zone*. This area—which extends ten feet in front of the bus, ten feet on each side of the bus, and behind the bus—is where children are at greatest risk of not being seen by the bus driver. Throughout the year, especially at the start of school, children need to be taught how to get on and off the school bus safely. Parents should help their children learn and follow these common-sense practices:

163

- Get to the bus stop at least five minutes before the bus is scheduled to arrive. Running to catch the bus is dangerous and can lead to injuries.

- When the bus approaches, stand at least five giant steps (10 feet) away from the curb, and line up away from the street.

- Wait until the bus stops, the door opens, and the driver says that it's okay before stepping onto the bus.

- If you have to cross the street in front of the bus, walk on the sidewalk or along the road to a point at least five giant steps ahead of the bus before you cross. Be sure that the bus driver can see you and you can see the bus driver when crossing the street. Stop at the edge of the bus and look left-right-left before crossing.

- Use the handrails to avoid falls. When getting off the bus, be careful that clothing with drawstrings and book bags and backpacks with straps don't get caught in the handrails or door.

- Never walk behind the bus.

- Walk at least five giant steps away from the side of the bus.

- If you drop something near the bus, tell the bus driver. Never try to pick it up, because the driver might not be able to see you.

Riding Safely

Students also need to behave safely during the school bus ride. Basic safety rules include the following:

- Always sit fully in the seat and face forward.

- Never distract the driver.

- Never stand on a moving bus.

- Obey the driver.

- Speak in a low voice, no screaming or shouting.

- Never stick anything out the window (arms, legs, head, book bags, etc.).

Safety Rules for Motorists

Motorists also need to observe traffic safety rules around school buses. First and foremost, they must know and understand the school bus laws in their state. In particular, they must be aware that it is illegal in all 50 states to pass a school bus that has stopped to load or unload students. (Ninety-five percent of the respondents in a recent telephone survey ranked this as the most dangerous of all illegal or unsafe driving practices. In fact, collisions involving motorists who illegally passed a stopped school bus accounted for almost one-fourth of the pedestrian fatalities in school bus-related crashes between 1989 and 1999.)

Motorists must learn the flashing signal light system that school bus drivers use to alert motorists that they are going to stop to load or unload students:

- Yellow flashing lights indicate the bus is preparing to stop to load or unload children. Motorists should slow down and prepare to stop their vehicles.

- Red flashing lights and extended stop arm indicate that the bus has stopped and that children are getting on or off. Motorists must stop their cars and wait until the red flashing lights are turned off, the stop arm is withdrawn, and the bus begins moving before they start driving again.

Motorists should also observe the following traffic safety rules:

- When backing out of a driveway or leaving a garage, watch out for children walking to the bus stop or walking or bicycling to school.

- When driving in neighborhoods and especially in school zones, watch out for young people who may be thinking about getting to school, but may not be thinking about getting there safely.

Part Three

Protection from
Child Abuse and Neglect

Chapter 17

Child Abuse and Maltreatment Statistics

Investigations of Child Abuse and Neglect

In 2000, three million referrals concerning the welfare of approximately five million children were made to Child Protective Services (CPS) agencies throughout the United States. Of these, approximately two-thirds (62%) were screened in; one-third (38%) were screened out. Screened-in referrals alleging that a child was being abused or neglected received investigations or assessments to determine whether the allegations of maltreatment could be substantiated. Some of the screened-out reports were referred to the attention of other service agencies.

Professionals, including teachers, law enforcement officers, social services workers, and physicians, made more than half (56%) of the screened-in reports. Others, including family members, neighbors, and other members of the community, made the remaining 44 percent of screened-in referrals.

Almost one-third of investigations or assessments (32%) resulted in a finding that the child was maltreated or at risk of maltreatment. The remaining investigations resulted in a finding that the maltreatment did not occur, the child was not at risk of maltreatment, or there was insufficient information to make a determination.

Excerpted from "National Child Abuse and Neglect Data System (NCANDS) Summary of Key Findings from Calendar Year 2000," Children's Bureau, Administration on Children, Youth and Families, http://www.calib.com/nccanch/pubs/factsheets/canstats.cfm, April 2002.

Victims of Maltreatment

Approximately 879,000 children were found to be victims of child maltreatment. Maltreatment categories typically include neglect, medical neglect, physical abuse, sexual abuse, and psychological maltreatment. Almost two-thirds of child victims (63%) suffered neglect (including medical neglect); 19 percent were physically abused; 10 percent were sexually abused; and 8 percent were psychologically maltreated.

The rate of child victims per 1,000 children in the population had been decreasing steadily from 15.3 victims per 1,000 children in the population in 1993 to 11.8 victims per 1,000 children in the population in 1999. The victimization rate increased slightly to 12.2 per 1,000 children in the year 2000. Whether or not this is a trend cannot be determined until additional data are collected.

Victimization rates declined as age increased. The rate of victimization for children in the age group of birth to 3 years old was 15.7 victims per 1,000 children of the same age. The rate of victimization for children ages 16 and 17 was 5.7 victims per 1,000 children of the same age in the population.

Victimization rates were similar for male and female victims (11.2 and 12.8 per 1,000 children respectively) except for victims of sexual abuse. The rate for sexual abuse was 1.7 victims per 1,000 female children compared to 0.4 victims per 1,000 male children.

More than half of all victims were White (51%); a quarter (25%) were African American; 15 percent were Hispanic. American Indian/Alaska Natives accounted for 2 percent of victims, and Asian/Pacific Islanders accounted for 1 percent of victims.

Perpetrators

Most states define perpetrators of child abuse or neglect as parents and other caretakers, such as relatives, babysitters, and foster parents, who have maltreated a child. Sixty percent of perpetrators were females and 40 percent were males. The median age of female perpetrators was 31 years; the median age of male perpetrators was 34 years.

More than 80 percent of victims (84%) were abused by a parent or parents. Mothers acting alone were responsible for 47 percent of neglect victims and 32 percent of physical abuse victims. Non-relatives, fathers acting alone, and other relatives were responsible for 29 percent, 22 percent and 19 percent, respectively, of sexual abuse victims.

Fatalities

Child fatalities are the most tragic consequence of maltreatment. Approximately 1,200 children died of abuse or neglect in the year 2000—a rate of 1.71 children per 100,000 children in the population. The increase in the rate of fatalities compared to earlier years is hypothesized to be largely attributable to improved reporting.

Youngest children were the most vulnerable. Children younger than one year old accounted for 44 percent of child fatalities, and 85 percent of child fatalities were younger than 6 years of age.

Services

Services to prevent the abuse or neglect of children were provided by various state and local agencies to an estimated three million children. Because of the difficulties in collecting these data, this may be an undercount.

More than half of the child victims (55% or an estimated 478,000) received services—including about one-fifth of all victims who were removed from their homes and placed in foster care—as a result of the investigation or assessment conducted by the child protective services agency. In addition, approximately one-fifth of children who were not found to be victims of maltreatment (19% or an estimated 385,000 children) also received services.

Summary

Child abuse and neglect continues to be a significant problem in the United States. These statistics can help us understand the scope of the problem, who is affected, and what type of services are being provided by state and local agencies.

Chapter 18

Defining Child Abuse

What Does Safety for My Child Mean?

We all want our children to be safe—keeping them safe means putting the child's best interests first. This means ensuring that the child is treated with respect and integrity—emotionally, socially, intellectually, physically, culturally, and spiritually.

When Is My Child Unsafe?

Young people are unsafe when someone uses his or her power or position to harm them either emotionally, physically, and/or sexually—this is abuse! Your child's safety is also at risk when she or he is threatened, intimidated, taunted, or subjected to racial slurs by a peer—this is harassment! Harassment can also occur when an adult discriminates against a youth.

The information in this chapter is excerpted from, Fair Play Means Safety for All: A Parents' & Guardians' Guide to Understanding Abuse & Harassment, produced and published by the Canadian Hockey Association with the assistance of Judi Fairholm, National Manager, Canadian Red Cross RespectED: Violence & Abuse Prevention, and Sally Spilhaus, Advisor on Rights and Responsibilities, Concordia University in Montreal, Quebec. ©2001 Canadian Hockey Association. Reprinted with permission. [For more information, or to view the full text of this booklet, visit the Canadian Hockey Association website at www.canadianhockey.ca.]

What Is Emotional Abuse?

Emotional abuse is a chronic attack on a child's self esteem; it is psychologically destructive behavior by a person in a position of power, authority, or trust. It can take the form of name calling, threatening, ridiculing, intimidating, isolating, hazing, or ignoring a child's needs! It is not:

- benching a player for disciplinary reasons
- cutting a player from a team after tryouts
- refusing to transfer a player
- limiting ice time
- yelling instructions from the bench

What Is Physical Abuse?

Physical abuse is when a person in a position of power or trust purposefully injures or threatens to injure a child or youth. This may take the form of slapping, hitting, shaking, kicking, pulling hair or ears, striking, shoving, grabbing, hazing or excessive exercise as a form of punishment.

What Is Neglect?

Neglect is the chronic inattention to the basic necessities of life such as clothing, shelter, nutritious diet, education, good hygiene, supervision, medical and dental care, adequate rest, safe environment, moral guidance and discipline, exercise, and fresh air. This may occur when injuries are not adequately treated, players are made to play with injuries, equipment is inadequate or unsafe, or road trips are not properly supervised.

What Is Sexual Abuse?

Sexual abuse is when a young person is used by an older child, adolescent, or adult for his or her own sexual stimulation or gratification. There are two categories:

Contact

- touched and fondled in sexual areas
- forced to touch another person's sexual areas

- kissed or held in a sexual manner
- forced to perform oral sex
- vaginal or anal intercourse
- vaginal or anal penetration with object or finger
- sexually oriented hazing

Non Contact

- obscene calls/obscene remarks on computer or in notes
- voyeurism
- shown pornography
- forced to watch sexual acts
- sexually intrusive questions or comments
- indecent exposure
- forced to pose for sexual photographs or videos
- forced to self-masturbate
- forced to watch others masturbate

What Is Harassment?

Harassment is a behavior which is insulting, humiliating, malicious, degrading, or offensive. Harassment can be a pattern of behavior, a "chilly" or "hostile" environment or a single event. Dealing with harassment can sometimes be difficult, as what is viewed as harassment by one person may be viewed as a joke by another person. But it is the impact of the behavior on the victim that is the most critical, not the intention of the person who is doing the harassing.

Like abuse, harassment is the misuse of power. Harassment can be non-criminal or criminal and falls into three categories: personal, sexual, or abuse of power and authority.

Personal Harassment

Personal harassment is any unwelcome behavior that degrades, demeans, humiliates, or embarrasses a person, and that a reasonable person should have known would be unwelcome. Examples are written or verbal abuse or threats, practical jokes which cause embarrassment

175

or endanger a person's safety, discriminating against a person, or use of degrading words to describe someone.

Sexual Harassment

Sexual harassment is unwelcome behavior of a sexual nature that negatively affects the person or the environment. Examples are questions about one's sex life, sexual staring, sexual comments, unwanted touching, persistence in asking someone for a date even after they have said "No," and sexual assault.

Abuse of Power or Authority

Abuse of power or authority is when someone uses the power of their position or authority to negatively control, influence, discriminate or embarrass another person. Examples are displays of favoritism or dis-favoritism, subtle put-downs, or ostracism.

What Is Hazing?

Hazing is a humiliating and degrading initiation rite in which a player is forced to participate in order to be accepted.

How Do I Know When My Children Are Being Abused or Harassed?

- by listening to them
- by believing them
- by observing them
- by watching their interactions with others
- by being aware of sudden changes in their behavior and/or anger in them
- by questioning unexplained bruises, marks on their faces, back, thighs, upper arms, heads, buttocks, genital areas

Recognizing Abusive and Vulnerable Situations

Who Would Hurt My Child?

Unfortunately, it is usually someone both you and your child know and trust.

- Harassers are usually peers who are insecure and want to feel power.

- Emotional and physical abusers have limited interpersonal skills and use their anger against children and youth.

- Sexual offenders "groom" children and youth by establishing trust relationships and then using them for sexual gratification.

Sexual offenders are/can be:

- most often male but may be female

- heterosexual, homosexual, or bisexual

- an older child, adolescent, or adult

- found in all levels of society and in all cultures

- either infrequent offenders or pedophiles who are fixated on children as sexual objects

- prone to rationalize and minimize their abusive behavior

Where is my child most at risk for all types of abuse? Basically your child is most vulnerable when he/she is alone with another person—this could be in the sports arena, dressing room, car, bus, home, office, outside—anywhere! In some situations, such as hazing, they are vulnerable in a group setting where there is inadequate supervision.

Recognizing Coping Mechanisms

How Do Children and Youth Cope with the Trauma of Abuse and Harassment?

- some pretend it never happened

- others convince themselves that it wasn't so terrible

- many find excuses as to why it happened

- some blame themselves

- some develop physiological defenses—headaches, body pains, and illnesses

- others escape through drugs, alcohol, food, or sex

- a few try to hide from their pain by being perfect

Why Do Kids Not Tell?

They may:

- be frightened
- believe they are responsible
- not want to get the offender into trouble
- be embarrassed and ashamed
- think no-one will believe them

Identifying Parents' and Guardians' Role

What Do I Do If a Child or Youth Tells Me He/She Is Being Harassed?

- listen
- believe
- talk with your coach or officials
- help the young person to learn effective ways of responding
- if it is mild harassment, try to resolve the situation informally
- if it is moderate or serious harassment, refer the complaint as specified in your organization's policy
- give the child or youth continuous support

How Do I Protect My Child or Youth against Hazing?

- talk with him/her about hazing; discuss peer pressure
- explain that he/she does not have to submit to hazing
- report it

What Do I Do If a Child or Youth Tells Me about an Abusive Situation?

Do:

- listen—take the time to hear what he/she is saying
- believe—"I believe you"

- reassure—"It's not your fault!"
- report—contact the appropriate authorities and make a report
- support—provide ongoing support to help the child or youth deal with the trauma of abuse
- take action—do not let the child or youth stay in a vulnerable situation

Don't:

- react with shock, horror or disbelief—even though you may feel like it
- promise to keep a secret—you are legally bound to report
- promise "everything will be fine"—there are many problems to resolve, it will take time
- assume the child or youth hates the abuser—there may be conflicting feelings
- put the responsibility of reporting on someone else—they may not do it
- press the child or youth for details—the matter may go to court, so it is important that evidence is not contaminated

What Do I Do If I Suspect My Child Is Being Abused?

- document your observations
- record behaviors, dates, times, and people involved
- identify vulnerable situations and be there to protect your child
- seek advice or information about abuse from a knowledgeable person
- tell your child your concerns
- listen to your child's fears about the situation
- do not promise that "everything will be fine"
- report if your suspicions are strong
- keep it confidential; do not get caught in the "rumor mill"
- support your child

Reporting

Anyone who has reasonable grounds to suspect that a youth is, or may be suffering, or may have suffered from emotional, physical abuse and neglect and/or sexual abuse should immediately report the suspicion and the information on which it is based to the local child protection agency and/or the local police detachment.

When I Report, What Questions Will Be Asked?

- the child's name, address, age, sex, and birth date
- parents'/guardians' names and addresses
- the name and address of alleged offender
- details of the incident(s) that prompted your report
- your name and address

What Happens When a Report Is Made?

- A social worker or police officer will decide if an investigation is needed.
- If the child is "at risk" and needs protection, an investigation is started as soon as possible.
- An experienced interviewer will conduct the interview.
- The primary concern is safety of the child.
- The social worker and/or police officer will decide what further action is required.

Why Don't People Report?

They don't report because they:

- are unaware of the reporting laws
- believe that they can take care of the problem themselves—it's their own business
- are fearful of retaliation from the abuser—or are friends with the abuser
- find it hard to believe
- assume someone else will make a report

- don't want "to tell" on someone
- want to protect their child from questions and embarrassment
- are not sure where or how to make a report
- just want it "all to go away"
- forget that the child's best interests are the priority

Do Children Ever Make False Allegations?

Yes, sometimes it happens. Some of the research shows that about 8% of disclosures are false. Most of the false allegations by children are encouraged by adults—e.g. custody cases, and others have been by adolescents who wanted "to get even." It is important to reinforce the truth—false allegations are devastating to the person accused!

Proactive Roles

How Do I Keep My Children Safe?

There are five essentials to keeping your child safe.

1. Communication

    - Listen, talk, believe, and reassure your children.
    - Provide opportunities for conversations with your children.
    - Be open to any questions; nothing is off limits.
    - Be open to discussing difficult subjects such as sexuality.
    - Develop frank and open communication with coaches.
    - If you have concerns, communicate them to the appropriate persons.
    - If you see or hear harassing or abusive behavior, speak out!

2. Knowledge

    - Make your children aware of vulnerable situations in a matter-of-fact way.
    - Review abuse and harassment policy and procedures.

- Be aware of the screening and selection process for staff and volunteers.

- Get to know the adults who are interacting with your children.

- Discuss with the coaches their expectations and the setting of boundaries: physical, sexual and social.

3. Skills

  - Teach your children specific ways to handle difficult situations.

  - Help your children define their personal boundaries.

  - Teach your children how to be assertive when their boundaries are crossed.

4. Build a safety plan

  - Develop check-ins, contingency plans, family codes.

  - Attend practices and games.

  - Be wary of regular private closed practices.

  - Be concerned of time spent alone with adults beyond training and game times.

5. Advocate

  - You are your children's strongest supporter.

  - Evaluate situations according to the "best interest of your child."

Chapter 19

Defining Physical Abuse

Physical abuse is the most visible form of child maltreatment and is defined as non-accidental trauma or physical injury resulting from punching, beating, kicking, biting, burning, or otherwise harming a child. While any of these injuries can occur accidentally when a child is at play, physical abuse should be suspected if the explanations do not fit the injury or if a pattern of frequency is apparent. The presence of many injuries in various stages of healing make it obvious that they did not all occur as a result of one accident.

The physical indicators of abuse include the presence of bruises, lacerations, swollen areas, or marks on the child's face, head, back, chest, genital area, buttocks, or thighs. Wounds like human bite marks, cigarette burns, broken bones, puncture marks, or missing hair may also indicate abuse. A child's behavior might signal that something is wrong. Behavioral indicators include withdrawn or aggressive behavioral extremes, complaints of soreness or uncomfortable movement, wearing clothing that is inappropriate for the weather, discomfort with physical contact, or becoming a chronic runaway.

It is difficult to imagine that any person would intentionally inflict harm on a child. Many times, physical abuse is a result of inappropriate or excessive physical discipline. An angry caretaker or parent may be unaware of the magnitude of force with which he or she strikes the child.

Excerpted from an undated web-page produced by American Humane Society, "Physical Abuse," http://www.americanhumane.org/children/factsheets/phys_abuse.htm. Downloaded August 2002.

183

There are better alternatives to use in disciplining children than physical punishment. Parents who discipline their children are motivated by their children's best interests. They want their children to be responsible, courteous, well-mannered, and more. Yet, kids will be kids. Children can be loud, unruly, and destructive. They will break things, interrupt telephone conversations, track mud through the house, not pick up their toys or clean their rooms, struggle over eating their vegetables, or pester routinely. Children will inevitably do things that may make their parents feel irritated, frustrated, disappointed, and mad. Changing a child's behavior is not easy. However, inflicting pain and injury does not cause change because the child does not learn what he or she is doing wrong. Children should be disciplined, but not through violence.

Raising a child is not easy. Denying children privileges when they do something that is unacceptable, as well as rewarding them when they do something good, serves to teach children that there are responsibilities and consequences for their actions.

Below are several more suggestions on alternatives to losing control. Make sure the child is in a safe place, or ask a neighbor to relieve you for a few minutes. Then try to calm down with the following suggestions:

- Take time out.
- Count to ten.
- Take deep breaths.
- Phone a friend.
- Look through a magazine or newspaper.
- Listen to music.
- Exercise.
- Take a walk (first make certain that children are not left without supervision).
- Take a bath.
- Write a letter.
- Sit down and relax.
- Lie down.

Other factors that can contribute to child abuse include the immaturity of parents, the lack of parenting skills, a parent's own poor childhood experiences, social isolation, frequent crises, and drug or alcohol problems. Child abuse is a symptom of difficulty coping with stressful situations. The problem will not go away unless an effort is made to treat it. Help is available for families at risk of abuse— through their local child protection agency, community center, church, physician, mental health facility, school, etc.

If you suspect physical abuse of a child is occurring, the first step to take toward protecting that child is to report it to your local child protective agency or law enforcement agency.

Chapter 20

Defining Neglect

What Is Neglect?

The NCANDS (The National Child Abuse and Neglect Data Sysem) report defines neglect as "a type of maltreatment that refers to the failure to provide needed, age-appropriate care." Unlike physical and sexual abuse, neglect is usually typified by an ongoing pattern of inadequate care and is readily observed by individuals in close contact with the child. Physicians, nurses, day-care personnel, relatives, and neighbors are frequently the ones to suspect and report neglected infants, toddlers, and preschool-aged children. Once children are in school, school personnel often notice indicators of child neglect such as poor hygiene, poor weight gain, inadequate medical care, or frequent absences from school. Professionals have defined four types of neglect—physical, emotional, educational, and medical.

- Physical neglect accounts for the majority of cases of maltreatment. It is estimated that 8 of every 1,000 children experience physical neglect. The definition includes the refusal of or extreme delay in seeking necessary health care, child abandonment, inadequate supervision, rejection of a child leading to expulsion from the home, and failing to adequately provide for the child's safety and physical and emotional needs. Physical

Excerpted from an undated web-page produced by American Humane Society, "Child Neglect," http://www.americanhumane.org/children/factsheets/ neg_abuse.htm. downloaded August 2002.

neglect can severely impact a child's development by causing failure to thrive; malnutrition; serious illnesses; physical harm in the form of cuts, bruises, and burns due to lack of supervision; and a lifetime of low self-esteem.

- Educational neglect occurs when a child is allowed to engage in chronic truancy, is of mandatory school age but not enrolled in school or receiving school training, and/or is not receiving needed special educational training. Educational neglect can lead to underachievement in acquiring necessary basic skills, dropping out of school, and/or continually disruptive behavior.

- Emotional neglect includes such actions as chronic or extreme spousal abuse in the child's presence, allowing a child to use drugs or alcohol, refusal or failure to provide needed psychological care, constant belittling, and withholding of affection. This pattern of behavior can lead to poor self-image, alcohol or drug abuse, destructive behavior, and even suicide. Severe neglect of infants can result in the infant failing to grow and thrive and may even lead to infant death.

- Medical neglect is the failure to provide for appropriate health care for a child although financially able to do so. In 1995, 3% of the substantiated cases of child maltreatment dealt with medical neglect. In some cases, a parent or other caretaker will withhold traditional medical care during the practice of certain religious beliefs. These cases generally do not fall under the definition of medical neglect, however, some states will obtain a court order forcing medical treatment of a child in order to save the child's life or prevent life-threatening injury resulting from lack of treatment. Medical neglect can result in poor overall health and compounded medical problems.

Although neglect is highly correlated with poverty, there is a distinction to be made between a caregiver's ability to provide the needed care due to the lack of financial resources, illness, or cultural norms, and a caregiver's knowing reluctance and/or refusal to provide care. Either way, children may be found to be in neglectful situations and in need of services even though the parent may not be intentionally neglectful. Whereas poverty may limit a parent's resources to adequately provide necessities for the child, services may be offered to assist families in providing for their children.

If you suspect child neglect is occurring, the first step to take toward protecting the child is to report it to the local child protective agency, often called "social services" or "human services," in your county or state. Professionals who work with children are required by law to report suspicion of neglect or abuse. Furthermore, there are 20 states that require every citizen who suspects abuse or neglect to report it. "Reasonable suspicion" based on objective evidence, which could be firsthand observation or hearing statements made by a parent or child, is all that is needed to report. If you are unsure which is the appropriate local agency to contact, you can call the Children's Division of the American Humane Association at 303-792-9900 to obtain the child protective agency number for your county or state.

Chapter 21

Defining Emotional Abuse

What Is Emotional Abuse?

There is no universally accepted definition of emotional abuse. Like other forms of violence in relationships, emotional abuse is based on power, and control. The following are widely recognized as forms of emotional abuse:

Rejecting—refusing to acknowledge a person's presence, value or worth; communicating to a person that she or he is useless or inferior; devaluing her/his thoughts and feelings. Example: repeatedly treating a child differently from siblings in a way that suggests resentment, rejection, or dislike for the child.

Degrading—insulting, ridiculing, name-calling, imitating and infantilizing; behaviour which diminishes the identity, dignity, and self-worth of the person. Examples: yelling, swearing, publicly humiliating, or labelling a person as stupid; mimicking a person's disability; treating a senior as if she or he cannot make decisions.

Terrorizing—inducing terror or extreme fear in a person; coercing by intimidation; placing or threatening to place a person in an unfit,

"What is Emotional Abuse?" Health Canada, 1996. Copyright © Minister of Public Works and Government Services Canada, 2002. http://www.hc-sc.gc.ca/hppb/familyviolence/html/emotioneng.html. Despite the age of this document, readers seeking information about emotional abuse will find this information useful.

or dangerous environment. Examples: forcing a child to watch violent acts toward other family members or pets; threatening to leave, physically hurt, or kill a person, pets or people she/he cares about; threatening to destroy a person's possessions; threatening to have a person deported or put in an institution; stalking.

Isolating—physical confinement; restricting normal contact with others; limiting freedom within a person's own environment. Examples: excluding a senior from participating in decisions about her or his own life; locking a child in a closet, or room alone; refusing a female partner, or senior access to her or his own money, and financial affairs; withholding contact with grandchildren; depriving a person of mobility aids, or transportation.

Corrupting/Exploiting—socializing a person into accepting ideas, or behaviour which oppose legal standards; using a person for advantage, or profit; training a child to serve the interests of the abuser, and not of the child. Examples: child sexual abuse; permitting a child to use alcohol, or drugs; enticing a person into the sex trade.

Denying emotional responsiveness—failing to provide care in a sensitive and responsive manner; being detached and uninvolved; interacting only when necessary; ignoring a person's mental health needs. Examples: ignoring a child's attempt to interact; failing to show affection, caring and/or love for a child; treating a senior who lives in an institution as though she/he is an object, or "a job to be done."

- Emotional abuse accompanies other forms of abuse, but also may occur on its own.

- No abuse—neglect, physical, sexual, or financial—can occur without psychological consequences. Therefore all abuse contains elements of emotional abuse.

- Emotional abuse follows a pattern; it is repeated and sustained. If left unchecked, abuse does not get better over time. It only gets worse.

- Like other forms of violence in relationships, those who hold the least power and resources in society, for example, women and children, are most often emotionally abused.

- Emotional abuse can severely damage a person's sense of self-worth and perception.

- In children, emotional abuse can impair psychological development, including: intelligence, memory, recognition, perception,
attention, imagination, and moral development. Emotional
abuse can also affect a child's social development, and may result in an impaired ability to perceive, feel, understand, and express emotions.

How Widespread Is Emotional Abuse?

Only a few studies provide insight about the prevalence of emotional abuse in Canada. Emotional abuse is difficult to research because:

- In comparison to other forms of abuse, its effects have only recently been recognized.

- There are no consistent definitions, and it is hard to define.

- It is difficult to detect, assess, and substantiate.

- Many cases of emotional abuse go unreported.

A recent study of Ontario investigations into child maltreatment found
that, in 1993, 10 percent of investigations alleged emotional abuse.
In 1993, 39 percent of women in abusive relationships reported that
their children saw them being assaulted.
In 1995, the Canadian Women's Health Test found that of 1000
women 15 years of age or over:

- 36 percent had experienced emotional abuse while growing up;
43 percent had experienced some form of abuse as children or
teenagers.

- 39 percent reported experiencing verbal/emotional abuse in a
relationship within the last five years.

Statistics Canada's 1993 Violence Against Women Survey showed
that among ever-married or common-law Canadian women aged 18
to 65 years, emotional abuse is widespread. The study found that:

- 35 percent of all women surveyed reported that their spouse
was emotionally abusive.

- 18 percent of women reported experiencing emotional abuse,
but not physical abuse in a relationship.

- 77 percent of women reported emotional abuse in combination with physical abuse.

In one Canadian study on abuse in university and college dating relationships, 81 percent of male respondents reported that they had psychologically abused a female partner.

In 1995, a study of seniors' client records from various agencies across Canada found that psychological abuse was the most prevalent form of abuse.

The 1990 National Survey on Abuse of the Elderly in Canada estimated that:

- 4 percent of seniors residing in private homes reported experiencing abuse and/or neglect.

- Questions about insults, swearing, and threats were asked as a measure of chronic verbal aggression. The study showed that 1.4 percent of seniors experienced these forms of emotional abuse in the year prior to the study.

- Chronic verbal aggression ranked as the second most prevalent form of mistreatment following material abuse.

Facts to Consider

Emotional abuse of children can result in serious emotional and/ or behavioural problems, including depression, lack of attachment, or emotional bond to a parent or guardian, low cognitive ability, and educational achievement, and poor social skills.

One study which looked at emotionally abused children in infancy, and then again during their preschool years consistently found them to be angry, uncooperative and unattached to their primary caregiver. The children also lacked creativity, persistence, and enthusiasm.

Children who experience rejection are more likely than accepted children to exhibit hostility, aggressive, or passive-aggressive behaviour, to be extremely dependent, to have negative opinions of themselves and their abilities, to be emotionally unstable, or unresponsive, and to have a negative perception of the world around them.

Parental verbal aggression (e.g., yelling, insulting), or symbolic aggression (e.g., slamming a door, giving the silent treatment) toward children can have serious consequences. Children who experience these forms of abuse demonstrate higher rates of physical aggressiveness, delinquency, and interpersonal problems than other children.

Children whose parents are additionally physically abusive are even more likely to experience such difficulties.

Children who see or hear their mothers being abused are victims of emotional abuse. Growing up in such an environment is terrifying, and severely affects a child's psychological and social development. Male children may learn to model violent behaviour while female children may learn that being abused is a normal part of relationships. This contributes to the intergenerational cycle of violence.

Many women in physically abusive relationships feel that the emotional abuse is more severely debilitating than the physical abuse in the relationship.

Repeated verbal abuse such as blaming, ridiculing, insulting, swearing, yelling, and humiliation has long-term negative effects on a woman's self-esteem and contributes to feelings of uselessness, worthlessness, and self-blame.

Threatening to kill or physically harm a female partner, her children, other family members, or pets establishes dominance, and coercive power on the part of the abuser. The female partner feels extreme terror, vulnerability, and powerlessness within the relationship. This type of emotional abuse can make an abused woman feel helpless, and isolated.

Jealousy, possessiveness, and interrogation about whereabouts, and activities are controlling behaviours which can severely restrict a female partner's independence, and freedom. Social, and financial isolation may leave her dependent upon the abuser for social contact, money, and the necessities of life.

Emotional abuse can have serious physical, and psychological consequences for women, including severe depression, anxiety, persistent headaches, back and limb problems, and stomach problems.

Women who are psychologically abused, but not physically abused are five times more likely to misuse alcohol than women who have not experienced abuse.

Senior abuse is still a new issue, and there is still little research in this field on emotional abuse.

We do know that senior emotional abuse and neglect can be personal or systemic and that it occurs in a variety of relationships, and settings, including abuse by:

- A partner.
- Adult, children, or other relatives.
- Unrelated, formal, or informal caregivers.
- Someone in a position of trust.

Seniors who are emotionally abused may experience feelings of extreme inadequacy, guilt, low self-esteem, symptoms of depression, fear of failure, powerlessness, or hopelessness. These signs may be easily confused with loss of mental capability so that a senior may be labelled as "senile," or "incapable" when in fact she, or he may be being emotionally abused.

Abusers may often outwardly display anger and resentment toward the senior in the company of others. They may also display a complete lack of respect, or concern for the senior by repeatedly interrupting or publicly humiliating her or him. Not taking into account a senior's wishes concerning decisions about her or his own life is an outward sign of abuse.

Table 21.1. Possible Indicators of Emotional Abuse and Neglect

Children	Adults
depression	depression
withdrawal	withdrawal
low self-esteem	low self-esteem
severe anxiety	severe anxiety
fearfulness	fearfulness
failure to thrive in infancy	feelings of shame and guilt
aggression	frequent crying
emotional instability	self-blame/self-depreciation
sleep disturbances	overly passive/compliant
physical complaints with no medical basis	social isolation
inappropriate behaviour for age or development	delay or refusal of medical treatment
overly passive/compliant	discomfort or nervousness around caregiver or relative
suicide attempts or discussion	suicide attempts or discussion
extreme dependence	substance abuse
underachievement	avoidance of eye contact
inability to trust	other forms of abuse present or suspected
stealing	
other forms of abuse present or suspected	

Detecting Emotional Abuse

Emotional abuse may be difficult to detect. However, personal awareness and understanding of the issue is key to recognizing it. The following indicators may assist in detecting emotional abuse.

Legal Interventions

Legal intervention in cases of child emotional abuse, and neglect is governed by provincial and territorial child protection legislation. All jurisdictions require that alleged or suspected child emotional abuse, or neglect be reported to child protection authorities or the police. In some jurisdictions, failure to report child emotional abuse or neglect may result in a fine or imprisonment.

Emotionally abusive behaviour such as repeatedly following the other person or someone known to her or him; repeatedly communicating, directly or indirectly, with the other person, or someone known to her or him; harassing the other person with telephone calls; besetting or watching the other person's house or place of work; and/or engaging in threatening conduct directed at the other person, or a member of her or his family is criminal harassment. These behaviours must cause a person to fear for her or his safety, or the safety of someone she or he knows. Other forms of emotional abuse such as insulting, isolating, infantilizing, humiliating, and ignoring, although serious, are not criminal behaviours and cannot be prosecuted under the Criminal Code of Canada.

What Can You Do?

If You Are Being Abused

Remember:

- You are not alone.
- It is not your fault.
- No one ever deserves to be abused.
- Help is available.

If You Suspect or Know That Someone Is Being Abused

- Listen.
- Believe.

- Support.

- Let the person know about available support services.

- Report suspected or known child abuse or neglect to a child welfare agency or the police.

If You Are a Service Provider

Work with other organizations to:

- Increase awareness of emotional abuse.

- Address the needs of those who have been or are being emotionally abused.

- Keep informed of resources and materials relating to intervention and prevention of abuse.

Where to Go for Support Services

- 24 hour help-line or distress line.

- Transition house or shelter.

- Social service agency.

- Child welfare or family services agency.

- Police.

- Legal aid service.

- Health professional (e.g., nurse, doctor, dentist).

- Community health centre.

- Public health department.

- Community counselling centre.

- Home support agency.

- Seniors' centre.

- Community living association.

- Friendship centre.

- Religious organization.

Chapter 22

Facts about Reporting Child Abuse

What Should I Know about Reporting Child Abuse and Neglect?

Taking the First Step

Deciding whether or not to report suspected child abuse can be a difficult and confusing process, yet it is the important first step toward protecting a child who might be in danger. Professionals who work with children are required by law to report suspected neglect or abuse. About 20 states require that every citizen who suspects a child is being abused or neglected must report. However, regardless of whether or not you are among those who are mandated to report, accurate reporting of the suspected maltreatment of any child is a moral obligation. "Reasonable suspicion" based on objective evidence is all that is needed to report. That evidence might be your firsthand observation or statements made by a parent or a child.

Unfamiliarity with state reporting laws and ignorance of the dynamics of abuse and neglect are two of the most frequent reasons given for non-reporting. Frustration with lack of response by child welfare

From an undated web page produced by American Humane Association (AHA), "What Should I Know About Reporting Child Abuse and Neglect?" http://www.americanhumane.org/children/factsheets/rep_abuse.htm, downloaded August 2002, and "Guidelines to Help Children Who Have Been Reported for Suspected Abuse and Neglect," AHA, http://www.americanhumane.org/children/factsheets/guidelines.htm, downloaded August 2002.

professionals to a complaint, and an unwillingness to "get involved" are other reasons given for failure to report. Others include not wanting to "make things worse for the child," an unwillingness to provide the time-consuming court testimony that might be necessary, or a reluctance to risk angering the family. All of these reasons are understandable, yet any one of them could lead to the death of a child that might otherwise have been prevented if the person with the information had only reported it.

What Happens after I Make the Decision to Report Suspected Child Abuse and/or Neglect?

Several events might take place before and after the initial complaint is filed. First of all, depending on where you live, you might report suspected abuse and/or neglect to your local child protective agency. These agencies are sometimes called Social Services, Human Rehabilitative Services, Human Welfare, or Children and Family Services. If you feel that a child is in an emergency situation, you should call your local law enforcement immediately.

The person responding to your call may ask you several questions about what you are reporting. This is done to ensure that enough information is available for the investigative team to be able to make decisions concerning whether or not abuse and/or neglect has occurred. You might be asked to give names of the family and child; your reasons for suspecting abuse; the names, addresses, and telephone numbers of other witnesses; your relationship to the alleged victim; any other previous suspicious injury to the child; or your name, address, and phone number. Anonymous reports can be made in every state, however, child welfare agencies generally try to discourage anonymity for many reasons. Not knowing the identity of the reporter denies the child welfare worker the opportunity to get more information during the investigative process or to call the reporter as a crucial evidentiary witness if the case goes to trial.

Unfortunately, over the last several years many child welfare agencies have been severely underfunded and understaffed. Sometimes the investigation of abuse and neglect complaints will be prioritized according to the immediate risk to the child. Be patient. You may have to call more than once.

Who Investigates Complaints of Child Abuse and Neglect?

The state or county agency that provides child protective services has the legal authority granted it by law or charter which gives them an obligation to provide services when needed and which grants them the right "to explore, study and evaluate" the facts. Child welfare workers base their decision on whether or not to remove a child from the family on two issues:

1. What is the immediate danger or risk to child?

2. What is the motivation, capacity, and intent of the alleged perpetrator?

During the investigative process, the child welfare worker may call on a variety of supportive assistance from individuals and organizations in the community. It then becomes the responsibility of the child welfare worker to organize or provide any needed services for the child and the family.

What Happens to the Child and Family?

With the enactment of Public Law 96–272, it is legally mandated that child welfare workers make all "reasonable efforts" to reunite the family whenever possible. If, after a thorough investigation, it is determined that the child is in need of substitute care, then the child is placed in temporary foster care or in another safe placement alternative until the immediate danger has passed and services can be provided for the child and family. Sometimes criminal child abuse charges have to be filed depending on the nature and the severity of the abuse/neglect. There is a range of legal penalties for child maltreatment that varies from ordering the perpetrator into therapy to incarceration.

Will I Be Able to Find out What Happens to the Child?

Persons who have reported suspected child maltreatment should be allowed to know whether or not their suspicions were founded and what steps the investigation agency took to protect the child. However, there is a great deal of confusion over whether or not information from child welfare cases should be shared. Legally, there is no impediment to providing general feedback to the child abuse/neglect reporter. Some states have even gone so far as to implement laws that require the child welfare agencies to report back to the reporters. Many times, child welfare agencies, overburdened with high caseloads and too many time demands, will not report back the results of their investigations. Other agencies will wrongly say that they cannot release the results of their investigations because the information is confidential. If the agency does not voluntarily provide such information to you, then you will have to request it. Mandated reporters of child abuse, because they have an ongoing legal obligation to report, need to know the circumstances of an investigation so that they can keep track of any conditions that might further endanger the child. Professionals who work with child victims may have to know information in order to treat the victims in their care. The most difficult confidentiality issue to resolve concerns the reporting individual's need to know vs. the family's right to privacy. So, the distinction is usually made to provide less specific information to individuals outside the child welfare professional community. This means that if the reporter is a family friend, neighbor, or relative, then the information won't be provided in detail. The child welfare agency may give feedback that indicates that the reporter was right in making a referral and that the agency will be working with the family.

What Happens If I Report and the Case Is Unsubstantiated?

All states have laws that protect the reporter of suspected abuse or neglect from legal liability as long as the report was made "in good faith" and not maliciously. Only a small percentage of reports are deliberately false. Another percentage of cases may be classified as "unsubstantiated." This means that there might not have been sufficient information regarding the allegation or the identity of the family, or that the state law contained narrow criteria for substantiating a case. In addition, a case may not be substantiated because services were provided to the child but no court action was taken, or because there was a lack of resources to assist the child or family. Criteria for substantiation varies from state to state because there is no uniform national system for case reporting.

If you are unsure of what the legal and societal definitions of abuse/neglect are in your community, contact your local child welfare agency for information. In addition, the American Humane Association can offer you more information on what you can do, and what we are doing to assure that children's interests and well-being are fully, effectively, and humanely guaranteed. Knowing how, when, and what to report about child abuse and neglect may make a life or death difference for a child.

Guidelines to Help Children Who Have Been Reported for Suspected Abuse and Neglect

How Important Is My Role?

School personnel, teachers, counselors, child care workers, Boy and Girl Scout troop leaders, coaches—all adults who interact with children on a regular basis have a tremendous influence on children. Although you may never know that a child in your care has been reported to your local child protective service agency or law enforcement for child abuse or neglect, oftentimes you are aware of children in such a situation. Learning how to help these children is an important contribution which you can make to help children overcome such tragedies. A caring adult can actually offset or reverse the harm caused by an abusing parent.

What Happens Once a Report Is Made?

When child protective services receives a report of child maltreatment, they may begin an investigation, or if the report is deemed inappropriate or incomplete, may refer the case to another resource agency. Depending on the particular situation, as well as the requirements of the local child protective services agency, those who reported the situation may have the opportunity to continue communicating with the child protective services worker regarding a child's progress. Educators, in particular, may be asked to share additional information to help determine the facts of the situation and develop a treatment plan. School personnel can be an excellent resource but must ensure confidentiality of information and ensure that the information is only shared with people designated by law. Obviously, rumors may further isolate the family and negatively affect efforts to help them.

How Should I Address the Parents?

Oftentimes, you will continue to have regular contact with the family after a report has been made. Parents who are suspected of child maltreatment can benefit from, or be hurt by, your influence as well.

- Be objective and supportive of the family. Remember that most parents want to be good parents but may need additional help and encouragement to do so.

- Do not blame or make judgments about the family.

- Limit conversation to the activities in which you are involved; it is not your responsibility to investigate suspected maltreatment.

- When talking to parents, be professional and objective. Do not allow yourself to be placed in the role of the adversary if parents get defensive and upset.

- Schools may be an ideal provider of support for parents through parent education programs, early childhood programs emphasizing child development, counseling programs such as job skills counseling, alcohol/drug abuse programs, and adult education programs.

- Families experiencing abuse or neglect are also often experiencing extreme stress from many factors. The program you are involved in may be a very important stress reducer to the child and parent.

How Should I Address the Needs of the Child?

The following tips can help you develop nurturing relationships with all the children with whom you interact, including abused and neglected children who often suffer from poor self-concepts.

- Children need positive adult role models. Warmth, sympathy, and interest can allow children to see adults in a positive, supportive, and caring role.

- Be an approachable, patient listener. Listen without being critical or negative toward the child or the child's parents. Do not pressure the child to self-disclose or reveal their experiences of maltreatment. Help the child realize that reluctance to talk about feelings is normal.

- Help children improve self-esteem. Give a lot of positive reinforcement and send him/her new messages about who they are and what they have to offer.

- Teach creative problem solving to help the child make more effective decisions and feel a sense of control over his/her own life.

- Teach conflict resolution; many abused or neglected children are unfamiliar with non-violent, controlled ways to deal with conflict.

- Be sensitive to their need for consistency, particularly regarding your behavior toward them.

- Design teaching segments on how to recognize feelings and properly express them. Use a "feeling barometer" that encourages children to move the indicator to show how they are feeling and discuss why.

- Victims of abuse and neglect may believe that it is their fault that they experience maltreatment, they are bad and if they were good, their parents would not hurt them again and again. Assure them that the abuse is not their fault.

- A child may try to protect him/herself from the real feelings by pretending the feelings do not exist. A child who wants very badly to be asked to play with others or join others may hide or avoid the situation. It is easier to pretend he/she does not care than to show interest and take a chance that others will reject him or her.

- When a child acts in ways that seem strange, remember to look for the feelings behind the actions.

- Always remember that maltreated children may be very loyal to the parent and, underneath any other feelings they may have, they love their parents and want to be loved and wanted in return.

- Do not display pity.

- Do not over-focus attention on the maltreated child. Children need to learn how to draw upon their own resources and fit in with other children. However, do not ignore the child because you are unsure or uncomfortable with the situation.

- Foster the child's relationships with peers by encouraging extra-curricular and school-related activities.

- Allow children to have possessions of their own for which they are responsible: their desk or work space, books, backpack, etc.

Specifically for Educators

Discover if your school system has a board policy or procedure for child abuse and neglect. To help maintain an open and professional relationship, the school should notify the parents as soon as a report is filed. Honestly inform them that a report has been filed and that there is legal authority for this action since, according to state law, teachers are mandated to report suspected child abuse and neglect. The parents should be assured that the school is supportive of them and interested in the well-being of the child.

• Maltreated children often have special educational, psychological, or medical needs. Help them access available resources for these needs.

• Devise individualized education plans tailored to the special educational needs of a maltreated child but be careful not to let the child know that he/she is being singled out for special treatment.

• Utilize programs which are already in place. One example is providing free or reduced breakfast and lunch, field trips, and extracurricular activities. Economic stress is often one factor which makes parenting difficult and may increase the risk for maltreatment.

How Do I Find out More about Child Abuse and Neglect?

Please contact the American Humane Association at 303-792-9900 if you need additional information about child abuse and neglect or help in identifying local resources for at-risk children and families.

Chapter 23

Responding to a Disclosure of Abuse

First Response to Victims of Crime 2001

Introduction

The victimization rate for children 12 through 19 is higher than that for any other age group. (Note: Criminal victimization data are not collected for children under 12 years of age.) In addition, according to the American Medical Association, approximately 1,100 children die each year from abuse and neglect while 140,000 are injured. Uniform Crime Report data indicate that almost 2,000 children under the age of 18 were murdered in 1996. Finally, murder and non-negligent manslaughter are the causes of death for approximately 17 percent of children under the age of 19.

When children are victimized, their normal physiological and psychological adjustment to life is disrupted. Furthermore, they must

This chapter contains text from "First Response to Victims of Crime 2001," U.S. Department of Justice www.ojp.usdoj.gov/ovc/infores/firstrep/2001/chldvics.html, December 2001; this chapter also contains text from the document, "Responding to a Disclosure of Abuse" by Jackie Reilly, M.S., Extension Youth Development Specialist/Associate Professor, University of Nevada Cooperative Extension, and Sally S. Martin, Ph.D., Family Life Specialist/Associate professor, Human Development and Family Studies, University of Nevada Cooperative Extension, ©1995. Reprinted with permission. For additional information, visit the web site of the University of Nevada Cooperative Extension at www.unce.unr.edu; for a listing of other publications related to child abuse and neglect, visit http://www.unce.unr.edu/publications/child.htm.

cope with the trauma of their victimization again and again in each succeeding developmental stage of life after the crime.

Child victims suffer not only physical and emotional traumas from their victimization. When their victimization is reported, children are forced to enter the stressful "adult" world of the criminal justice system. Adults—perhaps the same adults who were unable to provide protection in the first place—are responsible for restoring the children's sense that there are safe places where they can go, and safe people to whom they can turn. You can play a key role in this process, and lessen the likelihood of long-term trauma for child victims.

Tips for Responding to Child Victims

- Choose a secure, comfortable setting for interviewing child victims, such as a child advocacy center. If such an interview setting is not available, choose a location that is as comfortable as possible. Take the time to establish trust and rapport.

  - Preschool children (ages 2 through 6) are most comfortable at home—assuming no child abuse took place there—or in a very familiar environment. A parent or some other adult the child trusts should be nearby.

  - For elementary school-age children (ages 6 through 10), the presence of a parent is not usually recommended since children at this age are sometimes reluctant to reveal information if they believe they or their parents could "get into trouble." However, a parent or some other adult the child trusts should be close by, such as in the next room.

  - Preadolescents (ages 10 through 12 for girls, and 12 through 14 for boys) are peer-oriented, and often avoid parental scrutiny. For this reason, they may be more comfortable if a friend or perhaps the friend's parent(s) is nearby.

  - Since adolescents (generally, ages 13 through 17) may be fearful of betraying their peers, it may be necessary to interview them in a secure setting with no peers nearby.

- Realize that children tend to regress emotionally during times of stress, acting younger than their age. For example, 8-year-olds may suck their thumb.

- Use language appropriate to the victim's age. Remember your own childhood and try to think like the victim. Avoid "baby talk."

- Since young children often feel they may be blamed for problems, assure preschool, and elementary school-age children that they have not done anything wrong, and they are not "in trouble."

- Be consistent with the terms you use, and repeat important information often.

- Ask open-ended questions to make sure victims understand you.

- Use care in discussing sexual matters with preadolescent and adolescent children, as their embarrassment and limited vocabulary can make conversation difficult for them. At the same time, do not assume that victims, including elementary school-age children, are as knowledgeable about sexual matters as their language or apparent sophistication might indicate.

- Maintain a nonjudgmental attitude, and empathize with victims. Because elementary school-age children are especially affected by praise, compliment them frequently on their behavior and thank them for their help.

- Remember the limited attention span of children. Be alert to signs that victims are feeling tired, restless, or cranky. When interviewing preschool children, consider conducting a series of short interviews rather than a single, lengthy one. Also, consider postponing the interview until the victim has had a night's sleep. However, in this case, be sure not to wait too long before interviewing preschool children because victims at this age may have difficulty separating the events of the victimization from later experiences.

- Encourage preschool children to play, as it is a common mode of communication for them. You may find that as children play, they become more relaxed and thus more talkative.

- Limit the number of times victims must be interviewed. Bring together for interviews as many persons from appropriate public agencies as possible, including representatives from the prosecutor's office, child protective services, and the medical/health care community.

- Include victims—whenever possible—in decision-making, and problem-solving discussions. Identify, and patiently answer all of their questions. You can reduce victims' insecurity and anxiety by explaining the purpose of your interview, and by preparing them, especially elementary school-age children, for what will happen next.

- Show compassion to victims. Children's natural abilities to cope are aided immensely by caring adults.

- Although the immediate victim is the child, do not forget to comfort the non-offending parents. Referrals regarding how they can cope, what they can expect, as well as how to talk to, and with their child should be provided.

Responding to a Disclosure of Child Abuse

"My uncle burned me with his cigarette."

What do you say, what should you do... when children tell you they have been abused?

When a Child Discloses

Hearing a disclosure—a child telling you that someone has abused or hurt him—can be scary. How you respond can be critical. A lot of thoughts may run through your mind.

- You may be worried about the child, and yourself.

- You may be unsure of how to respond or what to say.

- You may be unsure of the child's comments, and information.

- You may not be sure if the child has been abused.

- You may be angry with the parent or alleged abuser.

- You may even want to take the child home with you. How you respond is very important. Responding to a disclosure of abuse or neglect is a big responsibility. This section has suggestions about how to respond in ways that help the child, her parents, and yourself.

Children Often Are Reluctant to Tell about Abuse

In over 80% of the cases of physical abuse, emotional abuse, or neglect the birth parents are the abusers. The majority of perpetrators in sexual abuse cases are non-related caregivers, that is, babysitters, stepparents, boyfriends, girlfriends, or adoptive parents.

Children often love the person who is abusing them, and simply want the abusive behavior to stop. Because they love and care about the person, they may be reluctant to get the person in trouble. Many perpetrators tell children to keep the abuse a secret, and frighten them with unpleasant consequences.

Children may start to tell someone about the abuse. If the person reacts with disgust or doesn't believe them, they will stop disclosing the events. Then they may not tell anyone about it until they feel brave enough or have established a sense of trust with someone. This may delay them from seeking help. If a child begins to tell you about possible abuse, please listen carefully.

He or She?

We give equal time and space to both sexes! That's why we take turns referring to children as "he" or "she". So keep in mind that even if we say "he" or "she" we are talking about all children.

Ideas that Can Help

- Find a place to talk where there are no physical barriers between you and the child.

- Be on the same eye level as the child.

- Don't interrogate or interview the child.

- Be tactful. Choose your words carefully; don't be judgmental about the child or the alleged abuser.

- Listen to the child. Do not project or assume anything. Let the child tell her own story.

- Find out what the child wants from you. A child may ask you to promise not to tell anyone. Be honest about what you are able to do for the child.

- Be calm; reactions of disgust, fear, anger, etc, may confuse or scare a child.

- Assess the urgency of the situation. Is the child in immediate danger? Safety needs may make a difference in your response.

- Confirm the child's feelings. Let him know that it is okay to be scared, confused, sad, or however he is feeling.

211

- Believe the child, and be supportive.

- Assure the child that you care. Some children will think you may not like them anymore if they tell you what happened. Let her know that you are still her friend, and that she is not to blame.

- Tell the child it is not his fault. Many children will think that the abuse happened because of something they did or did not do. Don't over dramatize.

- Tell the child you are glad he told you.

- Tell the child you will try to get her some help.

- Let the child know what you will do. This will help build a sense of trust, and he will not be surprised when he finds out that you told someone.

- Tell the child you need to tell someone whose job it is to help with these kinds of problems.

- Report your suspicions to the appropriate agency.

Chapter 24

Child Fatalities Fact Sheet

Children are one of the most vulnerable groups in our society. Child fatalities due to maltreatment represent the worst case scenario in attempts to protect children. Despite the efforts of the child protection system, child fatalities remain a serious problem. Although the untimely deaths of children due to illness and accidents have been closely monitored, the same cannot be said of children who have died as the result of physical assault or severe neglect. Intervention strategies targeted at resolving this problem face complex challenges.

Child Fatalities Due to Maltreatment Are Increasing

Although child deaths caused by abuse and/or neglect are relatively infrequent, the rate of child maltreatment fatalities, confirmed by Child Protective Services (CPS) to have been the result of child maltreatment, has steadily increased over the last decade. The National Child Abuse and Neglect Data System (NCANDS) reported that in 1997 there were an estimated 1,196 child fatalities, or 1.7 children per 100,000 in the general population. (This estimate was based on reports from 41 States that reported a total of 967 fatalities.) The U.S. Advisory Board on Child Abuse and Neglect in *A Nation's Shame: Fatal Child Abuse and Neglect in the United States*, reported that a

Excerpted from "Child Fatalities Fact Sheet," National Clearinghouse on Child Abuse and Neglect Information, http://www.calib.com/nccanch/pubs/factsheets/fatality.cfm, last updated April 2001.

more realistic estimate of annual child deaths as a result of abuse and neglect, both known and unknown to CPS agencies, is about 2,000, or approximately five children per day. Experts such as Ryan Rainey from the National Center for Prosecution of Child Abuse believe that the number of child deaths from maltreatment per year may be as high as 5,000.

The Actual Number of Child Fatalities May Be Under-Reported

Determining the actual numbers of children who die annually from abuse is complex. Many researchers and practitioners believe that child fatalities are under-reported because some deaths labeled as accidents, child homicides, and/or Sudden Infant Death Syndrome (SIDS) might be attributed to child maltreatment if more comprehensive investigations were conducted. It is difficult to distinguish a child who has been suffocated from a child who has died as a result of SIDS, or a child who was dropped, pushed, or thrown from a child who dies from a legitimate fall. Some researchers and practitioners have gone so far as to estimate that there may be twice the number of deaths as a result of abuse and/or neglect as are reported by NCANDS if cases unknown to CPS agencies are included.

There Is a Lack of Standard Terminology for Child Fatalities

To further complicate the issue, different terminology is used to discuss child fatalities, sometimes interchangeably. NCANDS defines "child fatality" as a child dying from abuse or neglect, because either (a) the injury from the abuse or neglect was the cause of death, or (b) the abuse and/or neglect was a contributing factor to the cause of death. Researchers such as Finkelhor and Christoffel use the term "child abuse homicide" to define a childhood death resulting from maltreatment (either assault or neglect) by a responsible caretaker. Law enforcement and criminal justice agencies also use the term "child abuse homicide," but their definition, while including the caretaker as perpetrator, also includes the "criminal act of homicide by non-caretakers" (death at the hands of another, felony child endangerment, and criminal neglect). More specifically, the term "infanticide" is increasingly used to define the murdering of children younger than 6 or 12 months by their parents.

Young Children Are the Most Vulnerable

Research supports that very young children (age 5 and younger) are the most frequent victims of child fatalities. NCANDS data for 1997 from a subset of States demonstrated that children 3 or younger accounted for 77 percent of fatalities. This population is the most vulnerable for many reasons including their small size and inability to defend themselves. The fatal abuse usually occurs in one of two ways: repeated abuse and/or neglect over a period of time (battered child syndrome) or in a single, impulsive incident of assault (drowning, suffocating, or shaking the baby, for example).

Primary Caretakers Are the Most Frequent Perpetrators

No matter how the fatal abuse occurs, one fact of great concern is that most of the perpetrators are, by definition, primary caretakers such as parents and other relatives.

Though there is no single profile for the perpetrator of fatal child abuse, there are consistent characteristics that reappear in studies. Frequently the perpetrator is a young adult in his/her mid-20s without a high school diploma, living at or below the poverty level, depressed, and who may have difficulty coping with stressful situations. In many instances, the perpetrator has experienced violence firsthand.

The Response to Fatal Child Abuse or Neglect Is Complex

The response to the problem is often hampered by inconsistencies:

- The inaccurate reporting of the number of children who die each year as a result of abuse and neglect.

- The lack of national standards for child autopsies or death investigations.

- The different roles that CPS agencies play in the investigation process.

- The use in many States of an elected coroner who is not required to have any medical or child abuse and neglect training, rather than a medical examiner.

215

Child Fatality Review Teams

To address some of these inconsistencies, multi disciplinary/multi agency Child Fatality Review Teams have emerged in many states to provide a coordinated approach to the investigation of child deaths. These teams are comprised of prosecutors, coroners, or medical examiners, law enforcement personnel, CPS workers, public health care providers, and others.

The teams review cases of child deaths and facilitate appropriate follow-up. The follow-up may include assuring that services are provided for surviving family members, providing information to assist in the prosecution of perpetrators, and developing recommendations to improve child protection and community support systems. In addition, teams can assist in determining avenues for prevention efforts and improving training for front-line workers. Well-designed, properly organized Child Fatality Review Teams appear to offer the greatest hope for defining the underlying nature and scope of fatalities due to child abuse and neglect and for offering solutions.

Prevention Services Are Key

When addressing the issue of child maltreatment, and especially child fatalities, prevention is a recurring theme. In 1995, the U.S. Advisory Board on Child Abuse and Neglect recommended a universal approach to the prevention of child fatalities that would reach out to all families through the implementation of several key strategies. These efforts would begin by providing services such as home visitation by trained professionals or paraprofessionals, hospital-linked outreach to parents of infants and toddlers, community-based programs designed for the specific needs of neighborhoods, and effective public education campaigns.

Chapter 25

Shaken Baby Syndrome

Alternative Names

Whiplash—shaken infant

Definition

This is a severe form of head injury caused by violently shaking an infant or child. It usually occurs in children younger than 2 years old, but may be seen in children up to the age of 5. The violent shaking may result in severe injuries to the infant including permanent brain damage or death.

Considerations

A baby's head is large and heavy in proportion to their body. For this reason, when a baby is dropped or thrown, he will tend to land on his head. There is space between the brain and skull to allow for growth and development. The baby's neck muscles and ligaments are weak and underdeveloped. All of these factors make infants highly vulnerable to whiplash forces.

When an infant or young toddler is shaken, the soft, pliable skull is not yet strong enough to absorb much of the force. The forces are thus transmitted to the brain, which then rebound against the skull causing bruising of the brain (cerebral contusion), swelling, pressure, and bleeding (intracerebral hemorrhage).

The large veins along the outside of the brain are also vulnerable to tear with these injuries which can lead to further bleeding, swelling, and increased pressure (subdural hematoma). This can easily cause permanent, severe brain damage, or death.

Shaking an infant or small child may also cause injuries to the neck and spine. Eye damage is very common and may result in loss of vision (retinal hemorrhage).

Causes

Shaken baby syndrome is almost always caused by non-accidental trauma (child abuse). It is caused by an angry parent or caregiver shaking a baby to punish or quiet them. Many times they do not intend to harm the baby.

In rare instances, this injury may be caused accidentally by actions such as tossing the baby in the air or jogging with a baby in a backpack. It does not result from gentle bouncing or play.

Symptoms

- Change in behavior, irritability.
- Lethargy, sleepiness, or loss of consciousness.
- Pale or bluish skin.
- Vomiting.
- Convulsions (seizures).
- Poor eating.
- Not breathing (apnea).

There are usually no outward physical signs of trauma, such as bruising, bleeding, or swelling. Examination by an ophthalmologist frequently reveals retinal hemorrhages.

Do Not

- Do not pick up the child or shake him to attempt to wake him up.
- Do not attempt to give anything by mouth.

Call Your Healthcare Provider If

- A child exhibits any of the above signs or symptoms.
- You suspect a child has sustained this type of injury.

First Aid

- For a severe head injury such as this, immediate emergency treatment is necessary. Activate the EMS system (call 911).
- If the victim stops breathing before emergency help arrives, begin CPR.
- If the victim is vomiting and you don't suspect a spinal injury, turn his or her head to the side to prevent choking and aspiration. If you suspect a spinal injury, carefully roll the whole body to the side as one unit (logrolling) while protecting the neck.
- If the victim has a convulsion, follow instructions for seizure-first aid.

Prevention

- Never shake a baby or child, whether in play or in anger.
- Do not hold your baby during an argument.
- If you find yourself becoming annoyed or angry with your baby, put him in the crib and leave the room. Try to calm down. Call someone for support.
- Call a friend or relative to come and stay with the child if you feel out of control.
- There are resources available such as a local crisis hotline or child abuse hotline.
- Seek the help of a counselor and attend parenting classes.
- Do not ignore the signs if you suspect child abuse in your home or the home of someone you know.

Chapter 26

Defining Proper Discipline Techniques

Appropriate Limits for Young Children: A Guide for Discipline, Part One

Denita is 5 years old. She whines not only when she is left in childcare, but also during most other times when she goes from one place to another. Once she gets interested in an activity, Denita's attention is completely focused until another child tries to join her or she is asked to put the activity away. Then she lashes out, usually throwing a toy, or disrupting a corner of the room. During group time, she cries until she is allowed to sit on the teacher's lap. Teachers give her time-outs in the beanbag chair, which she doesn't seem to mind. When it is time to go home, she cries. Her teachers and parents are frustrated.

How can Denita's teachers and parents work toward more desirable behavior?

Should she be punished or disciplined?

Punishment is taking some action against the child as pay back for a child's behavior.

Discipline is shaping a child; teaching the child to understand limits at home, or in other settings. While you can make rules for how they should behave, most children do not begin acting with self-control

From "Appropriate Limits for Young Children: A Guide for Discipline, Parts One and Two," by Karen DeBord, Ph.D., Associate Professor and Extension Child Development Specialist, North Carolina State University. © 1996. http://www.nncc.org/Guidance/limits1.html. Reprinted with permission until their middle childhood years (around ages 7 to 9). For children younger than this, discipline is learning self-control.

Children must pass through several learning and developmental stages as they mature. Discipline problems are a normal part of child development. While it appears that there are "good" and "bad" behaviors, each stage does have a positive, and a negative side. Parents and teachers alike must understand these developmental stages in order to determine what behavior they can realistically expect, and to decide whether a child's behavior is appropriate.

Why Do Children Misbehave?

According to some child development experts, children usually misbehave for one of four basic reasons: attention, power, revenge, or inadequacy.

Attention—When children believe they "belong" only when they are noticed. They feel important when they are commanding total attention.

While Mother was getting ready for work, Amanda jumped up from her breakfast and asked Mom to come help her in the bathroom. Encouraging her that she could manage alone, Amanda began to pull on Mom's leg and whine. "But I may not be able to." Mom replied, "Yes, you can, Amanda, just try it." After a few minutes, Amanda was back asking Mom to snap her pants. Helping her, Mom resumed her routine. Amanda called to her again, "Can you come here?"

Parents can respond by giving positive attention; at other times ignoring inappropriate behavior, setting up routines, encouraging, redirecting, or setting up special times.

Power—When children believe they belong only when they are in control or are proving that no one can "boss them around."

Whitney was ready to go shopping when Dad announced they were going to the mall. She grabbed her jar of pennies, ready to shop. At each store, she asked for items too costly for her budget. When she found an item for less than a dollar, she counted out the pennies and paid. Having spent her money, she continued to whine for other things "she needed." Mom said, "We will need to just leave if you can't quit asking for things." She begged not to leave, so browsing continued.

A short time later, she asked for another special item she had seen and loudly insisted she have it. This time Dad tried to get her quiet but had lost patience. "You're mean!" she screamed. She gave a glaring stare and mumbled "You don't love me." Dad took her hand and led her to the car. When she got home, the dollar toy was left in the car, forgotten.

Parents can respond with kind, but firm respect, giving limited choices, setting reasonable limits, encouraging, and redirecting the child to a more acceptable activity. When children test their limits and use a public display to assert themselves, parents can continue to stick to the basic rules letting them know their behavior is unacceptable. Leave the situation if possible—store or home in which you are a guest. Talk when things are calmer at a later time.

Revenge—When children believe they belong only by hurting others, since they feel hurt themselves.

Larry had been whining when Mom left him each morning with the childcare provider. That evening, Dad was cooking dinner while Mom worked late. Suddenly Logan screamed. Dad threw down the potato peeler and ran to see what the problem was. Larry had pinned Logan in a wrestling position and was twisting his ear. Dad hollered to Larry, saying "Why can't you leave your brother alone? Go to your room and wait for me!"

Sometimes the reason for misbehavior is not clear. When there is a new pattern of acting out, children and parents should talk about how they are feeling. Parents can respond by avoiding harsh punishment and criticism, building trust, listening, reflecting feelings, practicing sharing of feelings, encouraging strengths, and acting with care.

Inadequacy—When children believe they belong, only when they convince others not to expect anything of them since they are helpless or unable.

Jorge's teacher asked his parents what might be affecting Jorge's work at school. His teacher says, "He doesn't complete assignments and no matter how much I help him, he gets further behind." Mom replied, "He doesn't do anything at home either. I have quit asking him to do any chores at home because when he does them, he is so sloppy and does it so badly, I have to do it again."

Parents can respond by encouraging their children to try things, focusing on the child's strengths, not criticizing or giving in to pity, offering opportunities for success, and teaching skills in small steps.

Developmental Milestones

The First Two Years

From birth to about age 2, infants need to build close relationships with their parents, or other important people around them. These attachments make it possible for infants to build a sense of love and caring. They are learning to make sense out of permanent objects, and developing a sense of trust. Only as children experiment through touching, dropping, pushing, and pulling do they begin to learn.

During this time, children do not believe that things exist unless they can see them. This is why it is so difficult for them to be away from their parents.

To feel close to someone, infants need to be able to count on having their needs met in a timely manner. Gaining a sense of trust is the first stage of their emotional development.

The Preschool Years

These years are the most significant in a person's life. Language and social skills are developed. Children at this age also learn symbols. For example, they learn to see a picture of a ball and recognize that the picture represents a real ball. Recognizing symbols is an important step toward developing important skills such as the ability to read.

Toddling, exploring, and pounding may worry parents, but they are normal behaviors. When children touch, feel, look, mix, turn over, and throw, they are developing skills. Exploration is intellectually healthy, and helps children test their independence. Although these behaviors create a struggle between child and parent, they should be expected and planned for them.

Independence is an emotion to be encouraged during the early preschool years. The alternative is shame and doubt. Many significant events occur during these years—between 2 and 3, toilet training and language in particular. In responding to a child's misuse of language or accidents when toilet training, parents and caregivers should be sensitive to avoid using guilt and punishments for what are most likely normal acts of development.

Once children learn to handle independence, they are ready to develop a healthy sense of initiative. Initiative means starting activities, creating, and working. Children who learn to start their own activities lay the groundwork for positive and productive school experiences. Again, explorations, questions, and investigations play major roles in development.

Middle Childhood

From the time they begin school until around age 12, children are in middle childhood, when learning skills become better defined. Children at this stage have higher-order thinking skills and can use them to make more complex decisions. As children they have always believed what adults say as basically true, but they now begin to question the pedestal upon which they have placed adults.

Rules become more significant, and children learn not only rules for games, but rules that will help them understand math concepts and social rules, such as saying "please" and "thank you." Rules make formal education possible.

Closely on the heels of developing a sense of initiative in the preschool years is the development of a sense of industry. Groundwork is laid during this middle childhood for becoming productive members of society. Children can learn to be inferior (or inadequate). Adults should seek to build a sense of confidence that children in the middle childhood can do jobs well. Many children have their sense of industry undermined by well-meaning parents and teachers who mistakenly try to use criticism to motivate them.

Questioning Adult Responses: A Group Teaching Guide

Children spend their young years trying to figure out how they fit into the world. How independent or dependent will they be, allowed to be? What will be the consequences of various actions? Who will give them direction? Who will be their role models? In addition to the reasons for behaviors, parents must determine if they have provided a stable, loving, understanding place to help children learn and grow. The questions that follow may be used as small group activities or between parenting partners. It may be helpful to consider these questions:

Are Expectations for the Child Clear?

Children develop at different rates, have different interests, and certainly have different kinds of homes, and families. Are attempts made to prepare the child for new situations? Offer explanations of what the occasion is about, and what behavior will be expected so guessing isn't necessary. To prevent reactions, use continuous two-way communication and allow the child a certain amount of responsibility in setting his, or her own rules, or limits.

Is Behavior Driven by the Child's Need to Test the Boundaries of Particular Relationships?

There is security for children who realize that the adult will "still love them" if they are "bad." This may be particularly true when there have been many changes in the family home.

Are Consistent Limits Understood and Followed?

Children may resist limits if there is too much adult control and not enough room allowed for their choice. Discipline allows children to develop their own "inner voice," which will sensibly guide their behavior as they grow. Often adults must be careful that they, too, follow the rules they make for children. Consistency plays a major role in parenting.

Key Points

* Discipline is shaping and teaching a child to understand limits.
* Children may act out because they want attention.
* Children may act out because they need some control.
* Children may hurt others because they don't feel important.
* Parents can ask questions such as, "How can you behave differently the next time?"
* Parents can prepare the child for new situations by describing expected behaviors.
* Parents who understand stages of behavior will know better what to expect.

Appropriate Limits for Young Children: A Group Teaching Guide

The group leader sets the tone for the group to allow informal sharing, a sense of understanding and confidentiality without ridicule. Parenting is a very personal topic. Often to set the participants at ease and ease transitions, activities are needed. Some suggested activities are presented here as a stimulus for group leaders.

Activity

Ask the group participants to imagine a child with whom they have come in contact, one who they see daily or quite often. Ask them to think of ways to characterize this child. List these terms on easel paper or on a writing board before the group.

Activity

Scene setting descriptions of children to use for discussion. How would you respond to these situations:

Daryl is 4 years old. He cries when Mom leaves him at day care. He plays but is subdued. He can't seem to concentrate to finish puzzles and other tasks. He won't zip his jacket and tries to leave the group. The teacher shouts to the child to stay with the group and thinks he is just trying to get attention.

Marilyn is an attractive 2-year-old child with an advanced vocabulary. She enjoys most learning activities but has trouble sitting still during group time and during mealtime and naps. Marilyn is very loving but independent, often creatively precocious. When asked to "come here" by parents and teachers, she often plays games and runs away.

Activity

On index cards, ask parents to list the characteristics of ideal children, one characteristic per card. Take the cards and mix them up; then have each participant draw a card, and read that characteristic aloud.

Activity

Ask participants to describe their definition of discipline. After this has been discussed, ask for their definition of punishment.

Activity

Ask participants to brainstorm in small groups or as a large group regarding their ideas about why children misbehave.

Activity

Divide into small groups, allowing parents to share misbehavior incidents. Try to decide which goal may have generated the child's behavior at that time.

Appropriate Limits for Young Children: A Guide for Discipline, Part 2

Although researchers have characterized the three basic parenting styles as: authoritarian, permissive, and authoritative, many parents do not fit neatly into any of these categories. Parenting knowledge comes from a variety of sources, and parents combine many styles depending on any given situation. With this in mind, this section will examine these three parenting styles, referred to The Enforcer (authoritarian), The Negotiator (authoritative), and The Yielder (permissive). By examining the statements given for each parenting style, parents and caregivers can think about their basic style. Parenting styles influence the way in which children develop.

Parenting Styles

Group leaders may turn this section into a questionnaire as an alternate activity for parents to respond to their parenting style or beliefs.

The Yielder

- It is better to have no rules than to worry about breaking them.
- Children can get along pretty well if you just leave them alone.
- My work and home responsibilities are too stressful; I can't worry about what the children are doing.
- The children won't listen to me, so I have quit trying.
- Children should realize that my work is stressful, and I am tired at the end of the day.

These statements were written to describe the permissive parent, or the yielder. This parent makes few demands, administers little punishment, sets no guidelines, has little structure, and avoids asserting authority. He or she is often referred to as uninvolved, and spends minimal time and effort with the child. The parent sometimes uses stress and work to excuse himself or herself from spending time with the children; drugs and immaturity can also be reasons for their lack of involvement.

The child of this parent lacks self-control, is immature, may be aggressive at home, and may behave irresponsibly. These children tend to have poor self-esteem, low emotional development, and a low threshold for frustration. They may be school-skippers and resort to drugs, or become involved in legal problems in their search for attention.

The Enforcer

- Children should obey their parents and not talk back.

- Children should do as I say until they are old enough to make their own decisions.

- I was spanked when I was a child and I turned out okay.

- When children don't mind, I yell at them and threaten them with a variety of punishments.

- I expect my children to conform to my decisions without discussion.

These statements reflect the general nature of the enforcer or authoritarian style. This parent is demanding and strict, uses punishment, and generally doesn't allow choice or freedom of expression. They value obedience, tradition, and order, and discourage independence and individuality. These parents dislike having their authority questioned. They may use physical punishment, yelling, or threatening for disciplinary measures.

What kind of child comes from this discipline pattern? Research indicates an enforcer parent may produce a child who lacks spontaneity, curiosity, and creativity, and often has limited independence and assertiveness. These children don't learn how to decide for themselves, depending instead on others for their sense of control. They may have low self-esteem and be aggressive and defiant.

The Negotiator

- Children should be given choices.

- Sometimes children have a point. I try to listen to them.

- Although it takes hard work, parents and children should try to talk about family decisions, and let each person share his or her feelings.

- Children should be allowed to be individuals.

- I take care not to criticize my children or call names even when I cannot understand why they act as they do.

The negotiator (authoritative) parent, although not the perfect parent, has a better balance in discipline style, setting high standards and expectations for mature behavior, firmly enforcing rules, and encouraging independence and individuality. Children's individual rights are recognized and choices are given. There is better communication and listening, and a more democratic give-and-take arrangement.

Children of these parents generally are competent, responsible, and independent, have higher self-esteem and confidence, and are better able to control their aggression.

How to Reduce Discipline Problems

It is important for parents to realize that in order for children to grow up, they must pass through the experiences of childhood. There is no way around it. The experience of growing up causes distress and frustration. Reducing behavior problems can be best practiced through prevention. If parents can understand what to expect from children as they develop, this knowledge can be used to build a healthy environment and a clear set of expectations that can reduce some of the tensions.

Major concepts to remember are consistency, forethought, respect, recognition of a child's limits, cooperative relationships, common sense, and sense of humor. Discipline is guiding children toward learning behaviors and self-control for later life.

The following list may help parents and teachers to evaluate their environment as well as their interactions with children.

Prepare the Environment

- Are there enough supplies and materials so that children will not have to share too many items, and wait too long for others?

- Is the environment well organized? Are some areas cluttered?

- Are there areas where the child can feel in control (one-person corner, own room)?

- Are there a variety of play materials to allow choices?

- Do offered activities suit the child's ability?

- Can barriers to success be removed to avoid frustration (turn over the puzzle pieces)?

- Is waiting kept to a realistic level (for turns, meals, listening)?

- Is the area childproofed?

Set Limits

- Are older, school-age-children involved in designing limits or rules?

- Are limits reasonable?

- Are limits based on the child's ability to meet and understand limit?

- Are explanations and reasons for the limits appropriate to children's language skills?

- Is positive language used (do and should)?

- Is the child given time to comply with the limit?

- Are comparisons avoided to prevent resentment, and damaging self-esteem?

- Are adults acting as positive role models?

- Is moderation used in reactions? For example: "I like the way you are playing!" or "I see you are ready to begin. Here is the glue."

- Are desirable behaviors reinforced, remembering that the child is not a "good" or "bad" child?

Use Empathy

- Is support and kindness used in all communication?

- Are the child's words reflected to clarify understanding ("you mean")?

- Does the tone of voice and a smile convey empathy?

- Is a relationship being developed with the child?

- Is the child aware of the adult's "hot" button?

Share the Control

- Are children allowed some of the control, or is it important for the adult to call every shot?

- Are children listened to for their newly developing ideas?

- Is there an atmosphere of give-and-take?

- Is a menu of choices presented?

- Can incomplete sentences and open-ended questions be posed to compel the child to think, and formulate decisions? ("What do you think will happen if?")

- Are questions sincere? (How are you going to solve that? What should we do about that?)

Share the Reasoning

- Are children encouraged to figure out solutions?

- Are nods and positive responses given as children begin to make choices and decisions?

- Are options presented when guidance is required?

Use Choice

- Is choice allowed at an early age no matter how small the decision (such as sock color)?

- Is the child given two choices that the adult is willing to live with and experience?

- Are the choices given all safe ones?

Maintain Self-Control and Understand the Development of Self-Control

- Are discussions held following tantrums or angry out-bursts?

- Are outlets for anger provided?

- Is time-out used appropriately?

- Are alternatives and redirection used instead of threats and bribes?

Be Consistent

- Are personal consequences considered before making suggestions?

- Is there a plan for following through to check on these suggested activities?

- Is there trust between the child and adult?

Some Ways to Deal with Endless Undesirable Behaviors

Besides learning about child developmental stages, and planning ways to prevent situations that can lead to undesirable behavior, parents and teachers may need to decide how to manage some behaviors.

Natural Consequences

Many times, children learn as a result of natural consequences. For example, a child who will not eat supper during mealtime may feel hungry when he or she is not allowed to eat again until breakfast. Or a child who forgets to put skates away each night may, one-day find that they have been stolen.

Logical Consequences

When natural consequences are not safe or appropriate, logical consequences may be used. Children often can help set these (and are often stricter on themselves than a parent would have been). The consequences of behavior should relate somehow to the behavior. Referred to as logical consequences, the child can directly see how the behavior and the consequence relate. For example, if the child oversteps his or her boundaries when riding a bike, taking away the bike for a reasonable amount of time may be the consequences. Or if toys are not put away, a reasonable consequence may be to collect the toys for charity or at least put them in temporary storage.

Time-Out

In early childhood, children are very self-centered. It is normal. Children believe the world revolves around them! Children become confused and frustrated when they must face the fact that they are not the center of the universe. They need adult guidance as they begin to find appropriate ways to vent their feelings, and develop a sense of self-control.

Time-out is often used with children who have briefly lost self-control. Self-control is a developmental process. Until the young child has learned to see beyond themselves, and has the ability to see things through someone else's eyes, it is difficult to change self-centered behaviors.

Most children will be 7 and older before they can begin to talk about the consequences of and plan for their own behavior. A big part of self-evaluation is social comparison. Social comparison is the act of learning from role models, imitating them, and using appropriate behaviors in a variety of settings.

Time-out can be very effective when used sparingly and appropriately. Time alone gives the child a chance to calm down. Then the child may rejoin the activity. Children who view time out as a punishment may not use the time out situation as the caregiver intends. Rather than calming down or reflecting on how he or she should behave, the child may spend time figuring out how to get even!

These Questions May Help You Decide When to Use Time-Out

- Is time-out being used as a time for the child to regroup?

- Is time-out used as a retreat for the child; not the adult?

- Is time-out used as one answer among other alternatives?

- Are children given the chance to have some control by making choices about their daily activities?

Use time-outs sparingly. When a time-out is used, do so because the child needs it, and not because you are angry. Also, be sure the length of time is appropriate and is made clear to the child.

Instead of yelling "Go to the time-out area and sit there until I say to get up," try saying "I see you are having trouble keeping your feet to yourself. It hurts other children when they are kicked. You need to sit alone for 5 minutes. Then you will be able to come back to the group." Or you might say, "If you continue to play rough with the ball, you will have to sit out the rest of the game."

Think carefully about time-out as an aid in handling inappropriate or unsafe behaviors while preserving self-esteem and control for children and adults.

- Are assurances used to support the child who has lost self-control?

- Are assurances made by the adult to maintain self-control (mental counting, leaving the room)?

Redirection

Another way to help children gain control is to redirect them to another activity. This allows the child to get away from the problem situation, and yet still have something constructive to do. Redirecting children may be preferable to time-out.

Suggest an alternative activity or setting when a situation is about to get out of hand. Pose timely questions to avoid heated confrontation and conflict.

Setting Appropriate Limits for Young Children: A Group Teaching Guide

The group leader sets the tone for the group to allow informal sharing, a sense of understanding, and confidentiality without ridicule. Parenting is a very personal topic. Often to set the participants at ease and to smooth transitions, activities are needed. Some suggested activities are presented here as a stimulus for group leaders.

Activity

Ask the group participants to imagine a child with whom they have come in contact, one who they see daily or quite often. Ask them to think of ways to characterize this child. List these terms on easel paper, or on a writing board before the group.

Activity

In small groups, ask parents to work together to think of all the methods they use to discipline children.

Activity

On index cards, ask parents to list things about their child that they do not like; one characteristic per card. Take the cards and mix them up, then have each participant draw a card and read that characteristic aloud. Use this activity to turn that characteristic around into a positive aspect; such as talking back could mean that the child will learn to question things, which may come in handy during adolescence when tempted with illegal or immoral practices; or that asking for everything in sight in a store may mean that the child has not gained a sense of self-control yet.

Activity

Ask participants to describe their definition of discipline. After this has been discussed, ask for their definition of punishment.

Activity

Ask participants to brainstorm in small groups or as a large group about the types of parents with whom they have come in contact. Summarize characteristics. Define a "perfect" parent.

Activity

Discuss what you consider to be ongoing undesirable behavior. When do children's behaviors seem to be in need of "professional" counsel or parents in need of outside assistance?

Chapter 27

Is Your Child Ready to Stay Home Alone?

At Home Alone—Tips for Grownups

Introduction

Your ten-year-old comes home from school at 3:00, but you don't get home from work until 5:00. He's at home alone for those two hours every weekday. What does he do until you arrive?

Most likely, he gets a snack or talks on the phone. Maybe he watches TV, but since you're not there, you worry. Just like the majority of American parents who work, and have to leave their children on their own after school everyday, you are anxious about your child's safety.

But by following the safeguards listed below, you can help ease some of this worry and take measures that will protect your kids even when you're not around.

Are They Ready?

Can your children...

"At Home Alone—Tips for Grownups," from National Crime Prevention Council ©1995. Reprinted with permission. For more information regarding this topic go to http://www.mcgruff.org/alone.htm. Reprinted with permission from "Is Your Child Ready To Stay Home Alone?" originally published in the Summer 1999 issue of *The Daily Parent,* a newsletter produced by the National Association of Child Care Resource and Referral Agencies (NACCRRA), Washington D.C., and funded by the Citigroup Foundation. © 1999 NACCRRA. http://www.childcareaware.org/en/dailyparent/0399/.

- Be trusted to go straight home after school?
- Easily use the telephone, locks, and kitchen appliances?
- Follow rules and instructions well?
- Handle unexpected situations without panicking?
- Stay alone without being afraid?

What You Can Do

- Make sure your children are old enough and mature enough to care for themselves.
- Teach them basic safety rules.
- Know the three "W's":
  - Where your kids are.
  - What they're doing.
  - Who they're with.
- Don't forget to check on state law about the age at which children can be left at home alone.

Curiosity

Are there things you don't want your children to get into? Take the time to talk to them about the deadly consequences of guns, medicines, power tools, drugs, alcohol, cleaning products, and inhalants. Make sure you keep these items in a secure place out of sight, and locked up, if possible.

Teach Your "Home Alone" Children

- To check in with you or a neighbor immediately after arriving home.
- How to call 9-1-1, or your area's emergency number, or call the operator.
- How to give directions to your home, in case of emergency.
- To never accept gifts, or rides from people they don't know well.
- How to use the door and window locks, and the alarm system if you have one.
- To never let anyone into your home without asking your permission.

- To never let a caller at the door or on the phone know that they're alone. Teach them to say "Mom can't come to the phone—or door—right now."

- To carry a house key with them in a safe place (inside a shirt pocket or sock). Don't leave it under a mat or on a ledge outside the house.

- How to escape in case of fire.

- Not to go into an empty house or apartment if things don't look right—a broken window, ripped screen, or opened door.

- To let you know about anything that frightens them or makes them feel uncomfortable.

You Can Do More

- Work with schools, religious institutions, libraries, recreational and community centers, and local youth organizations to create programs that give children ages 10 and older a place to go, and something to do after school—a "homework haven," with sports, crafts, classes, and tutoring. Don't forget that kids of this age can also get involved in their communities. Help them design and carry out an improvement project!

- Ask your workplace to sponsor a survival skills class for employees' children. You can kick it off with a parent breakfast or lunch.

- Ask your community to develop a homework hotline latchkey kids can call for help or just to talk.

- Join or start a McGruff House or other block parent programs in your community to offer children help in emergencies or frightening situations. A McGruff House is a reliable source of help for children in emergency or frightening situations. For information call 801-486-8691.

Is Your Child Ready to Stay Home Alone?

For many families with older children between the ages of 9 and 12, the time comes when you must decide if your child is ready to care for himself. While some parents leave for work before school opens, others finish work long after school is over. Often there are few sitters or afterschool programs available at these times.

Some families may learn suddenly the babysitter is no longer available or that their child is unhappy with his child care arrangements. Some children ask to try new activities and stay home alone. Sometimes care is too expensive or certain child care arrangements are not available during school breaks. The transition to having your child stay home alone is a big step for every family.

While some children may be ready for the responsibility of staying home alone, many parents feel they need some time to prepare their child and themselves for this important transition. This text will help you take the steps towards safe and comfortable self care.

Is Your Child Ready?

Consider your child's maturity level and his ability to handle a variety of situations. If you answer "yes" to most of the following questions, this may indicate your child is ready to stay alone.

- Has he handled brief periods of being left alone well?

- Will he come straight home after school?

- Is he confident he will not be lonely or frightened by himself?

- Can he manage simple jobs like fixing a snack and taking phone messages?

- Is he physically able to unlock and lock the doors at home?

- Does he know when and how to seek outside help?

- Is he prepared to handle an accident or an emergency?

- Will he follow the rules set for him and use his time productively?

Self Care Options

As you begin to explore the idea of self care for your child, consider all options. For some families a combination of arrangements may be the best plan. You might enroll your child a couple of days in a local recreation or afterschool program. Many libraries, churches, and community centers also offer various activities, classes and school vacation programs for children.

Sometimes exchanging care with another parent works well. You might be able to offer before school care to someone who can supervise your child in the afternoon. Or, you might be able to arrange for evening care in exchange for care after school.

As your child spends time alone at home, you may want to schedule an activity at least one day a week. For some children an afternoon of sports, a music lesson, club meeting, or visit to a friend's house is wonderful to look forward to and breaks the routine of being alone.

When to Begin

There is no specific age when children are ready to stay home alone because children mature at different rates. It is most important to know if your child feels comfortable being home alone and has the levelheadedness to handle an emergency. Consider too the amount of support you can count on from neighbors, family, and friends.

Some states have laws regulating the age at which a child may be left home alone. You can find out what the law is where you live by calling the agency that oversees services for children and families.

The best way to begin is to have a conversation with your child. Listen to her feelings and concerns. If your child is anxious, you will want to proceed carefully with your arrangements. Starting self care may not be a good idea during a period of increased stress such as a move to a new home, a divorce, or death in the family.

Build up hours gradually by leaving your child briefly to run an errand or arranging to arrive home fifteen minutes later than usual from work. Ask your child if she felt comfortable and what she did with her time. Encourage her to tell you of any fears she may have no matter how trivial. With practice you will both be ready for her to spend longer periods of time alone and you can plan a regular schedule of self care.

Establishing House Rules and Routines

There are many important steps you can take to ease your worries and help protect your child while you're not around. Sit down with her and go over the rules of your home including what to do if a stranger comes to the door or if friends want to come over. Decide together what kinds of snacks are allowed and how much, what things are "off limits" until a parent is home, and how the time alone will be spent.

Some working parents ask their child to check in by telephone. This is both a safety precaution and a way to hear a bit about your child's day. Arrange a backup person at work when you can't take the call. You and your child should agree on specific times when she can and cannot talk with friends on the phone.

For many families some kind of central check-in center at home is helpful. This can be a bulletin board or message area with magnets on the refrigerator door. You can post reminders for the day as well as important phone numbers.

Chores and projects can be a part of your child's afternoon routine. You should decide on specific times for chores, homework and free time. Keep a weekly schedule and checklist for your child to use. This routine will help your child feel secure and responsible.

Putting It All Together

Making decisions for the care of your older child is a challenge for all parents. Take time to consider various ideas and options and resist making quick decisions. Every child is a unique individual and what works for one child may not necessarily work for yours.

Continually evaluate your arrangements and be flexible. Consider new ideas and change your choices if your plan doesn't work. Add or change rules if necessary. Your workable plan may breakdown along the way as activities and sports start and finish, a dance lesson is unexpectedly canceled, or there is a weather emergency.

Talk often with your child and listen to her likes and dislikes, fears and frustrations, joys and triumphs. This is a time of increased responsibility and independence for her. Together you can build on her ability and confidence to care for herself.

Safety Tips

Prepare your child to be ready for emergency situations. Go over the following together:

- His full name, address, and phone number.
- Your full name and the address and phone number at your job.
- The name and phone number of your designated backup person.
- The phone number for emergency services.
- Not to enter your home if a door or window is open or broken.
- What to do if someone knocks on the door.
- The location of a flashlight in good working order if the power should fail.
- How to exit your home quickly in case of a fire.
- The safety rules and routines of your home.
- Review basic first aid procedures and put together a first aid kit.

Chapter 28

Choosing Safe Child Care

Four Steps to Selecting a Child Care Provider

Step One: Interview Caregivers

Call first and ask:

- Is there an opening for my child?
- What hours and days are you open and where are you located?
- How much does care cost? Is financial assistance available?
- How many children are in your care?
- What age groups do you serve?
- Do you provide transportation?
- Do you provide meals (breakfast, lunch, dinner, snacks)?
- Do you have a license, accreditation, or other certification?
- When can I come to visit?

This chapter contains text from "Four Steps to Selecting a Child Care Provider," Child Care Bureau, The Administration for Children and Families, U.S. Department of Health and Human Services, http://www.acf.dhhs.gov/programs/ccb/faq1/4steps.htm, updated June, 2001, and the undated pamphlet "Be Sure Your Child Care Setting Is As Safe As It Can Be," Consumer Product Safety Commission, http://www.cpsc.gov/cpscpub/pubs/chldcare.html, downloaded July 2002.

Visit next (Visit more than once, stay as long as you can!). During your visit, look for the following:

- Responsive, nurturing, warm interactions between caregiver and children.

- Children who are happily involved in daily activities and comfortable with their caregiver.

- A clean, safe, and healthy indoor and outdoor environment, especially napping, eating and toileting areas.

- A variety of toys and learning materials, such as books, puzzles, blocks, and climbing equipment, that your child will find interesting and which will contribute to their growth and development.

- Children getting individual attention.

Ask the following during your visit:

- Can I visit at any time?

- How do you handle discipline?

- What do you do if a child is sick?

- What would you do in case of an emergency?

- What training have you (and other staff/substitutes) had?

- Are all children and staff required to be immunized?

- May I see a copy of your license or other certification?

- Do you have a substitute or back-up caregiver?

- May I have a list of parents (current and former) who have used your care?

- Where do children nap? Do you know that babies should go to sleep on their backs?

Step Two: Check References

Ask other parents:

- Was the caregiver reliable on a daily basis?

- How did the caregiver discipline your child?

- Did your child enjoy the child care experience?
- How did the caregiver respond to you as a parent?
- Was the caregiver respectful of your values and culture?
- Would you recommend the caregiver without reservation?
- If your child is no longer with the caregiver, why did you leave?

Ask the local child care resource and referral program or licensing office:

- What regulations should child care providers meet in my area?
- Is there a record of complaints about the child care provider I am considering and how do I find out about it?

Step Three: Make the Decision for Quality Care

From what you heard and saw, ask yourself....

- Which child care should I choose so that my child will be happy and grow?
- Which caregiver can meet the special needs of my child?
- Are the caregiver's values compatible with my family's values?
- Is the child care available and affordable according to my family's needs and resources?
- Do I feel good about my decision?

Step Four: Stay Involved

Ask yourself....

- How can I arrange my schedule so that I can...
    - Talk to my caregiver every day?
    - Talk to my child every day about how the day went?
    - Visit and observe my child in care at different times of the day?
    - Be involved in my child's activities?
- How can I work with my caregiver to resolve issues and concerns that may arise?

- How do I keep informed about my child's growth and development while in care?

- How can I promote good working conditions for my child care provider?

- How can I network with other parents?

Be Sure Your Child Care Setting Is As Safe As It Can Be

About 31,000 children, 4 years old and younger, were treated in U.S. hospital emergency rooms for injuries at child care/school settings in 1997. CPSC (Consumer Product Safety Commission) is aware of at least 56 children who have died in child care settings since 1990.

In a recent national study, CPSC staff visited a number of child care settings and found that two-thirds of them had one or more potentially serious hazards. Use the safety tips in this checklist to help keep young children safe.

Child Care Safety Checklist for Parents and Child Care Providers

Cribs. Make sure cribs meet current national safety standards and are in good condition. Look for a certification safety seal. Older cribs may not meet current standards. Crib slats should be no more than 2 3/8" apart, and mattresses should fit snugly.

This can prevent strangulation and suffocation associated with older cribs and mattresses that are too small.

Soft bedding. Be sure that no pillows, soft bedding, or comforters are used when you put babies to sleep. Babies should be put to sleep on their backs in a crib with a firm, flat mattress.

This can help reduce Sudden Infant Death Syndrome (SIDS) and suffocation related to soft bedding.

Playground surfacing. Look for safe surfacing on outdoor playgrounds—at least 12 inches of wood chips, mulch, sand or pea gravel, or mats made of safety-tested rubber or rubber-like materials.

This helps protect against injuries from falls, especially head injuries.

Playground maintenance. Check playground surfacing and equipment regularly to make sure they are maintained in good condition.

This can help prevent injuries, especially from falls.

Safety gates. Be sure that safety gates are used to keep children away from potentially dangerous areas, especially stairs.

Safety gates can protect against many hazards, especially falls.

Window blind and curtain cords. Be sure miniblinds and Venetian blinds do not have looped cords. Check that vertical blinds, continuous looped blinds, and drapery cords have tension or tie-down devices to hold the cords tight.

These safety devices can prevent strangulation in the loops of window blind and curtain cords.

Clothing drawstrings. Be sure there are no drawstrings around the hood and neck of children's outerwear clothing. Other types of clothing fasteners, like snaps, zippers, or hook and loop fasteners (such as Velcro), should be used.

Drawstrings can catch on playground and other equipment and can strangle young children.

Recalled products. Check that no recalled products are being used and that a current list of recalled children's products is readily visible.

Recalled products pose a threat of injury or death. Displaying a list of recalled products will remind caretakers and parents to remove or repair potentially dangerous children's toys and products.

Chapter 29

Parental Guidelines for Babysitting

Choosing and Instructing a Babysitter

Entrusting someone to care for your child can be difficult. Finding a qualified babysitter requires time and effort, but your reward is assurance that your child is in capable hands.

The recommendations of people you know and trust are your best bet for finding a reliable and capable babysitter. If you're new to the area and don't know how to go about finding a sitter, ask your neighbors or coworkers for recommendations, inquire at your place of worship, or talk to your child's doctor or nurse practitioner for suggestions. In addition, your local YMCA or American Red Cross chapter may have a list of babysitters who have completed their babysitting safety and infant and child CPR courses.

Interviewing prospective sitters and checking their references will help you narrow down your sitter choices. When talking with a sitter, you may want to find out about his or her experience caring for children and whether the sitter is certified in infant and child CPR. In addition, you may want to invite the sitter over for a dry run while you are at home so you can familiarize him or her with your household, and observe how he or she interacts with your child.

"Choosing and Instructing a Babysitter," provided by Kidshealth, one of the largest resources online for medically reviewed health information written for parents, kids, and teens. Found at http://www.kidshealth.org/parent/positive/family/babysitter.html. For more articles like this one, visit http://www.kidshealth.org, or http://www.teenhealth.org. © 2001 The Nemours Foundation. Reprinted with permission.

Babysitter Instructions

Before you walk out the door, prepare the sitter with the following information:

- Make sure the sitter knows where you will be and how to reach you at all times.

- Point out where the sitter can find the number for poison control (it should be posted in prominent location).

- Make sure the sitter knows what to do in an emergency. Provide an emergency phone list that includes neighbors, friends, relatives, and your child's doctor. Write your own phone number and address on the list, so that in case of an emergency, the sitter can provide that information to the police or paramedics.

- Show the babysitter where emergency exits, smoke detectors, and fire extinguishers are located. Demonstrate how to enable and disable security systems and alarms.

- Show the sitter where you keep the door keys in case your child locks herself inside a room.

- Let the sitter know of any special problems your child may have, such as an allergy to bee stings, certain foods, or household products, or the need for medication at a specific time (the directions for which should be clearly explained and written down). Show the sitter where first-aid items are kept.

- Teach your child the meaning of 911 and how to call for help, so that if something happens to your babysitter, your child knows what to do.

Let your babysitter know your child care expectations before you leave your home. If you'd prefer that the sitter not leave the house with your child, make that clear. If the phone and visitors are off limits, don't hesitate to discuss the restrictions with the sitter.

Sitter Safety

Make sure the sitter knows the following safety rules:

- Don't give your child any medicine without your written instructions.

- Don't leave your child alone in the house or yard, even for a minute.

- Don't leave your child unattended whenever she is near water. Infants and small children can drown in only a few inches of water.

- Don't feed your child under 4 years old nuts, popcorn, hard candy, raw carrots, or any hard, smooth foods that can block the windpipe and cause choking. Foods such as hot dogs or grapes should be chopped into small pieces.

- Don't let your child play with plastic bags, latex balloons, coins, or other small objects she could choke on.

- Don't let your child play near stairs, windows, stoves, or electrical outlets.

- After you return home, ask your child whether she enjoyed the sitter's visit. If your child has a reliable sitter with whom she enjoys staying, you can have a more relaxing and enjoyable time away from home.

Chapter 30

Child Abuse: Educators' Responsibilities

Introduction

There are many reasons why educators must become involved in the detection, treatment, and prevention of child abuse and neglect. In addition to professional and moral responsibility, school personnel have a unique opportunity to advocate for children in a way that no other adults except parents can. If the parent is the abuser, this need for advocacy on the part of the school becomes even more imperative.

Community Issues

It is becoming more obvious that dealing with abuse and neglect is, in fact, a community effort. Educators, though vital to the whole intervention picture, must be supported by other community members and agencies.

A good example of a community effort arose in one small city as a result of the report and later conviction of sexual abuse by a popular clergyman who had been quite involved with groups of Boy Scouts.

Excerpted from "The Role of Educators in the Prevention and Treatment of Child Abuse and Neglect," National Clearinghouse on Child Abuse and Neglect Information, http://www.calib.com/nccanch/pubs/usermanuals/educator/section2.cfm, 1992. A revision of this text is anticipated in late 2002, but was not yet available when the *Child and Youth Security Sourcebook* was being published. Watch the Clearinghouse web site for more information as it becomes available (http://www.calib.com/nccanch).

Once the initial shock had subsided, the church members joined with local school officials and other citizens to address the concerns of the children of the community as well as their parents. Support groups for abused and nonabused boys who knew the perpetrator, awareness programs, and educational programs enabled the stunned community to recover. As leaders in communities, educators are in an ideal position to initiate this type of teamwork.

Educational Issues

As educators, our primary goal is to enhance the learning of children and to remove barriers that make that learning difficult. Every year millions of dollars are authorized for this purpose under Public Law 94 142. This special education law protects the right of every child to individualized education. This law attests to our commitment to remove barriers to each child's ability to learn. Yet, the residual effects of child abuse and neglect are as much barriers to learning as any type of perceptual problem.

Educators are trained to recognize and intervene when children are not able to fully benefit from their educational opportunities. This training makes them uniquely qualified to detect cues that may indicate that children are being maltreated. Schools are the only places in which children are seen daily. Therefore, educators have a chance to see changes in their appearances and behaviors.

Legal Issues

State Policies

According to a 1984 survey done by the National Education Association, every state in the United States legally mandates that educators report suspected child abuse and neglect. However, the range of educators is defined broadly. Some states clearly define that teachers, principals, nurses, and counselors are included while other states designate all school personnel. In addition, almost every state levies a penalty against mandated reporters who choose not to report. This penalty ranges anywhere from a fine, a misdemeanor charge, to time spent in jail. (A mandated reporter is one who in his/her professional capacity is required by state law to report maltreatment to the designated state agency.) Until recently most states did not strictly enforce these penalties. This has changed within the last few years. A number of states have fined or otherwise sanctioned nonreporters to enforce reporting laws.

In addition to penalties for not reporting abuse and neglect, all states provide immunity from civil liability and/or criminal penalty for mandated reporters who do report in good faith.

In other words, the law is relatively simple. In general, it requires the involvement of educators in child abuse and neglect issues, provides protection for those educators who become involved, and penalizes those who fail to meet their obligations.

Local Policy

Local policy may also support the involvement of educators in the identification and treatment of child abuse and neglect. There is a growing trend across the Nation for school systems and boards of education to enact child abuse and neglect policies and regulations. These policies usually support state law by requiring educators to report suspected child abuse and neglect and may provide administrative penalties for noncompliance. Many further this by encouraging educators to become involved in the prevention and treatment of child abuse and neglect. Such policies may provide for periodic staff development or for representation on a community child abuse and neglect case consultation team; direct that staff support Child Protective Services (CPS) by participating in the initial CPS investigation; or offer direct service to involved families. Thus in many communities, administrative regulations also require the involvement of educators in the child abuse and neglect problem.

Individual School Policy

Each school system may respond differently to the mandate to report abuse and neglect. There are three important issues, however, that each school will want to address.

It is important that each school have in place a protocol to guide teachers and other school personnel in making reports. School staff should receive periodic training to ensure that everyone knows school policies and is able to implement policies when necessary.

Included in the protocol should be an indication of how problems with the implementation of the policy are handled (e.g., is there to be a troubleshooter or someone with final authority?).

Supports should be built in so that teachers do not feel vulnerable when reporting abuse and neglect.

Knowing the feelings and attitudes of those in their own school may help educators assess the types of supports and barriers they will encounter in the event that a maltreatment situation arises.

Ethical Issues

At the heart of the question of the involvement of educators in the child abuse and neglect problem may well be the ethical basis of the profession itself. Some of the strongest reasons for involvement come from professional responsibilities, basic principles of justice and democratic ideals, and personal commitment of educators to the well-being of the children and families they serve.

Professional Responsibility

Educators have a keen sense of professional responsibility to the children in their care. They are concerned about these children, about their health, safety, and happiness. Educators are aware that they themselves are models and examples for the children they teach, and that they are the only readily available source of support, concern, and caring for many children. Educators want to do what is best for the children in their care because their professional standards require it.

Justice and Democratic Ideals

In a very real sense, educators are symbols of the American principle of justice for all. They teach responsibility and respect for the democratic ideals of equal protection under the law and duty to uphold the law. When it comes to abused and neglected children, educators are obligated to practice what they teach. Ethics require their involvement in child abuse and neglect prevention and treatment.

Personal Commitment

For many educators, professional responsibility and respect for the law are supported by a deep personal commitment to the welfare of children. The value of this personal commitment must not be underestimated, for without it, child abuse and neglect prevention and treatment efforts can be no more than superficial academic exercises. It is this sense of personal responsibility to and for children that is perhaps the strongest reason for educators to become involved in the struggle against child abuse and neglect.

Personal Concerns

Educators Who Are Survivors

The helping professions, including education, sometimes attract those who would like to make the childhoods of others better than their own. Some educators were victims of abuses in their own families and these abuses may have left residual scars. The scars from childhood set up numerous conflicts which can color the way we approach our lives and work.

"I might have had a bit of a 'savior complex,'" one teacher said. "The kids I've taught over the years were special to me. I wanted their lives to be special, too. I didn't want them to have to go through the beatings I did as a kid. As a result I might have been too critical of their parents and too overprotective of the kids. It caused a few problems."

Another teacher described how the sexual abuse she experienced affected her contacts with her students.

"I felt as though my sense of reality was distorted somehow. I had experienced sexual abuse several different times and wasn't really sure what was appropriate or abusive and what was not. I had done a great deal of personal soul-searching, but still I think I missed signals that abused kids in my classroom were giving me just because of my own abuse."

As educators learn more about child maltreatment they may find themselves in conflict with their own experiences. The best solution is to not repress these feelings but rather to understand them. There are numerous books for people who have survived abusive childhoods. These may be of help. Educators may want to increase understanding through therapy. More and more therapists are skilled in talking with adult survivors. Whatever means they choose, educators owe it to themselves and their students to understand their own personal conflicts surrounding child maltreatment.

Knowing Whether to Touch Children

It is truly sad to learn how many day care centers and schools are requesting or even mandating that their staff not touch children because of fear that allegations of child abuse will be made against the educators.

Studies have shown that nurturing touch actually enhances learning. All children, and certainly those who are not nurtured at home, may be robbed of this important element.

Educators need not be afraid of normal touching. Touching is a concern if it is done in secrecy or isolation from others or for the sexual gratification of educators. Children need to be informed and empowered. Prevention programs are now designed to inform children about good, bad, and confusing touch. *Good touch* usually refers to hugs, encouraging pats, and other positive gestures. People may interpret these gestures differently, and this, too, is important to understand. For example, some people prefer not to be hugged; for them this is not *good touching*. *Bad touch* usually refers to hitting, punching, biting, and other acts designed to (or that unintentionally) hurt. *Confusing touch* refers to contact that may not feel quite right to children.

Once children are informed, empowerment requires that they be given permission to express their feelings about receiving such touches. Our culture teaches children not to express themselves freely around adults. Yet in this area especially they must be allowed to do so.

Children who are trained to recognize how certain touches feel to them and who are encouraged to express their feelings are allowed to tell the teacher when something does not feel good. While this may be simplistic on one level, training children to protect themselves can take a great deal of pressure off the teacher and reinstate positive touch as a part of learning. However, it is important that children not be made to feel that the entire burden of protection is on their own shoulders.

One type of touch used in some schools is corporal punishment. Currently only a few states have legally prohibited the practices of hitting, paddling, or in other ways punishing children with physical force, but hopefully more will soon.

There are several problems with physical punishment in schools. First, it often precludes the use of more creative sanctions. When children are "paddled," school personnel need not consider what might be more appropriate punishment. For example, one fourth grader was constantly vandalizing school property, e.g., writing on desks, etching words in wooden surfaces, and breaking equipment. For each offense he was sent to the principal's office for a "paddling." When his regular teacher was out for a prolonged illness, the long-term substitute found that this method was not working. At the next offense (etching obscene words in a wooden table), the boy was required to stay in during recess and after school to sand down and completely refinish the small table. After one or two similar gestures with similar punishments, his vandalism ceased. Not only was the punishment a lot of work, but he was also getting the individual company of the teacher as they were forced to be together during off hours. The teacher soon realized that it was this attention that the student craved, and the teacher found more positive methods for the student to request it.

In fact, children accustomed to being beaten at home may actually appear to invite such discipline, assuming that, like their home situation, it is the only attention they can get or to which they are entitled. Some commentators ask how society can condemn abusive parents for hitting children when schools continue the practice.

False Allegations

The issue of being accused of abuse was mentioned earlier in this section. This is certainly a fear of teachers in today's world. While it is true that those who have the inclination to abuse (especially sexually) are attracted to settings where children are easily available, the fact is that most educators are well meaning and intend no harm.

Mantell (a longtime consultant to the courts in Connecticut) cited six major types of erroneous allegations of child sexual abuse: simple misunderstandings, when adults misunderstand what children are trying to convey; simple misreporting, when the reporting process distorts the child's actual report by sifting it from adult to adult until the story changes; distortion through illness, a disturbed child making the report or a disturbed adult reporting the child's words in a distorted way; distortion by design, when adults who are intent upon revenge against other adults (e.g., custody cases) use reports of abuse to gain custody of the child; professional error, when children are asked leading questions by professionals who bias or distort the story; and misrepresentation, when people who apply to organizations for services recognize that an allegation of sexual abuse will elicit more immediate attention. Knowing how false allegations originate may actually be of some help in combating them.

While the incidence of educators being falsely accused is not high, this issue is of concern to many school personnel. Perhaps the best defense is in education.

As was previously mentioned, educating children about good and bad touch and how to talk about it is a first step. The educator should also learn about the social service system and how it functions. Are the local investigators adequately trained? Anyone accused of abuse has the right to the best trained professionals interviewing the child. If conducted by experienced individuals, these initial interviews are often enough to discount erroneous accusations. What is the process that is followed when a report is made? Knowing the process makes one feel less like a victim and allows one to be more alert to distortions caused by inconsistencies.

Children who falsely accuse usually do so for some reason. They may be disturbed, seeking attention, coached by someone else, seeking revenge, or just misinterpreted. Discovering the reason can often help with an adequate defense.

Part Four

Protection from Sexual Abuse

Chapter 31

What Is Sexual Abuse?

Child sexual abuse occurs when a child is used for sexual purposes by an adult or adolescent. It involves exposing a child to any sexual activity or behaviour. Sexual abuse most often involves fondling and may include inviting a child to touch or be touched sexually. Other forms of sexual abuse include sexual intercourse, juvenile prostitution, and sexual exploitation through child pornography. Sexual abuse is inherently emotionally abusive and is often accompanied by other forms of mistreatment. It is a betrayal of trust and an abuse of power over the child.

Child sexual abuse is a criminal offence in Canada. The Criminal Code clearly identifies those behaviours that are against the law. The Canada Evidence Act defines the forms of evidence that may be admitted in court. In recent years, both the Criminal Code and the Canada Evidence Act have been changed to provide better protection to children.

How Widespread Is the Problem?

Child sexual abuse is largely a hidden crime, so it is difficult to estimate the number of people who are sexually abused at some time during their childhood (the prevalence of child sexual abuse). Both adults and children may be reluctant to report sexual abuse for many reasons. Their reluctance may be related to the historical norm of keeping such behaviour secret because of the sense of shame associated with it. If the abuser is someone close to them in terms of kinship or other bonds, they may be deterred by the likelihood that criminal charges and penalties may be imposed. Finally, the fact that the victims are young and dependent tends to be a major obstacle to disclosure.

Research consistently reveals that, for reasons such as these, most child victims do not disclose their abuse. Even when they do, additional barriers may be encountered. For many of the same reasons that children do not report the abuse, their families may, in turn, not seek help. If the family does want help, they may still encounter difficulties finding the appropriate services.

There are few national statistics on child sexual abuse in Canada. A 1994 report, Child Welfare in Canada: The Role of Provincial and Territorial Authorities in Cases of Child Abuse, describes the provincial laws, definitions and child welfare systems that deal with child sexual abuse. A 1996 report, Child and Family Services Annual Report 1992-93 to 1994-95, presents statistical data on child welfare services in Canada. The available data cannot be directly or easily compared among the provinces because the information is collected according to different definitions and parameters in each province. For example, in some provinces, data on suspected cases are combined with those on confirmed cases. In other jurisdictions, sexual abuse is not distinguished from physical abuse.

Nonetheless, the following information provides some insight into the incidence of child sexual abuse.

- It is estimated that there were nearly 12,000 investigations of child sexual abuse in Ontario in 1993. Sexual abuse was substantiated in 29 percent of these cases and suspected in another 27 percent.

- In British Columbia, more than 500 complaints of sexual abuse were received in March 1992.

- The most extensive study of child sexual abuse in Canada was conducted by the Committee on Sexual Offences Against Children and Youths. Its report indicates that, among adult Canadians, 53 percent of women and 31 percent of men were sexually abused when they were children.

Facts to Consider

The Victim

- Victims of child sexual abuse are found in all classes and ethno-cultural communities. Children who have physical or mental disabilities are especially vulnerable to sexual abuse.

- Children are not able to give informed consent to sexual activity because they cannot fully understand adult-child sexual contact or predict the consequences, and because the adult is abusing a position of authority over the child.

- Children who are isolated from others are at greater risk of being sexually abused. These children have little contact with friends, brothers and sisters, or adults whom they can trust. Some abusers are able to take advantage of a child who is already isolated. Other abusers manage to isolate the child by manipulating people and situations. As a result of sexual abuse, some children may further isolate themselves because they feel different or afraid of what others will think.

- There is a greater possibility of serious distress to the child if the abuser is a family member, or if the child does not receive support from his or her non-abusive parent. The long-term consequences are also worse if force or the threat of force was used in the commission of the abuse, or if there were many incidents of abuse over a long period.

- As mentioned above, children find it difficult to break the silence. In a child's world, adults control most of the resources and seem to know all the answers. If the abuser threatens the child or someone the child loves, the child may not question the adult's power to carry out the threat.

- Children always want to tell about their abuse so that it can be stopped, but they are often afraid that they will not be believed or protected, or they are afraid of what might happen if they do tell. It is normal for children to delay telling about their abuse for a year or more after it occurs. They may talk about the abuse more readily if another victim discloses abuse by the same offender or if they are asked direct questions about the possibility of abuse.

- Especially in cases of incest, when the abuser is a close family member, children may not reveal their sexual victimization until they become adults. Many never tell even then. The abusers enforce secrecy and create in the child a fear of destroying the privacy and otherwise intact sense of security provided by the family.

- There is little evidence that many children deliberately make false allegations or misinterpret appropriate adult-child contact as sexual abuse. In the few recorded cases in which children appear to have made false allegations, it has usually been the result of manipulation by an adult.

- False denials of sexual abuse (saying it did not happen when it did) and recanting a disclosure of abuse (denying that it happened after having told someone about being abused) are much more common than false reports.

- Children sometimes recant truthful allegations of abuse. This is not surprising because the child naturally fears the impact that a disclosure will have on the family, or fears that he or she will not be believed. As well, the child may recant in fearful recognition of the fact that the offending adult has so much more power.

- When child victims receive professional support prior to giving testimony in court, their statements are more likely to be clear and accurately reflect the time and details of the event. The experience is also less stressful for the child who has received such support.

- Children vary in their responses to sexual abuse. The manner in which the adults react to the child's disclosure is an important factor in influencing how the child comes to view the abuse and his or her own role in it. Being believed and having family support can help the child to cope and adjust and can decrease some of the traumatic effects of sexual abuse.

- Adult women sexually molested as children are more likely than non-victims to suffer from both physical and psychological problems. Abusive and manipulative men may target these women as victims in adult relationships because of their vulnerability. Sexual abuse victims who were also physically or emotionally abused as children are the most likely to suffer from health problems and further abuse as adults.

- Men who were sexually abused as children may also suffer from depression, anxiety, and suicidal thoughts and behaviour, especially if they were abused more than once. Those who experienced both emotional abuse and multiple acts of sexual abuse are the most likely to have poor mental health and to report sexual interest in, or sexual contact with, children.

The Abuser

- Most offenders are not strangers to their victims. In most cases, they are well known to their victims. Approximately 25 percent of offenders are adolescents.

- Most of the reported abusers are male.

- It is the offender who initiates the sexual activity. The offender is responsible for the abuse no matter what the child does.

- A recent Canadian study revealed that more than 40 percent of convicted child molesters were sexually abused as children. They tended to choose victims close to the age at which they were first victimized.

- Offenders use a number of tactics to gain access to children and to ensure their victim's silence. These tactics include the use of threats, physical force, bribery, and other forms of physical and psychological coercion.

- Some offenders have abused more than 70 children before any of the victims disclosed the abuse. In cases in which one offender has abused a large number of victims, the abused children are more likely to be male.

- Incest offenders reflect the same range of education, religion, occupation, intelligence, and mental health status as can be found in a representative cross-section of the general population. Abusers are found among all ages, ethnocultural communities and social classes.

- Most sexual abuse takes place in the context of an ongoing relationship between the abuser and the child. This long-term relationship gives the offender opportunity to exploit the child's desires and fears. An incestuous father, for example, may give his child special privileges or gifts to obtain his or her cooperation and silence.

Reporting Child Sexual Abuse

If you believe you have reasonable grounds to suspect that a child is being sexually exploited or abused, promptly report your concerns to the child welfare agency, provincial or territorial social services department or police force in your community. In all cases, the person reporting is protected from any kind of legal action, provided the report is not falsely made and motivated by malice.

Where to Go for Support Services

Contact your local

- Child welfare agency.
- Police department.
- Social service agency.
- Hospital.
- Mental health centre.
- Sexual assault centre.
- Transition home.
- Distress centre.
- Other community service organization that provides counselling to children and families.

Many of these organizations are listed among the emergency telephone numbers on or near the first page of your local telephone directory.

Children who want help can also call the Kids' Help Phone at 1-800-668-6868.

What Can Be Done to Prevent Child Sexual Abuse?

- Lawyers, judges, psychologists, doctors, social workers, police, and other professionals who provide assistance to victims of child sexual abuse should receive specialized training.

- Children can best be protected by giving them the knowledge and skills necessary for their safety and well-being, and by creating in our families and communities an atmosphere in which they feel safe enough to come forward if they are being mistreated or abused.

- Children who are well informed about inappropriate touching, who are taught to trust their feelings about situations and people, and who know where to get help if they require it are less likely to be victims of any type of assault.

- Prevention education is particularly important for children who have been sexually abused, as they are at higher risk of revictimization than children who have not been sexually assaulted.

Chapter 32

Teach Children to Avoid Sexual Abuse

No parent wants to hear the words which I so vividly remember saying to my mother when I was 7 years old, "Mom, I have to tell you something."

My mother laughed and said, "Oh, God, what did you do now?" probably thinking I had just embarrassed myself at school again. "Mom, I'm serious. I need to talk to you," I said with my head down and my eyes full of tears.

I knew she had no idea what I was about to tell her—I had hid it so well for so long. I had protected my babysitter's husband who had molested me.

Why would anyone do that, you ask? No one had ever talked to me about sexual abuse, and I did not understand what had happened. I had really liked this guy before the incident occurred. He had been my friend and I didn't want to get him in trouble. I also didn't know how wrong it was, except for the funny feeling I got in my stomach whenever I thought about him after that day.

I was one of the lucky ones, though. Mine was a minor incident which never occurred again. Some kids aren't so lucky.

There are a few basic principles parents must understand to teach their children skills which can help protect them from this kind of abuse.

Lisa Edwards, "Abuse Prevention: Teach Children How to Protect Themselves from Sexual Abuse," ArmyLINK News, http://www.dtic.mil/armylink/news/Jun1997/a19970602techchld.html, June 1997. Despite the age of this document, readers seeking information about how to teach children to protect themselves from sexual abuse will find this information useful.

Teach Them That Their Bodies Belong to Them

The first is that their bodies belong to them—that they have a right to say who can touch them, where, and how. They need to feel comfortable with speaking up and saying no if someone touches them in any way that makes them feel uncomfortable (this will help protect them from both sexual abuse and physical abuse).

A good way to explain feeling uncomfortable to a child is that it is a funny feeling inside, a feeling that something is just not right. Let them know that no one should make them feel uncomfortable by touching any part of their body that their bathing suit would cover (a two-piece for girls and swimming trunks for boys).

It is important that they know that if someone ever does touch them there, then it is something you need to know about, even if it is supposed to be a secret. Yes, children need to be able to speak up to anyone—including Dad, Mom, siblings, baby-sitters, teachers, scout leaders, Sunday school teachers, and any other relative, friend, neighbor, etc.

Most cases of abuse are perpetrated by an adult that the child knows and trusts. It is usually a relative, family friend, or another adult whom the parents also trust. Teaching children to be assertive does not spoil them, it empowers them to protect themselves from being mistreated.

Teach Them What to Do If Abuse Happens

The second principle of abuse protection is teaching them what to do if someone does touch them in a way that makes them feel uncomfortable.

They need to be able to look that person straight in the eye with confidence, and tell him or her, "No, I don't like that," and then try to get away. This shows the abuser that the child is not going to just sit there and take the abuse. If the person does not stop the touching after the child says no, then the child needs to say, "I'm going to tell if you don't stop that." Then the abuser knows that this is not the child to mess with—this child knows what to do.

Ask the children who they would tell if this happened to them. Help them list all the people they could tell—parents, siblings, friends, teachers, doctors, nurses, etc. They need to know to keep telling until someone listens to them and helps them. Children also need to know that if they are touched in a way they don't like, it is not their fault—they did not ask for this person to touch them that way, nor did they do anything to deserve it.

Teach Them through Role-Playing

Children learn by doing. The "What if ..." game is an important part of teaching kids ways they can help defend themselves from harm. After teaching them when they should speak up and how, have them ask you "What if ..." questions.

Kids love to ask questions like "What if I couldn't get away?" Let them ask as many questions as they want, and ask them to try to answer their own questions before you help them out.

Then you can test them by giving example situations and asking what they would do. You could ask, "What if you were at the baby-sitter's house, and she kept hugging you really tight, and it really made you feel yucky inside?" Then role play the situations with them over and over again.

Teach them to react by looking you in the eye, telling you no (like they mean it), and getting away from you. Give them every possible situation you can think of. It is not necessary to scare them to get the point across. Just use hugs, squeezes, a peck on the cheek, etc. and have them pretend they're feeling uncomfortable.

Children actually love this "What if ..." game; they enjoy showing they know what to do. Have them do it over and over until they get it right. This role playing is probably the only thing that will really stick in the minds of young children and help them in the event of someone mistreating them.

When role playing, try to incorporate the tricks abusers often use to gain children's favor and trust. Ken Wooden, author of *Child Lures: A Guide to Prevent Abduction* lists the common lures.

- Conditional love is one, for example. "Oh, come on. Don't you love me? How can I love you if you won't even let me touch you?"

- A stranger may trick a child easily by asking for help, "Can you help me? My puppy ran away ... I need you to come help me catch him."

- Another possible lure is using authority, "Alex, I am your coach. You have to do what I tell you, or else you won't be on the team."

- Bribing with rewards such as candy, money, or toys is another common lure. I was offered a quarter.

- To lure a child into pornography, an adult may promise fame, "Trust me, beautiful, if you'll just put this on and do what I say, you'll be famous."

- Other child lures are fun and games. "Do you want to play a fun new game with me?"

- Older children may even be offered employment in exchange for sexual favors.

- Abusers can also use threats, "If you tell anyone about our little game, you will be in big trouble!"

- Children are also easily confused by the old stand-by "Jamie, get in the car! Your mommy has been in a bad accident and daddy sent me to bring you to the hospital!" This is why you need to have a code word with your kids. Then if this was a real situation, the family friend could say the code word, and the child would know that it was all right to go with them. It is important to stress with kids that only the parents and the children can know the code word, and that the parent will only tell someone who is picking up the child in an emergency. The code word will need to be changed if it is ever revealed to anyone else.

Teach Them How to Act around Strangers

The last principle of abuse protection is teaching children how to act around strangers. Kids are very confused about what the word stranger means. They often do not understand they need to be just as careful around strangers who are nice, or pretty, or who know their name, or who they have seen before. A stranger is simply someone who they don't know well; they can't tell a good stranger from a bad stranger.

Teach kids to drop what they're doing and stand up when a stranger comes into the yard or playground, and to always stay out of reach of any stranger. Also, teach them not to talk to strangers, not to go anywhere with strangers (unless the code word is used), and never to take anything from a stranger (then the child would be within an arm's reach).

Again, stress the importance of listening to that funny feeling inside to get away from a stranger if something doesn't seem right. Children should not try to help a stranger who claims to need their help; the stranger needs to find another adult to help.

Teach your children that they are responsible for keeping themselves safe when you cannot be with them. Kids also need to understand that they are never responsible for an adult mistreating them.

Conclusion

These basic principles of abuse prevention are recommended for teaching preschool through third-grade children, but are important for children of all ages to know. The most important rule about teaching children these skills is to be open and honest with them, without frightening them.

These teaching methods have been proven to change children's behavior, so that it is natural for them to protect themselves from abuse situations before the abuse occurs.

As with anything, these ideas and skills need to be reinforced to the children continually after the initial lessons, so that they are not forgotten.

Chapter 33

Parenting the Sexually Abused Child

What Is Child or Adolescent Sexual Abuse?

Child or adolescent sexual abuse is any forced or tricked sexual contact by an adult or older child with a child. Usually the adult or older child is in a position of power or authority over the child. Physical force is generally not used, since there is usually a trusting relationship between the adult or older child and the child who is abused.

There are various types of sexual activity which may take place. It can include open mouth kissing, touching, fondling, manipulation of the genitals, anus or breasts with fingers, lips, tongue or with an object. It may include intercourse. Children or adolescents may not have been touched themselves but may have been forced to perform sexual acts on an adult or older child. Sometimes children are forced or tricked into disrobing for photography or are made to have sexual contact with other children while adults watch.

Sexual abuse does not always involve physical touching. It can include any experience or attitude imposed on a child that gets in the way of the development of healthy sexual responses or behaviors. For example, a child may be a victim of emotional incest. If a mother tells her son, in great detail, about her sexual exploits, or if a father promises his daughter that she will be his life partner when she turns 18, these would be scenarios in which the child could be considered sexually

Excerpted from Rosemary Narimanian and Julie Marks, "Parenting the Sexually Abused Child," National Adoption Information Clearinghouse, http://www.calib.com/naic/pubs/f_abused.htm, 1990. Updated August 2, 2000.

abused. Siblings who are aware of a brother or sister's victimization, but are not actually abused themselves, may also suffer many of the same effects as an abused child.

In addition, some children experience ritualistic and/or satanic abuse. Ken Wooden, founder of the National Coalition for Children's Justice, defines ritualistic abuse as a bizarre, systematic, continuing abuse which is mentally, physically, and sexually abusive of children, and for the purpose of implanting evil.

How Often Does Child and Adolescent Sexual Abuse Occur?

Estimates are that approximately 1 in 4 girls and 1 in 8 boys experience sexual abuse in some way before they are 18. Data on how many of these children live in foster or adoptive homes are not available. Foster care and adoption social workers are now saying they believe the percentages of boys and girls in foster care who have been sexually abused are much higher than in the general population, perhaps as high as 75%. Many came into foster care initially because of sexual abuse and others are children who were re-victimized while in foster care, either by an older foster child or by an adult.

What Behaviors or Signs Might You See in a Child or Adolescent Who Has Been Sexually Abused?

While no one sign or behavior can be considered absolute proof that sexual abuse has occurred, you should consider the possibility of sexual abuse when one or several of these signs or behaviors are present.

Physical Signs

- scratches, bruises, itching, rashes, cuts or injuries, especially in the genital area
- venereal disease
- pregnancy in (young) adolescents
- blood or discharge in bedding or clothes, especially underwear

Behavioral Signs

- aggressive behavior towards younger children
- advanced sexual knowledge for the child's age

- seductive or "sexy" behavior towards adults or peers

- pseudo-mature behavior (for instance, a girl who is eight and dresses like a 16 year-old, wears makeup and generally acts "too old for her age," or a young boy who attempts to be his mother's "man" in every sense of the word)

- regressed behavior (for example, the child who has been toilet trained starts wetting the bed)

- excessive masturbation, masturbation in public places, difficulty with being re-focused to another behavior

- poor relationships with peers

- fear of a particular person, place, or thing (for example, if the abuse occurred in the bathroom, the child may show fear in that room)

- sudden or extreme changes in behavior (for instance, a previously good student starts having trouble with school work, a child who was not sad before starts crying frequently or acting sad, or a formerly cooperative child acts defiantly or is uncooperative or unusually overly cooperative)

- eating disorders (overeats, undereats)

Additional Behavioral Signs in Pre-Teens and Adolescents

- self-mutilation (the child may repeatedly pick at scabs, cut him/herself with a razor blade, bite his/her finger or arm, burn him/herself with a cigarette)

- threatening or attempting suicide

- using drugs or alcohol

- becoming promiscuous (a child is sexually active without discrimination, or just has that reputation)

- being prudish (the child avoids any sexuality, does not see him/herself as a sexual being in any way)

- prostitution

- fire-setting

- lying, stealing

- running away

- isolating self or dropping friends

- pre-occupation with death (the child may write poems about death, may ask a lot of questions about death, such as "What does it feel like and where do people go?")

Some Additional Behavioral Signs in Children Who Have Been Ritualistically/Satanically Abused

- bizarre nightmares

- sadistic play (for example, mutilation of dolls or small animals)

- self-mutilation

- pre-occupation with death

- increased agitation on certain dates which represent satanic high holy days

- a constant fear of harm and extreme fear of being alone

Do Boys Who Are Abused Have Special Issues?

Boys who are sexually abused face some additional problems because of persistent myths in our society. Males are rarely viewed as fitting the victim role. When boys get hurt, they are often told "act like a man," "don't be a sissy," "control your emotions." The message to boys is to stand on their own two feet and to take care of themselves. Under these circumstances, a male victim is less likely to tell and therefore cannot begin a healing process. This increases the chances that he may take on the role of the victimizer in an attempt to master his own experience.

A further complication for boys is that the media portray boys who have sexual experiences with older women as going through a "rite of passage" rather than as victims of sexual exploitation. Movies such as *Summer of '42* and *Get Out Your Handkerchiefs* are prime examples of this.

What about Juvenile Sex Offenders?

Some children who have been sexually abused go on to abuse other children. While this is a serious problem, the exact percentage of sexual abuse victims who become abusers is not known.

It is important to realize that these children are victims as well as offenders and need to receive counseling from qualified therapists who understand both aspects of the problem. The therapist must be able to be empathic and understanding of the victim but confrontational with the victimizer.

Victimizers have triggers that precede their behavior. For example, a child may abuse another child when he or she finds him or herself in a vulnerable or stressful situation. Sometimes this is because he or she lacks control or power. This may be when the child gets called a name at school or believes he or she is being punished unfairly. The therapist must help the child to not only recognize his/her own individual triggers but also, to understand the consequences of acting out these impulses.

In other instances, past experiences have left the child overly sexually stimulated. The child needs education and suggestions of alternative positive behaviors to replace the sexually victimizing behavior.

What Do Parents Need to Be Aware of about Themselves?

It is very important for you to be honest with yourselves and with others about a number of things:

Is there a history of sexual abuse in either the mother or father's past? If there is, how were those experiences resolved? Did you decide to just forget about it and chalk it up as one of those things that just happened? Or did you get help, from your parents, a teacher, a minister, a therapist, or someone who could help you work through your feelings about having been abused? Parents with unresolved abuse experiences in their history may be at greater risk for either abusing the child again, or for keeping too much physical and emotional distance, for fear of abusing the child. Both parents and survivors in local support groups regularly address these phenomena.

How comfortable are you as parents with your own sexuality and with your sexual relationship(s)? Can you talk comfortably about sex? Do you give yourselves permission to acknowledge your own sexual feelings, thoughts, fantasies, and fears? Do you have a well-established relationship which allows for direct and open communication? A child who has been sexually abused may need to talk about what happened to him or her. The child's behavior may be seductive or blatantly sexual at times. A parent must be able to deal with this.

What Do Parents Need to Be Aware of about Their Child Who Has Been Sexually Abused?

Children who have experienced sexual abuse will probably need help in learning new behaviors and ways of relating. Some of the behaviors and emotions you may see expressed by your child are:

Withdrawal. Overwhelmed by the feelings she or he has experienced, the child may retreat physically or emotionally. As a parent, you may feel confused or resentful. It can be very isolating to have someone close to you tune you out. Unless you think there is danger of physical harm to the child or others, the best course of action is to reassure the child that you care and that you will provide the limits and boundaries that your child needs.

Mood swings. A moment's tenderness can quickly explode into anger. The child may be full of confidence one day, only to sink into despair the next. It is difficult to see someone you care about in pain, but you cannot control the feelings of someone else. Point out that these mood swings are occurring. Do not allow yourself to be unfairly blamed. Try to stay calm and accepting that sometimes the child does not even know when or why his/her mood swings are occurring. Crying jags can be part of these mood swings. Accept that it is beyond your power to make it all better. Sometimes when a parent tries to rescue a child from his or her pain, he or she ends up feeling guilty, resentful, and frustrated when it does not work. When a caterpillar is emerging from the cocoon, it must have a period of time to build strength in its wings. If the butterfly is released from its cocoon before its time, its strength will be diminished and it will not be able to survive on its own.

Anger. The first target for the child's angry feelings may be the person he or she has come to feel the safest with—you. When a person's angry feelings are completely out of proportion to what is going on, it probably has nothing to do with the present situation. Something in the present is triggering and re-stimulating old memories and feelings. The safety of the current situation allows these feelings to be expressed. Recognize that this is actually a sign of health, but do not accept unacceptable behavior, and never expose yourself to physical violence.

You can assure your child that you are willing to work out the problem at hand, but in a safe and supportive manner. For example, a child may be offered a pillow to beat on in order to vent his or her anger.

Unreasonable demands. Some children learn the survival skills of manipulation and control. They may feel entitled to make unreasonable demands for time, money, or material goods. It is important not to play into or get trapped by these demands. You need to maintain a healthy relationship with your child. This will help the child reduce these demands.

Sexual behaviors. Since the abuse was acted out sexually, the child needs help in sorting out the meaning of abuse, sex, love, caring, and intimacy. Some children may try to demand sexual activity, while others may lose interest in any form of closeness. Think of all the needs that are met through sex: intimacy, touch, validation, companionship, affection, love, release, nurturing. Children need to be re-taught ways that these needs can be met that are not sexual.

A child who has been sexually abused may feel:

- I am worthless and bad.

- No person could care for me without a sexual relationship.

- I am "damaged goods" (no one will want me again).

- I must have been responsible for the sexual abuse because
    - it sometimes felt good physically.
    - it went on so long.
    - I never said "no."
    - I really wasn't forced into it.
    - I never told anyone.

- I hate my body.

- I am uncomfortable with being touched because it reminds me of the abuse.

- I think I was abused but sometimes I think I must have imagined it.

- I blame my (biological) mother or father for not protecting me but I can't talk about it; I don't want to hurt him/her.

A child who has been sexually abused will benefit from clear guidelines that set the rules both in the home and outside. These kinds of rules will help provide the structure, comfort, and security which all children need to grow into healthy adults. The following guidelines address topics with specific reference to children who have been sexually abused.

Privacy. Everyone has a right to privacy. Children should be taught to knock when a door is closed and adults need to role model the same behavior.

Bedrooms and bathrooms. These two locations are often prime stimuli for children who have been sexually abused, since abuse commonly occurs in these rooms.

By the time children enter first grade, caution should be used about children of the opposite sex sharing bedrooms or bath times.

It is not advisable to bring a child who has been sexually abused into your bed. Cuddling may be overstimulating and misinterpreted. A safer place to cuddle may be the living room couch.

Touching. No one should touch another person without permission. A person's private parts (the area covered by a bathing suit) should not be touched except during a medical examination or, in the case of young children, if they need help with bathing or toileting.

Clothing. It is a good idea for family members to be conscious of what they wear outside of the bedroom. Seeing others in their underclothes or pajamas may be overstimulating to a child who has been sexually abused.

Saying "no." Children need to learn that it is their right to assertively say "no" when someone touches them in a way they do not like. Help them to practice this.

Sex education. All children, including the child who has been sexually abused, need basic information about how they develop sexually. They also will benefit from an atmosphere in which it is OK to talk about sex. Appropriate words for body parts, such as penis, vagina, breasts and buttocks, will give the child the words to describe what happened to him or her. Suggestive or obscene language is sometimes a trigger for old feelings for a child who was sexually abused, and should not be allowed.

No "secrets." Make it clear that no secret games, particularly with adults, are allowed. Tell children if an adult suggests such a game, they should tell you immediately.

Being alone with one other person. If your child is behaving seductively, aggressively, or in a sexual manner, these are high risk situations. During those times, it is advisable not to put yourself in the vulnerable position of being accused of abuse. In addition, other children may be in jeopardy of being abused. Therefore, whenever possible during these high risk situations, try not to be alone with your child or allow him/her to be alone with only one other child.

Wrestling and tickling. As common and normal as these childhood behaviors are, they are often tinged with sexual overtones. They can put the weaker child in an overpowered and uncomfortable or humiliating position. Keep tickling and wrestling to a minimum.

Behaviors and feelings. Help children differentiate between feelings and behaviors. It is normal to have all kinds of feelings, including sexual feelings. However, everyone does not always act on all the feelings he or she has. Everyone has choices about which feelings he or she acts on, and everyone (except very young children) must take responsibility for his or her own behavior.

Will Our Child and Family Need Professional Help?

It is very likely that at some time or other parents of a child who was sexually abused will need professional help and support for themselves and their child. The type of therapy that will be the most helpful, that is, individual, couple, or family therapy, will depend on a family's particular situation. When a child is being seen in individual therapy, it is important that the parents, who have the primary responsibility for the child, be in close contact with the therapist, or included in the therapy. Try to choose a therapist who is knowledgeable about sexual abuse and with whom you feel comfortable. If parents are not familiar with the therapy resources in their area, they may want to ask their local mental health center for a referral.

Support groups for parents or sexually abused children and support groups for victims/survivors are another helpful resource. Parents who have had a chance to talk with others who understand the experience of parenting a sexually abused child say that this kind of sharing is very useful. Dr. Nicholas Groth, a leading psychologist in the field of sexual abuse, along with many children and adult victims/survivors, say that groups for children can be most effective in the healing process. The opportunity to talk and share with other children who have also experienced sexual abuse reduces a child's sense of isolation and belief that he/she is the only one to whom this has ever happened.

Is the Healing Ever Completed?

Recovery from child sexual abuse is an on-going process. As this process unfolds, the child will ideally move from victim to survivor to thriver. Developmental stages, particularly adolescence and young adulthood, may trigger old feelings about the abuse. For example, the time when an adolescent's body begins to develop physically, or when he or she marries, or becomes a parent may restimulate old feelings and memories.

As discussed earlier, so many factors can influence the extent of the damage to the abused child. While parents cannot erase what happened to their child earlier in his/her life, you have a wonderful opportunity to provide your child with new, healthier experiences. Those who have made the commitment to parenting a sexually abused child say that the rewards of helping a child grow into a healthy, vibrant adult are very satisfying indeed.

Chapter 34

Youth Sex Offenders

Who Are Adolescent Sex Offenders?

An adolescent sex offender is defined as any male or female between the ages of 12 and 17 years of age who commits any sexual act with a person of any age against the victim's will, without consent, or in an aggressive, exploitive, or threatening manner. Adolescent sex offenders come from all socio-economic, ethno-cultural, and religious backgrounds. They also vary widely in their level of intellectual functioning, their motivation, the victims they choose, and the behaviours they commit.

Some teens sexually abuse only younger children, others peer-aged victims. Some abuse only within their family. Others choose dating partners, acquaintances, strangers, and sometimes adults. Some use force or extreme violence while others trick, subtly pressure or manipulate their victims into sexual activity. Most adolescent sex offenders are known by their victims.

Some teens commit only "hands-off" sexual offences such as voyeurism (peeping), exposing their private parts to others, making obscene phone calls, frottage (rubbing against others in crowded places), or fetishism (such as stealing underwear). Others commit "hands-on" sexual offences such as fondling or penetration with a penis, finger, or objects.

Defining a behaviour as being sexual assault or abuse can sometimes be difficult. It is easy to identify a sexual offence when there is

From "Adolescent Sex Offenders," Health Canada, 1990, revised 1997. © Minister of Public Works and Government Services Canada, 2002.

287

a wide age gap between the teen perpetrator and the victim or the abuse involves force or penetration. But as the age gap narrows, and if the behaviour involves fondling or an absence of force or aggression, it is necessary to assess it in terms of coercion, consent, or power differences.

Coercion happens when one person tricks, pressures, or manipulates another to do something. If victims have been coerced, they have not really given full and informed consent.

If the perpetrator is in a position of power over or has responsibility for the victim, the relationship is not equal, so consent has not really been given. Power advantages can come from an offender being an older sibling, being a baby-sitter of the victim, being bigger in physical size or stronger, or having greater mental or emotional maturity.

How Widespread Is the Problem?

Precise estimates of the extent of adolescent sex offending behaviour in Canada are difficult to obtain. Detailed statistics on teen sex offending, are not readily available from treatment programs and services. Official national statistics do not reflect the fact that sometimes sexual assault charges are brought to court as common assault charges.

Nationally, between 15% and 33% of all sex offences in Canada are committed by persons under 21 years of age. Males represent approximately 90% of adult and adolescent sex offenders reported to authorities. In Ontario, between 1979 and 1984, nearly 1,400 persons between the ages of 16 and 19 were convicted of one or more sexual offences. A population survey done for the Badgley Commission on sexual offences against children found that almost one third of suspected or known offenders against children was under the age of 21.

Many victims do not report their abuse out of fear of revenge. Victims of sexual dating violence or acquaintance rape, or male victims of female offenders often do not define their experience as sexual assault or abuse therefore do not report it. Other victims are afraid of parental reactions, or are too embarrassed to report because they mistakenly believe that what happened to them is their fault. Some are sometimes reluctant to involve the police or other "officials" because they think they will bring shame or stigma to themselves or their family. Some victims are just too young, developmentally delayed, or immature to realize they were sexually assaulted or sexually abused.

Sexual acts by teens are still often dismissed or minimized as being just experimentation or harmless curiosity. Adolescent sex offenders rarely disclose their abusing behaviour or refer themselves to treatment. Many parents also do not report incidents of incest between siblings or other members of the family.

How Serious Are Their Offences?

When adolescents are caught sex offending it is generally assumed that this is not the first time they have done it or thought about doing it. Some teens begin by committing less serious kinds of sexual assault and, if not caught, progress to more serious offences. Serious forms of sexual behaviour typically have developed over a course of time. Sexual offences committed by teens range widely in their degree of seriousness. Penetration can account for as much as 37% or more of all reported offences.

Most, though not all, adolescent sex offenders are older than their victims. Force and threats are more typically used against older or peer aged victims, while misuse of power and authority, trickery, bribery, or blackmail may be used with younger victims and small children.

Where Do These Sexual Offences Occur?

It is generally believed that female sex offenders abuse more victims inside the family, while males abuse both siblings and others outside the family. Sex offences involving teen perpetrators occur most often in the victim's home, or the victim and offender's common home. Some happen while teens are baby-sitting siblings or other children. Others occur outside, in parks, alleys, and cars, and inside apartment or townhouse stairwells, elevators, and garages. Nearly 15% of all sexual offences involving teen perpetrators happen at school or on school property.

Why Do Adolescents Commit Sexual Offences?

Adolescents commit sex offences for a variety of reasons. Some teens who are awkward socially, have difficulty making friends, or have been rejected by other youth of their own age, sometimes turn to younger children for friendship or sex. The children they molest usually don t understand what is happening to them. They typically become scared or feel they cannot complain, so the teen may take this as a sign of consent and continue abusing them. Some teens offend out of anger or a need for power and control over others. Some teens may be developmentally delayed and unaware that what they are doing is wrong and abusive.

Some male teens in dating relationships possess distorted thinking about sex and relationships. They think that if their partner says "no" she only needs a little encouragement, verbal persuasion, or mild force. Adolescent sex offenders sometimes attempt to copy scenes they have seen in pornography media.

Many adolescent sex offenders grow up in abusive families where alcoholism, substance abuse, and inter-parental violence are commonplace. Seeing this everyday teaches a young person that anger, frustration, and personal needs can be dealt with by the use of force and violence.

Previous Victimization

A history of physical abuse, sexual abuse, or neglect can be found in the background of many adolescent sex offenders. One of the few Canadian studies on this subject found that about 33% of adolescent male offenders had experienced abuse or neglect in their childhood.

One American study found that 60% of abusers had been physically abused, 50% had been sexually abused, and 70% had experienced neglect in childhood. Over 50% of the adolescents had experienced a combination of these forms of abuse. Sexual victimization also shows up in the backgrounds of significant numbers of female adolescent sex offenders.

Adolescents who were themselves abused as children sometimes use sex offending as a way to get revenge. Some youth abused by parents and older siblings or family members may think that sex between older and younger persons is "normal."

Recent clinical research has shown that the relationship between previous victimization and future offending is complex and influenced to a significant degree by the quality of care and relationships child victims experience with their parents or caregivers. Not all sexual offenders were themselves abused as younger children. However, child sexual abuse victims are at greater risk of offending than are non-victims, though most child victims do not become offenders. Previous victimization is increasingly recognized as an important treatment issue.

Female Adolescent Sex Offenders

Though a majority of adolescent sex offenders are male, research emerging over the past ten years has begun to document female sex offending. Studies of hospital, child welfare agency, and treatment programs have found that females comprise between 3%–10% of the sex offender population. General population and victimization surveys report significantly higher numbers and extend the range up to 50% and even higher depending on the victim sample population studied.

Many of the behaviours of female adolescent sex offenders are hard to detect since few people question the close interactions of females with children. Much of the offending by females occurs when they are baby-sitting. Most victims are acquaintances and, primarily children. Twenty percent of sex offences against male siblings are committed by sisters, compared to 21% for brothers.

Adolescent females, like males, also offend against partners in same sex relationships. Research on same sex peer sexual assault among teens is only just beginning to be done.

Adolescent females commit many of the same types of offences as their male peers.

Some believe girls sex offend because they are forced to do so by male accomplices. However, some studies have not found this to be true. It is also believed that females use less force and violence to obtain compliance from their victims.

Offenders with an Intellectual Disability

Because research on adolescent sex offenders with an intellectual disability is lacking, it is difficult to provide a detailed picture. Early Canadian studies found varying degrees of intellectual disability in adolescent sex offenders that ranged between 24%–36%. The more severe the disability the more difficult it becomes to label the teen's behaviour as sex offending. Less than 3% of adolescent sex offenders could be considered seriously mentally disturbed or sociopathic.

Interventions with Adolescent Sex Offenders

Interventions with adolescent sex offenders are guided by four principles:

- Treatment must be directed at preventing further victimization.

- Legal accountability for offending behaviour must be acknowledged and communicated.

- Evaluation of the youth offender must include a thorough assessment conducted by a therapist trained to work with sex offenders.

- Treatment in peer groups designed specifically for teen sex offenders is the preferred mode of intervention.

Treatment programs for adolescent offenders should be staffed by persons trained to provide sex-offence specific interventions. All young offenders should be given a thorough assessment to develop an individualized program of care designed to meet their specific needs.

Professionals who work with adolescent sex offenders may choose a combination of individual, group, and family therapy, depending on the needs of the youth and the circumstances of the offence.

Teens in treatment are often provided with anger management and impulse control skills, basic sex education, relapse prevention techniques, life skills, and strategies to help them deal with their distorted thinking patterns.

Because the adolescent sex offender field is relatively new, we are still a long way from having all the information we need to be able to predict with a high degree of accuracy who will offend. Treatment providers, struggling with limited resources, are challenged to provide thorough assessments and comprehensive treatment interventions.

Prevention

We must be mindful of the words we use to discuss teen sex offending. Sexual offending behaviour is only one aspect of the young person's life. Labelling a youth a "sex offender" can have significant negative developmental consequences. We need to see the behaviour in a wider context of the youth's life and experience. We also need to recognize that teens often get their ideas about sex and sexuality from adults in the world around them. Currently, pornography is the principle source of information about sex and sexuality for young people.

We should understand a young person's curiosity about sex and learn to recognize the difference between appropriate sexual experimentation and problematic sexual behaviour.

Because many adolescents who offend were themselves victimized, we have to recognize the importance of dealing with the underlying harm caused by their own abuse. If we neglect to do so, we will have little success in treating their offending behaviour. Some adolescents begin sex offending before they reach 12 years of age. Many of these children are simply reacting to their own abuse. Others may copy sexual behaviour they have witnessed on the part of older siblings, adults, or in pornography. Therefore, early identification and treatment are essential for all young children who have been abused.

We need to take all problematic sexual behaviour of children and teens seriously. Holding abusers accountable, regardless of their age, is important for the well-being and healing of victims. It also brings abusers to the attention of those who can help stop them from harming themselves and others again.

While always potentially harmful to victims, some sex offending behaviour can start with curiosity and experimentation with younger children and siblings then gradually get out of hand. Parents and caregivers should closely monitor the sexual behaviours of children and provide gentle corrective feedback to them immediately.

There is a need to provide young people with appropriate, age-relevant information about sex and sexuality. Emphasis should be placed not simply on sex, birth control, or sexually transmitted diseases, but also include information about feelings, relationship-building, dating, power and control, sexual harassment, consent, and force.

The best teacher for a child or teen is a positive adult who models a sense of equality in relationships, possesses accurate information about sex, and is comfortable with his or her own sexuality. Such a person should use clear, concise, and direct language. Using vague or complicated terms reveals the adults discomfort and suggests to the youth that there is something shameful about sex.

Adults should carefully screen teenaged baby-sitters, both male and female, before using their services. Hire only mature and competent teens or adults. Obtain references from other families. Carefully observe the child's behaviour around this person, especially when returning home.

You can support local and national efforts in the media and popular entertainment to eliminate harmful sexual stereotypes, the sexualization of children and youth, the undue exploitation of male and female sexuality, and violent sexual images.

Experts in this field agree that there is a need to develop and support multi-disciplinary, coordinated continuum of care, including post-program supports or aftercare for these young offenders. Professionals within the continuum from child welfare and counsellors to police, probation officers, and the judiciary should possess a common understanding of the most current information available regarding adolescent sex offending behaviour and treatment.

Reporting Child Sexual Abuse

If you believe you have reasonable grounds to suspect that a child is being sexually exploited or abused, promptly report your concerns to the child welfare agency, provincial or territorial social services department or police force in your community. In all cases, the person reporting is protected from any kind of legal action, provided the report is not falsely made and motivated by malice.

Where to Go for Support Services

Contact your local

- Child welfare agency.
- Police department.
- Social service agency.
- Hospital.
- Mental health centre.
- Sexual assault centre.
- Transition home.
- Distress centre.
- Other community service organizations that provide counselling to children and families.

Many of these organizations are listed among the emergency telephone numbers on or near the first page of your local telephone directory.

Children who want help can also call the Kids' Help phone at 1-800-668-6868.

Chapter 35

Sibling Sexual Abuse

Child sexual abuse is a difficult thing to define. An adult having sexual contact with a child is easily defined as abuse, especially if that adult is related to the child. However, more difficult issues come into play when the perpetrator is another child in the family, especially when the child is 10 years old or younger. Cantwell (1988) reported several cases investigated in Denver in which children under the age of 10 years were molesting younger peers, sometimes siblings or cousins and sometimes unrelated children, in a variety of settings. These included multi-family households, school busses, and neighborhood children's homes. Parents may interpret this behavior at times as normal child sexual curiosity, and may ignore it. Other parents may spank the children to halt this behavior, but see nothing more to the incident. Often in these cases, the child perpetrators were abused themselves at a young age. However, due to the shock experienced on discovery of the abuse or the focus on the "victim," they did not receive services and their own history of abuse was not discovered until later.

Frequency

Typically sibling or cousin sexual contact is defined as "abuse" when it is marked by a five year difference between the children. When

Reprinted with permission from "Sibling Sexual Abuse," by Richard Niolon, Ph.D., the Director of Training at the Center for Personal Development in Chicago, Illinois, and an adjunct faculty member at the Chicago School of Professional Psychology. Additional information, as well as the text of this article including references, is available at www.psychpage.com. © 2000. Updated 2002.

the children are less than five years apart in age, the interaction is not deemed abusive unless force, coercion, injury, or penetration occurs. The criteria of force and/or coercion may be the most highly associated with negative outcomes, regardless of the specific sexual behavior (e.g., kissing, fondling, simulated intercourse, or exhibition) experienced (Haugaard and Tilly, 1988). Incidence of sibling or cousin sexual abuse varies greatly among studies, ranging from 10% to 40% among those reporting sexual abuse, although sibling and cousin sexual abuse are about equal in such samples (De Jong, 1988). Typically, the abuse begins when the victim is around six to seven years of age, and may be a one-time incident or may continue for some time.

It is unclear whether "non abuse" contacts always result in psychological harm or maladjustment. It may be that normal sexual curiosity between siblings and cousins that happens only once is not harmful. As to repeated sexual contact between the children, two models have typically been proposed. In the first model of contact, often called "nurturance-oriented," the children consensually seek sexual contact with each other over time, in part to provide nurturing and affection that is missing elsewhere in the family. It may begin with elements of loyalty, mutual satisfaction, and support, and may or may not turn coercive or lead to abuse outside the home as the child grows older. Some argue, however, that sibling sexual contact during preteen and teen years, even if consensual, interferes with the development of appropriate social skills and support systems beyond the family. This may prevent appropriate separation and differentiation from the family (Cicirelli, 1995).

The second model of contact entails a clear attempt by the abuser to experience some power, either for it's own sake or to possibly reenact and master their own experiences of abuse. Research has attempted to study this type of abuse and isolate its effects. However, such abuse is often associated with sexual abuse and promiscuity, as well as additional family dysfunction, and it is difficult to determine the effects of sibling abuse as separated from other forms of abuse (Cicirelli, 1995).

Consequences

Some of the research (Meiselman, 1978) comparing incest victims and non-abused women indicates that incest victims have more problems in romantic and family relationships, and more sexual problems. They appear to show no significant differences in regards to presence of depression, suicide risk, substance abuse, or anxiety, although they are likely to have more severe depression when it is present. Other studies (Herman, 1981) show that incest victims are more likely to suffer physical abuse in the family along with the sexual abuse, to experience teen pregnancy, to run away, and to make suicide attempts when compared to the average teen. Those attempting suicide are more likely to do so without obvious signs of depression, to attempt while using substances, and to attempt during the adolescent years between the ages of 14 and 16 (Goodwin, 1982). Finkelhor (1979, 1984) found college students reporting childhood sexual abuse had lower self-esteem, and others have found that incest victims were more likely to suffer other kinds of victimizing incidents over time, and to wait longer for treatment after disclosing the victimization.

Edwall and Hoffman studied teens admitting and denying incest, as previous research (Russell, 1986) found that 23% of adolescent girls entering treatment reported some intrafamilial abuse. They found incest victims:

- Were more likely to have experienced physical abuse, and their siblings were more likely to have experienced physical and sexual abuse.

- Were more likely to abuse substances in general, but alcohol and stimulants were typically their drugs of choice, and they often started abusing alcohol by the age of 9 years.

- Were more likely to have had a psychiatric hospitalization, to experience clinical levels of depression, and to be at risk for suicide.

- Were more likely to believe that their parents were ashamed of them and did not love them.

- Were more likely to have required police involvement and to have been picked up by police for running away.

- Were slightly more likely to experience abuse outside of the family, substance abuse by either or both parents, and divorce and remarriage in the family.

Higgs and colleagues (1992) offered that children who experienced more frequent incidents of incest, who had a close relationship with the abuser, who experienced violence during some of the abuse and consent during other sexual experiences, and who engaged in more serious sexual behavior (i.e., intercourse) were more likely to become abusers themselves. Further, failing to internalize aspects of a nurturing and psychologically aware parent can lead to a failure to develop the kind of empathy that would inhibit abuse of others.

Causes

De Jong (1988) and Daie et al (1989) present several factors in families that can lead to sibling or cousin abuse. Abuse can arise in an environment that:

- Fails to protect the child, through poor supervision/monitoring and poor choices regarding babysitters and surrogate caretakers; examples include allowing children to remain in the care of known siblings abusers, or a general lack of supervision of the children and knowledge about their activities in and out of the home.

- Fails to set appropriate boundaries through inappropriate sleeping arrangements and clear parent-child hierarchies for child care; examples include allowing older opposite-sex children to sleep with parents in the absence of the same-sex parent, or flagrant nudity or lack of privacy in the family. Inappropriate parental interests in children's sexual development and experiences, or extremely relaxed views of sex, can both lead to greater freedom to explore sexual relations with peers and siblings.

Others (Smith and Israel, 1987) argue that open parental sexual activity, especially in cases where one parent is having an affair, is an especially significant indicator. Parents turn outside the family for their needs, marking a disintegration of family structure and an increase in anxiety in siblings. This may promote a sexual relationship between siblings in an attempt to nurture each other. This is more likely to happen when:

- The home lacks supervision and care by two parents; the absence of a parent can arise through physical absence from the home (e.g., divorce, death, abandonment, or work), or emotional absence due to physical or psychological illness (e.g., hospitalization due to depression, alcoholism, or dependent personality disorder). This dynamic may be one of the most salient of sibling incest families.

- The home is a multi-familial home were older children have caretaking responsibility for younger children; combined with poor boundaries, this situation can allow older children to pressure younger children into meeting their sexual interests and needs.

* The family allows physical abuse and neglect over time; Daie cites a case in which a physically abused boy in turn abused his sister, with sexual abuse being a minor part at first, but becoming the predominant form of the abuse over time.

* The family has a rigid structure, discouraging open communication between children and parents, children and outsiders, and even between parents. They often show devaluing attitudes toward women, and enforce parental authority (often the father's power) unquestioningly over the family. This often leads to isolation, secretiveness, and enmeshment.

Smith and Israel (1987) also argued that extreme repressive attitudes toward sex may lead to increased interest on the part of the children in exploring sex with each other. Alternately, a history of child sexual abuse in one parent may lead to the kind of denial and repression that prevents the parent from noticing the signs of sibling sexual activity. In either case, a rigid and/or repressing environment can lead to sibling sexual abuse directly, or lead first to parent-child abuse. Brother-sister abuse, for example, can follow, modeling father-daughter abuse, as if the father's actions tacitly gave permission to the brother to abuse the girl as well.

Cicirelli (1995) notes that the stereotypes of incest occurring primarily in poor, less educated, ethnic minority families have not been supported by literature. Sibling abuse happens in families at all levels of income and education, and across ethnicities. Further, Smith and Israel (1987) note that there is no "type" of sibling who is likely to abuse, and personality characteristics are highly varied across abusers. Rather, sibling sexual abuse is the result of fragmenting and dysfunctional family processes, and not a cause of the family dysfunction. In response to the inadequacies of the family, a stronger and inappropriately close sibling bond may develop to compensate for the parents' dysfunction, or an abusive bond may develop and replicate the parents' dysfunction.

Responses

In families where abuse occurs, the dysfunction that led to the abuse may also lead to a poor response once the abuse is discovered. Wiehe (1990) noted that poorly responding families typically:

- Denied the allegations of abuse.

- Ignored or minimized the abuse, explaining it as normal child behavior.

- Acknowledged the abuse, but blamed or punished the abused child, and failed to protect the child and halt the abuse.

- Acknowledged the abuse, but their own dysfunction prevented them from responding to alter the environment.

Poorly responding families may be perpetuating the abuse in two ways. First, they fail to halt the abuse in the home, allowing it to spread through the child to other homes. Second, by failing in this, they create a sense that the child cannot be protected, and that the perpetrator was "chosen" over the victim. Such actions and the feelings of helplessness and rejection that result may prompt the abused child to become an abuser as well, seeking power and revenge (Johnson, 1989).

References

Cantwell, H., (1988). Child Sexual Abuse: Very Young Perpetrators. *Child Abuse and Neglect*, 12, 579-582.

Cicirelli, V. C. (1995). *Sibling Relationships across the Life Span.* New York: Plenum Press.

Daie, N., Witztum, E., and Eleff, M. (1989). Long-Term Effects of Sibling Abuse. *Journal of Clinical Psychiatry*, 50(11), 428-431.

De Jong, A. (1988). Sexual Interactions among Siblings and Cousins: Experimentation or Exploitation? *Child Abuse and Neglect*, 12(2), 271-279.

Edwall, G., and Hoffman, N. (1988). Correlates of Incest Reported by Adolescent Girls in Treatment for Substance Abuse. In Walker (Ed.), *Handbook on Sexual Abuse of Children: Assessment and Treatment Issues.* New York: Springer Publishing Company.

Finkelhor, D. (1979). *Sexually Victimized Children.* New York: Free Press.

Finkelhor, D. (1984). *Child Sexual Abuse: Theory and Research.* New York: Free Press.

Goodwin, J. (1982). Suicide Attempts: A Preventable Complication of Incest. In J. Goodwin, (Ed.), *Sexual Abuse: Incest Victims and Their Families.* Boston: John Wright.

Haugaard, J., and Tilly, C., (1988). Characteristics Predicting Children's Responses to Sexual Encounters with Other Children. *Child Abuse and Neglect,* 12, 209-218.

Herman, J. (1981). *Father-Daughter Incest.* Cambridge, MA: Harvard University Press.

Higgs, D. C., Canavan, M. M., and Meyer, W. J. (1992). Moving from Defense to Offense: The Development of an Adolescent Female Sex Offender. *Journal of Sex Research,* 29(1), 131-139.

Johnson, T. C. (1989). Female Child Perpetrators: Children Who Molest Other Children. *Child Abuse and Neglect,* 13(4), 571-585.

Meiselman, K. (1978). *Incest.* San Francisco: Jossey-Bass.

Russell, D. (1986). *The Secret Trauma: Incest in the Lives of Girls and Women.* New York: Basic Books.

Smith, H., and Israel, E. (1987). Sibling Incest: A Study of the Dynamics of 25 Cases. *Child Abuse and Neglect,* 11(1), 101-108.

Weihe, V. R. (1990). *Sibling Abuse: Hidden Physical, Emotional, and Sexual Trauma.* Lexington, MA: D. C. Heath.

Chapter 36

Dating Violence

What Is Dating Violence?

Dating violence is any intentional sexual, physical, or psychological attack on one partner by the other in a dating relationship. This definition reflects the belief that all forms of abuse are harmful and worth taking seriously. A wide range of harmful acts can occur in dating relationships that go beyond what people traditionally think of as "serious" abuse, that is, physical or sexual violence. Although both men and women may act abusively, the abuse of women by men is more pervasive and usually more severe.

Dating violence is more likely to happen when the aggressor has been drinking. This often leads people to blame alcohol for the problem. In fact, abusers themselves use alcohol as an excuse for being violent.

Sexual abuse includes unwanted sexual touching, using force or pressure to get a partner to consent to sexual activity, rape and attempted rape, and attempting or having intercourse with a person who is under the influence of alcohol or drugs. These kinds of abuse are more often directed at women. While all these acts are damaging emotionally, they vary in the extent to which they result in physical injury.

This chapter contains text from "Dating Violence," Health Canada, 1996. © Minister of Public Works and Government Services Canada, 2002, http://www.hc-sc.gc.ca/hppb/familyviolence/pdfs/violence.pdf, and "Teen Dating Violence," 1999, National Crime Prevention Council. © 1999 National Crime Prevention Council (NCPC). Reprinted with permission. Original NCPC document can be found at http://www.ncpc.org/publications/teendating.pdf.

Table 36.1. Myths about Dating Violence
(continued on next page)

Myth	Reality
Women are at a great risk of being assaulted by strangers.	Canadian, British and U.S. studies indicate that women are at far greater risk of being assaulted by men they know. Dating partners are more dangerous than strangers.
Jealousy is a sign of love.	Jealousy is the most common reason for assaults in dating relationships. When a man continually accuses a woman of flirting or having an affair, and is suspicious of everyone he sees with her, he is possessive and controlling.
When a woman gets hit by her partner, she must have provoked him in some way.	No one deserves to be hit. Whether or not there was provocation, violence is always wrong. It never solves problems, although it often silences the victim.
Women in abusive dating relationships stay because they enjoy being abused.	Women who are abused by their dating partner do not stay in the relationship because they like being bullied. Most victims want to improve their relationship rather than end it. Adolescent girls, in particular, feel social pressure to stick it out because having a "bad" boyfriend is better than having no boyfriend at all.
Men cannot control their sexual urges, and if a woman gets her date sexually aroused, she deserves what she gets.	Men are capable of controlling themselves. That's why forcing sex on a partner is illegal Even if a woman has consented to petting or necking, she still has the right to control her own body. When a woman says NO or NO MORE, then the man is required by law to stop.

Table 36.1. Myths about Dating Violence
(continued from previous page)

Myth	Reality
Men have the right to expect sexual favours if they pay for dates or if they have a long-standing relationship with a woman.	This myth is particularly persistent among teenagers. In fact, it is unreasonable to expect sex in return for initiating and paying for dates. And not every long-term relationship has to lead to "going all the way." Sex must be voluntary, and both partners have to agree on when they are ready.
Maybe things will get better.	Once violence begins in a dating relationship, it usually gets worse without some kind of intervention. Waiting and hoping he'll change is not a good strategy. Partners in an abusive relationship need help to break out of the pattern.
"Name calling" doesn't hurt anyone.	Emotional abuse is often considered harmless "name calling." But name calling hurts; that's why people use it. Emotional abuse lowers the victim's self-esteem, sometimes permanently. For many women it is the most damaging aspect of abusive relationships.
I can tell if a guy is going to be a "hitter" just by looking at him.	Abusers come in all sizes and shapes. They are not the stereotypical muscle-bound thugs portrayed in the media. They are in the classroom, at the dance, or living next door.
It'll never happen to me!	Dating violence can happen to you. It is not limited to a particular social class, or any single ethnic or racial group. Some women are victimized on their first date while others are assaulted after dating a long time. Everyone is at risk.

Sexual assault is particularly dangerous when the aggressor refuses to use condoms despite the risk of HIV (AIDS) infection. Such assaults cause extra distress to women because they must also deal with the fear of being infected.

Physical abuse includes shoving, slapping, choking, punching, kicking, biting, burning, hair pulling, using a weapon, threatening someone with a weapon, or forcibly confining someone.

These attacks cause both emotional and physical harm. Typically, men use physical force to assert control while women use it to protect themselves, to retaliate, or because they fear that their partner is about to assault them. Some women live in terror of such attacks. Men do not seem to fear assaults by their female partners. In general, men think of women's use of force as ineffectual.

Emotional abuse, like sexual and physical abuse, varies in its intensity and its consequences. It includes behaviour such as insulting or swearing at a partner, belittling them, threatening or terrorizing them, destroying their property or possessions, isolating them from friends and relatives, and treating them with irrational possessiveness or extreme jealousy. Emotional abuse originates in the aggressor's desire to control the other person's behaviour. By undermining the other person's self-confidence, the abuser tries to limit a dating partner's ability to act independently.

Both men and women use emotional abuse as a way to control their partners. Men are more likely to escalate the abuse when they think they are losing control. When words are no longer effective, men will sometimes resort to physical violence.

Both partners suffer emotional harm as a result. Society, however, too often downplays the effects of emotional abuse because there is no visible harm. As a result, communities offer little support to deal with emotional abuse by both men and women.

How Widespread Is the Problem?

Increased concern about interpersonal abuse in Canadian society is reflected in the increased number of studies on the topic. All of the studies show that dating abuse is a serious problem in Canada, but it is still difficult to assess its extent. This is because different surveys use different questions to determine if a person has been abused or abusive: some researchers use legal (i.e., Criminal Code) definitions of assault while others rely on a broader definition based on potential harm, both emotional and physical. In any case, between 16% and 35% of women surveyed say they have experienced at least one physical assault by a male dating partner.

Studies on sexual abuse in dating are even less clear-cut because the definition of sexual abuse varies, and responses from men and women differ so much. Kelly and DeKeseredy found that 27.8% of the women they surveyed reported at least one incident of sexual abuse in the 12 months preceding the study. Fully 45.1% of the women said they had been victimized since leaving high school. Based on Criminal Code definitions of sexual assault, 37% of Canadian women had experienced at least one sexual assault since the age of 16.

Warning Signs

The following are general warning signs of the potential for sexual or physical violence in dating relationships. Each warning sign is accompanied by facts or approaches that may help you reduce your risk of being victimized. This information may also help you to offer better support to women who are assaulted.

Warning sign: Your partner makes threats of violence.

Reducing the risk: Any threat should be taken seriously. Get help immediately when a partner threatens to use violence. It is not a joke or a game. Men who threaten will generally carry out their threats. You can get help from counsellors, women's shelters, teachers, and a variety of community groups. Your friends may also offer support, but be cautious. If the person you go to for advice trivializes your experience or tells you "boys will be boys," go elsewhere.

Warning sign: Your partner is obsessed with dominating and controlling you.

Reducing the risk: Exploring your partner's attitude to women is probably a useful technique for reducing risk. Knowing how he feels about issues like equality between partners or compromise in decision making is important. Look for early signs that he has to "have it all his own way."

Warning sign: Your partner is sexually possessive and often degrades or humiliates you.

Reducing the risk: Possessiveness should be addressed directly. You have to tell your partner that it will not be tolerated. Whether you are dating someone or not, you have the right to do what you want with your body. If he objects, he can always leave the relationship.

Warning sign: You know your dating partner abused a former girlfriend. His father is physically abusive. Your partner accepts or defends the use of violence.

Reducing the risk: Dating abuse is often part of a continuing pattern of behaviour. If your partner was abusive in a previous relationship, then the risk is very high that he will be abusive in this relationship. Men often become accustomed to violence because they see it as a way of life in their family or peer group. To break this pattern, urge your partner to get counselling.

Many men discuss their use of violence with their peers. Friends should tell friends that abuse is wrong. Women should be encouraged to report their experiences. When the victim is silent, the abuser may think he can "get away with it." Silence may also give him the message that his violence isn't really a problem.

What Can You Do?

If you are being abused, get out and get help. Informed counsellors can help you deal with the emotional and physical consequences of the abuse. If you want to stay and "work it out" with him, insist that he do more than just apologize. He needs to get counselling. Violent men do not just stop; the first blow is never the last.

If you suspect that someone you know is being abused, listen and be supportive. It is important not to blame her for the abuse. Tell her that what is happening is wrong and that he is responsible for his actions—she didn't provoke the violence or deserve it.

Let her know that he won't just stop. Both of them need help. She needs to heal, and he needs to be taught how to behave.

If you suspect that someone you know is being abusive, confront him about his use of violence. Tell him that it is wrong and illegal. Make him see that he is responsible for his actions; don't accept any excuses.

Tell him that sexual assault is any unwanted sexual contact and that includes taking advantage of a woman who has been drinking or taking drugs. Point out that a sexual assault conviction could mean 10 years in prison.

Where to Go for Help?

Most communities have services for victims of abuse and for abusers. These organizations will provide you with information and support. The YWCA may be one place to start. Local rape and sexual assault crisis centres can also be very helpful.

If you're still in school, ask a guidance counsellor or a teacher to help you find an agency that works with young people. Teenagers can also call the Kids Help Phone toll free at 1-800-668-6868.

If you want to end violence in dating relationships, don't be afraid to stand up for your beliefs. Tell those around you that violence is always wrong. Talk about other ways to deal with problems in relationships.

Support education programs in schools, universities, colleges, and the wider community that address issues of male violence against women and that seek to end violence by promoting greater equality in dating relationships. For example, the issues of jealousy and power and how they relate to sexual abuse in dating should be part of the school curriculum.

Join the campaign to persuade people that NO MEANS NO and that the men who deal the blows, not the women they hit, are responsible for the violence.

Teen Dating Violence

Dating violence or abuse affect one in four teens. Abuse isn't just hitting. It's yelling, threatening, name calling, saying "I'll kill myself if you leave me," obsessive phone calling or paging, and extreme possessiveness.

Are you going out with someone who...

- is jealous and possessive, won't let you have friends, checks up on you or won't accept breaking up?

- tries to control you by being bossy, giving orders, making all the decisions, or not taking your opinion seriously?

- puts you down in front of friends or tells you that you would be nothing without him or her?

- scares you? Makes you worry about reactions to things you say or do? Threatens you? Uses or owns weapons?

- is violent? Has a history of fighting, loses his or her temper quickly, brags about mistreating others? Grabs, pushes, shoves, or hits you?

- pressures you for sex or is forceful or scary about sex? Gets too serious about the relationship too fast?

- abuses alcohol or other drugs and pressures you to use them?

- has a history of failed relationships and always blames the other person for all of the problems?

- believes that he or she should be in control of the relationship?

- makes your family and friends uneasy and concerned for your safety?

If you answered yes to any of these questions, you could be a victim of dating abuse. Both males and females can be victims of dating violence, as can partners in heterosexual and homosexual relationships.

What If Your Partner Is Abusing You and You Want out?

- Don't put up with abuse. You deserve better.

- Know that you are not alone. Teens from all different backgrounds across the country are involved in or have been involved in a violent relationship.

- Understand that you have done nothing wrong. It is not your fault.

- Know that the longer you stay in the abusive relationship, the more intense the violence will become.

- Recognize that being drunk is not an excuse for someone to become abusive.

- Talk with your parents, a friend, a counselor, a faith leader or spiritual leader, or someone else you trust. The more isolated you are from friends and family, the more control the abuser has over you.

- Know that you can get help from professionals at rape crisis centers, health services, counseling centers, or your family's health care provider.

- Alert a school counselor or security officer about the abuse.

- Keep a daily log of the abuse for evidence.

- Remember that no one is justified in attacking you just because he or she is angry.

- Do not meet him or her alone. Do not let him or her in your home or car when you are alone.

- Avoid being alone at school, your job, or on the way to and from places.

- Always tell someone where you are going and when you plan to be back. Plan and rehearse what you will do if he or she becomes abusive.

How to Be a Friend to a Victim of Dating Violence

Most teens talk to other teens about their problems. If a friend tells you things that sound like his or her relationship is abusive, here are some suggestions on ways to help.

- Don't ignore signs of abuse. Talk to your friend.

- Express your concerns. Tell your friend you're worried. Support, don't judge.

- Point out your friend's strengths—many people in abusive relationships are no longer capable of seeing their own abilities and gifts.

- Encourage your friend to confide in a trusted adult. Offer to go with the friend for professional help.

- Find out what laws in your state may protect your friend from the abuser.

- Never put yourself in a dangerous situation with the victim's partner. Don't try to mediate or otherwise get involved directly.

- Call the police if you witness an assault. Tell an adult school principal, parent, guidance counselor, or school resource officer if you suspect the abuse but don't witness it.

Take Action

- Educate teens and adults in your community. Start a peer education program on teen dating violence.

- Encourage your school or a community organization to start a program to help abusers conquer their behavior. Teaching them how to be in a relationship without resorting to violence will help break the cycle.

- Read up on healthy relationships and dating violence. Ask your school library to purchase books about living without violence and the cycle of domestic violence.

- Inquire about having health, social studies, contemporary living, and other classes incorporate discussions of teen dating violence and its prevention.

Chapter 37

Date Rape Drugs

What Is the Date Rape Drug?

The date rape drug is the common name for Rohypnol, generically called flunitrazepam. Rohypnol is manufactured by Hoffman-La Roche and prescribed as a sleeping pill in countries outside of the United States. It is used as a short-term treatment for insomnia, as a sedative hypnotic and a pre-anesthetic. It has physiological effects similar to Valium (diazepam), but is approximately ten times more potent. It is used also as an illicit drug, often in combination with other drugs, such as heroin, cocaine, and alcohol. Common names for Rohypnol include the following: rophies, roofies, R2, roofenol, Roche, roachies, la rocha, rope, rib, circles, Mexican valium, roach-2, roopies, and ropies. A similar drug is known as clonazepam (Klonopin in the U.S. and Rivotril in Mexico.)

What Does Rohypnol Look Like?

Rohypnol tablets are white, scored on one side, with the word "ROCHE" and an encircled one or two (depending on the dosage) on the other. They are sold in pre-sealed bubble packs of one or two mg doses. Rohypnol can often be dissolved in a drink, and undetectable.

Excerpted from "'Date Rape' Drug (Rohypnol)," National Women's Health Information Center, Office on Women's Health, U.S. Department of Health and Human Services, http://www.4woman.gov/faq/rohypnol.htm, December, 2000.

Is Rohypnol Legal?

No, Rohypnol is not manufactured or sold legally in the United States. However, it is produced and sold legally by prescription in Europe and Latin America. It is smuggled into the United States by mail or delivery services.

Who Uses Rohypnol and How?

Rohypnol use has been reported on every inhabited continent. It is often used in conjunction with other drugs. It is usually ingested orally, but can be snorted. Teen use of Rohypnol is increasing. The most common pattern of use is by teenagers and young adults as an alcohol extender in an attempt to create a dramatic high most often in combination with beer, or as a drug to incapacitate a victim before a sexual assault.

Why Has There Been an Increase in Teen Use of Rohypnol?

First, Rohypnol is a low-cost drug, sold at less than $5.00 per tablet. Second, common misconceptions may explain the drug's popularity with young people: 1) many erroneously believe that the drug is unadulterated because it comes in pre-sealed bubble packs—and therefore tamper-proof and safe; 2) many mistakenly think its use cannot be detected by urinalysis testing.

What Happens When You Take Rohypnol? What Are the Side Effects?

Rohypnol intoxication is generally associated with impaired judgment and impaired motor skills and can make a victim unable to resist a sexual attack. The combination of alcohol and Rohypnol is also particularly hazardous because together, their effects on memory and judgment are greater than the effects resulting from either taken alone. Effects begin within thirty minutes, peak within two hours, and can persist for up to eight hours. It is commonly reported that persons who become intoxicated on a combination of alcohol and flunitrazepam have blackouts lasting eight to twenty-four hours following ingestion. Disinhibition (losing your social inhibitions) is another widely reported effect of Rohypnol, when taken alone or in combination with alcohol. Adverse effects of Rohypnol use include decreased blood pressure, memory impairment, drowsiness, visual disturbances, dizziness, confusion, gastrointestinal disturbances, and urinary retention.

Is Rohypnol Addictive?

Yes. Rohypnol can cause physical dependence. Withdrawal symptoms include headache, muscle pain, confusion, hallucinations, and convulsions. Seizures may occur up to a week after cessation of use.

Why Is Rohypnol Called the "Date Rape Drug"?

Rohypnol has been associated with date rape, and has also been called the "Forget Pill," "Trip-and-Fall," and "Mind-Erasers." In combination with alcohol, it can induce a blackout with memory loss and a decrease in resistance. Girls and women around the country have reported being raped after being involuntarily sedated with Rohypnol, which was often slipped into their drink by an attacker. The drug has no taste or odor so the victims don't realize what is happening. About ten minutes after ingesting the drug, the woman may feel dizzy and disoriented, simultaneously too hot and too cold, or nauseated. She may experience difficulty speaking and moving, and then pass out. Such victims have no memories of what happened while under the drug's influence.

Are There Other Date Rape Type Drugs?

Since about 1990, GHB (gamma-hydroxybutrate) has been abused in the U.S. for euphoric, sedative, and anabolic (bodybuilding) effects. As with Rohypnol, GHB has been associated with sexual assault in cites throughout the country. Common names include, "liquid ecstasy," "somatomax," "scoop," or "grievous bodily harm."

How Can I Avoid Becoming a Victim of Rape under the Influence of Rohypnol or GHB?

Here are a few suggestions for staying aware and alert:

* Be wary about accepting drinks from anyone you don't know well or long enough to trust.

* If you are accepting a drink, make sure it's from an unopened container and that you open it yourself.

- Don't put your drink down and leave it unattended, even to go to the restroom.

- Notify other females you know about the effects of this dangerous drug.

- If you think that you have been a victim, notify the authorities immediately.

Part Five

Missing and Abducted Children

Chapter 38

Missing Kids Statistics

Kidnaping of Juveniles: Patterns from NIBRS (National Incident-Based Reporting System)

Introduction

The kidnaping of children has generated a great deal of public concern, not to mention confusion and controversy. These crimes have been some of the most notorious and highly publicized news stories of recent history, occupying a central place in the fears and anxieties of parents. Yet, an ongoing debate has raged over how frequently such crimes occur, which children are most at risk, and who the primary offenders are.

Part of the problem has been confusion about the definition of kidnaping. While lengthy ransom abductions and the tragic recovery of bodies have molded the public's perception of the crime, in a strict legal sense, kidnaping also involves both short-term and short-distance displacements, acts common to many sexual assaults and robberies. Kidnaping occurs whenever a person is taken or detained

---

This chapter contains text from David Finkelhor and Richard Ormrod, "Kidnaping of Juveniles: Patterns From NIBRS," Office of Juvenile Justice and Delinquency Prevention, U.S. Department of Justice, http://www.ncjrs.org/html/ojjdp/2000_6_2/contents.html, June 2000, and John J. Wilson, "Children as Victims," Office of Juvenile Justice and Delinquency Prevention (OJJDP), http://www.ncjrs.org/pdffiles1/ojjdp/180753.pdf, May 2000.

against his or her will and includes hostage situations, whether or not the victim is moved. Moreover, kidnaping is not limited to the acts of strangers but can be committed by acquaintances, by romantic partners, and, as has been increasingly true in recent years, by parents who are involved in acrimonious custody disputes.

Confusion about kidnaping has been exacerbated by the absence of reliable statistics about the crime. Kidnaping is not one of the crimes included in the Federal Bureau of Investigation's (FBI) national Uniform Crime Reporting (UCR) system, and individual States or other jurisdictions have rarely made any independent tally of kidnaping statistics. As a result, a national picture of, or even a large data set about, this crime from the law enforcement perspective has been unavailable. In the past, several attempts were made to collect abduction data, but they were limited in scope or time. For example, OJJDP's 1988 National Incidence Studies of Missing, Abducted, Runaway, and Thrownaway Children (NISMART) estimated the number of family and non-family abductions for a single year but contained no police data on family abductions. The Washington State Attorney General's Office has compiled data on abduction homicides known to police, and the FBI has a database on the very serious kidnaping cases that have been reported to it. However, despite these various data sources, a broad picture covering the full spectrum of kidnaping offenses that are reported to and investigated by law enforcement has not been available.

The National Incident-Based Reporting System (NIBRS)

Fortunately, a comprehensive national database on kidnaping and other crimes is beginning to emerge. The FBI, in partnership with the Bureau of Justice Statistics, is supplanting the UCR with the more comprehensive National Incident-Based Reporting System (NIBRS), which collects detailed information on crimes known to the police. One of the improvements introduced by NIBRS is the inclusion of specific data on kidnaping. NIBRS offers an outstanding opportunity to learn more about the nature and extent of this crime, about which so few data have been available in the past.

This text describes the crime of kidnaping of juveniles (youth ages 17 and younger) as it appears in statistics reported by law enforcement agencies using NIBRS for 1997, the most recent reporting year for which NIBRS data are currently available. An analysis of data on 1,214 juvenile kidnapings from the jurisdictions in 12 States that participated in NIBRS in 1997 reveals the following:

- Kidnaping makes up less than 2 percent of all violent crimes against juveniles reported to police.

- Based on the identity of the perpetrator, there are three distinct types of kidnaping: kidnaping by a relative of the victim or *family kidnaping* (49 percent), kidnaping by an acquaintance of the victim or *acquaintance kidnaping* (27 percent), and kidnaping by a stranger to the victim or *stranger kidnaping* (24 percent).

- Family kidnaping is committed primarily by parents, involves a larger percentage of female perpetrators (43 percent) than other types of kidnaping offenses, occurs more frequently to children under 6, equally victimizes juveniles of both sexes, and most often originates in the home.

- Acquaintance kidnaping has features that suggest it should not be lumped with stranger kidnaping into the single category of non-family kidnaping, as has been done in the past.

- Acquaintance kidnaping involves a comparatively high percentage of juvenile perpetrators, has the largest percentage of female and teenage victims, is more often associated with other crimes (especially sexual and physical assault), occurs at homes and residences, and has the highest percentage of injured victims.

- Stranger kidnaping victimizes more females than males, occurs primarily at outdoor locations, victimizes both teenagers and school-age children, is associated with sexual assaults in the case of girl victims and robberies in the case of boy victims (although not exclusively so), and is the type of kidnaping most likely to involve the use of a firearm.

- Relatively little kidnaping involves weapons.

- Only one death and a few major injuries were associated with juvenile kidnaping reported to NIBRS.

NIBRS data on kidnaping have some important limitations. Conclusions drawn from these data must be used with caution. Although the patterns and associations discovered are real, they apply only to the jurisdictions reporting and are not necessarily representative of national patterns and dynamics of crime. Also, NIBRS relies on local law enforcement agencies to collect data, and it is not clear how systematic agencies are in their recording of kidnaping. Because kidnaping is not included in UCR data, agencies may not yet code for kidnaping as thoroughly as they might for other crimes. Moreover, jurisdictions may vary in how regularly they charge offenders with the crime of kidnaping. The elements of kidnaping exist in a wide range of criminal incidents—sexual assaults, robberies, and physical assaults—yet some jurisdictions, for a variety of possible reasons such as training, tradition, or local statutes, may charge or record the crime of kidnaping more or less frequently than other crimes.

Nonetheless, current NIBRS data provide a picture of the types of incidents law enforcement agencies in participating jurisdictions across the country are recording for statistical purposes as the crime of kidnaping. This perspective of current law enforcement practices is important in and of itself because, unlike public perceptions and prevailing stereotypes, it represents the actual juvenile kidnaping that police in these jurisdictions deal with on a day-to-day basis.

Juvenile Kidnaping—A Rare Occurrence

Data indicate that kidnaping of juveniles is a relatively rare crime in NIBRS jurisdictions. It constitutes only one-tenth of 1 percent of all the crimes against individuals, 1 percent of all crimes against juveniles, and 1.5 percent of all violent crimes against juveniles recorded in the database. Kidnaping is dwarfed by the much more common crimes of simple and aggravated assault, larceny, and sex offenses, which make up most of the crimes against juveniles. Both the limited coverage of NIBRS and the fact that kidnapings represent a very small percentage of all crimes make it impossible to project a reliable national estimate of kidnaping incidents. Nonetheless, the 1,214 juvenile kidnaping cases in the 1997 NIBRS data provide a larger database than has been previously available for examining the characteristics of this crime.

Kidnaping is widely recognized to involve very different dynamics and motives depending on the identity of the perpetrators and age of the victim. Previous research and current public policy divide kidnaping into two categories: family abductions and non-family abductions. Family abductions are usually committed by parents who, in the course of custodial disputes, take or keep children in violation of custody orders. Non-family abductions are generally thought to involve efforts, primarily by strangers, to isolate children in order to commit another crime, such as sexual assault or robbery.

Three Types of Perpetrators

In contrast, the criminal kidnaping of juveniles, as recorded by police in the NIBRS jurisdictions, is divided into three relatively large categories: family kidnaping (49 percent), acquaintance kidnaping (27 percent), and stranger kidnaping (24 percent). Compared with all violent crimes against juveniles, kidnaping has substantially higher percentages of both family and stranger perpetrators, but the high percentage of acquaintance kidnapings is striking given previous characterizations of this crime that have emphasized only the family and stranger elements.

In the NIBRS jurisdictions, family kidnaping perpetrators are usually parents (80 percent), almost always adults (98 percent), and often female (43 percent). Although not a majority of family kidnaping perpetrators, females commit a substantially larger portion of the family abductions than they do of acquaintance abductions (16 percent), stranger abductions (5 percent), or violent crimes in general (24 percent).

Stranger perpetrators are predominately males (95 percent) and predominately adults (90 percent). Acquaintance kidnaping has the largest proportion of juvenile offenders (30 percent) and a somewhat higher percentage of female offenders than stranger kidnaping (16 percent and 5 percent, respectively). Data from the NIBRS jurisdictions provide limited information about the characteristics of some offenders in the acquaintance category. Eighteen percent are categorized as boyfriend, which suggests a quite distinct dynamic, whereas two other subdivisions friend (7 percent) and acquaintance (73 percent) although more ambiguous, suggest different degrees of intimacy or familiarity.

Family perpetrators kidnap males and females in approximately equal proportions. Acquaintance perpetrators kidnap substantially more females than males (72 percent and 28 percent, respectively). Stranger perpetrators also kidnap more females than males but not quite so disproportionately as acquaintances (64 percent and 36 percent, respectively).

Victim Age Patterns

The three categories of kidnaping also have distinct patterns with respect to the age of victims. In the NIBRS incident reports, family kidnaping has its peak occurrence for children under age 6 (43 percent), while a large majority of acquaintance kidnaping victimizes teenagers (youth ages 12 to 17) (71 percent). Stranger kidnaping is more equally split between teenage and elementary school-age victims

(57 percent and 32 percent, respectively). However, the risks for children of different ages appear to have a complex interplay. Children under the age of 6 are primarily targets of family kidnaping, which peaks at about age 2 and declines thereafter. The risk of kidnaping by a stranger is comparatively low for preschoolers but rises throughout the elementary school years and reaches its peak around age 15. Acquaintance kidnaping is the predominant problem for teenagers, displacing stranger kidnaping as their biggest threat.

Location

NIBRS provides only crude data about the location of crimes, particularly a crime like kidnaping that may have an originating, intermediate, and destination locale (for example, a child taken from a street, driven in a car, brought into a residence, and then raped). NIBRS allows multiple-location coding for multiple-offense crimes, but only 1 percent of incidents involving kidnaping have multiple locations recorded in NIBRS data. The information on location does, however, show clear-cut associations between the offender's relationship to the victim and the location of the kidnaping.

In the NIBRS jurisdictions, family kidnaping, consistent with the stereotype, is associated primarily with homes and residences (84 percent). Stranger kidnaping, by contrast, is associated primarily with outdoor locations (58 percent) streets, highways, parks, waterways, and other public areas. Like family kidnaping, most acquaintance kidnaping takes place at homes and residences (63 percent), but unlike family kidnaping, a substantial percentage of acquaintance kidnaping also occurs in outside locations (22 percent). It is important to note that schools are an unusual site for abduction, even family abduction (only 5 percent of family, 4 percent of acquaintance, and 3 percent of stranger kidnaping occur at school).

Additional Offenses

In other studies, non-family kidnaping is generally associated with other offenses, such as robbery or sexual assault, and is in fact a means of facilitating those offenses. One advantage of NIBRS over UCR is its ability to code multiple crimes associated with a single incident. Overall, 19 percent of the juvenile kidnaping reported in NIBRS jurisdictions is associated with another violent crime. This makes it the most common crime to be paired with an additional offense. These additional offenses provide some perspective on the motives of kidnaping offenders.

Most additional offenses associated with kidnaping occur in conjunction with acquaintance and stranger kidnaping, but the types of offenses vary somewhat according to the gender of the victim. For female victims, sex crimes were the predominant adjunct to kidnaping, occurring in 23 percent of the kidnapings by acquaintances and 14 percent of the kidnapings by strangers reported to NIBRS in 1997. For male victims, robbery and assault were the additional offenses most likely to accompany kidnaping, although some sex offenses also occurred.

Family kidnaping tends not to be associated with any other crime. In this type of kidnaping, none of the offenses against boys and only 5 percent of the offenses against girls were linked to an additional violent crime.

Weapon Usage

For the most part in NIBRS jurisdictions, kidnaping is a weaponless crime. Approximately 14 percent of acquaintance kidnapings and about 23 percent of stranger abductions involved weapons, mostly guns. The use of weapons in family abductions was quite rare (less than 2 percent).

Injuries and Deaths

Injuries occurred in only 12 percent of all kidnapings recorded by police in participating jurisdictions. They were most frequent in acquaintance abductions (24 percent) and least frequent in family abductions (4 percent). Major injuries (for example, severe lacerations, broken bones, unconsciousness) were extremely rare, occurring in only 2 percent of all kidnapings. Only one fatal outcome to a kidnaping was recorded in the 1997 NIBRS data. When interpreting these facts, however, it must be kept in mind that these abductions were not necessarily crime episodes of long duration or ones in which a child was officially declared missing. They could have involved episodes during which a child was transported a short distance or into a building or car in order to accomplish a sexual assault or robbery. NIBRS has no usable information about whether the child victim was at any time in the episode reported missing or about the distance or duration of the kidnaping.

Time of Day

Rates for all crimes against children peak in the afternoon, and kidnaping is no exception: 41 percent of all juvenile kidnapings in

325

Table 38.1. Some categories of missing children are more numerous than others.

The term "missing children" has been used for many years to describe children involved in very different kinds of events, making it difficult to estimate the magnitude of these phenomena or to formulate appropriate public responses. NISMART 1 sought to measure the "missing child problem" by examining several distinct problems.

Broadly defined:

Defined as serious:

Parental/family abduction
354,100 children per year
A family member took a child or failed to return a child at the end of an agreed-upon visit in violation of a custody agreement/decree, with the child away at least overnight.

163,200 children per year
A family member took the child out of State or attempted to conceal/prevent contact with the child, or abductor intended to keep the child or permanently change custodial privileges.

Stranger/non-family abduction
3,200–4,600 children per year
Coerced and unauthorized taking of a child, or detention, or luring for purposes of committing another crime.

200–300 children per year
A non-family abduction where the abductor was a stranger and the child was gone overnight, or taken 50 miles or more, or ransomed, or killed, or the perpetrator showed intent to keep the child permanently.

Runaway
450,700 children per year
A child who left home without permission and stayed away at least overnight or who was already away and refused to return home.

133,500 children per year
A runaway who during a runaway episode was without a secure and familiar place to stay.

Thrownaway
127,100 children per year
A child who was told to leave home, or whose caretaker refused to let come home when away, or whose caretaker made no effort to recover the child when the child ran away, or who was abandoned.

59,200 children per year
A thrownaway who during some part of the episode was without a secure and familiar place to stay.

Otherwise missing
438,200 children per year
Children missing for varying periods depending on age, disability, and whether the absence was due to injury.

139,100 children per year
An otherwise missing child case where police were called.

NIBRS jurisdictions occur during afternoon hours (noon to 6 p.m.). The main difference among the three types of kidnaping is that acquaintance and stranger kidnaping are somewhat more likely than family kidnaping to occur in the evening (6 p.m. to midnight) or nighttime (midnight to 6 a.m.) hours (46 percent, 41 percent, and 30 percent, respectively).

Children as Victims

Editors note: The data presented below is from the first National Incidence Studies of Missing, Abducted, Runaway, and Thrownaway Children (NISMART 1), which was published in 1990. It provided the first nationally representative, comprehensive estimates of the incidence of missing children. Although information from the second Comprehensive Study of Missing Children (NISMART 2) is expected to be available soon, it was not available when the *Child and Youth Security Sourcebook* was being published. When information from NISMART 2 is available to the public it will be accessible at the National Criminal Justice Service website, http://www.ncjrs.org. NISMART 1 is still valuable to readers seeking information about national statistical trends of missing children in the U.S.

Who Are Runaways, and What Happens When They Are Away?

In NISMART 1, parents or guardians of runaways who were gone overnight provided information about the runaways and their experiences while gone.

Most runaways were teenage girls (58%); most were 16 or 17 years old (68%). Most came from families that were or had been broken; only 28% lived with both (natural or adoptive) parents.

Most runaways initially stayed with someone they knew (66%) or did so at some time during the episode (94%). Some had spent time in unfamiliar or dangerous situations: 29% spent at least part of the episode without a familiar and secure place to stay, and 11% spent at least one night without a place to sleep. Many runaways returned home within a day or two, but about half (52%) were gone for 3 days or more, and 25% were gone for a week or more. For about half of the runaways, the caretaker knew the child's whereabouts more than half of the time the child was away from home.

Many runaways had run away before, with 34% having run away at least once before in the past 12 months. Some traveled a long distance;

approximately 16% went more than 50 miles from home during the episode, and about 10% went more than 100 miles.

Who Are Thrownaways, and What Happens When They Are Away?

About half of thrownaway children were runaways whose parents or guardians made no effort to recover them, and about half were directly forced to leave home. Parents of thrownaway children reported that most (84%) were 16 years old or older. The vast majority stayed with friends at least part of the time while they were away (88%), although 13% spent at least one night without a place to sleep. A majority (68%) returned home within 2 weeks. For about three-quarters of thrownaway children, the caretaker knew the child's whereabouts more than half of the time the child was away from home.

Who Are Abducted Children, and What Happens When They Are Taken?

Parents of children abducted by a family member reported that most of these children were young: 33% were 2 to 5 years old, and 28% were 6 to 9 years old. Most were returned within a week: 62% were returned in 6 days or less, and 28% were returned in 24 hours or less. For just over half of children abducted by a family member, the care-taker knew the child's whereabouts more than half of the time the child was away from home.

Many family abductions appeared to fall into the serious category, with the abducting parent:

- preventing the child from contacting the care taking parent (41%)

- concealing the child (33%)

- threatening or demanding something of the care taking parent (17%)

- taking the child out of State (9%)

Non-family abductions were studied in the records of a national sample of police departments. In these cases, three-quarters of the children were teenage girls, and half were 12 years old or older. Most of the victims were not missing for long: most were gone for less than 1 day; an estimated 12% to 21% were gone for less than 1 hour. Nearly all of the victims were forcibly moved during the episode: most were taken from the street; 85% of the cases involved force (75% with a weapon). Researchers estimated that, of the 200–300 non-family abductions that fell into the serious category (stereotypical kidnapings), about 100 resulted in homicides.

Who Are Other Missing Children, and What Happens When They Are Missing?

Most lost or otherwise missing children tended to fall into one of two age groups: 4 years old or younger (47%) or 16 to 17 years old (34%). Of those incidences where the reason was known, most (57%) were missing for benign reasons (such as the child's forgetting the time or misunderstandings between parents and children about when the latter would return or where they would be). The next largest group (28%) involved children who had been injured while they were away from home. Nearly all of these children had returned within 24 hours.

Chapter 39

What to Do If Your Child Is Missing

Introduction

When your child is missing, your whole world seems to fall apart. You are bombarded by questions from friends, neighbors, the police, and the media and forced to make decisions that you never thought you would have to make. You feel desperate, confused, isolated. You may feel that you have nowhere to go for help or support.

Many parents who have faced similar crises have said that they wished they had a book to tell them where to turn when their child was missing. They felt that they were left on their own to figure out what to do. They longed for someone to give them direction or to tell them where to go for help and what needs to be done. They also wished they had known what to expect and how to respond.

The information contained in this chapter represents the shared knowledge and collective experiences of families who have faced similar situations in their lives. However, it is important to note that there is no right or wrong way to respond to the disappearance of a child, nor is there a right or wrong way to feel. The path you follow must be right for you. What makes sense for you will be based on your needs, your experiences, and your circumstances. Our hope is that this chapter will help you to make informed decisions about what you do and how you go about it.

Excercepted from "When Your Child Is Missing: A Family Survival Guide," by the National Center for Juvenile Justice, 1998. http://ojjdp.ncjrs.org/pubs/childismissing/contents.html.

You may find that the information in this chapter is overwhelming right now. If so, ask family members, friends, or other support persons to read it for you. They can help you take the steps needed to help recover your missing child.

Finally, as hard as it may seem, try to remain hopeful. Remember that hope is more than a wish, helping you to clear this hurdle. Hope is essential to your survival.

Checklist: What You Should Do When Your Child Is First Missing

The first 48 hours following the disappearance of a child are the most critical in terms of finding and returning that child safely home—but they also can be the most troublesome and chaotic. Use this checklist during those first hours to help you do everything you can to increase the chances of recovering your child—but if more than 48 hours have passed since your child disappeared, you should still try to tend to these items as quickly as possible. All of the action steps described here are covered in greater detail later in the chapter to help you gain a better understanding of what you should be doing and why.

The First 24 Hours

- Immediately report your child as missing to your local law enforcement agency. Ask investigators to enter your child into the National Crime Information Center (NCIC) Missing Persons File. There is no waiting period for entry into NCIC for children under age 18.

- Request that law enforcement put out a Be on the Look out (BOLO) bulletin. Ask them about involving the Federal Bureau of Investigation (FBI) in the search for your child.

- Limit access to your home until law enforcement arrives and has collected possible evidence. Do not touch or remove anything from your child's room or from your home. Remember that clothing, sheets, personal items, computers, and even trash may hold clues to the whereabouts of your child. The section "Checklist: Gathering Evidence in the First 48 Hours," included later in this chapter, contains detailed information about securing your child's room and preserving evidence.

- Ask for the name and telephone number of the law enforcement investigator assigned to your case, and keep this information in a safe and convenient place.

- Give law enforcement investigators all the facts and circumstances related to the disappearance of your child, including what efforts have already been made to search for your child.

- Write a detailed description of the clothing worn by your child and the personal items he or she had at the time of the disappearance. Include in your description any personal identification marks, such as birthmarks, scars, tattoos, or mannerisms that may help in finding your child. If possible, find a picture of your child that shows these identification marks and give it to law enforcement.

- Make a list of friends, acquaintances, and anyone else who might have information or clues about your child's whereabouts. Include telephone numbers and addresses, if possible. Tell your law enforcement investigator about anyone who moved in or out of the neighborhood within the past year, anyone whose interest in or involvement with the family changed in recent months, and anyone who appeared to be overly interested in your child.

- Find recent photographs of your child in both black and white and color. Make copies of these pictures for your law enforcement agency, the media, your State missing children's clearinghouse, the National Center for Missing and Exploited Children (NCMEC), and other nonprofit organizations.

- Call NCMEC at 800-THE-LOST (800-843-5678) to ask for help with photo distribution. Also, ask for the telephone numbers of other nonprofit organizations that might be able to help.

- Then, call your clearinghouse to find out what resources and services it can provide in the search for your child.

- Ask your law enforcement agency to organize a search for your child. Ask them about using tracking or trailing dogs (preferably bloodhounds) in the search effort.

- Ask your law enforcement agency for help in contacting the media.

- Designate one person to answer your telephone. Keep a notebook or pad of paper by the telephone so this person can jot down names, telephone numbers, dates and times of calls, and other information relating to each call.

- Keep a notebook or pad of paper with you at all times to write down your thoughts or questions and record important information, such as names, dates, or telephone numbers.

- Take good care of yourself and your family, because your child needs you to be strong. As hard as it may be, force yourself to get rest, eat nourishing food, and talk to someone about your tumultuous feelings.

The Second 24 Hours

- Talk with your law enforcement investigator about the steps that are being taken to find your child. If your law enforcement investigator does not have a copy of "Missing and Abducted Children: A Law Enforcement Guide to Case Investigation and Program Management," suggest that he or she call NCMEC at 800-THE-LOST (800-843-5678) to obtain one. Also, your law enforcement investigator can contact the Crimes Against Children Coordinator in the local FBI Field Office to obtain a copy of the FBI's Child Abduction Response Plan.

- Expand your list of friends, acquaintances, extended family members, yard workers, delivery persons, and anyone who may have seen your child during or following the abduction.

- Look at personal calendars, community events calendars, and newspapers to see if there are any clues as to who was in the vicinity and might be the abductor or a possible witness. Give this information to law enforcement.

- Expect that you will be asked to take a polygraph test, which is standard procedure.

- Ask your law enforcement agency to request that NCMEC issue a broadcast fax to law enforcement agencies around the country.

- Work with your law enforcement agency to schedule press releases and media events. If necessary, ask someone close to you to serve as your media spokesperson.

- Talk to your law enforcement agency about the use of a reward.

- Report all extortion attempts to law enforcement.

- Have a second telephone line installed with call forwarding. Get caller ID and call waiting. Ask law enforcement to install a trap-and-trace feature on your phone. Get a cellular phone or pager so you can be reached when you are away from home.

- Take care of yourself. Don't be afraid to ask others to take care of your physical and emotional needs and those of your family.

- Make a list of things that volunteers can do for you and your family.

- Call your child's doctor and dentist and ask for copies of medical records and x-rays. Give them to law enforcement.

Key Points

1. The actions of parents and of law enforcement in the first 48 hours are critical to the safe recovery of a missing child, but the rawness of emotion can seriously hinder the ability of parents to make rational decisions at this crucial time.

2. Your initial role in the search is to provide information to and answer questions from investigators and to be at home in the event your child calls.

3. Most of the initial searching of the area where the child is believed to have been last will be coordinated by law enforcement—either Federal, State, or local, depending on the circumstances of the disappearance.

4. An important aspect of law enforcement's job is to preserve and protect any evidence gathered during the search.

5. Keep the name and telephone number of your law enforcement coordinator in a safe, convenient place. Keep the lines of communication open between you and your search coordinator by asking questions, making suggestions, and airing differences of opinion.

6. Bloodhounds are the best choice for use in a search, because they have 60 times the tracking power of German shepherds,

can discriminate among scents, and can follow your child's scent in the air as well as on the ground—which means that they may be able to follow your child's scent even if he or she was carried in someone's arms or in a vehicle.

7. Established groups-rather than individual volunteers—should be recruited for the search, because they can gather together a large cadre of people very quickly, they have an inner chain of command that makes communication and training easier, and they have an internal screening mechanism that will help ensure volunteers' soundness of character.

8. The volunteer staging area should be located away from your home to protect your family from the accompanying traffic and chaos.

9. All volunteer searchers reporting for duty should be required to show their driver's licenses and to list in a log book their names, addresses, and organizational affiliations. If possible, law enforcement should run background checks on volunteers to guard against the involvement of misguided individuals.

10. Not all parents can or will want to be actively involved in the long-term search for a child. If you want to stay involved, develop a plan and set up a timetable with goals for continuing the search for your child, and set up a schedule of regular visits with your investigator to review the status of your child's case.

11. Keep the public aware of your plight by publicizing any new information about your child—such as a sighting or an interesting lead. Also, if your child has been missing for several years, ask NCMEC to develop an age-progressed picture, then place this picture next to the original picture on shirts, buttons, and posters.

12. Reread your notebook or journal periodically in case you find a passage that triggers a new idea or reminds you of something you had previously forgotten.

13. Consider hiring a private detective only if you are convinced that he or she can do something better than what is being done by law enforcement. Always ask for and check references to find out if the investigator is legitimate, make sure the

detective has experience working with law enforcement, insist that all expenses be itemized, and report to law enforcement any offers to bring your child back immediately for a specific sum of money.

14. Be extremely cautious before you allow a psychic to become involved in your child's case. Give all psychic leads to law enforcement for thorough investigation.

Checklist: Gathering Evidence in the First 48 Hours

One of the most critical aspects in the search for a missing child is the gathering of evidence that may hold clues about a child's disappearance or whereabouts. The mishandling of evidence can adversely affect an investigation. Similarly, the collection and preservation of evidence are key to finding a missing child. Parents play a vital role in finding a missing child by providing critical information to law enforcement, by protecting evidence in and around the home, and by gathering information about persons or situations that might hold clues. The following are some tips on what you should do to help law enforcement conduct a thorough and complete investigation.

- Secure your child's room. Even though your child may have disappeared from outside the home, your child's room should be searched thoroughly by law enforcement for clues and evidence. Don't clean the child's room, wash your child's clothes, or pick up your house. Don't allow well meaning family members or friends to disturb anything. Even a trash bin or a computer may contain clues that lead to the recovery of the child.

- Do not touch or remove anything from your child's room or from your home that might have your child's fingerprints, DNA, or scent on it. This includes your child's hairbrush, bed linens, worn clothing, pencil with bite marks, diary, or address book. With a good set of fingerprints or a sample of DNA from hair, law enforcement may be able to tell whether your child has been in a particular car or house. With good scent material, tracking dogs may be able to find your child.

- Do not allow anyone else to sleep in your child's bed, play with his or her toys, or use his or her bedroom for any purpose. Law enforcement dispatch should advise you not to disturb any part of the house until a thorough search of the scene has been conducted. Investigators should let you know when their search is complete.

• Be prepared to give investigators all the facts and circumstances related to the disappearance of your child. This includes knowing where your child was last seen, where your child normally went to play, what your child was wearing, and what personal possessions your child had with him or her.

• Describe in detail the clothing your child was wearing and any personal items in the child's possession at the time of the disappearance. Specify color, brand, and size. If possible, have someone obtain replicas of clothing, hats, purses, backpacks, or other items your child had or wore at the time of the disappearance. Give these articles to law enforcement for them to release to the media and to show to searchers. Make sure you mark these items as duplicates or replicas.

• Make a list of personal identification marks and specific personality traits. Describe birthmarks, scars, tattoos, missing teeth, eyeglasses, contacts, speech patterns, and behavioral traits. If possible, find photographs that show these unique features. If you have fingerprints of your child or a DNA blood sample, also give these to law enforcement.

• Gather together personal items, such as baby teeth, old baseball caps, or old toothbrushes. These items may contain hair or blood samples that may be useful as DNA evidence. Also look for pencils or toys that contain impressions of your child's teeth.

• Think about your child's behavior and routine. Be prepared to discuss where your child played or hung out, what was the usual route taken to and from school, and what other paths of travel might have been taken. Be specific about what your child did for recreation, including playing outdoors, surfing the Internet, and other activities.

• Try to remember any changes in your child's routine or any new experiences. Look at personal and family calendars to see if they contain clues as to your child's whereabouts or the identity of the abductor. For example, during the past year, did your child join a soccer team, change teams, or get a new coach? Did your child start playing or hanging out in a different area? Did your child keep a diary that might hold clues?

- Try to remember if your child mentioned any new friends. Talk with your child's friends and teachers to see if they know of any new friends or other contacts your child recently made.

- Find recent photographs of your child in both color and black and white, then have someone make multiple copies of the photographs and keep the originals in a safe place. Check your cameras for undeveloped film, because the most recent photos of your child may be found there. Ask family members and friends to do the same. Give law enforcement multiple photos showing different poses. Steer away from formal or posed photos that do not look like your child. Being careful not to damage the photo, marks the back of each picture with your child's name, address, date of birth, and age when the picture was taken.

- Find videotapes or movies of your child and make copies. Also ask family members and friends if they have videotapes or movies of your child, perhaps at birthday parties, soccer games, and so forth. Give law enforcement copies that show your child's expressions and mannerisms.

- Make a list of family members, friends, acquaintances, coaches, teachers, and other school staff. Write down as many telephone numbers and addresses as you can. Offer information for prior in-laws and relatives as well. Include on your list anyone you feel might have something against you or your family.

- Make a list of everyone who routinely comes to your home. Your list should include postal workers, meter readers, garbage collectors, repair persons, salespeople, pizza delivery persons, and so forth.

- Make a list of new, different, or unusual people or circumstances in and around your home or school within the past year. Think about if you or any of your neighbors had any home remodeling or house repairs done within the past year. Were any houses listed for sale in your neighborhood in the past year? Has there been any road construction or building in the area? Have any traveling carnivals passed through the area?

- Ask your child's doctor and dentist for copies of the child's medical and dental records and x-rays. Give copies of all medical and dental records to law enforcement for use in the investigation.

Law Enforcement

Few parents have had experience working with law enforcement agencies. Perhaps you have had contact previously with law enforcement as a result of a traffic ticket or an accident. If so, you probably saw law enforcement as the enforcer of rules that had been broken-not as a lifeline.

But when your child is missing, you and law enforcement become partners pursuing a common goal-finding your lost or abducted child. As partners, you need to establish a relationship that is based on mutual respect, trust, and honesty. As partners, however, you do not have to agree on every detail. This section provides insight into the relationship you are entering into with law enforcement—what you can expect from the investigation, what types of questions you are likely to be asked, and what situations you and your family are likely to encounter in the process.

Your Partnership with Law Enforcement

Most people do not believe that they will be victims of crime, or that their children will be victimized. But if a young member of your family becomes a victim, you will likely wonder what law enforcement expects of you and what you can expect of law enforcement. Understanding these expectations will deepen your knowledge of law enforcement's role, establish a sound basis for your relationship with the agencies and organizations that are there to help, and assist you in handling this all-too-sudden change in circumstances.

Make sure law enforcement understands that your child is in danger and that his or her absence is likely to be involuntary. If your child is 10 years old or younger, it will not be hard to show that your child is in danger. However, if your child is older than 10, it is important to let law enforcement know that your child's absence is not normal behavior and that you would be surprised if your child had disappeared voluntarily.

Check to see if any money, clothing (other than what your child was wearing), or other personal items are missing. If nothing else is missing, be sure law enforcement is aware of this.

Let law enforcement know how your child is doing in school, and if your child has quarreled recently with you or a friend. If you can establish that there is nothing to indicate that your child ran away, it will expedite law enforcement's classification of your child as abducted or endangered.

Be honest, complete, and forthcoming in your statements and answers to law enforcement. Fully disclose all recent activities of and conversations with your child. What may seem insignificant to you may be important to an investigator.

Be prepared for hard, repetitious questions from investigators. As difficult as it may be, try not to respond in a hostile manner to questions that seem personal or offensive. The fact is that investigators must ask difficult and sensitive questions if they are to do their jobs effectively.

Don't feel guilty about relaying suspicions concerning someone you know. It is not often that a total stranger takes a child. You may not want to believe that it is someone that you know, but keep an open mind and consider all the possibilities. Above all else, trust your feelings, instincts, and gut reactions and share them with law enforcement so they can be checked out.

Do everything possible to get you and your family removed from the suspect list. As painful as it may be, accept the fact that a large number of children are harmed by members of their own families, and therefore you and your family will be considered suspects until you are cleared. To help law enforcement move on to other suspects, volunteer early to take a polygraph test. Insist that both parents be tested at the same time by different interviewers, or one after another. This will help to deflect media speculation that one of you was involved in the disappearance.

Insist that everyone close to your child be interviewed. Encourage everyone—including family members, friends, neighbors, teachers, and coaches—to cooperate in the investigatory process. Although polygraph testing is voluntary, refusal to take a polygraph can cause law enforcement to spend time trying to eliminate an individual from the suspect list through other means and, as a result, take valuable time away from finding the real suspect.

Leave the interviewing of your other children to law enforcement. Do not question your children yourself. Especially with younger children, insist that a law enforcement officer who is trained to interview children conduct the questioning. Many law enforcement agencies have a child abuse unit with officers who are specially trained to work with children.

You can also ask to have a child advocate sit in on the interview with your child. Child advocates are specially trained volunteers who provide assistance and support to children involved in the legal process. Child advocates are normally housed in the district attorney's office, the court, or the law enforcement agency. Ask law enforcement for information about your local child advocate office. If your child is very young, you may be asked to sit in on the interview. Don't be alarmed, however, if law enforcement prefers to interview your children alone.

Be prepared for constant law enforcement presence in your home. For the protection of you and your family, an officer may be assigned to your home on a 24-hour basis. Although this presence may feel intrusive, welcome the officer, and recognize that this person is there to answer calls and take leads, protect you and other members of your family from potential harm, and provide support. If your law enforcement agency is small, however, it may not have the resources to place an officer in your home 24 hours a day. In those circumstances, it is still reasonable for you to ask for added law enforcement protection in your home.

Talk regularly with your primary law enforcement contact. The officer who responded initially to your call for help may not be your permanent family contact. If there is a good chance that your child has run away, for example, your primary law enforcement contact may work in the missing persons unit. If it is suspected that force was used to abduct your child, your case may be handled by a detective from homicide. Find out who your primary law enforcement contact is and get his or her phone and beeper numbers. Make sure that you find out the name of the backup person to call when your primary law enforcement contact is not available.

Pick a time of day for your contact to call you with information. But realize that there will be days when your investigator has nothing to report. Also, designate one person to serve as the primary law enforcement contact for the family. If your investigator is bombarded with telephone calls from family members and friends, valuable time will be taken away from the investigation.

Make sure investigators know that you expect to hear about significant developments in the case from them, not from the media. The flip side of this is that you must honor law enforcement's request not to disclose some pieces of information to the media. Understand, however, that law enforcement may not be able to tell you everything about the case because full disclosure might jeopardize the investigation.

Satisfy yourself that law enforcement is handling your child's case properly. All of the agencies involved in the investigation should be cooperating with one another in pursuit of one goal-finding your missing child and getting the predator off the street. The more you understand the investigatory process, the better able you will be to ask questions about it.

However, you should be aware that most law enforcement officers do not have firsthand experience working on a missing child case. If your primary contact cannot answer a question, find out who can. Also, if you feel that your child's disappearance has been classified inappropriately, ask to speak to the officer's supervisor or to someone else who may have more experience in these types of cases. Don't take no for an answer if you feel strongly that something else needs to be done.

Finally, learn about the services that are available from NCMEC, from your state's missing children's clearinghouse, and from the television show America's Most Wanted.

Chapter 40

Protect Your Child from Abduction and Exploitation

Preventing Child Abduction

Thousands of children are reported missing every year in America. Some children will be found and returned home. Some will not.

Child abduction is a tragedy that devastates parents and touches all of us. These tips tell you how to keep your children safer.

What to Do

- Know where your children are at all times.

- Never leave children alone in cars.

- Establish strict procedures for picking up children at school, after movies, at friend's homes, etc. Don't let your children accept rides from people with whom you haven't made prior arrangement, even if they say they are police officers, teachers, or friends of the family.

- Teach your children their full names, your full name, address, and telephone number. Teach them how to reach either you or a trusted adult and how to call for police assistance. Make sure they know how to make local and long distance telephone calls.

From, "Preventing Child Abduction," California Governor's Office of Criminal Justice Planning. Downloaded from http://www.ocjp.ca.gov/publications/pub-abdu.pdf, August 2002.

Even small children can learn to dial 9-1-1 or 0 for an operator to get help.

- Tell your children about the abduction problem in a calm and simple way, as if you were teaching any other important coping skill.

- Listen attentively when your children discuss anyone they've encountered in your absence.

- Establish a family code word. Tell your children never to go with anyone who does not know the code word.

- Have photographs taken of your children four times a year (especially for preschoolers). Make note of birthmarks or other distinguishing features. This won't protect you child, but will help to make it easier to identify them whether they are found safe, injured, or deceased.

- Have fingerprints taken of your children. Most law enforcement agencies have child fingerprint programs. Like the previous tip, this won't protect your child, but will help to make it easier to identify them whether they are found safe, injured, or deceased.

Teach Your Children

- Never to leave the yard without your permission. Very small children should play only in the backyard or in a supervised play area.

- Not to wander off, to avoid lonely places, and not to take short-cuts through alleys or deserted areas.

- They are safer walking or playing with friends.

- Always to come straight home from school unless you've made other arrangements.

- Never to enter anyone's home without your prior approval. (Exception: A block parent or safe house.)

- To scream, run away and tell you or a trusted adult if anyone attempts to touch or grab them.

- Not to give any information over the telephone, particularly their name and address, or that they are alone.

- Never to go anywhere with anyone who does not know the family code word.

- To keep all doors locked and admit only authorized people into the house.

The Safe House Program

A safe house is a temporary haven for children who find themselves in emergencies or frightening situations such as being bullied, followed, or hurt while walking in the neighborhood. Individuals who volunteer their homes for a safe house program agree to make emergency phone calls for children in trouble and watch out for neighborhood children going to and from school. A safe house is not a medical-aid station, a restaurant, or a public rest room. The program is not an escort service or a place for long term protection. It is a short-term interaction between an adult helper and a child needing help. It is also an effective way for a community to protect children.

Chapter 41

International Child Abduction

Introduction

Parental child abduction is a tragedy. When a child is abducted across international borders, the difficulties are compounded for everyone involved. This chapter is designed to assist the adult most directly affected by international child abduction, the left-behind parent.

Prevention: How to Guard against International Child Abduction

How Vulnerable Is Your Child?

You and your child are most vulnerable when your relationship with the other parent is troubled or broken, the other parent has close ties to another country, and/or the other country has traditions or laws that may be prejudicial against a parent of your gender or to non-citizens in general. However, anyone can be vulnerable.

Cross-Cultural Marriages: Should You or Your Child Visit the Country of the Other Parent?

Many cases of international parental child abduction are actually cases in which the child traveled to a foreign country with the approval

Excerpted from "International Parental Child Abduction," U.S. Department of State, Pub. No. 10862, http://travel.state.gov/int'lchildabduction.html, revised July 2001.

of both parents, but was later prevented from returning to the United States. Sometimes the marriage is neither broken nor troubled, but the foreign parent, upon returning to his or her country of origin, decides not to return to the U.S. or to allow the child to do so. A person who has assimilated a second culture may find a return to his or her roots disturbing and may feel pulled to shift loyalties back to the original culture. Furthermore, a person's behavior may change when he or she returns to the culture where he or she grew up.

In some societies, children must have their father's permission and a woman must have her husband's permission to travel. If you are a woman, to prevent your own or your child's detention abroad, find out about the laws and traditions of the country you plan to visit or plan to allow your child to visit, and consider carefully the effect that a return to his traditional culture might have on your child's father; in other societies, children need the permission of both parents to travel and the refusal of one parent to give that permission may prevent the departure of a child from that country. For detailed advice in your specific case, you may wish to contact an attorney in your spouse's country of origin. Many U.S. Embassies/Consulates list attorneys on their web-sites, accessible via http://travel.state.gov.

Precautions That Any Parent Should Take

In international parental child abduction, an ounce of prevention is worth a pound of cure. Be alert to the possibility and be prepared:

- Keep a list of the addresses and telephone numbers of the other parent's relatives, friends, and business associates both here and abroad.

- Keep a record of important information about the other parent, including: physical description, passport, social security, bank account, and driver's license numbers; and vehicle description and plate number.

- Keep a written description of your child, including hair and eye color, height, weight, fingerprints, and any special physical characteristics.

- Take full-face color photographs and/or videos of your child every six months—a recent photo of the other parent may also be useful.

If your child should be abducted, this information could be vital in locating your child.

In addition, the National Center for Missing and Exploited Children (NCMEC), suggests that you teach your child to use the telephone, memorize your home phone number, practice making collect calls, and instruct him or her to call home immediately if anything unusual happens. Discuss possible plans of action with your child in the case of abduction. Most important, however, if you feel your child is vulnerable to abduction, seek legal advice. Do not merely tell a friend or relative about your fears.

The Importance of a Custody Decree

Under the laws of the United States and many foreign countries, if there is no decree of custody prior to an abduction, both parents may be considered to have equal legal custody of their child. Even though both parents may have custody of a child, it still may be a crime for one parent to remove the child from the United States against the other parent's wishes. If you are contemplating divorce or separation, or are divorced or separated, or even if you were never legally married to the other parent, ask your attorney, as soon as possible, if you should obtain a decree of sole custody or a decree that prohibits the travel of your child without your permission or that of the court. If you have or would prefer to have a joint custody decree, you may want to make certain that it prohibits your child from traveling abroad without your permission or that of the court.

How to Draft or Modify a Custody Decree

A well-written custody decree is an important line of defense against international parental child abduction. NCMEC, in its publication *Family Abduction: How to Prevent an Abduction and What to Do If Your Child is Abducted*, makes several recommendations to help prevent the abduction of your child if your spouse is a legal permanent resident alien or a U.S. citizen with ties to a foreign country. For instance, it may be advisable to include court-ordered supervised visitation and a statement prohibiting your child from traveling without your permission or that of the court. If the country to which your child might be taken is a member of the Hague Convention on the Civil Aspects of International Child Abduction (Hague Convention), your custody decree should state that the terms of the Hague Convention apply if there is an abduction or wrongful retention. The American Bar Association (ABA) also suggests

351

having the court require the non-citizen parent or the parent with ties to a foreign country to post a bond. This may be useful both as a deterrent to abduction and, if forfeited because of an abduction, as a source of revenue for you in your efforts to locate and recover your child.

Obtain several certified copies of your custody decree from the court that issued it. Give a copy to your child's school and advise school personnel to whom your child may be released.

U.S. Passports

The Department of State's Passport Lookout Program can help you determine if your child has been issued a U.S. passport. You may also ask that your child's name be entered into the State Department's Children's Passport Issuance Alert Program. This will enable the Department to notify you or your attorney if an application for a U.S. passport for the child is received anywhere in the United States or at any U.S. embassy or consulate abroad. If you have a court order that either grants you sole custody, joint legal custody, or prohibits your child from traveling without your permission or the permission of the court, the Department may also refuse to issue a U.S. passport for your child. The Department may not, however, revoke a passport that has already been issued to the child. There is also no way to track the use of a passport once it has been issued, since there are no exit controls of people leaving the U.S.

To inquire about a U.S. passport or to have your child's name entered into the passport alert program, complete the request form found at http://travel.state.gov/int'lchildabduction.html and mail or fax it to:

Office of Children's Issues
Children's Passport Issuance Alert Program (CPIAP)
2401 E Street, N.W., Room L127
Washington, D.C. 20522
Phone: 202-736-7000
Fax: 202-312-9743

Change in Passport Regulations

A new law, which took effect in July 2001, requires the signature of both parents prior to issuance of a U.S. passport to children under the age of 14.

Requirements

Both parents, or the child's legal guardians, must execute the child's passport application and provide documentary evidence demonstrating that they are the parents or guardians; or the person executing the application must provide documentary evidence that such person has sole custody of the child; has the consent of the other parent to the issuance of the passport; or is acting in place of the parents and has the consent of both parents, of a parent with sole custody over the child, or of the child's legal guardian, to the issuance of the passport.

Exceptions

The law does provide two exceptions to this requirement: (1) for exigent circumstances, such as those involving the health or welfare of he child, or (2) when the Secretary of State determines that issuance of a passport is warranted by special family circumstances. For additional information, see the Bureau of Consular Affairs home page on the Internet at http://travel.state.gov.

Foreign Passports — the Problem of Dual Nationality

Many United States citizen children who fall victim to international parental abduction possess, or may have a claim to dual nationality. While the Department of State will make every effort to avoid issuing a United States passport if the custodial parent has provided a custody decree, the Department cannot prevent embassies and consulates of other countries in the United States from issuing their passports to children who are also their nationals. You can, however, ask a foreign embassy or consulate not to issue a passport to your child. Send the embassy or consulate a written request, along with certified complete copies of any court orders you have which address custody or the overseas travel of your child. In your letter, inform them that you are sending a copy of this request to the United States Department of State. If your child is only a United States citizen, you can request that no visa for that country be issued in his or her United States passport. No international law requires compliance with such requests, but some countries may comply voluntarily.

The United States government does not have exit controls at the border. There is no way to stop someone with valid travel documents at the United States border. The U.S. government does not check the names or the documents of travelers leaving the United States. Many foreign countries do not require a passport for entry. A birth certificate is sufficient to enter some foreign countries. If your child has a valid passport from any country, he or she may be able to travel outside the United States without your consent.

What the State Department Can and Cannot Do When a Child Is Abducted Abroad

When a United States citizen child is abducted abroad, the State Department's Office of Children's Issues (CA/OCS/CI) works with United States embassies and consulates abroad to assist the child and left-behind parent in a number of ways. Despite the fact that children are taken across international borders, child custody disputes remain fundamentally civil legal matters between the parents involved, over which the Department of State has no jurisdiction. If a child custody dispute cannot be settled amicably between the parties, it often must be resolved by judicial proceedings in the country where the child is located.

What the State Department Can Do

- Act as the primary point of contact for left-behind parents.

- Act as a liaison with federal and state agencies, including law enforcement officials.

- In cases where the Hague Convention on the Civil Aspects of International Child Abduction applies, assist parents in filing an application with foreign authorities for return of or access to the child.

- Attempt to locate, visit, and report on the child's general welfare.

- Provide the left-behind parent with information on the country to which the child was abducted, including its legal system, custody laws, and a list of local attorneys willing to accept American clients.

- Inquire as to the status of judicial or administrative proceedings overseas.

- Assist parents in contacting local officials in foreign countries or contact them on the parent's behalf.

- Provide information concerning how federal warrants against an abducting parent, passport revocation, and extradition from a foreign country may affect return of a child to the United States.

- Alert foreign authorities to any evidence of child abuse or neglect.

- If the child is in the Children's Passport Issuance Alert Program, contact the left-behind parent when application is made for a new U.S. passport for the child.

What the State Department Cannot Do

- Intervene in civil legal matters between the parents.

- Enforce an American custody agreement overseas (United States custody decrees are not automatically enforceable outside of United States boundaries).

- Force another country to decide a custody case or enforce its laws in a particular way.

- Assist the left-behind parent in violating foreign laws or re-abducting the child to the United States.

- Pay legal or other expenses.

- Act as a lawyer, give legal advice, or represent parents in court.

- Take custody of the child.

- Revoke the child's passport.

How to Search for a Child Abducted Abroad

Where to Report Your Missing Child

1. If your child is missing or has been abducted, file a missing person report with your local police department and request that your child's name and description be entered into the "missing person" section of the National Crime Information Center (NCIC) computer. This is provided for under the National Child Search Act of 1990. The abductor does not have to be charged with a crime when you file a missing person report. It is not always a good idea to file criminal charges against the abducting parent at the same time you file a missing person

report, although local law enforcement authorities may urge you to do so. In addition, through INTERPOL, the international police organization, your local police can request that a search for your child be conducted by the police in the country where you believe your child may have been taken. If your local law enforcement is unaware of the legal requirements for immediate entry into NCIC please contact the Office of Children's Issues at 202-736-7000.

2. Contact the National Center for Missing and Exploited Children (NCMEC) at 1-800-THE LOST/1-800-843-5678. With the searching parent's permission, the child's photograph and description may be circulated to the media in the country to which you believe the child may have been taken.

3. Request information about a possible United States passport and have your child's name entered into the United States Children's Passport Issuance Alert Program. A United States passport for a child under 16 years expires after 5 years. If you do not know where your child is, but information about the child is in the name check system, it may be possible to locate him or her through the passport application process. All United States passport agencies and United States embassies and consulates are on-line with the name check system.

After Your Child Is Located

A consular officer overseas, working with this information, will try to confirm the location of your child. If the consular officer is unable to find the child based on the information provided, he or she may also request information from local officials on your child's entry or residence in the country. Please note, however, that most countries do not maintain such records in a retrievable form, and some countries will not release such information.

The Department of State may also ask you for photographs of both your child and the abducting parent because these are often helpful to foreign authorities trying to find a missing child.

The Department of State, when requested to do so, may conduct visits to determine the welfare and whereabouts of American citizens abroad. The Office of Children's Issues communicates such requests to the United States embassy or consulate responsible for the area to which you believe your child has been abducted. A welfare and whereabouts visit cannot be conducted if the abducting parent refuses access.

Further Steps to Take in Your Search

It is possible that none of the institutions mentioned (the police, the NCMEC, or the Department of State) will succeed in locating your child right away and you will need to carry on the search on your own. As you search, you should, however, keep these institutions informed of your actions and progress.

- One of the best ways to find your child overseas is through establishing friendly contact with relatives and friends of the other parent, either here or abroad. You may have more influence with such persons than you suspect, and their interest in your child's welfare may lead them to cooperate with you.

- The United States Department of Health and Human Services, Office of Child Support Enforcement maintains the Federal Parent Locator Service (FPLS). The primary purpose of this service is to locate parents who are delinquent in child support payments, but the service will also search for parental abductors when requested to do so by an authorized person. Generally speaking, an authorized person is a state court judge, police officer, prosecutor, or other state official seeking to enforce a child custody order. Please ask your local law enforcement to request a search. To learn how to access the services of the FPLS, contact your local or state Child Support Enforcement office. These offices are listed under government listings in your telephone directory.

- You can contact the principal of the school to obtain information on requests that may have been made by the abductor to your child's school for the transfer of your child's records.

- You can find out from the National Center for Missing and Exploited Children how to prepare a poster on your child. A poster may assist foreign authorities in attempting to locate your child.

- You can ask your district attorney to contact the United States Postal Inspection Service to see if a "mail cover" can be put on any address that you know of in the United States to which the abductor might write.

- It may be possible for local law enforcement authorities to obtain, by subpoena or search warrant, credit card records that may show where the abductor is making purchases. Check with state and local authorities if anything can be done. In the same manner, you can try to obtain copies of telephone bills of the abductor's friends or relatives who may have received collect calls from the abductor. Law enforcement may also be able to track usage of a cell phone or e-mail the abductor may be sending.

The Best Solution: Settling out of Court

Promoting Communication between Parents and Children

Legal procedures can be long and expensive. You may have greater success negotiating with the abducting parent. In some cases, friends or relatives of the abductor may be able to help you reach a compromise with the abductor. A decrease in tension might bring about the return of your child, but, even if it does not, it can increase your chances of being able to visit the child and participate in some way in the child's upbringing. In some cases compromise and some kind of reconciliation are the only realistic option.

Obtaining Information on Your Child's Welfare

If you know your child's location and your child is a United States citizen you can request that a United States consular officer attempt to visit your child. If the consul obtains the other parent's permission to visit the child, he or she will do so and report back to you about your child. Sometimes consular officers are also able to send you letters or photos from your child. Contact the Office of Children's Issues (CA/OCS/CI) at 202-736-7000 to request such a visit.

Working with Foreign Authorities

In child abduction cases, consular officers routinely maintain contact with local child welfare and law enforcement officers. If there is evidence of abuse or neglect of the child, the United States embassy or consulate may request that local authorities become involved.

The Question of Desperate Measures/Re-Abduction

Consular officers cannot take possession of a child abducted by a parent or aid parents attempting to act in violation of the laws of a foreign country. Consular officers must act in accordance with the laws of the country to which they are accredited. The Department of State strongly discourages taking desperate and possibly illegal measures to return your child to the United States. Attempts to use self-help measures to bring an abducted child to the United States from a foreign country may endanger your child and others, prejudice any future judicial efforts you might wish to make in that country to stabilize the situation, and could result in your arrest and imprisonment in that country. In imposing a sentence, the foreign court will not necessarily give weight to the fact that the would-be abductor was the custodial parent in the United States or otherwise had a valid claim under a United States court order (e.g., failure of the foreign parent to honor the terms of a joint custody order). Should you be arrested, the United States Embassy will not be able to secure your release.

If you do succeed in leaving the foreign country with your child, you and anyone who assisted you may be the target of arrest warrants and extradition requests in the United States or any other country where you are found. Even if you are not ultimately extradited and prosecuted, an arrest followed by extradition proceedings can be very disruptive and disturbing for both you and your child.

Finally, there is no guarantee that the chain of abductions would end with the one committed by you. A parent who has re-abducted a child may have to go to extraordinary lengths to conceal his or her whereabouts, living in permanent fear that the child may be re-abducted again. Please consider how this might affect the child.

If you are contemplating such desperate measures, you should read the information available from the National Center for Missing and Exploited Children (NCMEC) about the emotional trauma inflicted on a child who is a victim of abduction and re-abduction. The NCMEC advises against re-abduction not only because it is illegal, but also because of possible psychological harm to the child.

One Possible Solution: The Hague Convention

One of the most difficult and frustrating elements for a parent of a child abducted abroad is that United States laws and court orders are not automatically recognized abroad and therefore are not directly enforceable abroad. Each country has jurisdiction within its own territory and over people present within its borders. No country can tell another country how to decide cases or enforce laws. Just as foreign court orders are not automatically enforceable in the United States, United States court orders are not automatically enforceable abroad.

At the Hague Conference on Private International Law in 1976, 23 nations agreed to draft a treaty to deter international child abduction. Between 1976 and 1980, the United States was a major force in preparing and negotiating the Hague Convention on the Civil Aspects of International Child Abduction (Hague Convention or the Convention). The Convention was incorporated into U.S. law and came into force for the United States on July 1, 1988. As of July 2001, the Convention is in force between the United States and 50 other countries. The Convention applies to wrongful removals or retentions that occurred on or after the date the treaty came into force between those two countries. The dates vary for each country and more countries are considering signing on to the Convention all the time. Check the most recent list prepared by the Office of Children's Issues to learn whether the Convention was in force in a particular county at the time of the wrongful removal or retention. You can find the list on the Department of State web site, http://travel.state.gov.

What Is Covered by the Convention

The Hague Convention is a civil legal mechanism available to parents seeking the return of, or access to, their child. As a civil law mechanism, the parents, not the governments, are parties to the legal action.

The countries that are party to the Convention have agreed that a child who is habitually resident in one party country, and who has been removed to or retained in another party country in violation of the left-behind parent's custodial rights, shall be promptly returned to the country of habitual residence. The Convention can also help parents exercise visitation rights abroad.

There is a treaty obligation to return an abducted child below the age of 16 if application is made within one year from the date of the wrongful removal or retention, unless one of the exceptions to return apply. If the application for return is made after one year, the court may use its discretion to decide that the child has become resettled in his or her new country and refuse return of the child. In any case, a court may refuse to order a child returned if any of the following conditions apply (note: interpretation of these exceptions varies from country to country):

- A grave risk that the child would be exposed to physical or psychological harm or otherwise placed in an intolerable situation in his or her country of habitual residence.

- If the child objects to being returned and has reached an age and degree of maturity at which the court can take account of the child's views (the treaty does not establish at what age children reach this level of maturity: that age and the degree of weight given to children's views varies from country to country).

- If the return would violate the fundamental principles of human rights and freedoms of the country where the child is being held.

How to Use the Hague Convention

The Convention provides a legal mechanism for you to seek return of your child or exercise your visitation rights. You do not need to have a custody decree to use the Convention. However, to apply for the return of your child, you must have had and been actually exercising a "right of custody" at the time of the abduction, and you must not have given permission for the child to be removed, or, in the case of a retention, to be retained beyond a specified, agreed-upon period of time. The Convention defines "rights of custody" as including "rights relating to the care of the person of the child and, in particular, the right to determine the child's place of residence." This right need not be sole custody. If there was no court order in effect at the date of the abduction, these "rights of custody" may be established by the law in the state in which your child was living before his or her removal. In some cases it may be advisable to get a determination in your local court that 1) you have a right of custody to your child, and 2) the removal or retention was wrongful. Use of the Convention is not restricted to U.S. citizens.

An application should be submitted as soon as possible after an abduction or wrongful retention has taken place. As stated above, there is a time factor of one year involved. Do not wait until you get a custody order. That order would be irrelevant anyway. Copies of the application form can be found at http://travel.state.gov/int'lchildabduction.html.

Each country that is party to the Convention has designated a Central Authority to carry out specialized duties under the Convention. The Central Authority for the United States is the Department of State's Office of Children's Issues (CA/OCS/CI). You may submit your application directly to the Central Authority or foreign court of the country where the child is believed to be held, but, in order to ensure that you receive all available assistance it is best to submit your application to the U.S. Central Authority.

Chapter 42

What Is Parental Abduction?

Richie was only four when his non-custodial father abducted him. When he was located a year later, his vocabulary had diminished and he was suffering from a fungal skin condition caused by a lack of hygiene. The boy screamed in terror at the sight of his mother because he had been told she had abandoned him.

Richie and his mother are two of the victims of the estimated 354,100 parental abductions that take place in the United States each year.

Conducted in 1988, National Incidence Studies of Missing, Abducted, Runaway, and Thrownaway Children (NISMART) estimated that 3,200 to 4,600 nonfamily abductions involved coercion, detention of the child for more than one hour, or the luring of the child for the purpose of committing another crime. Of the 354,100 family abductions

Excerpted from Ronald Laney, "Parental Kidnaping," Office of Juvenile Justice and Delinquency Prevention (OJJDP), fact sheet #34, http://www.ncjrs.org/txtfiles/fs-9534.txt, 1995. Regarding the data presented here from the first National Incidence Studies of Missing, Abducted, Runaway, and Thrownaway Children (NISMART 1), which was published in 1990: It provided the first nationally representative, comprehensive estimates of the incidence of missing children. Although information from the second Comprehensive Study of Missing Children (NISMART 2) is expected to be available soon, it was not available when the *Child and Youth Security Sourcebook* was being published. When information from NISMART 2 is available to the public it will be accessible at the National Criminal Justice Service website, http://www.ncjrs.org. NISMART 1 is still valuable to readers seeking information about national statistical trends of missing children in the U.S.

that NISMART estimated took place that year, 163,200 involved concealment, interstate transportation of the child, or evidence the abductor intended to alter custodial privileges permanently.

Impact

Recent research suggests that children endure adverse consequences from being abducted. Besides emotional turmoil, children may suffer from inadequate schooling, poor nutrition, unstable lifestyles, and neglect. Some are abandoned, only to be discovered living in foster homes. In the most egregious cases, children suffer long-term harm that may leave them scarred for life.

Faced with the demands of rising violent crime and dwindling budget resources, law enforcement agencies are hard-pressed to make parental abductions a priority. The belief that a child is safe with a parent lessens the chance of aggressive investigation by law enforcement. Yet one study reported 49 percent of abductors have previously established criminal histories and 75 percent of abducting fathers have a history of violent behavior.

Research reveals diverse motivations when a parent kidnaps children in violation of custody or visitation rights. Children are often used as pawns in contentious divorces in a parental game of one-upmanship. Some abductors kidnap children as an extension of battering, seeking to control their spouse by depriving them of visitation or custodial rights. One of the most difficult claims for police and prosecutors to investigate is the allegation that domestic violence or abuse motivates the abduction. Abductors may flee to avoid further abuse to themselves or children, or the abuser may abduct in an attempt to intimidate a battered parent who is attempting to leave the relationship.

Strategies

The National Center for Missing and Exploited Children (NCMEC) recommends that law enforcement officers investigate allegations of abuse and parental kidnaping separately and comprehensively. To neglect one charge in favor of the other places children at risk. NCMEC's *Missing and Abducted Children: A Law Enforcement Guide to Case Investigation and Program Management* contains an investigative checklist and a complete discussion of issues associated with parental abduction investigations. In cases where no civil custodial determinations are in place, NCMEC recommends that investigating officers, at a minimum, enter the child into the FBI's National Crime Information Center (NCIC) Missing Person File. Once a State or local court establishes custody, investigators may proceed with a criminal investigation as appropriate.

Recognizing the possibility of custody violations when one parent flees domestic violence, the National Council of Juvenile and Family Court Judges' Family Violence Project recommends the following four steps to law enforcement and prosecutors:

1. Issue a warrant for the fleeing parent.

2. Ensure that there is an adequate investigation of the potential impact of family violence on the flight.

3. Maintain existing child custody orders until such investigation is complete.

4. Initiate orders to protect the children until final resolution.

Federal Response

The Parental Kidnaping Prevention Act (PKPA) authorizes the issuance of federal warrants for unlawful flight to avoid prosecution in parental abduction cases. The PKPA also provides access to authorized persons, including law enforcement officers, to the Federal Parent Locator Service. This service, which searches such Federal agency databases as Social Security Administration, Internal Revenue Service, and State Employment Agencies, can help find abducting parents.

The PKPA authorizes the Federal Bureau of Investigation to investigate parental kidnaping cases when an unlawful flight to avoid prosecution (UFAP) warrant has been issued. FBI investigation of parental abduction cases that cross state boundaries can be crucial to the resolution of these crimes.

The Office of Juvenile Justice and Delinquency Prevention (OJJDP) has established a partnership with NCMEC. Established in 1984, NCMEC provides lead information, case management, photo distribution, age progression, publications, and technical assistance to law enforcement, prosecutors, parents, and other interested parties. NCMEC maintains a toll-free hotline and works closely with local law enforcement and state clearinghouses to prevent abductions, find abducted children, and facilitate their return to the custodial parent.

Chapter 43

Preventing Parental Abduction

Introduction

"You'll never see your child again!" When are these words an idle threat spoken in anger and frustration and when are they a warning that a parent intends to abduct his or her child, depriving the child and the other parent of future contact?

Although custody laws vary from state to state, abducting one's own child is a crime in every state. If a parent or other family member takes, hides, or keeps a child away from a parent with custody or visitation rights, then he or she may have committed a crime. More important, a child often is harmed by life on the run and by being deprived of his or her other parent. Prior to abduction, many of these children have been exposed to neglectful and abusive behaviors in their homes and have witnessed high levels of conflict between their parents. These children are at risk for psychological harm.

The U.S. Department of Justice, Office of Juvenile Justice and Delinquency Prevention, funded a research study on prevention of family abduction through early identification of risk factors to answer the following questions:

- What type of parent abducts his or her child?

Excerpted from "Early Identification of Risk Factors for Parental Abduction," Office of Juvenile Justice and Delinquency Prevention (OJJDP), http://www.ncjrs.org/html/ojjdp/2001_3_1/contents.html, March 2001.

- What role does family violence play in increasing the likelihood of abduction?

- How can one identify which child is at risk of being abducted by a parent or other family members?

- What can be done to prevent family abductions and protect the child?

Six descriptive profiles of parents at risk for abducting their children emerged from the findings of the study.

Profiles of Parents at Risk for Abducting Their Children

Profile 1: When There Has Been a Prior Threat of or Actual Abduction

When a parent has made credible threats to abduct a child or has a history of hiding the child, withholding visitation, or snatching the child from the other parent, there is great distrust between the parents and a heightened risk of further custody violation. This risk profile is usually combined with one or more of the other profiles. In these cases, the underlying psychological and social dynamics that motivate the abduction need to be understood and addressed. When other risk factors are present, one or more of the following are general indicators of an imminent threat of flight with the child:

- The parent is unemployed, homeless, and without emotional or financial ties to the area.

- The parent has divulged plans to abduct the child and has the resources or the support of extended family and/or friends and underground dissident networks needed to survive in hiding.

- The parent has liquidated assets, made maximum withdrawals of funds against credit cards, or borrowed money from other sources.

Profile 2: When a Parent Suspects or Believes Abuse Has Occurred and Friends and Family Members Support These Concerns

Many parents abduct their child because they believe that the other parent is abusing, molesting, or neglecting the child. These abducting parents feel that the authorities have not taken them seriously or properly investigated the allegations. Repeated allegations increase the hostility and distrust between the parents. Parents who have the fixed belief that abuse has occurred and will continue to occur then "rescue" the child, often with the help of supporters who concur with their beliefs, justify their actions, and often help with the abduction and concealment. Supporters might include family members, friends, or underground networks (usually women) that help "protective" parents (usually women) obtain new identities and find safe locations.

In a large number of cases, the child has been previously exposed to neglectful, endangering, or violent environments (e.g., domestic violence or substance abuse). In these cases, the courts and child protective services may have failed to protect the child and the concerned parent or family member. They may have trivialized the allegations, dismissing them as invalid or the product of a contentious divorce. Often, however, the allegation of sexual abuse by a father or stepfather that motivates a mother to abduct her child is unsubstantiated. In these cases, the abduction can psychologically harm the child and the other parent, possibly leaving their relationship in serious need of repair.

Profile 3: When a Parent Is Paranoid Delusional

Although only a small percentage of parents fit this profile, these parents present the greatest risk of physical harm or death to the child, regardless of whether an abduction occurs. Parents who fit the paranoid profile hold markedly irrational or psychotic delusions that the other parent will definitely harm them and/or the child. Believing themselves to be betrayed and exploited by their former partner, these parents urgently take what they consider to be necessary measures to protect themselves and the child.

Psychotic parents do not perceive the child as a separate person. Rather, they perceive the child as part of themselves that is, as a victim (in which case they take unilateral measures to rescue the child) or they perceive the child as part of the hated other parent (in which case they may precipitously abandon or even kill the child). Marital separation and/or the instigation of the custody dispute generally triggers an acute phase of danger for these psychotic individuals. The result can be not only parental abduction, but also murder and suicide.

Profile 4: When a Parent Is Severely Sociopathic

Sociopathic parents are characterized by a long history of flagrant violations of the law and contempt for any authority including that of the legal system. Their relationships with other people are self-serving, exploitive, and highly manipulative. These people are also likely to hold exaggerated beliefs about their own superiority and entitlement and are highly gratified by their ability to exert power and control over others. As with paranoid and delusional parents, sociopathic parents are unable to perceive their children as having separate needs or rights. Consequently, they often use their children as instruments of revenge or punishment or as trophies in their fight with the former partner. Sociopathic parents have no qualms about continuing coercive, controlling, and abusive behavior or abducting their child, nor do they believe that they should be punished for their actions. Like paranoia, a diagnosis of severe sociopathy is rare.

Profile 5: When a Parent Who Is a Citizen of Another Country Ends a Mixed-Culture Marriage

Parents who are citizens of another country (or who have dual citizenship with the United States) and have strong ties to their extended family in their country of origin have long been recognized as potential abductors. The risk of abduction is especially acute at the time of parental separation and divorce, when these parents may feel cast adrift from their mixed-culture marriage and may need to return to their ethnic or religious roots to find emotional support and reconstitute a shaken self-identity. Often in reaction to being rendered helpless or feeling rejected and discarded by the former spouse, such parents may try to take unilateral action by returning with the child to their family of origin. This is a way of insisting that the abducting parent's cultural identity be given preeminent status in the child's upbringing.

Profile 6: When Parents Feel Alienated from the Legal System and Have Family/Social Support in Another Community

Many subgroups of potential abductors feel alienated from the judicial system. Listed below are five such subgroups.

- Subgroup 1. Parents who are indigent and poorly educated lack knowledge about custody and abduction laws and cannot afford the legal representation or psychological counseling that would help them resolve their disputes. Those parents who have extended family or other social, emotional, and economic support in another geographical community may be at risk for abducting their children.

- Subgroup 2. Many parents cannot afford and are unaware of the need to access the court system. In addition, those who have had prior negative experiences with civil or criminal courts do not expect family courts to be responsive to their values or their plight.

- Subgroup 3. Parents who belong to certain ethnic, religious, or cultural groups may hold views about child rearing that are contrary to the prevailing custody laws that emphasize gender neutrality and the rights of both parents. These parents instead turn to their own social networks for support and use informal self-help measures rather than the courts in disputes over the children.

- Subgroup 4. A mother who has a transient, unmarried relationship with her child's father often views the child as her property, and her extended family supports this belief. Many of the women in this subgroup assume they have sole custody of their child and are genuinely surprised when they are informed that the father by law in California and most other states has joint rights to the child.

- Subgroup 5. Parents who are victims of domestic violence are at risk of abducting their child, especially when the courts and community have failed to take the necessary steps to protect them from abuse or to hold the abuser accountable. Joint custody, mediated agreements, and visitation orders often leave victims vulnerable to ongoing violence, despite separation from the abuser. When such victims abduct their child, the violent partners may successfully obscure the facts about the abuse and activate the abduction laws to regain control of their victims.

Preventive Interventions for Custody Violation and Parental Abduction

Profile 1: When There Has Been a Prior Threat of or Actual Abduction

- Obtain certified copy of custody/visitation order specifying access and jurisdiction.

- Obtain restraining order that prohibits leaving area without permission.

371

- Flag passports or school, medical, and birth records so that both parents need to approve the release of or at least be advised of the other parent's request to see these materials.

- Supervise visits or use electronic surveillance.

- Require that potential abducting parent post bonds.

- Provide family counseling and mediation of impasse.

Profile 2: When a Parent Suspects or Believes Abuse Has Occurred and Friends and Family Members Support These Concerns

- Undertake a timely, thorough investigation of allegations.

- Inform concerned social network.

- Coordinate all professionals involved to share perspectives and conclusions.

- Implement temporary supervised visits to protect abused child or falsely accused parent. If investigation is inconclusive, appoint co-parenting counselor-arbitrator to provide counseling, rebuild trust, and monitor situation.

- Provide the child with therapy.

Profile 3: When a Parent Is Paranoid Delusional

- Assess lethality!

- Conduct emergency ex parte hearing for psychiatric screening; appoint legal representation for child and deluded parent.

- Suspend visits or supervise with high security.

- Award temporary custody to other parent or to third party.

- Provide adult psychiatric treatment and child therapy.

Profile 4: When a Parent Is Severely Sociopathic

- Have the parent obtain appropriate restraining orders.

- Engage decisive use of court authority; obtain explicit court orders and rapid sanctions for contempt; fine or jail.

- Suspend or supervise access and resume unsupervised visits contingent on conforming behavior.

Profile 5: When a Parent Who Is a Citizen of Another Country Ends a Mixed-Culture Marriage

- See "Profile 1: When There Has Been a Prior Threat of or Actual Abduction."

- Require that parent departing with child post bonds to ensure return from visiting homeland; hold passport and monitor airlines.

- Obtain mirror custody orders with country of origin; inform families of consequences of aiding custody violation.

- Provide culturally sensitive divorce counseling, including child's need for both parents and both cultural identities.

- Provide emotional/financial support.

Profile 6: When Parents Feel Alienated from the Legal System and Have Family/Social Support in Another Community

- Provide access to legal services, *pro se* clinics, and translation assistance.

- Advocate community services.

- Provide culturally sensitive divorce and custody counseling/mediation.

- Educate parent and social network regarding abduction laws.

Chapter 44

Preventing Infant Abduction

Stolen and Switched Babies: How to Keep Your Newborn Safe

The chances are slim, but the result can be devastating to a family. If you deliver at a hospital, how can you make sure your newborn is not stolen or switched at birth?

Loss of Innocence

On Friday, June 12, 1992, I reported after work for my usual volunteer duty at Alta Bates Hospital in Berkeley, California. I worked in the nursery as a "cuddler," holding and touching the ill and premature infants. Normally I signed in at the desk, entered the nursery, scrubbed in, and then reported to the various nurseries to see who needed some TLC—tender loving care—that day.

But that summer day was different. There was security at the nursery entrance and a stressed, hyper-aware atmosphere. Though it had only just hit the news, there had been an infant abduction that day. The nurses weren't really allowed to speak of the incident.

The next morning's paper carried the details: Jessica Mammini had handed her two-day-old daughter over to a kind woman who had introduced herself as a social worker. Jessica was told the baby needed to be weighed before financial aid could be approved. The woman then disappeared with "Baby Kerri."

The following September, a tip led police to Karen Lea Hughes, a woman who had apparently taken Kerri to soothe her upset over an earlier miscarriage. The baby was healthy and had been reasonably cared for and was returned to her frantic parents. In those few months, however, hospital nurseries nationwide wised up and implemented newer, more stringent security measures. (Hughes, sentenced to eight years in prison, served three before being released on parole in March 1997.)

Less than two years later after Baby Kerri was abducted, I delivered my first daughter at that same hospital.

The Numbers

According to the National Center for Missing and Exploited Children (NCMEC), the number of infant thefts are conservatively estimated at between 12 and 18 per year. Add to that number the equally high-profile cases of switched infants.

Even one stolen or switched infant is too many. How can you protect your newborn? Here are some tips.

Before Birth

Before delivering, take a hospital a tour or attend orientation so that you are familiar with the hospital and appearance of the staff. Before birth, take the time to inquire about nursery routines as well as security procedures. If you wait until you're in labor to become acquainted with these details, you may find it difficult to be very attentive to the finer points.

After the Baby Is Born

Immediately after your baby is born, you, your baby, and your partner/support-person will receive matching identification bracelets. Personally verify that the bands have matching numbers and make sure your baby's band—usually around the ankle, or two bands, one each around ankle and wrist—is not loose enough to slip off. If you cannot keep your baby with you at all times, double-check these numbers to ensure they are the same.

Make a note of your baby's appearance and vital statistics: hair color and amount, weight, length. Some hospitals take photographs of the baby shortly after birth.

If you can't keep your baby with you at all times—"rooming in"—see if your partner or another family member can accompany the baby to the nursery (where bathing and other examinations may take place).

When Baby Isn't in Your Arms

Never leave your baby unattended and alone in your room for even a minute. This includes while you take a nap, go to the bathroom or have a shower—if you or a family member can't keep a constant eye on the baby, ask to have the baby taken to the nursery. While in your room, it is preferable to keep your baby on the far side of your bed, away from the door. When you have a lot of visitors, you may get distracted.

Do not give your baby to anyone without proper identification: usually a combination of attire and a hospital photo ID badge, and usually a separate badge identifying him or her as nursery staff. If you have doubts, trust your instinct and don't take chances—call the nursing station and ask someone on the staff to come in and verify. Do not feel as if you are being unreasonable: this is your baby, and you have the right, and responsibility to protect your newborn.

If anyone unfamiliar enters your room or asks about your baby, feel free to question them to satisfy yourself that they're on the hospital staff.

Before Leaving

The hospital staff should check your matching ID bands before you are discharged, but take it upon yourself to again check your baby's ID bands for yourself. Look at the baby, for the features you first identified after birth: hair color and amount, and weight. Also take a quick peek into the diaper to check gender, and whether or not the baby is circumcised. If you have photos, also use those to compare this baby to the one you delivered.

When You're Home

The risk of baby theft doesn't end when you leave the hospital: public birth announcements can trigger baby theft. That means: avoid the lawn signs, the "It's a Girl!" balloons on the mailbox, and other banners announcing the new arrival. It's hard to contain your joy at having a wonderful new family member, so dispense that energy in other ways: hang the balloons and banners indoors instead.

Keep in mind that some hospitals provide information about new births to the local newspapers, or parents/family members supply the details themselves. Don't send out birth announcements to your friends, family and co-workers, and don't take unnecessary risks.

You and Your Baby

Like many things in life, the buck stops with you. It's up to you to be extra cautious, to make yourself aware of any potentially improper situations, and to listen to your intuition. It's worth it for the peace of mind, and besides, there's almost nothing else as wonderful bringing a new baby home.

Part Six

Protection from Youth Substance Abuse

Chapter 45

Teaching Children and Youth to Say No to Drugs

Introduction

We, as parents, are the most important role models in our children's lives. What we say and do about drugs matters a lot when it comes to the choices our children make. We can:

- set a positive example and get involved in our children's lives

- get involved in their activities, know their friends, know where they're going and what they're doing

- create clear, consistent expectations and enforce them

- talk early and often about drugs

- discuss the consequences of drug use

- show we care enormously about what choices our children make about drugs

Children learn by example. They adopt the values we demonstrate through our actions. As they grow, they're impressed by our concern for others when we bring soup to a sick neighbor and by our honesty when we admit making a mistake.

Although we believe these traits are important, it's not always easy to be consistent. Telling a friend you're younger than you really are

Excerpted from "Growing Up Drug-Free," U.S. Department of Education, http://www.pueblo.gsa.gov/cic_text/children/drgfree/drugfree.htm, 1998.

sends a confusing message to your child—isn't it wrong to lie? If you forbid smoking in the house, how can you allow your friends to break the rules? If you say that drinking alcohol is a serious matter, how can you laugh uproariously at TV and movie drunks? Because alcohol is off-limits for children, even asking them to fetch a beer from the refrigerator or to mix drinks at an adult party can be confusing.

Children who decide not to use alcohol or other drugs often make this decision because they have strong convictions against the use of these substances—convictions based on a value system. You can make your family's values clear by explaining why you choose a particular course of action and how that choice reflects your values. If you're walking down the street together and spot a blind person attempting to cross, you can both offer to help him and then take the opportunity to discuss why it's important to support those in need. You can also explore moral issues by posing hypothetical questions at the dinner table or in the car, for example, "What would you do if the person ahead of you in the movie line dropped a dollar bill?" or "What would you do if your friend wanted you to skip class with him and play video games instead?" Concrete examples like these make the abstract issue of values come alive.

Planning for Togetherness

Sometimes it's frustrating how few chances there are to have conversations about drugs with our children. In our busy culture, with families juggling the multiple demands of work, school, after-school activities, and religious and social commitments, it can be a challenge for parents and children to be in the same place at the same time. To ensure that you have regular get togethers with your children, try to schedule:

- Family meetings. Held once a week at a mutually-agreed-upon time, family meetings provide a forum for discussing triumphs, grievances, projects, questions about discipline, and any topic of concern to a family member. Ground rules help. Everyone gets a chance to talk; one person talks at a time without interruption; everyone listens, and only positive, constructive feedback is allowed. To get resistant children to join in, combine the get-together with incentives such as post-meeting pizza or assign them important roles such as recording secretary or rule enforcer.

- Regular parent-child rituals. These eliminate the need for constant planning and rearranging. Perhaps you can take the long way home from school once a week and get ice cream or make a weekly visit to the library together. Even a few minutes of conversation while you're cleaning up after dinner or right before bedtime can help the family catch up and establish the open communication that is essential to raising drug-free children.

Making Your Position Clear

When it comes to dangerous substances like alcohol, tobacco, and other drugs, don't assume that your children know where you stand. They want you to talk to them about drugs. State your position clearly; if you're ambiguous, children may be tempted to use. Tell your children that you forbid them to use alcohol, tobacco, and drugs because you love them. (Don't be afraid to pull out all the emotional stops. You can say, "If you took drugs it would break my heart.") Make it clear that this rule holds true even at other people's houses. Will your child listen? Most likely. According to research, when a child decides whether or not to use alcohol, tobacco, and other drugs, a crucial consideration is "What will my parents think?"

Also discuss the consequences of breaking the rules—what the punishment will be and how it will be carried out. Consequences must go hand-in-hand with limits so that your child understands that there's a predictable outcome to his choosing a particular course of action. The consequences you select should be reasonable and related to the violation. For example, if you catch your son smoking, you might ground him, restricting his social activities for two weeks. You could then use this time to show him how concerned you are about the serious health consequences of his smoking, and about the possibility that he'll become addicted, by having him study articles, books, or video tapes on the subject. Whatever punishment you settle on shouldn't involve new penalties that you didn't discuss before the rule was broken—this wouldn't be fair. Nor should you issue empty threats ("Your father will kill you when he gets home!"). It's understandable that you'd be angry when house rules are broken, and sharing your feelings of anger, disappointment, or sadness can have a powerfully motivating effect on your child. Since we're all more inclined to say things we don't mean when we're upset, it's best to cool off enough to discuss consequences in a matter-of-fact way.

Contrary to some parents' fears, your strict rules won't alienate your children. They want you to show you care enough to lay down the law and to go to the trouble of enforcing it. Rules about what's acceptable, from curfews to insisting that they call in to tell you where they are, make children feel loved and secure. Rules about drugs also give them reasons to fall back on when they feel tempted to make bad decisions. A recent poll showed that drugs are the number-one concern of young people today. Even when they appear nonchalant, our children need and want parental guidance. It does not have to be preachy. You will know best when it is more effective to use an authoritarian tone or a gentler approach.

Always let your children know how happy you are that they respect the rules of the household by praising them. Emphasize the things your children do right instead of focusing on what's wrong. When parents are quicker to praise than to criticize, children learn to feel good about themselves, and they develop the self-confidence to trust their own judgment.

What Your Own Alcohol, Tobacco, and Drug Use Tells Your Children

Drinking alcohol is one of the accepted practices of adulthood. It is legal for adults to have wine with dinner, beer at the end of a long week, or cocktails at a dinner party. But drinking to the point of losing control sends the wrong message to children, as does reaching for a drink to remedy unhappiness or tension.

Although it is legal for adults to smoke cigarettes, the negative impact tobacco has on a smoker's health is well documented. If a child asks his parents why they smoke, they may explain that when they began, people didn't understand how unhealthy smoking is and that once a smoker starts, it's very hard to stop. Young people can avoid making the same mistake their parents did by never starting and risking addiction. When parents smoke marijuana or use other illegal drugs, they compromise not only their children's sense of security and safety, but the children's developing moral codes as well. If you use illegal drugs, it is self-deluding to imagine that your children won't eventually find out. When they do, your parental credibility and authority will go out the window. If their parents—their closest and most important role models—don't respect the law, then why should they? Parents who abuse alcohol or other drugs should seek professional help. This help is available at treatment centers and from support groups such as Alcoholics Anonymous and Narcotics Anonymous. Their children also may benefit from professional counseling and support from groups such as Families Anonymous, Al- Anon, and Nar-Anon.

What to Say When Your Child Asks, "Did You Ever Use Drugs?"

Among the most common drug-related questions asked of parents is "Did you ever use drugs?" Unless the answer is "no," it's difficult to know what to say because nearly all parents who used drugs don't want their children to do the same thing. Is this hypocritical? No. We all want the best for our children, and we understand the hazards of drug use better than we did when we were their age and thought we were invincible. To guide our children's decisions about drugs, we can now draw on credible real-life examples of friends who had trouble as a result of their drug use: the neighbor who caused a fatal car crash while high; the family member who got addicted; the teen who used marijuana for years, lost interest in school, and never really learned how to deal with adult life and its stresses.

Some parents who used drugs in the past choose to lie about it, but they risk losing their credibility if their children discover the truth. Many experts recommend that when a child asks this question, the response should be honest.

This doesn't mean that parents need to recount every moment of their experiences. As in conversations about sex, some details should remain private, and you should avoid providing more information than is actually sought by your child. Ask clarifying questions to make sure you understand exactly why and what a child is asking before answering questions about your past drug use, and limit your response to that information.

This discussion provides a good opportunity for parents to speak frankly about what attracted them to drugs, why drugs are dangerous, and why they want their children to avoid making the same mistake. There's no perfect way to get this message across, only approaches that seem more fitting than others. Some suggestions:

- "I took drugs because some of my friends used them, and I thought I needed to in order to fit in. In those days, people didn't know as much as they do now about all the bad things that can happen when you smoke marijuana or do other drugs. If I'd known then what I know now, I never would have tried them, and I'll do everything I can to keep you away from drugs."

- "Everyone makes mistakes, and when I used drugs, I made a big one. I'm telling you about this, even though it's embarrassing, because I love you, and I want to save you from making the

385

same stupid decision that I made when I was your age. You can learn from my mistakes without repeating them."

• "I did drugs because I was bored and wanted to take some risks, but I soon found that I couldn't control the risks—they were controlling me. There are much better ways of challenging yourself than doing drugs."

• "At your age, between homework, friends, sports, and other interests, there are a lot of fun things going on. If you get into taking drugs, you're pretty much giving up those other things, because you stop being able to concentrate, and you can't control your moods or keep to a schedule. You'll miss out on all these great experiences, and you'll never get those times back."

• "You don't know how your body will react to drugs. Some people can get addicted really quickly and can get really sick even using a drug for the first time."

• "I started drinking/doing drugs when I was young, and I've been battling them ever since. They made me miss a big part of growing up, and every day I have to fight with myself so they don't make me miss more—my job, my relationships, and my time with you. I love you too much to watch you set yourself on the same path."

How Grandparents Can Help Raise Drug-Free Children

Grandparents play a special part in a child's life and, unlike parents, grandparents have had years to prepare for their role. They've been through the ups and downs of child-rearing and bring a calmer, more seasoned approach to their interactions with their grandchildren. They, as well as other extended family members, can serve as stable, mature role models, especially if they need to step in to assume some of the responsibilities of the child's parents. These important elders have one advantage over parents: Their relationships with their grandchildren are less complicated, less judgmental, and less tied to day-to-day stresses. Grandparents can use their positions of trust and intimacy to reinforce the same lessons in self-respect and healthy living that children are learning from their parents. When grandparents show concern with questions like "Has anyone ever tried to sell you drugs?" or "Why are your eyes so red?" they may be more likely to hear honest answers especially if they indicate that they are willing to listen in confidence, and will not be quick to judge or punish. Their grand-children may be less defensive and more likely to listen closely to their advice about avoiding drugs. Grandparents can also help reinforce positive messages and praise their grandchildren when they do well.

Talking with Your Children Effectively

As soon as your child begins to talk, the questions come: "Why is the grass green?" "What's wrong with that man sitting in the park?" If you show your child that you're ready to give answers at any time, even if the topics make you uncomfortable, you'll forge a trusting re-lationship, and your child will feel comfortable coming to you with concerns because she knows you take her seriously.

Being a good listener also gives you insight into your child's world. Your child will tell you about the sights and sounds that influence him every day—he's the expert about fashion, music, TV, and movies that people his age follow. Ask him what music groups are popular and what their songs are about, what his friends like to do after school, what's cool and what's not and why. Encourage him with phrases such as "That's interesting" or "I didn't know that," and by asking follow-up questions.

In these conversations, you can steer the talk to drugs and why they're harmful. If you can ingrain this information in your children well before they are faced with making difficult choices, experts say they'll be more likely to avoid rather than use. In fact, teenagers who say they've learned a lot about the risks of drugs from their parents are much less likely to try marijuana than those who say they learned nothing from them. You needn't fear that by introducing the topic of drugs, you're putting ideas into your children's heads, any more than talking about traffic safety might make them want to jump in front of a car. You're letting them know about potential dangers in their environment so that when they're confronted with them, they'll know what to do. To introduce the topic, ask your child what he's learned about drugs in school and what he thinks of them. He may even men-tion people who might be using them. If you hear something you don't like (perhaps a friend smokes marijuana or your child confesses to trying beer at a party), it is important not to react in any way that cuts off further discussion. If he seems defensive or assures you that he doesn't know anyone who uses drugs, ask him why he thinks people use them. Discuss whether the risks are worth what people may get out of using them and whether he thinks it would be worth it to take the risks. Even without addiction, experimentation is too great a gamble. One bad experience, such as being high and misjudging how long it takes to cross a busy street, can change or end a life forever. If something interrupts your conversation, pick it up the next chance you get.

Teachable Moments

Another way to talk about drugs is to take advantage of everyday teachable moments:

- If you and your child are walking down the street and you see a group of teenagers drinking and hanging out, talk about the negative effects of drinking alcohol.

- Newspapers are full of the consequences of alcohol and drug abuse. Take your examples right off the front page. Ask your child if she heard about the mother who used drugs and was arrested. Who will take care of her baby now? Did she make a good decision when she used drugs?

- Watch TV with your children, and ask them what they think. Do the programs and advertising make drug use look acceptable and routine, or do they show its downside? When you see a news item involving drug use, point out the story's full implications to families and all of society: Drug addiction can cause or aggravate many tragedies involving child neglect and abuse, family violence and rape, HIV transmission, teenage suicide, and teenage pregnancy.

- Whenever you see an anti-drug commercial on TV, use it as an opening to talk with your children about drugs. Ask them what they think about the commercial. The White House Office of National Drug Control Policy, in conjunction with the Partnership for a Drug-Free America, has embarked upon an unprecedented national anti-drug media campaign that will provide many opportunities to discuss drugs with your children.

When There's a Family History of Alcoholism or Drug Abuse

If your family had a tendency for high blood pressure, you'd tell your children they might inherit it. In the same way, they need to know about recurring patterns of substance abuse, particularly if you, your spouse, or their grandparents have had problems with alcohol or other drugs. Children of substance abusers are much more likely to become addicted if they use drugs; they may have inherited genes that make them react to alcohol and drugs differently, and they may have had more difficult upbringings. When you use the example of a family member to illustrate why your children should be careful about trying alcohol and other drugs, you make a compelling argument.

Try to find a positive perspective. If substance abuse is a persistent problem in your family, you might tell your children that being aware of the challenge that the future holds better equips them to plan ahead and avoid potentially unhealthy situations.

The Drugs in Your Kitchen Cabinet

Ordinary household products such as nail polish remover, cleaning fluid, hair spray, gasoline, spray paint, and the propellant in aerosol whipped cream can be abused as dangerous inhalants. Inhalants pose a difficult challenge to parents because they can't be banished from the household.

Because inhalants are easily available, they are a popular drug for younger users; more than one in five children report having used inhalants by the eighth grade, the year during which usage peaks. Parents need to tell children about the deadly consequences of abuse. Inhalants starve the body of oxygen and can cause unconsciousness, severe damage to the brain and nervous system, and even death.

Helping Your Child Say No to Drugs

No matter where children grow up or who their friends are, nearly all of them are confronted at some time or another by friends with bad ideas—ways of testing limits, getting in trouble, and doing things they'll regret later. It's not so hard saying "No thanks, I have to go now" to a stranger. But it's a lot tougher when a child's friend—especially one whose approval means a lot to him—tries to get him to do something he knows is wrong.

Even good kids occasionally pester their friends into skipping a class or lying about why they were out together so late. But if friends or acquaintances entice your children to try tobacco, alcohol, or drugs, the consequences can be more serious. The best way to prepare children to succeed in these encounters is to role play—practice similar scenarios in advance. With the right words at the tip of their tongue, children can assert their independence while making it clear that they're rejecting their friends' choices and not the friends themselves.

389

You need to have these practice sessions before your child finds herself in any new situation. If your child hasn't asked you what she should do in such situations, find the time to bring it up yourself. Stress that you're working together on a skill that comes in handy whenever someone doesn't want to take no for an answer. You might, for instance, take the role of a boy she likes and try to persuade her to share a six-pack of beer with you. What can she say? "You're such a jerk!" is alienating. "I don't know..." leaves the door open and sounds like she could be coaxed. The middle ground, in which she's firm but friendly, works best. Help her rehearse key phrases that give reasons for why she simply won't have a beer:

- "My parents would kill me if they found out, and they always find out!"

- "No, I'm not into that stuff."

- "I tried it once, and I hate the taste."

- "My parents trust me to not drink, and I don't want to break that trust."

Or she could state the consequences of drinking:

- "I tried it once and ended up vomiting on everything!"

- "Drinking would make me feel out of control, and I hate that."

She'll need to be prepared for protests. She can meet them with the "broken record" technique, in which she repeats her reason for not drinking over and over until attempts at persuading her cease. Or she can make it clear that the discussion about beer is over by changing the subject: "Did you watch the basketball game last night?" or "Hey, do you know if that concert's sold out?" If all else fails, she should leave the scene, saying, "I've got to go."

Questions Children Frequently Ask about Drugs

Why Would People Want to Put Bad Things into Their Bodies?

One answer might be that they might not realize how dangerous the bad things are; another is that they are not taking care of themselves. Sometimes people start using a drug just to see what it feels like, but it can turn into an addiction (like cigarettes) and it's very hard to stop.

Why Are Some Drugs Good for You and Some Drugs Wrong for You to Take?

You can discuss how drugs are powerful chemicals that change the way you feel. Doctors prescribe medicine to make sick people better— these are good drugs. Bad drugs are ones that aren't given by doctors and don't make you better; in fact, they can harm your body. That is why it is wrong to take these bad drugs.

Why Can't I Taste That Grown up Drink?

A small amount of alcohol has a much greater negative effect on a child's body than on an adult's; even a small amount can sicken a child.

Did You Smoke Marijuana When You Were Young?

Don't give your child more information than necessary. If the answer is yes, give the reasons why you feel you made a mistake; for instance, it made you feel out of control, you missed schoolwork, messed up in sports, let down your friends or lost touch with them. Also explain that more is known about the harmful effects of marijuana and other drugs now.

When Your Child Enters Middle School or Junior High

This year is both an exciting and challenging time for children. They're little fish in a big pond and desperately want to fit in. Because your children may now see older students using alcohol, tobacco, and other drugs and may think they are cool and self-assured, your children may be tempted to try drugs, too. Drug use goes up dramatically in the first year of middle school or junior high.

No matter where you live, your children will be exposed to all kinds of drugs from now on, so you need to be familiar with all the information about drugs that they may be receiving.

At this time when peer approval means everything, your children may make you feel unwelcome. But while your children are pulling away from you to establish their own identities or may seem to be embarrassed by you, they need you to be involved in their lives more than ever before.

To help your children make good choices during this critical phase, you should:

- make sure they're well-versed in the reasons to avoid alcohol, tobacco, and drugs

- get to know their friends by taking them to and from after-school activities, games, the library, and movies (while being sensitive to their need to feel independent)

- volunteer for activities where you can observe your child at school

- get acquainted with the parents of your children's friends and learn about their children's interests and habits. If it seems that your child is attracted to those with bad habits, reiterate why drug use is unacceptable.

Drug Myths vs. Reality

While you are teaching the facts about drugs, your child is getting lots of misinformation and mythology from peers. Be aware and be ready to address the half-truths and misinformation that children hear and believe, such as:

Myth: Marijuana is not harmful because it is all natural and comes from a plant.

Truth: Marijuana smoke contains some of the same cancer-causing compounds as tobacco, sometimes in higher concentrations.

Myth: It's okay to use marijuana as long as you're not a chronic user or stoner.

Truth: Occasional use can lead to frequent use.

Myth: Because sniffing powdered heroin doesn't require needles, it isn't very risky (40% of the high school seniors polled do not believe there is a great risk in trying heroin).

Truth: Heroin is dangerous no matter how it's ingested. Once addicted to heroin, users may eventually switch to injecting the drug because it's cheaper.

Myth: Drugs are not that dangerous and I can handle it.

Truth: Drug use is extremely unpredictable and affects people differently. Anyone can become addicted to drugs.

Myth: Everyone is doing it.

Truth: Research shows that more than four out of five eighth graders have not used drugs in the past month. Even among high school seniors (the group with the highest rate of marijuana use), only a quarter of those polled in a national study reported using the drug in the last month. In any given school, most students aren't doing drugs.

Medical Marijuana Update

If your teen is interested in the debate about whether or not marijuana should be legal in certain circumstances, you can state the facts: Voters' referenda are appearing in some states to legalize marijuana for medical use.

Some supporters of medical marijuana are genuinely concerned with exploring the potential for providing sick people with relief from their suffering; others are using the issue to change drug laws in America and to legalize illegal drugs, principally marijuana.

To protect consumers, medical protocol is set by health authorities and not determined by popular vote. The Food and Drug Administration withholds approval of a drug until studies strongly indicate that it is safe and effective for its intended use. Unless such studies determine that marijuana used medically fits that description, the American Medical Association recommends that the drug not be prescribed or used for medical purposes.

Tobacco and Teens: A Bad Combination

Unfortunately, increased awareness about the hazards of tobacco smoking has not deterred many teens. One reason may be that teenagers are notorious for not worrying about death—it seems a long way off. They may even convince themselves that by the time they're adults, cancer and the other heart and lung diseases that smoking causes will be cured.

If you discover your son or daughter smoking, experts say you should tell him or her to quit immediately and that smoking is not tolerated. You need to be firm but supportive; let your child know you realize that breaking tobacco addiction is difficult for anyone, regardless of age. Understand that a child who is an addicted smoker may relapse and will need encouragement. Although relapses on the road to abstinence may recur, always make it clear that quitting is imperative. If your child can't seem to quit independently, seek help from your family physician who may prescribe medication or direct your child to an anti-smoking program.

Chapter 46

Detecting and Addressing Suspected Drug Abuse

Signs That Your Child Might Be Using Drugs

Since mood swings and unpredictable behavior are frequent occurrences for preteens and teenagers, parents may find it difficult to spot signs of alcohol and drug abuse. But if your child starts to exhibit one or more of these signs (which apply equally to sons and daughters), drug abuse may be at the heart of the problem:

- She's withdrawn, depressed, tired, and careless about personal grooming.
- He's hostile and uncooperative; he frequently breaks curfews.
- Her relationships with family members have deteriorated.
- He's hanging around with a new group of friends.
- Her grades have slipped, and her school attendance is irregular.
- He's lost interest in hobbies, sports, and other favorite activities.
- Her eating or sleeping patterns have changed; she's up at night and sleeps during the day.
- He has a hard time concentrating.
- Her eyes are red-rimmed and/or her nose is runny in the absence of a cold.

Excerpted from "Growing Up Drug-Free," U.S. Department of Education, http://www.pueblo.gsa.gov/cic_text/children/drgfree/drugfree.htm, 1998.

- Household money has been disappearing.

The presence of pipes, rolling papers, small medicine bottles, eye drops, or butane lighters in your home signal that your child may be using drugs. Other clues include homemade pipes and bongs (pipes that use water as a filter) made from soda cans or plastic beverage containers. If any of these indicators show up, parents should start discussing what steps to take so they can present a united front. They may also want to seek other family members' impressions.

Acting on Your Suspicions

If you suspect that your child is using drugs, you should voice your suspicions openly—avoiding direct accusations—when he or she is sober or straight and you're calm.

This may mean waiting until the next day if he comes home drunk from a party, or if her room reeks of marijuana. Ask about what's been going on—in school and out—and discuss how to avoid using drugs and alcohol in the future. If you encounter reluctance to talk, enlist the aid of your child's school guidance counselor, family physician, or a local drug treatment referral and assessment center—they may get a better response. Also, explore what could be going on in your child's emotional or social life that might prompt drug use. Taking the time to discuss the problem openly without turning away is an important first step on the road to recovery. It shows that your child's well-being is crucial to you and that you still love him, although you hate what he's doing to himself. But you should also show your love by being firm and enforcing whatever discipline your family has agreed upon for violating house rules. You should go over ways to regain the family's trust such as calling in, spending evenings at home, and improving grades.

Even in the face of mounting evidence, parents often have a hard time acknowledging that their child has an alcohol, tobacco, or drug problem. Anger, resentment, guilt, and a sense of failure are all common reactions, but it is important to avoid self-blame. Drug abuse occurs in families of all economic and social backgrounds, in happy and unhappy homes alike. Most important is that the faster you act, the sooner your child can start to become well again.

Addiction

No one who begins to use drugs thinks he or she will become addicted. Addiction is a disease characterized by compulsive drug-seeking behavior regardless of the consequences. Research conducted by the National Institute on Drug Abuse clearly shows that virtually all drugs that are abused have a profound effect on the brain. Prolonged use of many drugs including cocaine, heroin, marijuana, and amphetamines can change the brain in fundamental and long-lasting ways, resulting in drug craving and addiction.

If and when a drug abuser becomes addicted depends on the individual. Research shows that children who use alcohol and tobacco are more likely to use marijuana than children who do not use these substances. Children who use marijuana are more likely to use other addictive drugs. Certain genetic, social, and environmental risk factors make it more likely that certain individuals will become addicted to alcohol, tobacco, and other drugs. These include:

- children of alcoholics who, according to several studies, may have inherited genes that make them more prone to addiction, and who may have had more stressful upbringings

- sensation-seekers who may like the novelty of feeling drunk or high

- children with psychological problems, such as conduct disorders, who self-medicate to feel better

- children with learning disabilities, and others who find it difficult to fit in or become frustrated learning

- children of poverty who lack access to opportunities to succeed and to resources when they're in trouble

The more risk factors children have, the greater their vulnerability. And everyone has a different ability to tolerate drugs and alcohol—what if your child's tolerance is very low?

Regardless of how cool drugs may look, there is nothing glamorous about the reality of addiction, a miserable experience for the addict and everyone around him. Addiction causes an all-consuming craving for drugs, leading an otherwise responsible, caring person to destroy relationships, work, and family life.

Finding the Right Treatment

Certified drug and alcohol counselors work with families to find the program best suited to a child's needs. To find a good certified counselor you can consult your child's doctor, other parents whose children have been treated for drug abuse, the local hospital, a school social worker, the school district's substance abuse coordinator, or the county mental health society.

You can also call the U.S. Department of Health and Human Services Center for Substance Abuse Treatment (800) 662-HELP for referrals. Counselors will discuss treatment options such as individual or group out-patient programs, prescription medication, and residential programs. Counselors may also have information on whether a particular treatment center will accept third-party, partial, or no payment for services (Some residential centers reserve a number of government-financed beds for patients who are unable to afford treatment). Counselors may also be able to suggest support groups that can steer families to sources of funding such as local church programs.

Addiction Is a Treatable Disease

The success of any treatment approach depends on a variety of factors such as the child's temperament and willingness to change, and the extent and frequency of use. Drug addiction is now understood to be a chronic, relapsing disease. It is not surprising, then, that parents may have to make a number of attempts at intervention before their child can remain drug-free, and they should not despair if their first try does not produce long-lasting results. Even if it is not apparent at the time, each step brings the child closer to being healthy.

Advice from a Teen in Treatment (Name Has Been Changed)

Jamal, 17, treatment client in a residential program in Encinitas, California:

"My mom and dad are both addicts. When I was 15, I was living with my uncle, and we got into a fight. I went to stay overnight at a friend's, and he was using marijuana. So we got high on pot. But pot got old, and a bunch of us went to our dealer's house, gave him all the money we had, and he bought hard liquor for us. It made me feel on top of the world, and alcohol became my drug of choice."

"I started ditching school, and I got suspended. I only went to get high anyway. But now I couldn't graduate. I was living with my grandmother at the time, and a peer counseling teacher from school recommended a residential treatment center."

"When I got here, I didn't think I'd stay. I thought I'd just come to cool down. But they started forcing me to change. The staff made me see that I was out of control. In about six months, I started changing. The counselors threw my issues in my face—I had been molested and abused when I was young, and I had had problems with my mom. I made commitments that I had to keep. I plan to graduate and move back to New York, and I hope to attend college."

"My advice to anyone doing drugs is that if you feel vulnerable, find someone—your best friend or someone you know who cares—and do what is hardest: Talk about your pain. The people who take care of you shouldn't be dictators too; they should share their own experiences and let kids know that they're there for them. I wish my parents had talked to me about their own drug problems."

A Family Triumphs (Name Has Been Changed)

Andrea M., married; a New Jersey mother of a daughter, 16, and son, 18:

"Both my kids were fun-loving and good students, but when my son was almost 16, his behavior changed. He was having trouble in school, he found a different set of friends, his personal appearance suffered, he slept all day and he was wide awake all night. I thought this was just typical teenage stuff. I didn't notice any changes in my daughter, but it turns out that she had started around the same time and was just better at hiding her drug abuse."

"We began getting phone calls at night, and my money started disappearing, but my husband and I disagreed about what to do, so we did nothing. Finally, about a year ago, my son and daughter got caught together trying to sell tabs of acid to the police in a sting operation."

"They both received two years' probation, which is mandatory in our state for a first drug offense. My husband decided that day that our kids needed a full-force intervention program, so we brought them to a treatment facility not too far from our home in the suburbs. Both kids attended sessions there several times per week after school. We were shocked to learn that they had been using drugs much more than we'd ever imagined—marijuana, acid, crystal meth and Ketamine."

"The parents attend the program on a regular basis, too. We learn the three Cs: that you didn't Cause, can't Control and can't Cure your kids' problems. But you can't ignore the problems because they won't go away by themselves."

"My daughter graduated from the program first. She's clean and has a boyfriend and is working on her SATs so she can go to college the year after next. My son lives at home, too, and is trying to juggle the commitments of a girlfriend, work, and college. They both go to

Narcotics Anonymous meetings, which is a continuation of the treatment program. We're relieved, but we still take it one day at a time."

Parent-School Partnerships

Parents do not need to feel they are alone in helping their children stay drug-free. For the first time ever, there are preventative intervention programs that have been proven to be effective and are available to schools, families, and communities.

Children have the best prospects for leading healthy, drug-free lives when schools support parents in their anti-drug message. There should be nothing confusing or contradictory in what children learn about drugs from the adults in their lives, and school policies need to reflect the same attitude toward alcohol and drugs that you express at home: Drug use is not acceptable. Drugs diminish a child's ability to concentrate and follow through on academic responsibilities, they cause absenteeism and a loss of motivation, and students who use them can be disruptive and drain teachers' time and energy. The best way to ensure that the anti-drug policies at your child's school are strong is to be involved. You can:

- Learn about the current policies regarding alcohol and other drugs at your child's school. If there's no anti-drug policy in place, attend Parent Teacher Association (PTA) or curriculum review meetings, or schedule an interview with the principal to help develop a policy. The policy should specify what constitutes an alcohol, tobacco, or other drug offense, spell out the consequences for failing to follow the rules, and describe procedures for handling violations.

- Familiarize yourself with how drug education is being taught in your child's school. Are the faculty members trained to teach about alcohol, tobacco, and other drug use? Is drug education taught in an age-appropriate way at each grade level throughout the year or only once during a special week? Is drug education taught during health class, or do all the teachers incorporate anti-drug information into their classes? Is there a parent education component? Is the school's program based on current research?

- Immerse yourself in the school's drug education program at home. Ask your child to show you any materials distributed during or outside class and take the opportunity to review them together.

- Find out if your child's school conducts assessments of its drug problem and whether these results are used in the program.

- Ask what happens to those who are caught abusing drugs. Does the school offer a list of referrals for students who need special help?

- Request and examine any existing materials. Do they contain a clear message that alcohol, tobacco, and other drug use is wrong and harmful? Is the information accurate and up to date?

- Investigate whether your school's drug program is being evaluated for success. Research indicates that some of the most effective programs emphasize the value of life skills such as coping with anxiety, being assertive, and feeling comfortable socially. When these lessons are combined with drug education and media literacy (being able to critically evaluate the media's messages), students confronted with drugs are better equipped to resist them.

Help from the Community

Drug-free sons and daughters not only strengthen their families but their communities, too. As a result, many towns have found ways to help local young people stay healthy. Some offer teens alternatives to familiar rituals, such as alcohol- and drug-free proms, and special dry events such as First Night festivities on New Year's Eve. Others support student-run clubs where teens can hang out, listen to music, and play sports in the evening.

Reclaiming Our Neighborhoods Block by Block

Contrary to a common misperception, drug-use rates for urban African-American children have typically been lower than rates for the population as a whole. But children in less affluent urban areas are more often exposed to drugs and the street-level drug culture. When dealers make themselves at home in a neighborhood, they often bring with them a number of other blights: crime, truancy, a higher drop-out rate, increased drug use, the physical deterioration of buildings and common areas, and despair. Residents, however, often don't realize the tools at their command to discourage drug dealing. Dealers tend to avoid neighborhoods in which the community stands united against them. Here's how we can demonstrate our commitment to reclaiming our streets:

- Form a community patrol, block association, or Neighborhood Watch. Members can take turns patrolling the streets and recording license-plate numbers of cars cruising for drugs.

- Increase two-way communication with the police by inviting them to neighborhood meetings and by keeping them informed about suspicious drug activities, which can be reported anonymously.

- Fill the streets with volleyball games, block parties, and other events that make a strong, united showing to dealers.

- Call the city public works department for help in cleaning up. Blazing lights, litter-free streets, and newly-planted flowers tell drug dealers that residents care too much about their neighborhood to hand it over.

- Provide positive outlets for the energies of local young people so they won't be attracted to drug-dealing—an activity that increases the likelihood that they'll become users.

- Continue to reassure our children that we love them and don't want them to do drugs. Even in neighborhoods where a walk to the grocery store can mean exposure to a drug dealer, children whose parents reinforce strong anti-drug attitudes stand a better chance of growing up drug-free.

Parents Supporting Each Other

Parents have no stronger allies in their fight against drug abuse than each other. Many parents find it useful to meet regularly in support of each other. It's helpful to be able to turn to other parents at the same stage of child-rearing with questions like "My daughter wants to go to a party where the chaperone will be a 20-year-old cousin—are you allowing your son to go?" If you haven't met many parents in your area with whom you can share anti-drug plans, you might want to contact a parent or community group with resources for parents. These organizations also provide interested families with information about drug prevention and referrals for treatment.

No matter how good school and community anti-drug efforts are, a parent's prevention campaign is still the most powerful. Gail Amato Baker, former president of Bowling Green Parents for Drug-Free Youth, who is now a community service representative for the Passage Group in Knoxville, Tennessee, tells why: "People often ask me why I think parents are the answer, and I think it's because we have the most to lose. Schools can help, churches can help, law enforcement can help, but no one can replace the family. Being involved with drug and alcohol prevention lets our children know that we care. It strengthens the family and helps us to be the kind of parents our children need us to be."

What You Can Do

Your child's transition from elementary school to middle school or junior high calls for special vigilance. Children are much more vulnerable to drugs and other risky behavior when they move from sixth to seventh grade than when they were younger.

Continue the dialogue on drugs that you began when your child was younger, and stay involved in your child's daily life by encouraging interests and monitoring activities. Use the specific actions below to significantly reduce the chance of your child becoming involved with drugs. Some of these actions, like being sure your child is supervised in the hours after school, may seem like common sense. And some may meet with resistance from preteens who are naturally striving to achieve independence from their parents. But all the measures listed below are critically important in making sure that your child's life is structured in such a way that drugs have no place in it.

- If possible, arrange to have your children looked after and engaged from three to five p.m. Encourage them to get involved with youth groups, arts, music, sports, community service, and academic clubs.

- Make sure children who are unattended for periods during the day feel your presence. Give them a schedule and set limits on their behavior. Give them household chores to accomplish. Enforce a strict phone-in-to-you policy. Leave notes for them around the house. Provide easy-to-find snacks.

- Get to know the parents of your child's friends. Exchange phone numbers and addresses. Have everyone agree to forbid each others' children from consuming alcohol, tobacco, and other drugs in their homes, and pledge that you will inform each other if one of you becomes aware of a child who violates this pact.

- Call parents whose home is to be used for a party. Make sure they can assure you that no alcoholic beverages or illegal substances will be dispensed. Don't be afraid to check out the party yourself to see that adult supervision is in place.

- Make it easy for your child to leave a place where substances are being used. Discuss in advance how to contact you or another designated adult in order to get a ride home. If another adult provides the transportation, be up and available to talk about the incident when your child arrives home.

- Set curfews and enforce them. Weekend curfews might range from 9 p.m. for a fifth-grader to 12:30 a.m. for a senior in high school.

- Encourage open dialogue with your children about their experiences. Tell your child, "I love you and trust you, but I don't trust the world around you, and I need to know what's going on in your life so I can be a good parent to you."

Chapter 47

Alcohol and Youth

How Does Alcohol Affect the World of a Child?

Ask Yourself

As Parents

- Do you know how to discuss alcohol use with your child and where to get information to help you?

- Do you know your child's friends, and do you feel that they provide positive influences on your child's activities?

- Do you know the extent of drinking by children in your neighborhood and how to find local organizations that are working on the issue?

- Do you know the legal consequences if your child is caught drinking alcohol?

The Child

- Almost 42% of ninth grade students reported having consumed alcohol before they were 13.

This chapter contains text from "How Does Alcohol Affect the World of a Child?" National Institute on Alcohol Abuse and Alcoholism (NIAAA), National Institutes of Health (NIH), http://www.niaaa.nih.gov/publications/yourself-text.htm, 1999, and "Make a Difference, Talk to Your Child about Alcohol," NIAAA, NIH Pub. No. 00-4314, http://www.niaaa.nih.gov/publications/children.pdf, 2000.

- About 44% of ninth grade students reported drinking in the past month. In contrast, only 33% of ninth graders reported smoking in the past month.

- One fourth (25%) of ninth grade students reported binge drinking (having had five or more drinks on one occasion) in the past month.

- Rates of drinking differ among racial and ethnic minority groups. Among ninth graders, binge drinking was reported by 27% of non-Hispanic white students and 30% of Hispanic students, but only 15% of African American students and 5% of Asian-Pacific Islander students.

- The gap between alcohol use by boys and girls has closed. Girls consume alcohol and binge drink at rates equal to boys.

- Forty percent of children who start drinking before the age of 15 will become alcoholics at some point in their lives. If the onset of drinking is delayed by 5 years, a child's risk of serious alcohol problems is decreased by 50%.

Family

- Current research suggests children are less likely to drink when their parents are involved with them and when they and their parents report feeling close to each other.

- Adolescents drink less and have fewer alcohol-related problems when their parents discipline them consistently and set clear expectations.

- Nearly 17% of children under 14 and 20% of children under 18 live with a parent (or responsible adult) who drinks heavily or has an alcohol problem.

- Parents' drinking behaviors and favorable attitudes about drinking have been associated with adolescents' initiating and continuing drinking.

- The immediate family members of alcoholics are 2 to 7 times more likely than the general population to develop problems with alcohol during their lifetime.

- Drinking during pregnancy has been associated not only with fetal alcohol syndrome but with offspring learning and behavioral problems into adolescence.

- Elevated rates of alcoholism are consistently found in parents of youth with Attention Deficit/Hyperactivity Disorder (ADHD).

School

- Evidence suggests that alcohol use by peers is a strong predictor of adolescent use and misuse of alcohol.

- According to a 1995 national survey of fourth through sixth graders who read the *Weekly Reader*, 30% of students reported that they received "a lot" of pressure from their classmates to drink beer.

- Three-quarters of eighth graders reported having friends who use alcohol. In fact, one-fourth of eighth graders said that most or all of their friends drink.

- Among eighth graders, students with higher grade point averages reported less alcohol use in the past month.

- Among eighth graders, higher truancy rates were associated with greater rates of alcohol use in the past month.

- One national study found that students are less likely to use alcohol if they are close to people at school, are a part of their school, and if they feel that teachers treat students fairly.

- According to the 1995 Weekly Reader survey, over half (54%) of fourth through sixth graders reported learning about the dangers of illicit drugs at school, but less than a third (30%) learned about the dangers of drinking and smoking at school.

- In 1995, 76% of seventh through twelfth grade teachers polled felt that underage student drinking was a serious or somewhat serious problem.

Impact on Children's Health and Safety

- Among 12-to 17-year-old current drinkers, 31% had extreme levels of psychological distress, and 39% exhibited serious behavioral problems.

- Current drinkers among a nationally representative sample of youth aged 12–16 had higher levels of diastolic blood pressure than did their non-drinking counterparts.

- Adolescent females who drink exhibit higher levels of estradiol (an estrogen) and testosterone than non-drinking girls. High levels of estrogen may contribute to increased risk for specific diseases, including breast cancer, and high levels of testosterone are associated with an increased risk of substance use.

- Girls, aged 12–16, who were current drinkers were four times more likely than their non-drinking counterparts to suffer depression.

Make a Difference, Talk to Your Child about Alcohol

Introduction

Kids who drink are more likely to be victims of violent crime, to be involved in alcohol-related traffic accidents, and to have serious school-related problems. You have more influence on your child's values and decisions about drinking before he or she begins to use alcohol. Parents can have a major impact on their children's drinking, especially during the preteen and early teen years.

With so many drugs available to young people these days, you may wonder, "Why focus on helping kids avoid alcohol?" Alcohol is a drug, as surely as cocaine and marijuana are. It's also illegal to drink under the age of 21. And it's dangerous. Kids who drink are more likely to:

- be victims of violent crime.

- have serious problems in school.

- be involved in drinking-related traffic accidents.

Keep in mind that the suggestions on the following pages are just that—suggestions. Trust your instincts. Choose ideas you are comfortable with, and use your own style in carrying out the approaches you find useful. Your child looks to you for guidance and support in making life decisions—including the decision not to use alcohol.

"But my child isn't drinking yet," you may think. "Isn't it a little early to be concerned about drinking?" Not at all. This is the age at which some children begin experimenting with alcohol. Even if your child is not yet drinking, he or she may be receiving pressure to drink. Act now. Keeping quiet about how you feel about your child's alcohol use may give him or her the impression that alcohol use is OK for kids.

It's not easy. As children approach adolescence, friends exert a lot of influence. Fitting in is a chief priority for youth, and parents often feel shoved aside. Kids will listen, however. Study after study shows that even during the teen years, parents have enormous influence on their children's behavior. The bottom line is that most children don't yet drink. And parents' disapproval of youthful alcohol use is the key reason children choose not to drink. So make no mistake: You can make a difference.

Kids and Alcohol: The Risks

For young people, alcohol is the number one drug of choice. In fact, youth use alcohol more frequently and heavily than all other illicit drugs combined. Although most children ages 10 to 14 have not yet begun to drink, early adolescence is a time of special risk for beginning to experiment with alcohol.

While some parents and guardians may feel relieved that their youth is "only" drinking, it is important to remember that alcohol is a powerful, mood-altering drug. Not only does alcohol affect the mind and body in often unpredictable ways, but kids lack the judgment and coping skills to handle alcohol wisely. As a result:

- Alcohol-related traffic accidents are a major cause of death and disability among youth. Alcohol use also is linked with youthful deaths by drowning, fire, suicide, and homicide.

- Youth who use alcohol are more likely to become sexually active at earlier ages, to have sexual intercourse more often, and to have unprotected sex than youth who do not drink.

- Young people who drink are more likely than others to be victims of violent crime, including rape, aggravated assault, and robbery.

- Youth who drink are more likely to have problems with school work and school conduct.

- An individual who begins drinking as a young teen is four times more likely to develop alcohol dependence than someone who waits until adulthood to use alcohol.

The message is clear: Alcohol use is very risky business for young people. And the longer children delay alcohol use, the less likely they are to develop any problems associated with it. That's why it is so important to help your child avoid any alcohol use.

A Young Person's World

Early adolescence is a time of enormous and often confusing changes for your child, which makes it a challenging time for both your youngster and you. Being tuned in to what it's like to be a youth can help you stay closer to your child and have more influence on the choices he or she makes—including decisions about using alcohol.

Thinking skills. Most youth are still very "now" oriented and are just beginning to understand that their actions (such as drinking) have consequences. They also tend to believe that bad things won't happen to them, which helps to explain why they often take risks. Therefore, it is very important for adults to invest time in helping kids understand how and why alcohol-related risks do apply to them.

Social and emotional changes. As children approach adolescence, friends and "fitting in" become extremely important. Youth increasingly look to friends and the media for clues on how to behave and begin to question adults' values and rules. Given these normal developments, it is perhaps not surprising that parents often experience conflict with their kids as they go through early adolescence. During this sometimes stormy time, perhaps your toughest challenge is to try to respect your child's growing drive for independence while still providing support and appropriate limits.

The Bottom Line: A Strong Parent-Child Relationship

You may wonder why a chapter on preventing youth alcohol use is putting so much emphasis on parents' need to understand and support their children. But the fact is, the best way to influence your child to avoid drinking is to have a strong, trusting relationship with him or her. Research shows that youth are much more likely to delay drinking when they feel they have a close, supportive tie with a parent or guardian. Moreover, if your son or daughter eventually does begin to drink, a good relationship with you will help protect him or her from developing alcohol-related problems.

The opposite is also true: When the relationship between a parent and youth is full of conflict or is very distant, the youth is more likely to use alcohol and to develop drinking-related problems. This connection between the parent-child relationship and a child's drinking habits makes a lot of sense when you think about it. First, when children have a strong bond with a parent, they are apt to feel good about themselves and therefore be less likely to cave in to peer pressure to use alcohol. Second, a good relationship with you is likely to influence your children to try to live up to your expectations, because they want to maintain their close tie with you. Here are some ways to build a strong, supportive bond with your child:

- Establish open communication. Make it easy for your youth to talk honestly with you.

- Show you care. Even though youth may not always show it, they still need to know they are important to their parents. Make it a point to regularly spend one-on-one time with your child—time when you can give him or her your loving, undivided attention. Some activities to share: a walk, a bike ride, a quiet dinner out, or a cookie-baking session.

- Draw the line. Set clear, realistic expectations for your child's behavior. Establish appropriate consequences for breaking rules and consistently enforce them.

- Offer acceptance. Make sure your youth knows that you appreciate his or her efforts as well as accomplishments. Avoid hurtful teasing or criticism.

- Understand that your child is growing up. This doesn't mean a hands-off attitude. But as you guide your child's behavior, also make an effort to respect his or her growing need for independence and privacy.

Tips for Communicating with Your Youth

Developing open, trusting communication between you and your child is essential to helping your child avoid alcohol use. If your child feels comfortable talking openly with you, you'll have a greater chance of guiding him or her toward healthy decision making. Some ways to begin:

Encourage conversation. Encourage your child to talk about whatever interests him or her. Listen without interruption and give your child a chance to teach you something new. Your active listening to your child's enthusiasms paves the way for conversations about topics that concern you.

Ask open-ended questions. Encourage your youth to tell you how he or she thinks and feels about the issue you're discussing. Avoid questions that have a simple "yes" or "no" answer.

411

Control your emotions. If you hear something you don't like, try not to respond with anger. Instead, take a few deep breaths and acknowledge your feelings in a constructive way.

Make every conversation a "win-win" experience. Don't lecture or try to "score points" on your youth by showing how he or she is wrong. If you show respect for your child's viewpoint, he or she will be more likely to listen to and respect yours.

Talking to Your Teen about Alcohol

For many parents, bringing up the subject of alcohol is no easy matter. Your young teen may try to dodge the discussion, and you yourself may feel unsure about how to proceed. To boost your chances for a productive conversation, take some time to think through the issues you want to discuss before you talk with your child. Also, think about how your child might react and ways you might respond to your youngster's questions and feelings. Then choose a time to talk when both you and your child have some "down time" and are feeling relaxed.

Keep in mind, too, that you don't need to cover everything at once. In fact, you're likely to have a greater impact on your child's drinking by having a number of talks about alcohol use throughout his or her adolescence. Think of this discussion with your child as the first part of an ongoing conversation.

And remember, do make it a conversation, not a lecture! Following are some topics for discussion:

Your child's views about alcohol. Ask your young teen what he or she knows about alcohol and what he or she thinks about youth drinking. Ask your child why he or she thinks kids drink. Listen carefully without interrupting. Not only will this approach help your child to feel heard and respected, but it can serve as a natural "lead-in" to discussing alcohol topics.

Important facts about alcohol. Although many kids believe they already know everything about alcohol, myths and misinformation abound. Here are some important facts to share:

- Alcohol is a powerful drug that slows down the body and mind. It impairs coordination; slows reaction time; and impairs vision, clear thinking, and judgment.

- Beer and wine are not "safer" than hard liquor. A 12-ounce can of beer, a 5-ounce glass of wine, and 1 ounce of hard liquor all contain the same amount of alcohol and have the same effects on the body and mind.

- On average, it takes 2 to 3 hours for a single drink to leave the body's system. Nothing can speed up this process, including drinking coffee, taking a cold shower, or "walking it off."

- People tend to be very bad at judging how seriously alcohol has affected them. That means many individuals who drive after drinking think they can control a car but actually cannot.

- Anyone can develop a serious alcohol problem, including a youth.

The magic potion myth. The media's glamorous portrayal of alcohol encourages many youth to believe that drinking will make them popular, attractive, happy, and "cool." Research shows that youth who expect such positive effects are more likely to drink at early ages. However, you can help to combat these dangerous myths by watching TV shows and movie videos with your child and discussing how alcohol is portrayed in them. For example, television advertisements for beer often show young people having an uproariously good time, as though drinking always puts people in a terrific mood. Watching such a commercial with your child can be an opportunity to discuss the many ways that alcohol can affect people—in some cases bringing on feelings of sadness or anger rather than carefree high spirits.

Good reasons not to drink. In talking with your child about reasons to avoid alcohol, stay away from scare tactics. Most youth are aware that many people drink without problems, so it is important to discuss the consequences of alcohol use without overstating the case. For example, you can talk about the dangers of riding in a car with a driver who has been drinking without insisting that "all kids who ride with drinkers get into accidents." Some good reasons that youth shouldn't drink:

- You want your child to avoid alcohol. Be sure to clearly state your own expectations regarding your child's drinking and to establish consequences for breaking rules. Your values and attitudes count with your child, even though he or she may not always show it.

413

- To maintain self-respect. In a series of focus groups, youth reported that the best way to persuade them to avoid alcohol is to appeal to their self-respect—letting them know that they are too smart and have too much going for them to need the crutch of alcohol.

- Drinking is illegal. Because alcohol use under the age of 21 is illegal, getting caught may mean trouble with the authorities. Even if getting caught doesn't lead to police action, the parents of your child's friends may no longer permit them to associate with your child. If drinking occurs on school grounds, your child could be suspended.

- Drinking can be dangerous. One of the leading causes of teen injuries and death is drunk driving. Alcohol is also a major factor in other types of fatal accidents among youth, such as drownings, burns, falls, and alcohol poisoning from drinking too much, too fast. Drinking also makes a young person more vulnerable to sexual assault and unprotected sex. And while your youth may believe he or she wouldn't engage in hazardous activities after drinking, point out that because alcohol impairs judgment, a drinker is very likely to think such activities won't be dangerous.

- You have a family history of alcoholism. If one or more members of your immediate or extended family has suffered from alcoholism, your child may be somewhat more vulnerable to developing a drinking problem. Your child needs to know that for him or her, drinking may carry special risks.

How to handle peer pressure. It's not enough to tell your youth that he or she should avoid alcohol—you also need to help your child figure out how. What can your daughter say when she goes to a party and a friend offers her a beer? Or what should your son do if he finds himself in a home where kids are passing around a bottle of wine and parents are nowhere in sight? What should their response be if they are offered a ride home with an older friend who has been drinking? Brainstorm with your youth for ways that he or she might handle these and other difficult situations, and make clear how you are willing to support your child. An example: "If you find yourself at a home where kids are drinking, call me and I'll pick you up and there will be no scolding or punishment." The more prepared your child is, the better able he or she will be to handle high-pressure situations that involve drinking.

414

Mom, Dad, did you drink when you were a kid? This is the question many parents dread yet it is highly likely to come up in any family discussion of alcohol. The reality is that many parents did drink before they were old enough to legally do so. So how can one be honest with a child without sounding like a hypocrite who advises, "Do as I say, not as I did"?

This is a judgment call. If you believe that your drinking or drug use history should not be part of the discussion, you can simply tell your child that you choose not to share it. Another approach is to admit that you did do some drinking as a teenager, but that it was a mistake and give your youth an example of an embarrassing or painful moment that occurred because of your drinking. This approach may help your child better understand that youthful alcohol use does have negative consequences.

How to Host a Teen Party

- Agree on a guest list and don't admit party crashers.

- Discuss ground rules with your child before the party.

- Encourage your youth to plan the party with a responsible friend so that he or she will have support if problems arise.

- Brainstorm fun activities for the party.

- If a guest brings alcohol into your house, ask him or her to leave.

- Serve plenty of snacks and non-alcoholic drinks.

- Be visible and available but don't join the party!

Six Ways to Say No to a Drink

At some point, your child will be offered alcohol. To resist such pressure, youth say they prefer quick "one-liners" that allow them to dodge a drink without making a big scene. It will probably work best for your youth to take the lead in thinking up comebacks to drink offers so that he or she will feel comfortable saying them. But to get the brainstorming started, here are some simple pressure-busters from the mildest to the most assertive.

- No thanks.

- I don't feel like it—do you have any soda?

- Alcohol's not my thing.
- Are you talking to me? Forget it.
- Why do you keep pressuring me when I've said no?
- Back off!

Taking Action! Prevention Strategies for Parents

While parent-child conversations about drinking are essential, talking isn't enough—you also need to take concrete action to help your child resist alcohol. Research strongly shows that active, supportive involvement by parents and guardians can help youth avoid underage drinking and prevent later alcohol misuse.

In a survey of sixth graders, over half said it would be easy for a kid their age to get alcohol at a party. And in a recent national survey, 75 percent of eighth graders said alcohol was "fairly easy" or "very easy" to get. The message is clear: Youth still need plenty of adult supervision. Some ways to provide it:

Monitor alcohol use in your home. If you keep alcohol in your home, keep track of the supply. Make clear to your child that you don't allow unchaperoned parties or other youth gatherings in your home. If possible, however, encourage him or her to invite friends over when you are at home. The more entertaining your child does in your home, the more you will know about your child's friends and activities.

Connect with other parents. Getting to know other parents and guardians can help you keep closer tabs on your child. Friendly relations can make it easier for you to call the parent of a youth who is having a party to be sure that a responsible adult will be present and that alcohol will not be available. You're likely to find out that you're not the only adult who wants to prevent youthful alcohol use—many other parents share your concern.

Keep track of your child's activities. Be aware of your youth's plans and whereabouts. Generally, your child will be more open to your supervision if he or she feels you are keeping tabs because you care, not because you distrust him or her.

Develop family rules about youth drinking. When parents establish clear "no alcohol" rules and expectations, their children are less likely to begin drinking. While each family should develop agreements

416

about youth alcohol use that reflect their own beliefs and values, some possible family rules about drinking are:

- Kids will not drink alcohol until they are 21.

- Older siblings will not encourage younger brothers or sisters to drink and will not give them alcohol.

- Kids will not stay at youth parties where alcohol is served.

- Kids will not ride in a car with a driver who has been drinking.

Once you have chosen rules for your family, you will need to establish appropriate consequences for breaking those rules. Be sure to choose a penalty that you are willing to carry out. Also, don't make the consequences so harsh that they become a barrier to open communication between you and your youth. The idea is to make the penalty "sting" just enough to make your child think twice about breaking the rule. A possible consequence might be temporary restrictions on your child's socializing.

Finally, you must be prepared to consistently enforce the consequences you have established. If your children know that they will lose certain privileges each and every time an alcohol use rule is broken, they will be more likely to keep their agreements.

Set a good example. Parents and guardians are important role models for their children—even children who are fast becoming teenagers. Studies indicate that if a parent uses alcohol, his or her children are more likely to drink themselves. But even if you use alcohol, there may be ways to lessen the likelihood that your child will drink. Some suggestions:

- Use alcohol moderately.

- Don't communicate to your child that alcohol is a good way to handle problems. For example, don't come home from work and say, "I had a rotten day. I need a drink."

- Instead, let your child see that you have other, healthier ways to cope with stress, such as exercise; listening to music; or talking things over with your spouse, partner, or friend.

- Don't tell your kids stories about your own drinking in a way that conveys the message that alcohol use is funny or glamorous.

- Never drink and drive or ride in a car with a driver who has been drinking.

- When you entertain other adults, make available alcohol-free beverages and plenty of food. If anyone drinks too much at your party, make arrangements for them to get home safely.

Don't support youth drinking. Your attitudes and behavior toward youth drinking also influence your child. Avoid making jokes about underage drinking or drunkenness, or otherwise showing acceptance of youth alcohol use. In addition, never serve alcohol to your child's underage friends. Research shows that kids whose parents or friends' parents provide alcohol for youth get-togethers are more likely to engage in heavier drinking, to drink more often, and to get into traffic accidents. Remember, too, that it is illegal in most states to provide alcohol to minors who are not family members. You can also join school and community efforts to discourage alcohol use by youth. By working with school officials and other members of your community, you can help to develop policies to reduce alcohol availability to youth and to enforce consequences for underage drinking.

Help your child build healthy friendships. If your child's friends use alcohol, your child is more likely to drink too. So it makes sense to try to encourage your youth to develop friendships with kids who do not drink and who are otherwise healthy influences on your child. A good first step is to simply get to know your child's friends better. You can then invite the kids you feel good about to family get-togethers and outings and find other ways to encourage your child to spend time with those youth. Also, talk directly with your youngster about the qualities in a friend that really count, such as trustworthiness and kindness, rather than popularity or a "cool" style. When you disapprove of one of your child's friends, the situation can be tougher to handle. While it may be tempting to simply forbid your child to see that friend, such a move may make your child even more determined to hang out with him or her. Instead, you might try pointing out your reservations about the friend in a caring, supportive way. You can also limit your child's time with that friend through your family rules, such as how after-school time can be spent or how late your child can stay out in the evening.

Encourage healthy alternatives to alcohol. One reason kids drink is to beat boredom. Therefore, it makes sense to encourage your child to participate in supervised after-school and weekend activities that are challenging and fun. According to a recent survey of youth, the availability of enjoyable, alcohol-free activities is a big reason for deciding not to use alcohol.

If your community doesn't offer many supervised activities, consider getting together with other parents and youth to help create some. Start by asking your child and other kids what they want to do, since they will be most likely to participate in activities that truly interest them. Find out whether your church, school, or community organization can help you sponsor a project.

Could My Child Develop a Drinking Problem?

While this chapter is mainly concerned with preventing youth alcohol use, we also need to pay attention to the possibility of youthful alcohol abuse. Certain children are more likely than others to drink heavily and encounter alcohol-related difficulties, including health, school, legal, family, and emotional problems. Kids at highest risk for alcohol-related problems are those who:

- Begin using alcohol or other drugs before the age of 15.

- Have a parent who is a problem drinker or an alcoholic.

- Have close friends who use alcohol and/or other drugs.

- Have been aggressive, antisocial, or hard to control from an early age.

- Have experienced childhood abuse and/or other major traumas.

- Have current behavioral problems and/or are failing at school.

- Have parents who do not support them, do not communicate openly with them, and do not keep track of their behavior or whereabouts.

- Experience ongoing hostility or rejection from parents and/or harsh, inconsistent discipline.

The more of these experiences a child has had, the greater the chances that he or she will develop problems with alcohol. Having one or more risk factors does not mean that your child definitely will develop a drinking problem. It does suggest, however, that you may need to act now to help protect your youngster from later problems. For example, if you have not been openly communicating with your child, it will be important to develop new ways of talking and listening to each other. Or, if your child has serious behavioral difficulties, you may want to seek help from your child's school counselor, physician, and/ or a mental health professional. Some parents may suspect that their child already has a drinking problem. While it can be hard to know for sure, certain behaviors can alert you to the possibility of an alcohol problem. If you think your child may be in trouble with drinking, consider getting advice from a health care professional specializing in alcohol problems before talking with your youth. To find a professional, contact your family doctor or a local hospital. Other sources of information and guidance may be found in your local Yellow Pages under "Alcoholism."

Warning Signs of a Drinking Problem

While the following behaviors may indicate an alcohol or other drug problem, some also reflect normal teenage growing pains. Experts believe that a drinking problem is more likely if you notice several of these signs at the same time, if they occur suddenly, and if some of them are extreme in nature.

- Mood changes: flare-ups of temper, irritability, and defensiveness.

- School problems: poor attendance, low grades, and/or recent disciplinary action.

- Rebelling against family rules.

- Switching friends, along with a reluctance to have you get to know the new friends.

- A "nothing matters" attitude: sloppy appearance, a lack of involvement in former interests, and general low energy.

- Finding alcohol in your child's room or backpack, or smelling alcohol on his or her breath.

- Physical or mental problems: memory lapses, poor concentration, bloodshot eyes, lack of coordination, or slurred speech.

Action Checklist

- Establish a loving, trusting relationship with your child.

- Make it easy for your youth to talk honestly with you.

- Talk with your child about alcohol facts, reasons not to drink, and ways to avoid drinking in difficult situations.

- Keep tabs on your young teen's activities, and join with other parents in making common policies about youth alcohol use.

- Develop family rules about youth drinking and establish consequences.

- Set a good example regarding your own alcohol use and your response to youth drinking.

- Encourage your child to develop healthy friendships and fun alternatives to drinking.

- Know whether your child is at high risk for a drinking problem; if so, take steps to lessen that risk.

- Know the warning signs of a youth drinking problem and act promptly to get help for your child.

- Believe in your own power to help your child avoid alcohol use.

Chapter 48

Tobacco and Youth

Facts on Youth Smoking, Health, and Performance

Among young people, the short-term health effects of smoking include damage to the respiratory system, addiction to nicotine, and the associated risk of other drug use. Long-term health consequences of youth smoking are reinforced by the fact that most young people who smoke regularly continue to smoke throughout adulthood.

- Smoking hurts young people's physical fitness in terms of both performance and endurance—even among young people trained in competitive running.

- Smoking among youth can hamper the rate of lung growth and the level of maximum lung function.

- The resting heart rates of young adult smokers are two to three beats per minute faster than those of nonsmokers.

- Among young people, regular smoking is responsible for cough and increased frequency and severity of respiratory illnesses.

This chapter contains text from "Facts on Youth Smoking, Health, and Performance," Centers for Disease Control and Prevention (CDC), http://www.cdc.gov/tobacco/research_data/youth/ythsprt.htm, page last reviewed November 02, 2000, and "Parents—Help Keep Your Kids Tobacco-Free," CDC, http://www.cdc.gov/tobacco/educational_materials/Yuthfax1.htm, page last reviewed November 02, 2000.

- The younger people start smoking cigarettes, the more likely they are to become strongly addicted to nicotine.

- Teens who smoke are three times more likely than nonsmokers to use alcohol, eight times more likely to use marijuana, and 22 times more likely to use cocaine. Smoking is associated with a host of other risky behaviors, such as fighting and engaging in unprotected sex.

- Smoking is associated with poor overall health and a variety of short-term adverse health effects in young people and may also be a marker for underlying mental health problems, such as depression, among adolescents. High school seniors who are regular smokers and began smoking by grade nine are

  - 2.4 times more likely than their nonsmoking peers to report poorer overall health.

  - 2.4 to 2.7 times more likely to report cough with phlegm or blood, shortness of breath when not exercising, and wheezing or gasping.

  - 3.0 times more likely to have seen a doctor or other health professional for an emotional or psychological complaint.

Parents—Help Keep Your Kids Tobacco-Free

Know the Facts about Youth and Tobacco Use

- Kids who use tobacco may cough and have asthma attacks more often and develop respiratory problems leading to more sick days, more doctor bills, and poorer athletic performance. They are more likely to use alcohol and other drugs such as cocaine and marijuana, as well as becoming more addicted to tobacco and find it extremely hard to quit.

- Spit tobacco and cigars are not safe alternatives to cigarettes; low-tar and additive-free cigarettes are not safe either.

- Tobacco use is the single most preventable cause of death in the United States causing heart disease, cancers, and strokes.

Take a Stand at Home Early and Often

- Despite the impact of movies, music, and TV, parents can be the greatest influence in their kids' lives.

- Talk directly to children about the risks of tobacco use; if friends or relatives died from tobacco-related illnesses, let your kids know.

- If you use tobacco, you can still make a difference. Your best move, of course, is to try to quit. Meanwhile, don't use tobacco in your children's presence, don't offer it to them, and don't leave it where they can easily get it.

- Start the dialog about tobacco use at age 5 or 6 and continue through their high school years. Many kids start using tobacco by age 11, and many are addicted by age 14.

- Know if your kids' friends use tobacco. Talk about ways to refuse tobacco.

- Discuss with kids the false glamorization of tobacco on billboards, and other media, such as movies, TV, and magazines.

Make a Difference in Your Community

- Vote with your pocketbook. Support businesses that don't sell tobacco to kids. Frequent restaurants and other places that are tobacco-free.

- Be sure your schools and all school events (i.e., parties, sporting events, etc.) are tobacco-free.

- Partner with your local tobacco prevention programs. Call your local health department or your cancer, heart, or lung association to learn how you can get involved.

Chapter 49

Information about Specific Drugs

Depressants

Alcohol

- *Street Terms:* Beer, wine, liquor, cooler, malt liquor, booze

- *Administration:* Orally

- *Potential Consequences:*
  - Addiction (alcoholism)
  - Dizziness
  - Slurred speech
  - Disturbed sleep

Figure 49.1. Alcohol

Excerpted from "Growing up Drug-Free: A Parent's Guide to Prevention," U.S. Department of Education, 1998. The information in this chapter can be found at the following webpages: http://www.pueblo.gsa.gov/cic_text/children/drgfree/drug%20tables/stimulants/depressant-stimulants_table.htm, http://www.pueblo.gsa.gov/cic_text/children/drgfree/drug%20tables/stimulants/stimulants_table1.htm, http://www.pueblo.gsa.gov/cic_text/children/drgfree/drug%20tables/stimulants/stimulants_table2.htm, http://www.pueblo.gsa.gov/cic_text/children/drgfree/drug%20tables/opiates/opiates_table.htm, http://www.pueblo.gsa.gov/cic_text/children/drgfree/drug%20tables/hallucinogens/hallucinogens_table.htm, http://www.pueblo.gsa.gov/cic_text/children/drgfree/drug%20tables/others/other_drugs_table.htm. Despite the age of this document, readers seeking information about drugs will find this information useful.

- Nausea
- Vomiting
- Hangovers
- Impaired motor skills
- Violent behavior
- Impaired learning
- Fetal alcohol syndrome
- Respiratory depression and death (high doses)
- *Other Facts:* 25% of 8th graders have admitted to being intoxicated at least once.

Stimulants

Amphetamines

- *Street Terms:* Speed, uppers, ups, hearts, black beauties, pep pills, copilots, bumble bees, benzedrine, dexedrine, footballs, biphetamine
- *Administration:* Orally, injected, snorted, or smoked
- *Potential Consequences:*
  - Addiction
  - Irritability
  - Anxiety
  - Increased blood pressure
  - Paranoia/psychosis
  - Depression
  - Aggression
  - Convulsions
  - Dilated pupils and blurred vision
  - Dizziness
  - Sleeplessness
  - Loss of appetite; malnutrition
  - Increased body temperature
  - Increased risk of exposure to HIV (Human Immunodeficiency Virus), hepatitis, and other infectious diseases if injected

- *Other Facts:* Chronic use can induce psychosis with symptoms similar to schizophrenia such as visual and auditory hallucinations, and paranoia.

Methamphetamine

- *Street Terms:* Speed, meth, crank, crystal ice, fire, croak, crypto, white cross, glass

- *Administration:* Orally, injected, snorted, or smoked

- *Potential Consequences:*
  - Addiction
  - Irritability
  - Anxiety
  - Increased blood pressure
  - Paranoia/psychosis
  - Aggression
  - Nervousness
  - Hyperthermia
  - Compulsive behavior
  - Stroke
  - Depression
  - Convulsions
  - Heart and blood vessel toxicity
  - Insomnia
  - Loss of appetite; malnutrition
  - Hallucinations
  - Formication: the sensation of insects creeping on or under the skin
  - Arrhythmia
  - Increased risk of exposure to HIV, hepatitis, and other infectious diseases if injected

- *Other Facts:*
  - Some users avoid sleep for 3 to 15 days.
  - "Ice" is the street name for smokable methamphetamine.

Ecstasy (methylenedioxy amphetamine)

- *Street Terms:* XTC, Adam, MDMA

- *Administration:* Orally

- *Potential Consequences:*

  - Psychiatric disturbances including panic, anxiety, depression, and paranoia

  - Muscle tension

  - Nausea

  - Blurred vision

  - Sweating

  - Increased heart rate and blood pressure

  - Hallucinations

  - Reduced appetite

  - Sleep problems

  - Fainting

  - Chills

Figure 49.2. *Ecstasy in pill and powder form.*

- *Other Facts:* Ecstasy is popular at all-night dance parties (called "raves") and is the most common "designer drug."

Ritalin (methylphenidate)

- *Street Terms:* Speed, west coast

- Note: Ritalin, a legally prescribed medication for treating attention deficit disorder and hyperactivity, is sometimes sold and abused as a street drug.

- *Administration:* Tablet is crushed, and the powder is snorted or injected

- *Potential Consequences:*

  - Loss of appetite

  - Fevers, convulsions, and severe headaches

  - Increased risk of exposure to HIV, hepatitis, and other infectious diseases if injected

- Irregular heartbeat and respiration
- Paranoia, hallucinations, delusions
- Excessive repetition of movements and meaningless tasks
- Tremors, muscle twitching
- *Other Facts:* Some children buy or steal the drug from their classmates.

Herbal Ecstasy/Ephedrine

- *Street Terms:* Herbal ecstacy, cloud 9, rave energy, xphoria, X

- *Administration:* Orally

- *Potential Consequences:*
  - Increased heart rate and blood pressure
  - Seizures
  - Heart attacks
  - Stroke
  - Death

Figure 49.3. Herbal ecstasy tablets.

- *Other Facts:* The active ingredients in herbal ecstasy are caffeine and ephedrine.

Designer Drugs (Fentanyl-based)

- *Street Terms:* Synthetic heroin, goodfella

- *Administration:* Injected, sniffed, or smoked

- *Potential Consequences:*
  - Instant respiratory paralysis
  - Potency creates strong possibility for overdose
  - Increased risk of exposure to HIV, hepatitis, and other infectious diseases if injected
  - Many of the same effects as heroin

- *Other Facts:* Designer drugs are created by changing the molecular structure of an existing drug or drugs to create a new substance.

GHB *(Gamma Hydroxybutyric Acid)*

- *Street Terms:* Liquid ecstasy, somatomax, scoop, grievous bodily harm, liquid x, Georgia home boy, goop

- *Administration:* Snorted, orally in liquid form, smoked, or mixed into drinks

- *Potential Consequences:*
  - Liver failure
  - Vomiting
  - Tremors
  - Seizures
  - Comas
  - Fatal respiratory problems

- *Other Facts*: Sometimes the user transports the drug in empty hotel shampoo or eye-dropper bottles.

Cocaine

- *Street Terms:* Coke, snow, nose candy, flake, blow, big C, lady, white, snowbirds

- *Administration:* Snorted or dissolved in water and injected

- *Potential Consequences:*
  - Addiction
  - Pupil dilation
  - Elevated blood pressure and heart rate
  - Increased respiratory rate
  - Increased risk of exposure to HIV, hepatitis, and other infectious diseases if injected
  - Paranoia
  - Seizures
  - Heart attack
  - Respiratory failure
  - Constricted peripheral blood vessels
  - Restlessness, irritability, anxiety

- Loss of appetite
- Tactile hallucinations
- Insomnia
- Increased body temperature
- Death from overdose

- *Other Facts:*
  - Cocaine is a powerfully addictive drug.
  - Heavy use may produce hallucinations, paranoia, aggression, insomnia, and depression

Crack

- *Street Terms:* Rock, freebase
- *Administration:* Heated and smoked in a pipe
- *Potential Consequences:* Same as cocaine
- *Other Facts:* A cheaper form of cocaine that may be more addicting

Opiates/Opiate-Like

Heroin

- *Street Terms:* Smack, horse, mud, brown sugar, junk, black tar, big H, dope
- *Administration:* Injected, smoked, or snorted
- *Potential Consequences:*
  - Addiction
  - Slowed and slurred speech
  - Slow gait
  - Constricted pupils, droopy eyelids, impaired night vision
  - Vomiting after first use and at very high doses
  - Decreased sexual pleasure, indifference to sex
  - Reduced appetite
  - Constipation

- "Nodding off" (at high doses)
- Respiratory depression or failure
- Increased risk of exposure to HIV, hepatitis, and other infectious diseases if injected
- Dry, itching skin and skin infections
- Death from overdose

- *Other Facts:* Heroin users quickly develop a tolerance to the drug and need more and more of it to get the same effects, or even to feel well.

Rohypnol

- *Street Terms:* Roach, roofies, the forget pill, rope, rophies, ruffles, R2, roofenol, la roche, rib

- *Administration:* Orally in pill form, dissolved in a drink, or snorted

- *Potential Consequences:*
  - Addiction
  - Blackouts with a complete loss of memory
  - A sense of fearlessness and aggression
  - Dizziness and disorientation
  - Nausea
  - Difficulty with motor movements and speaking
- *Other Facts:*
  - Referred to as the "date-rape" drug.
  - Creates a drunk feeling that lasts two to eight hours.

"Special K" (Ketamine Hydrochloride)

- *Street Terms:* Vitamin K, new ecstasy, psychedelic heroin, Ketalar, Ketaject, super-K, breakfast cereal

- *Administration:* Snorted or smoked

- *Potential Consequences:*
  - Delirium
  - Amnesia

- Impaired motor function
- Potentially fatal respiratory problems
- *Other Facts:*
  - Popular at raves.
  - Used as an anesthetic for animals.

Hallucinogens

PCP (Phencyclidine)

- *Street Terms:* Angel dust, ozone, rocket fuel, peace pill, elephant tranquilizer, dust
- *Administration:* Snorted, smoked, orally, or injected
- *Potential Consequences:*
  - Hallucinations
  - "Out-of-body" experiences
  - Impaired motor coordination
  - Inability to feel physical pain
  - Respiratory attack
  - Depression
  - Anxiety
  - Disorientation
  - Fear, panic, paranoia
  - Aggressive behavior and violence
  - Increased risk of exposure to HIV, hepatitis, and other infectious diseases if injected
  - Death
- *Other Facts:* Marijuana joints can be dipped into PCP without the smoker's knowledge.

LSD (Lysergic Acid Diethylamide)

- *Street Terms:* Acid, microdot, tabs, doses, trips, bits, sugar cubes
- *Administration:* Tabs taken orally or gelatin/liquid put in eyes

- *Potential Consequences:*
  - Elevated body temperature and blood pressure
  - Suppressed appetite
  - Sleeplessness
  - Tremors
  - Chronic recurring hallucinations
- *Other Facts:*
  - LSD is the most common hallucinogen.
  - LSD tabs are often decorated with colorful designs or cartoon characters.

Mushrooms (Psilocybin)

- *Street Terms:* Shrooms, caps, magic mushrooms
- *Administration:* Eaten or brewed and drunk in tea
- *Potential Consequences:*
  - Increased blood pressure
  - Sweating
  - Nausea
  - Hallucinations
- *Other Facts:* Many mushroom users purchase hallucinogenic mushroom spores via mail order.

Other Drugs

Inhalants

- *Street Terms:* Nitrous oxide, laughing gas, whippets, aerosol sprays, cleaning fluids, solvents
- *Administration:* Vapors are inhaled.
- *Potential Consequences:*
  - Headache, muscle weakness, abdominal pain
  - Severe mood swings and violent behavior
  - Numbness and tingling of hands and feet
  - Decrease or loss of sense of smell

- Nausea
- Nosebleeds
- Liver, lung, and kidney damage
- Dangerous chemical imbalances in the body
- Fatigue, lack of coordination
- Loss of appetite
- Decreases in heart and respiratory rates
- Hepatitis or peripheral neuropathy from long-time use

- *Other Facts:*
  - Hundreds of legal household products can be sniffed or "huffed" to get high.
  - All inhalants can be toxic.

Figure 49.4. *Hundreds of legal household products can be sniffed or "huffed" to get high.*

Marijuana/Hash

- *Street Terms:* Weed, pot, reefer, grass, dope, ganja, Mary Jane, sinsemilla, herb, Aunt Mary, skunk, boom, kif, gangster, chronic, 420

- *Administration:* Smoked or eaten

- *Potential Consequences:*
  - Bloodshot eyes
  - Dry mouth and throat
  - Impaired or reduced comprehension
  - Altered sense of time
  - Reduced ability to perform tasks requiring concentration and coordination, such as driving a car
  - Paranoia
  - Intense anxiety or panic attacks
  - Altered cognition, making acquisition of new information difficult
  - Impairments in learning, memory, perception, and judgment—difficulty speaking, listening effectively, thinking, retaining knowledge, problem solving, and forming concepts

- *Other Facts:*
  - The average age teens first use of marijuana is 14.
  - Marijuana can be smoked using homemade pipes and bongs made from soda cans or plastic beverage containers.

Steroids

- *Street Terms:* Rhoids, juice

- *Administration:* Orally or injected into muscle

- *Potential Consequences:*
  - Liver cancer
  - Sterility
  - Masculine traits in women and feminine traits in men
  - Aggression
  - Depression
  - Acne
  - Mood swings

- *Other Facts:* Steroid users subject themselves to more than 70 potentially harmful side effects.

Tobacco

- *Street Terms:* Smoke, bone, butt, coffin nail, cancer stick

- *Administration:* Cigarettes, cigars, pipe, smokeless tobacco (chew, dip, snuff)

- *Potential Consequences:*
  - Addiction
  - Heart and cardiovascular disease
  - Cancer of the lung, larynx, esophagus, bladder, pancreas, kidney, and mouth
  - Emphysema and chronic bronchitis
  - Spontaneous abortion, pre-term delivery, and low birth weight

- *Other Facts:* One in five 12th graders is a daily smoker.

Chapter 50

Marijuana

What Is Marijuana? Are There Different Kinds?

Marijuana is a green, brown, or gray mixture of dried, shredded leaves, stems, seeds, and flowers of the hemp plant (*Cannabis sativa*). Before the 1960s, many Americans had never heard of marijuana, but today it is the most often used illegal drug in this country.

Cannabis is a term that refers to marijuana and other drugs made from the same plant. Strong forms of cannabis include sinsemilla (sinseh-me-yah), hashish ("hash" for short), and hash oil.

All forms of cannabis are mind-altering (psychoactive) drugs; they all contain THC (delta-9-tetrahydrocannabinol), the main active chemical in marijuana. They also contain more than 400 other chemicals.

Marijuana's effect on the user depends on the strength or potency of the THC it contains. THC potency has increased since the 1970s but has been about the same since the mid-1980s. The strength of the drug is measured by the average amount of THC in test samples confiscated by law enforcement agencies.

- Most ordinary marijuana has an average of 3 percent THC.

- Sinsemilla (made from just the buds and flowering tops of female plants) has an average of 7.5 percent THC, with a range as high as 24 percent.

Excerpted from "Marijuana: Facts Parents Need to Know," National Institute on Drug Abuse (NIDA), National Institutes of Health (NIH), http://www.nida.nih.gov/MarijBroch/MarijParentstxt.html, revised November, 1998.

439

- Hashish (the sticky resin from the female plant flowers) has an average of 3.6 percent, with a range as high as 28 percent.

- Hash oil, a tar-like liquid distilled from hashish, has an average of 16 percent, with a range as high as 43 percent.

What Are the Current Slang Terms for Marijuana?

There are many different names for marijuana. Slang terms for drugs change quickly, and they vary from one part of the country to another. They may even differ across sections of a large city.

Terms from years ago, such as pot, herb, grass, weed, Mary Jane, and reefer, are still used. You might also hear the names Aunt Mary, skunk, boom, gangster, kif, or ganja.

There are also street names for different strains or "brands" of marijuana, such as "Texas tea," "Maui wowie," and "Chronic." A recent book of American slang lists more than 200 terms for various kinds of marijuana.

How Is Marijuana Used?

Most users roll loose marijuana into a cigarette (called a joint or a nail) or smoke it in a pipe. One well-known type of water pipe is the bong. Some users mix marijuana into foods or use it to brew a tea. Another method is to slice open a cigar and replace the tobacco with marijuana, making what's called a blunt. When the blunt is smoked with a 40 ounce bottle of malt liquor, it is called a "B-40."

Lately, marijuana cigarettes or blunts often include crack cocaine, a combination known by various street names, such as "primos" or "woolies." Joints and blunts often are dipped in PCP and are called "happy sticks," "wicky sticks," "love boat," or "tical."

How Many People Smoke Marijuana? At What Age Do Children Generally Start?

A recent government survey tells us:

- Marijuana is the most frequently used illegal drug in the United States. Nearly 69 million Americans over the age of 12 have tried marijuana at least once.

- About 10 million had used the drug in the month before the survey.

- Among teens 12 to 17, the average age of first trying marijuana was 14 years.

A yearly survey of students in grades 8 through 12 shows that 23 percent of 8th-graders have tried marijuana at least once, and by 10th grade, 21 percent are "current" users (that is, used within the past month). Among 12th-graders, nearly 50 percent have tried marijuana/ hash at least once, and about 24 percent were current users.

Other researchers have found that use of marijuana and other drugs usually peaks in the late teens and early twenties, then declines in later years.

How Can I Tell If My Child Has Been Using Marijuana?

There are some signs you might be able to see. If someone is high on marijuana, he or she might

- seem dizzy and have trouble walking
- seem silly and giggly for no reason
- have very red, bloodshot eyes
- have a hard time remembering things that just happened

When the early effects fade, over a few hours, the user can become very sleepy.

Parents should be aware of changes in their child's behavior, although this may be difficult with teenagers. Parents should look for withdrawal, depression, fatigue, carelessness with grooming, hostility, and deteriorating relationships with family members and friends. In addition, changes in academic performance, increased absenteeism or truancy, lost interest in sports or other favorite activities, and changes in eating or sleeping habits could be related to drug use. However, these signs may also indicate problems other than use of drugs.

In addition, parents should be aware of:

- signs of drugs and drug paraphernalia, including pipes and rolling papers
- odor on clothes and in the bedroom
- use of incense and other deodorizers
- use of eye drops
- clothing, posters, jewelry, etc., promoting drug use

Why Do Young People Use Marijuana?

Children and young teens start using marijuana for many reasons. Curiosity and the desire to fit into a social group are common reasons. Certainly, youngsters who have already begun to smoke cigarettes and/or use alcohol are at high risk for marijuana use.

Also, our research suggests that the use of alcohol and drugs by other family members plays a strong role in whether children start using drugs. Parents, grandparents, and older brothers and sisters in the home are models for children to follow.

Some young people who take drugs do not get along with their parents. Some have a network of friends who use drugs and urge them to do the same (peer pressure). All aspects of a child's environment—home, school, neighborhood—help to determine whether the child will try drugs.

Children who become more heavily involved with marijuana can become dependent, and that is their prime reason for using the drug. Others mention psychological coping as a reason for their use—to deal with anxiety, anger, depression, boredom, and so forth. But marijuana use is not an effective method for coping with life's problems, and staying high can be a way of simply not dealing with the problems and challenges of growing up.

Researchers have found that children and teens (both male and female) who are physically and sexually abused are at greater risk than other young people of using marijuana and other drugs and of beginning drug use at an early age.

Does Using Marijuana Lead to Other Drugs?

Long-term studies of high school students and their patterns of drug use show that very few young people use other drugs without first trying marijuana. The risk of using cocaine has been estimated to be more than 104 times greater for those who have tried marijuana than for those who have never tried it. Although there are no definitive studies on the factors associated with the movement from marijuana use to use of other drugs, growing evidence shows that a combination of biological, social, and psychological factors are involved.

Marijuana affects the brain in some of the same ways that other drugs do. Researchers are examining the possibility that long-term marijuana use may create changes in the brain that make a person more at risk of becoming addicted to other drugs, such as alcohol or cocaine. While not all young people who use marijuana go on to use other drugs, further research is needed to determine who will be at greatest risk.

What Are the Effects of Marijuana?

The effects of marijuana on each person depend on the

- type of cannabis and how much THC it contains
- way the drug is taken (by smoking or eating)
- experience and expectations of the user
- setting where the drug is used
- whether drinking or other drug use is also going on

Some people feel nothing at all when they first try marijuana. Others may feel high (intoxicated and/or euphoric).

It's common for marijuana users to become engrossed with ordinary sights, sounds, or tastes, and trivial events may seem extremely interesting or funny. Time seems to pass very slowly, so minutes feel like hours. Sometimes the drug causes users to feel thirsty and very hungry—an effect called "the munchies."

How Is Marijuana Harmful?

Marijuana can be harmful in a number of ways, through both immediate effects and damage to health over time.

Marijuana hinders the user's short-term memory (memory for recent events), and he or she may have trouble handling complex tasks. With the use of more potent varieties of marijuana, even simple tasks can be difficult.

Because of the drug's effects on perceptions and reaction time, users could be involved in auto crashes. Drug users also may become involved in risky sexual behavior. There is a strong link between drug use and unsafe sex and the spread of HIV (Human Immunodeficiency Virus), the virus that causes AIDS (Acquired Immunodeficiency Syndrome).

Under the influence of marijuana, students may find it hard to study and learn. Young athletes could find their performance is off; timing, movements, and coordination are all affected by THC.

What Are the Long-Term Effects of Marijuana?

While all of the long-term effects of marijuana use are not yet known, there are studies showing serious health concerns. For example, a group of scientists in California examined the health status of 450 daily smokers of marijuana but not tobacco. They found that the marijuana smokers had more sick days and more doctor visits for respiratory problems and other types of illness than did a similar group who did not smoke either substance.

Findings so far show that the regular use of marijuana or THC may play a role in cancer and problems in the respiratory, immune, and reproductive systems.

Cancer

It is hard to find out whether marijuana alone causes cancer because many people who smoke marijuana also smoke cigarettes and use other drugs. Marijuana smoke contains some of the same cancer-causing compounds as tobacco, sometimes in higher concentrations. Studies show that someone who smokes five joints per week may be taking in as many cancer-causing chemicals as someone who smokes a full pack of cigarettes every day.

Tobacco smoke and marijuana smoke may work together to change the tissues lining the respiratory tract. Marijuana smoking could contribute to early development of head and neck cancer in some people.

Immune System

Our immune system protects the body from many agents that cause disease. It is not certain whether marijuana damages the immune system of people. But both animal and human studies have shown that marijuana impairs the ability of T-cells in the lungs' immune defense system to fight off some infections. People with HIV and others whose immune system is impaired should avoid marijuana use.

Lungs and Airways

People who smoke marijuana often develop the same kinds of breathing problems that cigarette smokers have. They have symptoms of daily cough and phlegm (chronic bronchitis) and more frequent chest colds. They are also at greater risk of getting lung infections such as pneumonia. Continued marijuana smoking can lead to abnormal function of the lungs and airways. Scientists have found signs of lung tissue injured or destroyed by marijuana smoke.

Can a Person Become Addicted to Marijuana?

Yes. While not everyone who uses marijuana becomes addicted, when a user begins to seek out and take the drug compulsively, that person is said to be dependent on the drug or addicted to it.

Some heavy users of marijuana show signs of dependence because when they do not use the drug, they develop withdrawal symptoms. Some subjects in an experiment on marijuana withdrawal had symptoms, such as restlessness, loss of appetite, trouble with sleeping, weight loss, and shaky hands.

According to one study, marijuana use by teenagers who have prior serious antisocial problems can quickly lead to dependence on the drug. That study also found that, for troubled teenagers using tobacco, alcohol, and marijuana, progression from their first use of marijuana to regular use was about as rapid as their progression to regular tobacco use, and more rapid than the progression to regular use of alcohol.

What Is "Tolerance" for Marijuana?

"Tolerance" means that the user needs increasingly larger doses of the drug to get the same desired results that he or she previously got from smaller amounts. Some frequent, heavy users of marijuana may develop tolerance for it.

Are There Treatments to Help Marijuana Users?

Up until a few years ago, it was hard to find treatment programs specifically for marijuana users. Treatments for marijuana dependence were much the same as therapies for other drug abuse problems. These include detoxification, behavioral therapies, and regular attendance at meetings of support groups, such as Narcotics Anonymous.

Recently, researchers have been testing different ways to attract marijuana users to treatment and help them abstain from drug use. There are currently no medications for treating marijuana dependence. Treatment programs focus on counseling and group support systems. From these studies, drug treatment professionals are learning what characteristics of users are predictors of success in treatment and which approaches to treatment can be most helpful.

Further progress in treatment to help marijuana users includes a number of programs set up to help adolescents in particular. Some of these programs are in university research centers, where most of the young clients report marijuana as their drug of choice. Others are in independent adolescent treatment facilities. Family physicians are also a good source for information and help in dealing with adolescents' marijuana problems.

How Can I Prevent My Child from Getting Involved with Marijuana?

There is no magic bullet for preventing teenage drug use. But parents can be influential by talking to their children about the dangers of using marijuana and other drugs, and remain actively engaged in their children's lives. Even after teenage children enter high school, parents can stay involved in schoolwork, recreation, and social activities with their children's friends. Research shows that appropriate parental monitoring can reduce future drug use, even among those adolescents who may be prone to marijuana use, such as those who are rebellious, cannot control their emotions, and experience internal distress. To address the issue of drug abuse in your area, it is important to get involved in drug abuse prevention programs in your community or your child's school. Find out what prevention programs you and your children can participate in together.

Resources for Talking to Your Children about Marijuana

As this chapter has shown, marijuana is clearly a dangerous drug which poses a particular threat to the health and well-being of children and adolescents at a critical point in their lives—when they are growing, learning, maturing, and laying the foundation for their adult years. As a parent, your children look to you for help and guidance in working out problems and in making decisions, including the decision not to use drugs. As a role model, your decision to not use marijuana and other illegal drugs will reinforce your message to your children.

There are numerous resources, many right in your own community, where you can obtain information so that you can talk to your children about drugs. To find these resources, you can consult your local library, school, or community service organization.

The National Clearinghouse for Alcohol and Drug Information (NCADI) offers an extensive collection of publications, videotapes, and educational materials to help parents talk to their children about drug use. For more information on marijuana and other drugs, contact:

National Clearinghouse for Alcohol and Drug Information (NCADI)
P.O. Box 2345
Rockville, MD 20847
Toll-free: 800-729-6686
TDD: 800-487-4889

Chapter 51

Club Drugs

Club Drugs Aren't "Fun Drugs"

Across the country, teens and young adults enjoy all-night dance parties known as "raves" and increasingly encounter more than just music. Dangerous substances known collectively as club drugs— including Ecstasy, GHB, and Rohypnol—are gaining popularity. These drugs aren't "fun drugs."

Although users may think these substances are harmless, research has shown that club drugs can produce a range of unwanted effects, including hallucinations, paranoia, amnesia, and, in some cases, death. When used with alcohol, these drugs can be even more harmful. Some club drugs work on the same brain mechanisms as alcohol and, there-fore, can dangerously boost the effects of both substances. Also, there are great differences among individuals in how they react to these substances and no one can predict how he or she will react. Some people have been known to have extreme, even fatal, reactions the first time they use club drugs. And studies suggest club drugs found in party settings are often adulterated or impure and thus even more dangerous.

Because some club drugs are colorless, tasteless, and odorless, they are easy for people to slip into drinks. Some of these drugs have been

---

This chapter contains text from Alan I. Leshner, Ph.D., "Club Drugs Aren't Fun Drugs," National Institute on Drug Abuse, http://www.drugabuse.gov/ Published_Articles/fundrugs.html, January 2001, and "Club Drugs, an Update," U.S. Drug Enforcement Administration, http://www.dea.gov/pubs/intel/01026/ index.html, September 2001, and "Tips for Parents: The Truth about Club Drugs," U.S. Department of Justice, http://www.ojp.usdoj.gov/docs/clubdrug.pdf, 2001.

associated with sexual assaults, and for that reason they are referred to as "date rape drugs."

An Introduction to Club Drugs

"X," "Adam," and "MDMA" are slang names for Ecstasy, which is a stimulant and a hallucinogen. Young people may use Ecstasy to improve their moods or get energy to keep dancing; however, chronic abuse of Ecstasy appears to damage the brain's ability to think and regulate emotion, memory, sleep, and pain.

"G," "Liquid Ecstasy," "Georgia Home Boy" or Gamma-hydroxybutyrate (GHB) may be made in homes by using recipes with common ingredients. At lower doses, GHB can relax the user, but, as the dose increases, the sedative effects may result in sleep and eventual coma or death.

"Roofie" or "Roche" (Rohypnol) is tasteless and odorless. It mixes easily in carbonated beverages. Rohypnol may cause individuals under the influence of the drug to forget what happened. Other effects include low blood pressure, drowsiness, dizziness, confusion, and stomach upset.

"Special K" or "K" (Ketamine) is an anesthetic. Use of a small amount of ketamine results in loss of attention span, learning ability, and memory. At higher doses, ketamine can cause delirium, amnesia, high blood pressure, depression, and severe breathing problems.

"Speed," "Ice," "Chalk," "Meth" (Methamphetamine) is often made in home laboratories. Methamphetamine use can cause serious health concerns, including memory loss, aggression, violence, psychotic behavior, and heart problems.

"Acid" or Lysergic Acid Diethylamide (LSD) may cause unpredictable behavior depending on the amount taken, where the drug is used, and on the user's personality. A user might feel the following effects: numbness, weakness, nausea, increased heart rate, sweating, lack of appetite, "flashbacks," and sleeplessness.

Club Drugs: An Update

The dangers associated with this emerging drug market are that drug quality may vary significantly, and customers are often unaware that drug substitutions may occur when suppliers are unable to provide the drug currently in demand. This has been a problem with MDMA in some markets across the United States because "look-alike" substances, such as paramethoxyamphetamine (PMA) and dextromethorphan (DXM), are sold as MDMA. In addition, in a small percentage of cases, MDMA tablets have been found to contain other substances such as ketamine, PCP, caffeine, ephedrine, or methamphetamine. Since club drug users usually do not have a steady distribution network on which to depend, they unwittingly risk taking dangerous combinations of drugs. Not only can this lead to a greater risk of drug overdose, the lack of knowledge regarding what drug was ingested can complicate the task of emergency medical response personnel.

Raves

The use of synthetic drugs has become a popular method of enhancing the club and rave experience, which is characterized by loud, rapid-tempo "techno" music (140 to 200 beats per minute), light shows, smoke or fog, and pyrotechnics. Users of drugs such as MDMA report that the effects of the drugs heighten the user's perceptions, especially the visual stimulation. Quite often, users of MDMA at clubs will dance with light sticks to increase their visual stimulation. Legal substances such as Vick's nasal inhalers and Vick's VapoRub are often used to enhance the effects of the drugs.

Raves originated in England and on the Island of Ibiza (off the coast of Spain) and the culture rapidly spread to the United States, along with techno music. Raves are either legal or illegal, the former run by professional promoters with the requisite permits and licenses, while the latter are amateur operations at unapproved sites (such as warehouses or open fields). Attendance can range from several hundred to many thousands, and admission varies from $10 to over $50 but is sometimes free. Raves often are advertised on the Internet and by word-of-mouth. Advertisements range from simple black-and-white flyers to elaborate artwork designed to portray the freedom and social awareness that these events espouse. Event attendance is heavily determined by the disc jockeys working the shows.

While these events were not originally intended to serve as a nexus for illicit drug sales, the culture surrounding the events has created a favorable environment for illegal drug trafficking. Although raves may have been the traditional venue for drug purchases throughout the early 1990s, more recently these drugs are being purchased at clubs and brought back to college dorms, high school parties, and more rural party venues.

The Truth about Club Drugs: Tips for Parents

Effects common to all club drugs can include anxiety, panic, depression, euphoria, loss of memory, hallucinations, and psychotic behavior. Drugs, traces of drugs, and drug paraphernalia are direct evidence of drug abuse. Pacifiers, menthol inhalers, surgical masks, and other such items could also be considered indicators.

Where Do You Go for Help?

If you suspect your child is abusing drugs, monitor behavior carefully. Confirm with a trustworthy adult where your child is going and what he or she is doing. Enforce strict curfews. If you have evidence of club drug use, approach your child when he or she is sober, and if necessary, call on other family members and friends to support you in the confrontation.

Once the problem is confirmed, seek the help of professionals. If the person is under the influence of drugs and immediate intervention is necessary, consider medical assistance. Doctors, hospital substance programs, school counselors, the county mental health society, members of the clergy, organizations such as Narcotics Anonymous, and rape counseling centers stand ready and waiting to provide information and intervention assistance.

Part Seven

Protection from Social Harm

Chapter 52

Preventing Destructive Behavior by Harnessing the Power of Peers

Tragic events such as school shootings have presented us with images of adolescent aggressive and antisocial behavior. There is a national search for answers. Fortunately, a long-term commitment to basic behavioral research at National Institute of Mental Health (NIMH) is now paying off with the development and implementation of interventions to address these vexing problems.

Data from the National Youth Survey (NYS), a long-term study of violent offenders, point compellingly to the influence of deviant peers on a young person's tendency to engage in aggressive and violent behavior. This means that interventions must pay attention to the peer group, a key factor influencing whether a young person will lead a young adulthood characterized by violent and aggressive behaviors.

In 1976, the NYS began to follow a nationally representative sample of 1,725 boys and girls, ages 11 to 17. NYS investigators have monitored participants' self-reports of serious violent behaviors as well as official records of law violations. At the time of the most recent interview, the survey participants were between ages 27 and 33. More than half of all participants with records of violent behavior began to engage in such behavior between the ages of 14 and 17, although a substantial number began as young as age 12. After age 20, the risk

---

Excerpted from "Teens: The Company They Keep," National Institute of Mental Health, National Institutes of Health, http://www.nimh.nih.gov/publicat/teens.cfm, updated January 2001.

of initiating a pattern of violent behavior was found to be close to zero. In addition, they found that association with delinquent peers precedes the initiation and progression to serious violent offenses in 90 percent of cases. This finding was true of young people of all races.

Many well-intended attempts to "reform" severely delinquent youths have had few positive effects and even negative outcomes. Typically, these programs place delinquent youth with other delinquents in settings such as "group homes." One alternative based on the new under-standing of peer influence is the Therapeutic Foster Care program, a treatment model for serious and chronic delinquents (i.e., with an average of 14 arrests, including 4 for felonies). In this program, severely delinquent youths are placed in the homes of "therapeutic foster parents," carefully selected couples who are specially trained in science-based procedures for working with these troubled youngsters and are given round-the-clock support as well. The combination of this family-based care with specialized treatment interventions is intended to create a therapeutic environment in the context of the family home.

Evaluations of the Therapeutic Foster Care program have shown that it is more effective in reducing delinquency than the usual placement in group homes. It is also significantly less expensive, and has fewer runaways and fewer program failures. The Foster Family-based Treatment Association, developed under NIMH leadership, now has some 400 agency members across the U.S. who promote the use of this science-based and effective model. The research and its effective application seriously challenge the policies, programs and procedures that bring problem youth together.

Today's research is also suggesting new ways to prevent antisocial behavior through an array of interventions for youth that is aimed at peers and other key components of their social environment. Classroom and school-based programs are creating curriculums that include peer training, problem solving, conflict management, violence prevention, as well as programs for promoting social and emotional development in general school populations. These sorts of universal and targeted interventions compliment each other, and are designed to reduce violence across entire communities.

This continuing research has revealed that although there are identifiable and escalating pathways to antisocial behavior, and possibly some biological factors placing some children at risk, they are not set in stone, and individuals can make a long-term difference in the lives of troubled and troubling children.

References

Elliot DS, Huizinga D, Morse B. Self-reported violent offending — a descriptive analysis of juvenile violent offenders and their offending careers. *Journal of Interpersonal Violence*, 1986; 1: 472-514.

Elliot DS. Serious violent offenders: onset, developmental course, and termination — the American Society for Criminology 1993 Address. *Criminology*, 1994; 32: 1-21.

Dishion TJ, McCord J, Poulin F. When interventions harm: peer groups and problem behavior. *American Psychologist*, 1999; 54(9): 755-64.

Chamberlain P, Mihalic SF. Multidimensional treatment foster care. In: Elliott DS, ed. *Book Eight: blueprints for violence prevention*. Boulder, CO: Institute of Behavior Science, University of Colorado at Boulder, 1998.

Stroul BA, Friedman RM. Caring for severely emotionally disturbed children and youth. Principles for a system of care. *Children Today*, 1988; 17(4): 11-5.

Aos S, Phipps P, Barnoski, R, et al. The comparative costs and benefits of programs to reduce crime: a review of national research findings with implications for Washington State (Publication No. 99-05-1202). Olympia, WA: Washington Institute for Public Policy, 1999.

Chamberlain P, Reid J. Comparison of two community alternatives to incarceration for chronic juvenile offenders. *Journal of Consulting and Clinical Psychology*, 1998; 6(4): 624-33.

Chapter 53

Conflict Resolution Overview

Irritated? Frustrated? Angry? Ready to explode? You're not alone. Whether it's an argument with a friend, aggravation because a driver cut in front of you, or rage because your ex-girlfriend or -boyfriend is going out with your best friend—conflict is part of everyday life.

Anger leads to conflict, produces stress, hurts friendships, and can lead to violence. We can't always avoid anger or conflict, but we can learn to manage it without violence.

Steps to Managing Conflict

* Understand your own feelings about conflict. This means recognizing your triggers words or actions that immediately cause an angry or other emotional response. Your trigger might be a facial expression, a tone of voice, a finger being pointed, a stereotype, or a certain phrase. Once you know your triggers, you can improve control over your reactions.

* Practice active listening. Go beyond hearing only words; look for tone, body language, and other clues to what the other person is saying. Pay attention instead of thinking about what you're going to say next. Demonstrate your concentration by using body

"Making Peace: Tips on Managing Conflict," 1999, National Crime Prevention Council. © 1999 National Crime Prevention Council (NCPC). Reprinted with permission. Original NCPC document can be found at http://www.ncpc.org/publications/conflict.pdf.

language that says you are paying attention. Looking at the ground with your arms crossed says you're uninterested in what the other person is telling you. Look the other person in the eye, nod your head, and keep your body relaxed and your posture open.

- Come up with your own suggestions for solving the problem. Many people can think of only two ways to manage conflict— fighting or avoiding the problem. Get the facts straight. Use your imagination to think up ways that might help resolve the argument.

Moving toward Agreement

- Agree to sit down together in a neutral place to discuss the problem.

- Come to the discussion with a sincere willingness to settle the problem.

- State your needs—what results are important to you—and define the problem. Talk about the issues without insulting or blaming the other person.

- Discuss various ways of meeting needs or solving the problem. Be flexible and open-minded.

- Decide who will be responsible for specific actions after reaching agreement on a plan. Write the agreement down and give both people a copy.

Confronting the Issue

Good communication skills are a necessity throughout our lives. They allow us to resolve issues before they become problems and help keep us from getting angry. When talking to people, especially those who are acting confrontational,

- Look and feel relaxed.

- Keep your voice calm.

- Be direct and specific about what's bothering you. Use "I" statements—statements that emphasize how you feel, rather than blaming the other person. Instead of yelling, "You always interrupt me! You don't care what I think," try saying "I feel frustrated when I can't finish making my point. I feel as though my opinions don't matter."

- Ask, don't demand. Instead of saying, "Get away from me," try asking, "Would you please leave me alone right now? I am trying to talk to my friends."

- Make your statement once, then give it a rest. Don't repeat your point endlessly.

If You Can't Work It out... Get Help

Mediation. Many schools offer programs that train students to act as mediators for their peers. Mediators do not make decisions for people—they help people make their own decisions. Mediators encourage dialog, provide guidance, and help the parties define areas of agreement and disagreement.

Student courts. Many schools have implemented teen courts to help students solve disputes. Teens serve as judges, juries, prosecutors, and defenders in each case. Students caught fighting on campus can use the courts to settle arguments, and teen juries can "sentence" those students to detention or community service, rather than imposing suspension or expulsion.

Anger management. How to recognize attitudes, actions, and circumstances that trigger an angry reaction and how to control that reaction are skills that many teens and even some adults have not learned. Anger management training helps individuals take command of their emotional reactions instead of allowing their emotions to take command of them.

Arbitration. In arbitration, a neutral third party determines an action. Disputing parties agree on an arbitrator who then hears evidence from all sides, asks questions, and hands down a decision.

Where to Find Help

- Schools (check on whether they have peer mediation programs), colleges, and universities.

- Community or neighborhood dispute resolution centers.

- Local government family services.

- Private organizations listed in the telephone directory's Yellow Pages under "arbitration" or "mediation services."

- Law school legal clinics.

Chapter 54

Mentoring among Youth

What Is Peer Mentoring?

Peer mentoring programs match older youth with young students in one-on-one relationships to provide guidance for the children. Through this special relationship, peer mentors provide advice and support and serve as role models for younger people who need help. Challenges facing those being mentored include problems with schoolwork; social issues, such as pressure to drink or smoke; family problems or tension; and other typical difficulties of growing up. A peer mentor can also simply be someone for a younger student to hang out with.

Mentoring programs, when carefully designed and well run, provide positive influences for younger people who may need a little extra attention or who don't have a good support system available to them. For example, a young person who has recently lost a parent or close family member or who has experienced neglect or abuse or who simply feels lonely or uncomfortable in large group situations may especially benefit from the support, attention, and kindness of a peer mentor, along with other supports.

What Does Mentoring Do to Prevent or Reduce Crime?

For many children, having an older youth to talk to and spend time with—someone who provides encouragement and friendship—can

Exerpted from "Make a Friend—Be a Peer Mentor," *Youth in Action*, # 08, U.S. Department of Justice, Office of Justice Programs, Office of Juvenile Justice and Delinquency Prevention, July 1999.

mean the difference between dropping out of school and graduating, or between getting involved with drugs and developing the strength and self-confidence to resist such pressures. Youth involved in mentoring programs, in fact, have been shown to be less likely to experiment with drugs, less likely to be physically aggressive, and less likely to skip school than those not involved in such programs. Peer mentors provide the important extra support that many younger people need to make it through a difficult period in their lives when peer pressure and the desire to fit in are strong influences.

What Does It Take to Start a Mentoring Program?

To be effective, a mentoring program requires training for potential mentors, careful matching of mentors and children being mentored, and ongoing support to maintain and improve the mentoring relationship. To meet these goals, your group should learn about and develop ties to organizations in your community that offer services or provide information that would be helpful for you and those you are mentoring. Inform your mentors of available resources and encourage them to use them and recommend them to others as appropriate. In many areas, local Big Brothers Big Sisters organizations have set up a program called High School Bigs in which high school students volunteer to be Big Brothers or Big Sisters to elementary, middle, or junior high school students in their community.

With about 100 High School Bigs programs already in place across the Nation, you're likely to find one in your area. Contact Big Brothers Big Sisters of America to find out how to link up with one of these efforts to take advantage of existing training, matching resources, and support services.

If you decide to start your own program, get in touch with national and local mentoring organizations such as The National Mentoring Partnership, to find out how they began and how they currently operate. Also contact national service organizations such as the Corporation for National Service and AmeriCorps for general advice and guidance on mentoring and a wide variety of other volunteer work. The IdeaList Web site (www.idealist.org) is another great source of information on mentoring, listing 16,000 volunteer organizations and numerous books, organizations, and services that your volunteers may find useful. [See the Additional Help and Information section of this *Sourcebook* for contact info for many of the organizations listed above.]

When starting your mentoring program, decide what the minimum (weekly or monthly) time commitment for mentors should be. Include time required for training, meeting with the young person being mentored, following up on any issues that arise, attending sessions with other mentors, and learning about available resources. Emphasize to your volunteer mentors that they must not only serve as role models, but be able to provide sound advice and accurate information on issues ranging from schoolwork to family relationships to peer pressure. If tutoring will be part of your program, recognize that you will need to match the academic and interpersonal skills of the mentor with the educational needs of the youth being tutored. Obviously, personal compatibility is at the core of the match. You may have to assign pairs more than once before finding just the right match.

Next, consider where and how you will recruit or identify younger people to be mentored. A school's guidance office or a community day care or recreation center may be able to work with your program and supply names of students in need of support or guidance. Sometimes you can work with or "adopt" a single elementary, middle, or junior high school in your area and mentor students from that school only. In that case, you may be able to develop strong ongoing relationships with teachers, counselors, and administrators in the school and meet regularly in the school's cafeteria, auditorium, or classrooms. In addition, fewer transportation obstacles will exist when dealing with only one school. Having safe activities in convenient locations is essential.

Once you have decided whom you will be mentoring, talk with the parents or guardians of these children to secure their understanding of and commitment to your program. Explain how the mentoring process will work and the potential benefits to the children being mentored.

One of the most important steps in creating a mentoring program is training your volunteer mentors. To do so, think about the following questions:

- What kinds of activities are popular with the students you will be mentoring?

- How much help should mentors give with schoolwork?

- What should mentors do if they suspect a problem in the home of a child assigned to them?

- What do mentors do if a younger person says that he or she has been a victim of crime or has committed a crime? What if the child has experienced abuse or neglect?

- What can mentors do to influence their young friends' lives in a positive and lasting way?

The answers to these questions will help you create a framework for both your training program and your ongoing program activities. Spending time observing or working with an established mentoring program can also give you many good ideas.

Considering the complexities of organizing a mentoring program, you may want to work with a school counselor or a community group that can provide initial assistance with management and training. Starting the program with a small number of matched pairs is another good idea. As your program staff become more experienced and as interest grows, you can increase participation.

What Does It Take to Keep a Mentoring Program Going?

Mentors should schedule routine visits with those they are mentoring and should be absolutely committed to keeping those appointments. Because they play such an important role in the lives of their assigned young friends, mentors need to treat every scheduled meeting, tutoring session, and outing—even something as casual as meeting to share a soda after school—as a high priority.

Most mentoring programs recommend that pairs meet at least once a month, and more frequently in the beginning of a relationship. The Office of Juvenile Justice and Delinquency Prevention's (OJJDP) Juvenile Mentoring Program (JUMP) calls for a significantly greater time commitment, recommending that mentors meet with their assigned young friends three times a month for 4 hours each time (a total of 12 hours per month) and requiring no less than 1 to 2 hours per week (totaling 4–8 hours per month).

Whatever time commitment you decide on, your program coordinators will need to check regularly with mentors and make sure that they are meeting this requirement. Mentors helping with schoolwork may need to arrange more frequent meetings.

Your training program should show mentors how to take advantage of all kinds of situations—even running errands with the younger person—to create opportunities for learning and thoughtful, caring communication. Supply mentors ideas for social outings. Recommend, for example, participating in a book group for youth at a local library; visiting a museum or park; attending a concert, movie, or sporting event; taking part in community festivals; or doing volunteer work together for elderly or needy residents in your community. Encourage mentors to help their young friends develop new interests and have exciting new experiences. It may be possible for members of your group to obtain discount tickets to programs or shows at theaters, concert halls, museums, or other community establishments.

The primary element required for an effective mentoring program is time. Every mentor agrees to a minimum time commitment, as does the younger person being mentored.

Community support is another important ingredient. Volunteers can staff the program (as mentors, trainers, coordinators), but support from persons outside your group is also required for the program to be a success. Adults may form an advisory board or resource group to offer ideas and serve as a link to community training, services, and activities for your program. Teachers, administrators, counselors, and librarians from your local schools, for example, may agree to meet with mentors once a month to answer questions, provide lesson plans, and offer tips on how best to show support and provide guidance to the children being mentored.

What Are Some of the Challenges of a Mentoring Program?

Investment of self and time is a major challenge for mentors, and it should not be taken lightly. Failing to follow through with a relationship by canceling or not showing up for a meeting or by just not demonstrating enough attention and support to someone who depends on and looks up to you is worse than never getting involved in the first place. It is sometimes difficult for volunteers to understand this. Before you assign them to someone, make sure that your mentors appreciate the importance of the role they'll be playing and that they're ready and able to keep their commitment to a younger person.

Compatibility is another challenge for mentoring programs. Your group should have a plan for dealing with situations in which the mentor and youth just don't get along. When that happens, each person needs to understand that there is no blame, simply a need for a different match. A new match should be made as soon as possible.

Mentors need to be patient. It is difficult to realize that a younger person may not be immediately grateful for your kindness, attention, and friendship. Positive changes may not show up for several months. A friendship may grow steadily for a while and at other times may seem stuck. In either case, both parties need to give the mentoring relationship a chance to grow. Relationships between mentors and the parents of children being mentored are also occasionally sensitive. Though they sometimes feel jealous of or threatened by mentors, parents need to understand that mentors are not trying to take over the role of parents. Mentors, in turn, need to respect and support parents' rules and concerns for the children while building their own relationships.

What Are Some of the Rewards?

Successful mentors may earn satisfaction from knowing that they have helped their young friends to develop strong relationships with older peers, learn life skills, or master academic subjects. They may see significant improvements in academic performance, behavior, or communication skills in the young people they are working with and know that they have played a part in those changes. The youth being mentored also receive a variety of rewards. These range from such short-term benefits as higher grades and positive feedback from teachers, parents, and friends to such long-term benefits as greater self-confidence, stronger communication skills, and the strength to resist peer pressure—all of which will make them more likely to become productive, happy adults and assets to their communities.

How Can a Mentoring Program Be Evaluated?

Evaluating your project can help you learn whether it has met its goals, but only if you decide up front what you want to evaluate and how you will go about doing so. The purpose of conducting any evaluation is to answer practical questions of decision-makers who want to know whether to continue a program, extend it to other areas, improve it, or close it down. In particular, you will want to be able to show that your mentoring program does one or all of the following:

- Improves the grades or other measures of academic performance of the youth being mentored.

- Improves school attendance for those being mentored.

- Reduces rates of truancy, suspension, expulsion, and dropout for those being tutored.

- Improves mentored youth's self-esteem and confidence.

- Teaches mentors valuable communication skills.

- Teaches mentors the importance of commitment and sensitizes them to the needs, experiences, and situations of other members of their community.

- Strengthens community ties by creating opportunities for youth to work with and learn from younger and older members of the community.

- Dispels or reduces stereotypes, misconceptions, or fears that members of different age groups in the community may have held about others prior to the program.

Evaluating a peer mentoring program requires both short- and long-term perspectives. In the short term, regular check-ins with mentoring pairs and careful monitoring of recruitment and training will help to keep the program on the right path. In the long term, following up with youth who were mentored to determine how the relationship affected them can provide important data on the program's success.

In addition, both mentors and the youth being mentored should have a regular opportunity to evaluate the program. Ask them what they find most valuable and what they believe should be changed. Secure such input by administering a survey every month (or week) or by having a hotline or suggestion box available at all times. The following are examples of questions to ask both mentors and the persons being mentored when evaluating your program:

- How did the peer mentoring program help you?

- What were some of your favorite activities with the program?

- What were some of your least favorite activities?

- How did the program compare with your expectations?

- How do you think the program could be improved?

- Would you recommend this program to your peers?

- What did your mentor do especially well?

- In what areas did he or she need improvement?

In evaluating your peer mentoring program, also consider whether and how it meets the following more general crime prevention goals:

- Reduces crime or fear of crime.

- Educates and informs a target audience.

- Is cost effective.

- Has a lasting impact.

- Attracts support and resources.

- Makes people feel more positive about being a member of their school or community.

Be sure to include an evaluation step in your mentoring program's overall plan. Ask yourself what you can do to meet the many different needs of the youth being mentored and how you can recruit more mentors and provide services to a greater number of young persons in your community. Take a good look at the input you receive from mentors and the children being mentored. Then, make adjustments to strengthen your program.

Learning to evaluate the things you do is a good skill, one you can apply to all aspects of your life. Good luck with your mentoring project and be a good role model!

Chapter 55

Peer Mediation in Youth

What Is Mediation?

In a process called mediation, a person trained as a mediator helps two (or more) people resolve a conflict or disagreement. The conflict being resolved might be as simple as who should pay for a damaged locker. Or it might be as complex as which parent should receive custody of a child in the case of a divorce. In either situation, mediation involves solving the dispute through peaceful means. The mediator, however, does not simply listen to the conflict and draw up the terms of a solution; the people with the conflict (the participants or disputants) do that. In addition, it is the participants, not the mediator, who enforce the agreed-upon solution.

The mediator plays a special role. He or she doesn't decide what is right or wrong or find people guilty or innocent, as a judge would in a courtroom. Instead, the mediator tries to help the disputants find and agree upon a peaceful way to resolve their conflict.

How Does Mediation Prevent or Reduce Crime?

As you know, conflict is an unavoidable part of life. Passengers in a car might disagree about a wrong turn on a road trip. A person may play music more loudly than others would like. Friends may argue over who is to blame for a broken possession. These are all types of conflict.

Exerpted from "Want to Resolve a Dispute? Try Peer Mediation," *Youth in Action*, # 13, U.S. Department of Justice, Office of Justice Programs, Office of Juvenile Justice and Delinquency Prevention, March 2000.

Conflicts are not always minor and harmless. Assaults or threatened assaults often happen between people who know each other and, in many of these cases, start off with small arguments or disagreements. The mediation process provides a way for these people to resolve their disagreements before either party resorts to violence. It also helps people reach agreements without feeling they have had to "give in." In this way, both sides in mediation come out winners!

Mediation has helped to reduce violence in neighborhoods and in schools. Using peers as mediators—a process known as "peer mediation"—is a popular way of handling conflicts and preventing violence in middle schools and high schools. Schools using this process recruit and train students interested in being peer mediators. Guidance counselors or other trained professionals teach the young mediators how to listen to both sides of an argument, offer unbiased impressions, and help students in conflict find a workable solution to their problem. For example, the Peer Mediation in Schools Program, developed by the New Mexico Center for Dispute Resolution, trains school staff and students in peer mediation. This program uses selected students as peer mediators and includes:

- Curriculum focused on conflict resolution.

- Staff orientation designed to help teachers exhibit the communication skills they are trying to instill in their students.

Peer mediators help the disputants rechannel anger and reach peaceful agreements. When a disagreement or conflict arises, a teacher, an administrator, a concerned student, or the fighting students themselves can refer the issue to peer mediation. A peer mediator is quickly assigned, and the mediation process begins, resolving the issue and preventing further discord. Playground mediators in elementary schools similarly help prevent fights and resolve disagreements between much younger students.

Mediation programs run for and by youth have enjoyed great success across the Nation. Students in Buncombe County, NC, for example, have conducted more than 1,100 mediation hearings at middle schools and high schools. The disputes were handled by more than 330 student mediators, all of whom received training and technical assistance from the Mediation Center of Asheville, NC. According to Buncombe County school officials, the mediation sessions were a huge success. They eliminated 742 days of in-school suspension and 1,220 days of out-of-school suspension. The school system also reported reduced violence in the schools as a result of the mediation program.

Warning

If you are planning a mediation program, be sure to work closely with your local community mediation program, police department, sheriff's office, or school administration. Some disputes are too complex or potentially violent to be solved by peer mediation alone.

What Does It Take to Start a Mediation Program?

Any effective crime prevention program requires careful planning. To make your mediation program a success, follow these six critical planning steps.

Step 1: Identify the Types of Conflict to Address

When planning your mediation program, first identify the types of conflict you want to help solve. Are there particular places, organizations, or programs in your community where people need extra help resolving disputes or frequently experience conflict? What kinds of disputes tend to arise? Family problems? Conflicts involving school rules or policies? Fights over possessions? Arguments between students of different races or ethnic groups? After examining the types of conflict in your school and community, determine which ones can be subject to mediation. Check to see if there is a community mediation center in your area, and ask the center's staff what they have learned about community conflict.

Step 2: Decide When to Use Mediation

After taking a good look at the types of problems that exist in your school, community, facility, or organization and determining which type of problem or conflict your program will address, decide when mediation should be used. Talk to your school administrators, teachers, peers, and adults about how mediation might help in your school or community. Should it be used only on an emergency basis or only when the possibility of violence exists? Who should refer disputes? How quickly after a referral will mediation take place?

Step 3: Recruit Mediators

Your next important planning activity is to recruit potential mediators. They could be just a few family members or friends or an entire

471

group. Whatever the case, identify and recruit people who have the time and desire to complete all necessary training. Volunteers need to understand that they will be helpers, not judges. They will not determine guilt or innocence or impose punishments. Rather, they will help disputants find the best possible solution to their particular conflict. Mediators do not impose their ideas on the people in disagreement. They help others decide on solutions that are best for them.

Step 4: Train Mediators

Training mediators is the single most important step when planning a mediation program. To mediate effectively, a person must be a good listener, one who will not take sides in a dispute. A mediator must also be able to help disputants come up with several different ways to resolve their conflict. He or she must understand how to guide the mediation process and keep disputants focused. Although disputants may want concentrate only on their differences of opinion, they must be kept moving toward their goal—an agreed-upon solution to their problem.

Adult mediators may volunteer to help youth start mediation programs. Sometimes courts or bar associations will supply names of local mediators who can donate time or services. (See the Resources chapter at the end of this *Sourcebook* for names of organizations that can help.) Some communities have community mediation centers that provide training; some have school mediation projects that have many services. Local law schools may also be able provide training or volunteers.

It is hard to estimate how much time is needed to train your mediators. Training youth mediators can take anywhere from 20 to 60 hours. The number of hours needed depends on how old the disputants and mediators are, how complex the conflicts are likely to be, and how experienced your mediators are. Whatever the age and experience of your mediators may be, everyone can learn the basic principles.

Be sure each specific part of the training is well planned. Such planning will help ensure the success of your effort. Professional trainers know that preparation and organization are critical steps for good training.

Step 5: Identify Disputants

You begin by identifying people who need help to settle conflicts or arguments peacefully. Finding parties with conflicts appropriate for your mediation program requires support from school officials, community leaders, or other adults. Those individuals can help refer disputes to your program. They can also help you to explain the value of mediation to disputants and determine the kinds of disagreements your program will handle.

Step 6: Select a Neutral Location for Mediation Hearings

When planning your mediation program or seeking a place to resolve any kind of disagreement, it is important to choose a neutral location. If your program focuses on disputes between students and school administrators, you won't want to meet in the principal's conference room. If you're trying to settle an argument between members of rival sports teams, you similarly won't want to meet on one team's playing field. The place selected should not be associated with any single group, clique, gang, or attitude. A guidance counselor, school administrator, neighborhood leader, or youth group officer can help you think of possible places and find out if they're available.

Make sure that the location you choose allows everyone involved in the mediation to feel physically comfortable.

- Are there windows?
- Is the lighting sufficient?
- Can the temperature be adjusted?
- Is the room large enough to seat at least three people?
- Is there a large table, or would disagreeing parties have to sit side by side?
- Is there enough room for the mediator and the participants to get up and walk around?
- Is there a private room or space nearby if a disputant needs to make a phone call or be alone for a period of time?
- Is the location easily accessible to your mediators and likely disputants?

Answering the questions above and selecting a neutral location are necessary to ensure that your mediation sessions are as unbiased and confidential as possible.

What Does It Take to Keep a Mediation Program Going?

Recruit New Mediators

One of the biggest challenges to any crime prevention program operated by youth is a high turnover rate among volunteers. Peer mediation programs are no different. Your mediation program will eventually lose its mediators as these trained volunteers graduate from high school, get paying jobs, move on to college (perhaps out of the area), or simply get too old to be youth mediators. They may remain an asset to your program by training new mediators or continuing to volunteer their time, but they will no longer be peers of your community's youth. Thus, it is vital to keep recruiting and training new mediators to continue and expand your program.

As you recruit mediators, explain to them what it means personally to be a mediator. Resolving disputes fairly requires putting aside one's own judgments and feelings about an issue, facilitating discussion and fact-finding, being positive, listening carefully, and offering encouragement.

Provide Ongoing Training

In addition to training new mediators, it's important to provide refresher and skills improvement training to current mediators. Mediators should have opportunities to share their abilities and experiences and learn from one another. This is a good way for mediators to develop new skills.

Demonstrate and Share Your Program's Success

It's important to be able to demonstrate your program's success. Positive information about the results and effects of your program is critical to proving that the program has had an impact and deserves continued (or increased) support. Publicizing positive results will also help you recruit new mediators and disputants and attract additional resources to improve and expand your program.

Recognition by the community is also vital. Mediators and other volunteers need to know that their efforts are appreciated and valued, not just by the program, but by the community as a whole. Placing an article in a school or community newspaper, posting thank you letters from disputants, and scheduling public celebrations are good ways to recognize volunteers. Providing T-shirts, hats, or other such "uniforms" with your program's logo or motto printed on them can also help build a strong group identity and a sense of teamwork.

What Are Some of the Challenges You Will Face?

For conflict mediation to be successful, both parties must want to settle their disagreement before it develops into a larger one. This

474

means that disputants may have to compromise or set aside some of their personal interests. One of the mediator's biggest challenges, therefore, is to separate the disputants' real interests from their stated positions. While a person may claim to want what's best for his or her school, his or her judgment may be clouded by other factors, such as ego, reputation among peers, or potential financial benefits.

Mediators must also work hard to avoid getting sidetracked. The positions of the disputants should not get in the way of developing a reasonable solution. If disputants are not encouraged to reveal and discuss their real interests, any agreement they reach will be built on shaky ground.

What Are Some of the Rewards?

Successful mediation brings a great sense of accomplishment to both the disputants and the mediator. Two parties who were previously close to fighting now agree on a nonviolent way to settle their problems. Even an ultimately unsuccessful mediation may create some sense of accomplishment if the process allowed participants to better understand one another's perspective and what is really important to them. Mediating conflicts makes your school, neighborhood, and community less violent while helping people take responsibility for their actions.

Mediation will also make the people involved with the process— mediators, other volunteers, disputants—better able to resolve conflicts in their lives peacefully. Conflicts arise every day at school, in the workplace, in the community, and at home. Seeing another person as a disputant in a mediation and considering his or her interests and needs makes it easier to see that person as another human being with perceptions that may differ from yours. With that understanding, it's easier for people to find common ground.

How Can You Evaluate Your Program?

Evaluating your mediation program can help you learn whether it has met its goals, but only if you decide up front what you want to evaluate and how you'll go about doing so. The purpose of conducting an evaluation is to answer practical questions of decision-makers and program implementors who want to know whether to continue a program, extend it to other sites, modify it, or close it down.

There are many different aspects of mediation that you can examine and evaluate. Keep track of how many mediators have been

475

trained and how many hours of service they contribute each year. Also keep records of how many disputes they have mediated and whether those disputes ended with a signed agreement.

When evaluating your program, also examine the quality of every mediation session. Always ask for and secure feedback at the end of the session to find out what can be done to improve the process.

- Were participants satisfied with the outcome? Why or why not?

- What did they learn?

- What was helpful?

- Did the mediator succeed in helping the parties find an acceptable solution? If so, how? If not, why not?

- What were the mediator's strengths and weaknesses?

- Would the disputants participate in mediation again? Why or why not?

Lasting agreements are signs of success. Arrange to contact disputants 2 weeks or a month after they have signed an agreement. Ask them whether the conflict remains solved. Survey participants in past mediations as well.

When evaluating your program, also consider its effect on your community as a whole. Are there fewer fights in schools since your program started? Have disturbance complaints with your police department or sheriff's office dropped? Are assault charges down? Do people in your school or neighborhood feel there has been less fighting in the hallways or in public places?

In evaluating your mediation program, also consider whether and how well it meets the following more general crime prevention goals:

- Reduces crime.

- Reduces fear of crime.

- Is cost effective.

- Has a lasting impact.

- Attracts support and resources.

- Makes people feel safe and better about being in your school or community.

Be sure to include an evaluation step in your overall plan. Learning to evaluate the things you do is a good skill, one you can apply to all aspects of your life. Ask yourself how you can better reach your goals, involve more people, and spread your message to a wider audience. Then, adjust your activities to strengthen your project.

Developing, carrying out, and evaluating a mediation project can help youth, children, and adults in your community. Good luck with mediation and resolve some conflicts!

Sample Mediation Session

Step 1: Introduction

The mediator's first job is to make the parties feel at ease and explain the ground rules. The mediator's role is not to make a decision but to help the parties reach agreement. The mediator explains that he or she will not take sides.

Step 2: Telling the Story

Each party tells what happened. One person tells his or her side of the story first. No interruptions are allowed. The other party then explains his or her version of the facts. Again, no interruptions are allowed. Any of the participants, including the mediator, may take notes during the process. The mediator's notes are thrown away at the end of the session to ensure confidentiality.

Step 3: Identifying Facts, Issues, and Interests

The mediator next attempts to identify any agreed-upon facts and issues and the issues that are important to each person. The mediator listens to each side, summarizes each party's view, and checks to make sure each party understands the other's view.

Step 4: Identifying Alternative Solutions

During this step, the participants (with help from the mediator) think of all possible solutions to their problem. Because the opposing sides to the dispute probably arrived at the mediation session with a desired outcome in mind, it is often difficult for them to consider other solutions. The mediator makes a list of solutions and asks each party to explain his or her feelings about each one.

Step 5: Revising and Discussing Solutions

On the basis of feelings expressed by each party, the mediator revises the list of possible solutions and tries to identify a solution that both parties may be able to agree on.

Step 6: Reaching an Agreement

The mediator helps the parties to reach an agreement by choosing a solution that has been discussed and that both parties agree on. After the parties have decided on a solution, an agreement should be put in writing. The written agreement should be as specific as possible, stating exactly what each party has agreed to do and when he or she will do it. The agreement should also explain what will happen if either disputant breaks the agreement. Some agreements require parties to appear for additional mediation; others call for the payment of money or the performance of services when an agreement is broken. In most instances, the parties themselves are responsible for enforcing the contract by bringing examples of breached agreements to the attention of the mediation program. Once it is finalized, the agreement, which usually takes the form of a contract, is signed by both parties.

Chapter 56

Preventing Youth Hate Crime

Responding to Hate-Motivated Behavior in Schools

Introduction

Racial tension and violent behavior among students are prevalent in schools today. Despite the fact that many hate-motivated crimes go unreported, the number of reported incidents is up. When students in informal surveys nationwide acknowledge that fighting and violence in school is one of their major concerns, we know that we have a national problem. Students and faculty want safe places in which to teach and learn, but often racial tension results in fights, name-calling, graffiti, and other bias-related incidents. These acts of hatred often represent a much deeper-rooted expression of hostility against a person or property because of race, religion, nationality, gender, ethnicity, or sexual orientation than we would like to admit. Schools and other institutions need to learn to recognize and address bias-related incidents. Educators must encourage students to speak up when they see or experience something hateful, and teachers and students must learn to do something about the problem.

The information in this chapter is reprinted from "Hate Hurts: Tips for Teachers/Parents," by the Anti-Defamation League (ADL). Further information about this subject is available on the ADL website at www.adl.org. © 2000. Reprinted with permission of the Anti-Defamation League.

Definition of a Hate Incident

Hate-motivated incidents are defined as an expression of hostility against a person or property because of the victim's race, religion, disability, gender, ethnicity, or sexual orientation. However, hate-motivated incidents include those actions that are motivated by bias, but do not meet the necessary elements required to prove a crime. This may include such behavior as non-threatening name-calling, using racial slurs or disseminating racist leaflets. Protected classifications vary from state to state.

Definition of a Hate Crime

Hate crimes are defined under specific penal code sections as an act or an attempted act by any person against the person or property of another individual or group which in any way constitutes an expression of hostility toward the victim because of his or her race, religion, sexual orientation, national origin, disability, gender, or ethnicity. (This includes, but is not limited to, threatening phone calls, hate mail, physical assaults, vandalism, cross burning, destruction of religious symbols, and fire bombings. Protected classifications vary from state to state.)

Plan Ahead

1. Work with your school administration to establish a plan for responding promptly to hate incidents and hate crimes.

2. Educate school staff on how to recognize hate-motivated incidents and hate crimes.

3. Establish procedures for reporting hate-motivated incidents/crimes.

4. Establish school policies which clearly indicate that hate-motivated behavior will not be tolerated.

Response Strategies

1. Respond promptly to incidents.

2. Conduct a complete investigation of the incident, including the questioning of victim(s), witnesses, and perpetrators. Report hate-motivated crimes to law enforcement. If there is

physical damage—defacing, spray-painting, etc.—take photographs. As soon as law enforcement personnel have viewed the damage and photographs have been token, have the damage repaired. If hate literature has been distributed, collect the literature for evidence.

3. Train school counselors to assist hate-motivated crime victims and/or provide referral sources to community agencies. Reassure the victim and/or her family that the incident will be treated seriously.

4. Determine proper disciplinary action according to school protocols.

5. If your district has a reporting policy, submit a hate-motivated crime/incident report to the appropriate district offices.

6. Determine whether or not additional follow-up activities are necessary, e.g., staff and student awareness activities, responses to the media, etc.

Factors in Identifying Acts as Bias Related

The motivation behind the act determines whether an incident is bias related. Although no one factor is conclusive, the following criteria, applied singly or in combination, should be used to determine if probable cause exists to believe that an incident was motivated entirely or in part by animosity toward the victim because of his or her race, religion, sexual orientation, ethnicity, or national origin.

1. Were words, symbols or acts which are or may be offensive to an identifiable group used by the perpetrator, or are they present as evidence? For example, is there a burning cross or a pointed swastika, or were derogatory words or slurs or graffiti directed at a particular racial, religious, ethnic, or other group?

2. Are the victim and the suspected perpetrator members of different racial, religious, or ethnic groups?

3. Has the victim or the victim's group been subjected to post incidents of a similar nature? Has there been tension or hostility between the victim's group and another particular racial, religious, or ethnic group?

4. Is the victim the only minority group member in the neighborhood or one of just a few such persons?

5. Did the victim recently move into the area? Is the victim acquainted with neighbors and/or local community groups? Has there been evidence of hostility toward the victim by neighbors?

6. When multiple incidents occur at the same time, are all victims of the some race, ethnicity, religion, national origin, or sexual orientation?

7. Does a meaningful portion of the community perceive and respond to the situation as a bias related incident?

8. Does the incident appear to be timed to coincide with a specific holiday or date of significance (e.g., Martin Luther King Day, Rosh Hashanah, Ramadan)?

9. Has the victim been involved in recent public activity that would possibly make him or her a target? For example, has the victim been associated with any prominent recent or past activities relating to his or her race, ethnicity, religion or sexual orientation (e.g., NAACP, gay rights rally, demonstrations by or against the Ku Klux Klan)?

10. Has there been prior/recent news coverage of events of a similar nature?

11. What were the manner and means of attack (e.g., color of point, symbols or signs utilized, unusual spelling of the words used)? Is the *modus operandi* similar to other documented incidents?

12. Is there an ongoing neighborhood problem that may have initiated or contributed to the act (i.e., could the act be retribution for some conflict between neighbors or with area juveniles)?

13. Does the perpetrator responsible have a true understanding of the impact of the crime/incident on the victim or other group members? Are the perpetrators juveniles?

14. Does the crime/incident indicate possible involvement by an organized hate group (e.g., Ku Klux Klan, American Nazi Party)? For example: Is the literature printed or handwritten? Does it

contain an identifiable hate group symbol or insignia or hate group address? Is there any documented or suspected organized hate group activity in the area?

Holiday Activities Guidelines

Be Accurate and Sensitive

Religious holidays offer excellent opportunities throughout the year for teaching about religion and its historical importance. However, in order to avoid student embarrassment, don't ask children to explain their own religious practices or observances or to bring religious objects to class as a basis of discussion. Be aware that some religions teach that celebrating holidays—or birthdays—is wrong. Children should always be permitted not to participate and should have the opportunity to engage in optional, enjoyable activities. Remember that writing a letter to Santa may be uncomfortable for the non-Christian child who is "not on his list." An option that is true to the spirit of the winter holidays might be encouraging children to write to merchants, or other children, seeking donations for children who lack any toys.

Avoid Stereotyping

Not all members of the same religious group observe a holiday in the same way. Make sure that you do not treat some holidays as regular and others as exotic, nor that you introduce an ethnic group only in terms of its holiday observances. Multicultural activities that focus only on foods and holidays have been justifiably labeled the tourist approach. Better to share the holiday's name, when it occurs, who participates and how this holiday reveals the historical experiences and culture of its followers. Because some holiday customs incorporate stereotypes, help children, for example, to identify stereotypes of Native Americans on Thanksgiving cards and decorations, and to understand why Thanksgiving can be a reminder of promises broken and dispossession for some while it represents togetherness and thanks for others. Spend time creating new cards and decorations that celebrate the holiday with respect for all.

Be Constitutionally Appropriate

Holiday observances, if held under public school auspices, violate the First Amendment's separation-of-church-and-state mandate. Joint celebrations (Christmas-Chanukah, for example) do not solve the problem, as they only serve to introduce religious observances into the schools, They also tend to pit holidays in competition, with each other and distort the significance of each. While recognizing a diverse group of holidays validates children and their families, bringing religious leaders into a public setting is not appropriate. The use of religious symbols such as a cross, menorah, crescent, Star of David, crèche, symbols of Native American religions, the Buddha, among others, that are part of a religious tradition is permitted as a teaching aid, provided such symbols are displayed only as an educational example of the culture and religious heritage of the holiday and are temporary in nature. They may not be used as decorations.

Use holiday activities as a way of enhancing respect for religions and traditions different from one's own, but stress common themes, as well. Many religions focus on festivals of light, including Christmas, Chanukah, Kwanzaa, Santa Lucia Day and Diwali. Liberation is the theme of such holidays as the Fourth of July, Passover, Cinco de Mayo, Juneteenth and Martin Luther King Jr.'s Birthday. By connecting holiday themes, you communicate that holidays are a valid expression of cultural and religious pride. You also convey that it's okay to be different.

What Is Anti-Bias Education?

All members of U.S. society are expected to be responsible citizens. A pluralistic and free society is sustained when all people are treated with respect, dignity, equality, and fairness regardless of differences. School communities have always had as part of their educational mission a mandate to create learning opportunities in which the development of responsible citizenship is a primary goal.

Changing demographics, economic disparity, and societal tensions foster climates of distrust and fear among people who lack the knowledge and skills to be successful in a pluralistic society. The potential for conflict, discrimination, and scapegoating is high when prejudice and stereotypes go unchallenged or are ignored. Biased behavior is learned behavior. Left unexamined, biased attitudes can lead to biased behaviors, which have the potential to escalate into violent acts of hate.

Biased behavior can be subtle or overt. In schools, name-calling and acts of social exclusion are the most common examples of discriminatory behavior and prejudicial thinking. Although children are not born prejudiced, by preschool they have already acquired stereotypes or negative attitudes toward those they perceive as "others." In an attempt to minimize the development of prejudice, well-meaning adults often teach children to ignore differences and focus only on similarities. Just as common experiences are part of the glue that holds communities together, understanding and respecting differences are essential for successful multicultural societies.

Anti-bias education incorporates the philosophy of multicultural education while expanding to include other forms of bias, stereotypes, and misinformation. Anti-bias education not only addresses race and ethnicity but also includes gender, language, religious diversity, sexual orientation, physical, and mental abilities and economic class. Anti-bias education takes an active, problem solving approach that is integrated into all aspects of an existing curriculum and a school's environment. An anti-bias curriculum promotes an understanding of social problems and provides students with strategies for improving social conditions.

Educators who seek to challenge stereotypes and biases can provide students with factual, concrete information and positive interpersonal experiences. Teachers can also learn how to effectively address biased behavior when it occurs. A comprehensive program of staff development, curricular materials, and school assessment tools can help teachers, students, parents and other community members create and sustain a cohesive community where positive and equitable relationships are established across cultural barriers.

Creating a Positive Environment in Which to Raise Diversity Issues

"I don't discuss those issues in my classroom... I am sure that if I did it would only open a whole Pandora's box that I just don't have time to deal with."

Sound familiar? The above statement expresses the sentiments of many teachers. Time is always a factor in the school day, and teachers are not wrong to safeguard it as a precious commodity.

At the same time, there are teachers whose reasons for not addressing diversity issues in the classroom have less to do with time than with fear of conflict and concern about their competency to handle such discussions. In addition, there are teachers whose own life experiences have not included many opportunities for interaction with diverse populations, who can feel uncomfortable addressing issues of differences in light of their limited firsthand experiences.

Racism is a word often spoken in hushed tones, as though it were an unmentionable subject, like a fatal disease. And to make matters more difficult, schools of education, administrators, and colleagues often do not provide much expertise or support in this arena for teachers.

Recognizing that there are many legitimate reasons for teachers to be apprehensive about raising diversity issues in the classroom, the following list of teaching practices is offered to assist those who want to begin creating a safe classroom climate conducive to an honest exchange of ideas. The list is not meant to be comprehensive; rather it is intended to provide a good place to begin the journey.

Know Yourself

Examine your own cultural biases and assumptions. Ask yourself if your understanding of cross-cultural miscommunication includes the idea that such misunderstandings are the result of a clash between two cultures, and not caused solely by the person whose ethnicity is not of the dominant mainstream culture.

Lay Foundation

Lay a foundation by establishing ground rules and by defining terms. The ground rules serve as community norms that everyone in the class agrees to abide by. Ask students to develop these norms by thinking about what classroom conditions would have to exist in order for them to feel they can share their ideas and feelings openly. Keep these guidelines posted in your room at all times, and remind students that every person, not just the teacher, is responsible for seeing that the ground rules are adhered to. Define terms so that students develop an appropriate vocabulary for discussing equity issues.

Integrate

Integrate diversity issues into all aspects of your regular teaching. Don't relegate addressing equity issues to "special" or "multicultural" time. "Valuing Difference" should never be a unit of study or a weekly, monthly, or yearly theme; the concept is so basic it should be on integral part of everything that occurs in the school.

Allow for Maturation

Allow time for the class to mature. Introduce less complex topics first, and create time to establish trust. Recognize that the long history of mistrust between people in different groups will not dissipate overnight.

Establish Goodwill

Establish an environment that allows for mistakes. Since most of us were acculturated into racist, sexist, anti-Semitic, and homophobic (to name a few!) ways of thinking unconsciously and unwittingly, we must acknowledge that intolerant thinking will surface from time to time in ourselves and others. Create a climate in the classroom where such behavior can be addressed without fear of retribution. Model nondefensive behavior in the face of being told that something you said or did was offensive to someone. Make assuming goodwill a common practice in your classroom. Recognize that assuming goodwill is harder for people who are usually on the receiving end of discriminatory treatment than for those who are not.

Keep Learning

Be a model of lifelong learning. Keep abreast of current issues such as affirmative action and the "English Only" movement. Clip articles from newspapers and magazines and post them in your classroom. Make sure your words and actions match your expressed beliefs. Let students know that you consider yourself a learner in these issues, and that you see yourself as part of the learning process.

Avoid Preaching

Avoid preaching to students about how they should behave. According to research, preaching and exhorting do not work with students. In fact, such methodology often produces a result opposite from the desired effect. The same holds for books and videos that convey an over-simplified "brotherhood message." Such material makes it easy for students to tune out because they already know the "right" answer. Provide opportunities for students to resolve conflicts and solve problems

Use Emergency Lessons

Interrupt name-calling, slurs, jokes, teasing, excluding, or other prejudicial behavior whenever you see it occur. A teacher's failure to address an incident of prejudice can signal to students that such behavior is acceptable. Create an "emergency" lessons file in which you keep lessons that address issues of prejudice and discrimination.

Share Personal Experiences

Sharing life experiences in class can help students develop empathy. Make your classroom a place where students' experiences are not marginalized, trivialized, or invalidated. Be careful not to create a hierarchy of oppressions where students will be vying for victim status based on their membership in targeted groups. At the same time, acknowledge that experiences in which prejudice and/or discrimination have occurred are unique and cannot be equated one with another.

Review Resources

Review materials so that classroom displays and bulletin boards are inclusive of all people. Insure that the books and videos you use do not reinforce existing stereotypes; point out such examples to students when you see them. Don't trivialize culture so that it is reduced to the three usual F's: foods, festivals, and famous men.

And Finally...

Always remember the awesome power we have as teachers; let us use it wisely and well.

"As a teacher, I possess a tremendous power to make a child's life miserable or joyous. I can be a tool of torture or an instrument of inspiration. I can humiliate or humor, hurt or heal. In all situations, it is my response that decides whether a crisis will be escalated and a child humanized or dehumanized."

—Hiam Ginott

Chapter 57

What to Tell Your Child about Prejudice and Discrimination

Introduction

Prejudice. Attitudes or opinions about a person or group simply because the person belongs to a specific religion, race, nationality, or other group. Prejudices involve strong feelings that are difficult to change. Prejudice is pre-judging. A person who thinks, "I don't want (name of group) living in my neighborhood," is expressing a prejudice.

Discrimination. When people act on the basis of their prejudices or stereotypes, they are discriminating. Discrimination may mean putting other people down, not allowing them to participate in activities, restricting their access to work or to live in certain neighborhoods, or denying them something they are entitled to by right and law.

Stereotype. Oversimplified generalization about a group of people. When people say that all members of a specific nationality, religion, race, or gender are "cheap," "lazy," "criminal," or "dumb," they are expressing stereotypes. All groups have both cheap and generous individuals. All groups have individuals who commit crimes. To label an entire group based on the actions of some is to engage in stereotyping.

The information in this chapter is reprinted from What to Tell Your Child About Prejudice and Discrimination, a brochure produced and published by the National Parent Teacher Association (National PTA) and the Anti-Defamation League (ADL). © 1999. Reprinted with permission from National PTA and ADL.

Even when a stereotype is positive, such as when people in one racial group are thought to be superior athletes, the consequences of stereotyping are negative.

Scapegoating. Blaming an individual or group when the fault actually lies elsewhere. Prejudicial attitudes and discriminatory acts can lead to scapegoating.

The population of our nation is becoming increasingly diverse. Here are some suggestions to help your child get along with people of varied backgrounds and abilities in the United States today.

The Center for Immigration Studies reports that by the year 2000, one-third of all U.S. citizens will be people of color. [Editor's Note: Updated population figures based on the 2000 U.S. census data are available online at www.census.gov.] Today, one-third of the children in public schools are from what have traditionally been called "minority" groups. Schools are increasingly challenged to educate children who come from a wide range of backgrounds, abilities, and experiences. So-called "minorities" have become the numerical majority in 50 cities. The workforce of the near future will be composed of a majority of women and people of color.

While today's changing demographics are compelling, historically the United States has always been challenged to find effective ways for its diverse populations to live and work well together. To ensure their potential for success, we must prepare all children to live and work harmoniously and productively alongside others who represent various and many racial and cultural groups, backgrounds, and abilities in our society. One of the greatest obstacles to creating such a future is prejudice. While many of us would like to believe that prejudice is a problem of the past, this is not the case. Incidents of prejudice and discrimination occur every day. For example, on a daily basis:

- Some people are called hurtful names or are excluded from participating in events.
- Some people are unfairly excluded from jobs, neighborhoods, bank loans, educational opportunities, social events, and clubs.
- Some people are attacked and beaten.
- Some people's homes, places of worship, or cemeteries are vandalized.
- Some people are unfairly paid less than others for doing equal work.

Such instances of discrimination are far from rare. If we are to have a just society, it is up to each of us to take a stand against such unfair practices and attitudes. We must teach our children that there is no place for prejudice or discrimination in our communities, homes, schools, or places of work.

Learning Prejudice

Despite the best efforts of many parents and teachers, children still learn prejudice and practice discrimination. How does this happen?

Prejudice is learned through living in and observing a society where prejudices exist. Children's opinions are influenced by what the people around them think, do, and say. Even if you, as a parent, are a model of tolerance, your children are still exposed to other people who may not respect differences.

A child may observe that some people won't associate with members of certain groups or that members of some groups rarely, if ever, occupy influential positions in the school or community. It does not escape children's notice that all of the U.S. presidents so far have been white and male. A child may overhear some people or groups put down by jokes. If no one addresses these instances of exclusion, a child may grow up thinking that this is the way it is supposed to be, and that people who have been discriminated against deserve this treatment because they are inferior in some way. This is why it is so important to address issues of prejudice and discrimination when and wherever they occur, to point out inequities, and to let children know such ideas and actions are unacceptable in a democratic society.

Media Influence and Self-Image

Children also observe and are exposed to prejudice by watching television, reading books and magazines, or even studying school textbooks that present stereotyped views of various groups of people. In addition to stereotypes, some books present misinformation; others exclude important information about some groups in any positive way. Television shows and books exert undue influence when they are the only exposure a child has to certain groups. Although some improvements have been made, it is not difficult to find TV shows that depict some well-established stereotypes.

Children who have poor self-images are more vulnerable to developing prejudices. They may try to bolster their own worth by finding a group of people whom they can put down. An insecure child might think, "I may not be very good but I am better than those people." For some, putting down others may serve a psychological function, allowing them to feel more important and powerful than those they put down.

Some children may exclude or make fun of others because they believe it is the popular thing to do. Children may begin to use unkind names for different groups if they feel it will help them to be more accepted by their peers. Over time, such actions can result in prejudice and discrimination against specific groups. All children notice differences. This is developmentally appropriate and, by itself, not a problem; but when negative values are attached to those differences, problems occur.

Responding to Children's Questions and Comments

Find out more about what your children think in order to know what misconceptions may need to be corrected. After you have determined what they think, respond with a simple, "I'm trying to understand why you said that, but I don't see it that way." Be direct. Be brief. Use language your children will understand. Questions that might be addressed include the following:

How is a prejudice different from a dislike? Prejudice is having an opinion or idea about a member of a group without really knowing that individual. A dislike is based on information about and experiences with a specific individual.

Why don't people like those people? Why do people call them names? One answer could be: "Some people make judgments about a whole group people without knowing very much about them. Sometimes people are afraid of those who seem different from them and, unfortunately, they express that with name-calling and negative treatment. When people grow up with these ideas, sometimes it's hard to get rid of them."

It is important for children to know that they can help to overcome racism, sexism, and all forms of bigotry. Show them how the choices they make can help to create a fairer world: "When a lot of children like you grow up, differences will become less and less important, and people will respect each other even for their differences."

Why do those people look (or act) so funny? Why can't he walk? Why do they believe such strange things? Children need to realize that all people are different. It is important to communicate to children that we often think others are different simply because they are unfamiliar to us. We don't think our own beliefs and appearances are strange or funny because they are what we're used to. Point out that we must appear different to others, too.

I don't like (name of group) people. Such a comment needs to be handled carefully. It is important that you address such comments without making your children become defensive. With young children, the tone of the discussion should be one of exploring their thinking. A discussion might go as follows:

"You sound as if you know all the people who are (name of group), and that you don't like any of them. You can only like or dislike people you know. If you don't know someone, you can't have a good reason for liking or not liking them. There are children you may not like to play with, but their skin color (religion, accent, appearance, size, etc.) should have nothing to do with it." Discuss with your children the character traits they look for in their friends, such as kindness, honesty, etc.

Name-calling? I didn't mean anything! Often young children do not know the meaning of the words they use, but they do know that the words will get a reaction from the victim. Children need to learn that such language can hurt other people, and is as bad as throwing rocks. Children who yell a racist or other hurtful name in anger should be talked to right away. They must learn not to throw objects at or say hurtful words to other children. Children need to understand that they have made a mistake and have hurt someone. A discussion might include the following ideas:

"You were angry at Tom and you called him a hurtful name. You need to know that words can hurt. When people get hurt by words, they don't get cuts or bruises on the outside, but they are hurt on the inside. You may have been really upset at something Tom did; but instead of telling him what you didn't like, you called him a word that is used to hurt people. If you told Tom what you didn't like, it might have helped him to change his behavior. Name-calling is unfair. It hurts people, and it doesn't solve anything." Help children think about solutions. Try to elicit a few options from them, and then ask which ones they would like to try. "If you are angry with Tom, what can you do to let him know how you feel without calling him a name?"

In an effort to educate the name caller, it is important not to ignore the child who has been called hurtful names. Be sure to give time and attention to children who have been victimized by name-calling;

they need to be reassured that their race, religion, gender, accent, disability, sexual orientation, or appearance do not make them deserving targets.

What Can Parents Do about Prejudice?

- Accept each of your children as unique and special. Let your children know that you recognize and appreciate their individual qualities. Children who feel good about themselves are less likely to be prejudiced. Also, notice unique and special qualities in other people and discuss them with your children.

- Help your children become sensitive to other people's feelings. Studies indicate that caring, empathic children are less likely to be prejudiced. Share stories and books with your children that help them to understand the points of view of other people. When personal conflicts occur, encourage your children to think about how the other person might be feeling.

- Make sure your children understand that prejudice and discrimination are unfair. Make it a firm rule that no person should be excluded or teased on the basis of race, religion, ethnicity, accent, gender, disability, sexual orientation, or appearance. Point out and discuss discrimination when you see it.

- Teach your children respect and an appreciation for differences by providing opportunities for interaction with people of diverse groups. Studies show that children playing and working together toward common goals develop positive attitudes about one another. Sports teams, bands, school clubs, and community programs are examples of activities that can help to counter the effects of homogeneous neighborhoods. In addition to firsthand experiences, provide opportunities for children to learn about people through books, television programs, concerts, or other programs that show positive insights into other cultures.

- Help children recognize instances of stereotyping, prejudice, and discrimination. Make sure they know how to respond to such attitudes and behaviors when they see them in action. Television news and entertainment shows, movies, and newspapers often provide opportunities for discussion. According to recent studies, encouraging children's critical thinking ability may be the best antidote to prejudice.

- Encourage your children to create positive change. Talk to your children about how they can respond to prejudiced thinking or acts of discrimination they observe. Painting over racist graffiti, writing letters to a television producer who promotes stereotyped programming, or confronting a peer's discriminatory behavior are all appropriate actions. Confronting classmates is particularly hard for children, so they need to have a ready made response to such instances. If another child is called a hurtful name, an observer might simply say, "Don't call him/her that. Call him/her by his/her name." Or, if your child is the victim, "Don't call me that. That's not fair." or "You don't like to be called bad names and neither do I." In all cases, try to help your child to feel comfortable in pointing out unfairness.

- Take appropriate action against prejudice and discrimination. For example, if other adults use bigoted language around you or your children, you should not ignore it. Your children need to know that such behavior is unacceptable even if it is from a familiar adult. A simple phrase will do: "Please don't talk that way around me or my children." or "That kind of joke offends me." Adults need to hold themselves to the same standards they want their children to follow.

Chapter 58

Gangs

Introduction

The expansion of the American youth gang problem during the past decade has been widely documented. National survey findings that have noted the spread of gangs throughout the United States indicate that law enforcement agencies across the country are acknowledging the presence of youth gangs in their communities. In particular, recent survey results have documented the presence of youth gangs in rural areas. Most of these rural gangs appear to be primarily homegrown problems and not the result of the social migration of urban gang youth.

The emergence of youth gangs in rural areas and in cities previously without gangs coincided with the juvenile violent crime wave of the 1980's and early 1990's. The issue of whether youth gangs were responsible for the juvenile violent crime wave in the United States is beyond the scope of this chapter. However, given the relationship between gang membership and violent offending, it makes sense to examine the youth gang problem within the larger context of youth violence.

American society demonstrated a heightened concern about juvenile violence during the past 30 years. Demographic consequences of

Excerpted from "Preventing Adolescent Gang Involvement," Office of Juvenile Justice and Delinquency Prevention (OJJDP), Office of Justice Programs, U.S. Department of Justice, September 2000. The complete text of this document, including references, may be found at the following website: http://www.ncjrs.org/html/ojjdp/2000_9_2/contents.html.

the baby boom were, in large part, responsible for this concern. During the 1960's, the number of individuals ages 13–17 rose to 10 percent of the total population, leading to a corresponding increase in the number of crimes occurring within this cohort. By the mid-1980's, youth in this age range had fallen to 7 percent of the total population. However, the number of juvenile crimes did not see a similar decrease, resulting in an increase in the juvenile crime rate. Public concern continued to focus on juvenile violence, drug use, and delinquent behavior. Following an apparent hiatus of youth gangs during the 1970's, American society witnessed a reemergence of youth gang activity and media interest in this phenomenon in the 1980's and 1990's. *Colors*, *Boyz in the Hood*, other Hollywood productions, and MTV brought Los Angeles gang life to suburban and rural America. Recent research also suggests that youth gangs now exist in Europe and other foreign localities.

Concurrent with the reemergence of gangs, the juvenile homicide rate doubled and crack cocaine became an affordable drug of choice for urban youth. In spite of the decline in juvenile violence during the 1990's, concern about this issue continued as a dominant topic in public discourse. Fox (1996) and DiIulio (1995) were among the more widely cited authors who warned of an impending blood bath as a new cohort of super-predators (young, ruthless, violent offenders with casual attitudes about violence) would cause an increase in homicides in the 21st century. The media quickly spread this gloomy scenario. Zimring (1998), however, disputed these doomsday predictions by highlighting the erroneous assumptions underlying them. For example, the predictions were based on the belief that 6 percent of the population would become serious delinquents. DiIulio argued that by 2010, the population of boys under age 18 in the United States would grow from 32 million to 36.5 million, and that this increase would result in an additional 270,000 serious delinquents. However, this estimate suggested that 1.9 million super-predators already existed in the United States (6 percent of 32 million). Zimring noted, "That happens to be more young people than were accused of any form of delinquency last year in the United States."

How is this discussion relevant to a chapter on gang prevention programs? Just as the super-predator notion took on a life of its own in the media, so too has the image of the drug-crazed, drug-dealing, gang-banging gang member. In fact, the tendency is to consider gang members and super-predators as one and the same. This depiction of youth gang members as marauding, drug-dealing murderers has underlying errors similar to those inherent in the super-predator concept.

For the majority of the time, gang youth engage in the same activities as other youth—sleeping, attending school, hanging out, working odd jobs. Only a fraction of their time is dedicated to gang activity. Klein summarized gang life as being "a very dull life. For the most part, gang members do very little—sleep, get up late, hang around, brag a lot, eat again, drink, hang around some more. It's a boring life." In his book about Kansas City, MO, gang members, Fleisher (1998) provided numerous descriptive accounts of this lifestyle. Although gang life may not be as exciting or as violent as media portrayals might suggest, one consistent finding across all research methodologies is that gang youth are in fact more criminally involved than other youth. Illegal behavior attributed to youth gangs is a serious problem for which hype and sensationalism are neither required nor warranted. Regardless of study design or research methodology, considerable consensus exists regarding the high rate of criminal offending among gang members. With the increase in gang membership and in the violent juvenile crime rate during the past decade, and with the availability of increasingly lethal weapons, criminal activity by gang members has taken on new importance for law enforcement and prevention efforts.

What Is Known about American Youth Gangs?

Although this chapter focuses on gang prevention programs, it is essential to first review what is known about American youth gangs. Aside from the high rate of criminal activity among gang members, what is known about this adolescent phenomenon? What risk factors are associated with the emergence of gangs, and who joins these gangs once they have formed? Are gang members stable or transient? Are they delinquent prior to their gang associations? Are there identifiably different social processes (reasons for joining the gang or expected benefits from gang life) involved for girls and boys who join gangs? These are some of the questions that should help to shape gang prevention efforts.

In spite of years of research and years of suppression, intervention, and prevention efforts, considerable disagreement exists regarding the nature and extent of youth gangs. Debate still centers on how to define gangs. For instance, how many youth constitute a gang? Must the gang members commit crimes as a gang to be considered a gang? Must gangs have an organizational structure? Should skinhead groups, white supremacist groups, and motorcycle gangs be considered part of the youth gang problem? These definitional questions reveal both a lack of consensus about the magnitude of the gang problem and confusion about what policies might best address it.

Generally, for a group to be classified a youth gang, the following elements should exist:

- The group must have more than two members. Given what is known about youth offending patterns (most offenses are committed in groups of two or more) and what has been learned from studying gangs, a gang seldom consists of only two members.

- Group members must fall within a limited age range, generally acknowledged as ages 12 to 24.

- Members must share some sense of identity. This is generally accomplished by naming the gang (often referring to a specific geographic location in the name) and/or using symbols or colors to claim gang affiliation. Hand signs, graffiti, specific clothing styles, bandannas, and hats are among the common symbols of gang loyalty.

- Youth gangs require some permanence. Gangs are different from transient youth groups in that they show stability over time, generally lasting a year or more. Historically, youth gangs have also been associated with a particular geographical area or turf.

- Involvement in criminal activity is a central element of youth gangs. While some disagreement surrounds this criterion, it is important to differentiate gangs from noncriminal youth groups such as school and church clubs, which also meet all of the preceding criteria.

What Are the Risk Factors?

To prevent gangs from forming and to keep juveniles from joining existing gangs, it is necessary to understand the causes of gang formation and the underlying attraction of gangs. The following sections provide an overview of the research examining risk factors associated with gang membership. They focus on the following five domains: individual and family demographics, personal attributes, peer group, school, and community.

Individual and Family Demographics

Traditionally, the typical gang member is male, lives in the inner city, and is a member of a racial or ethnic minority. Although these characteristics may be prevalent among gang members, it should not be assumed that all, or even the overwhelming majority of, gang members share these demographic qualities. In addition to changes in the geographical distribution of gangs, research in the past 20 years has highlighted the presence of girls in gangs. Evidence also shows that gang membership is not restricted to youth from racial and ethnic minorities.

Gang behavior has been described almost exclusively as a male phenomenon. Law enforcement estimates generally indicate that more than 90 percent of gang members are male. Early references to female gang members were usually restricted to their involvement in sexual activities or as tomboys; they were rarely included in any serious discussions about gangs. The little that was said about gang girls suggested that they were socially inept, maladjusted, and sexually promiscuous and that they suffered from low self-esteem.

Recent survey research, however, suggests that females may account for more than one-third of youth gang members. In addition, a number of contemporary researchers have moved beyond the stereotypical notion that female gang members are merely auxiliary members of male gangs and have proposed gender-specific explanations of gang affiliation. Some researchers have explored the possibility that girls join gangs in search of a sense of belonging to a peer "familial" group. For example, in an ethnographic study of Latina gang members in male-dominated Hispanic gangs in the San Fernando Valley of California, Harris (1988) concluded that Latina gang members were lost between two worlds—Anglo and Mexican American society and culture. The complex social and cultural roles of Latinas are displayed in Latina gang membership and behavior in which females found peers with whom they could relate. The females would "fight instead of flee, assault instead of articulate, and kill rather than control their aggression."

Another myth about the demographics of gang youth is that they are almost exclusively members of ethnic or racial minorities. Some law enforcement estimates and studies based on law enforcement samples indicate that 85 to 90 percent of gang members are African American or Hispanic. However, more recent law enforcement estimates from the 1998 National Youth Gang Survey indicate that earlier estimates may overstate the minority representation of gang members. The survey revealed that the race or ethnicity of gang members is closely tied to the size of the community. While Caucasians constituted only 11 percent of gang members in large cities (where most gang research has taken place), they accounted for approximately 30 percent of gang members in small cities and rural counties. Lending credence to law enforcement estimates are ethnographers' depictions of gang youth, usually based on research conducted in socially disorganized communities (that is, characterized by high rates of poverty, mobility, welfare dependency, and single-parent households) in Los Angeles, New York, or other urban areas with high concentrations of minority residents. More general surveys that examine youth gangs also tend to be restricted to specific locations that do not include diverse population samples. For example, longitudinal studies in Denver and Rochester, part of the Office of Juvenile Justice and Delinquency Prevention (OJJDP) funded Program of Research on the Causes and Correlates of Delinquency, were concentrated in high-risk neighborhoods that (by definition) included disproportionate representation of racial and ethnic minorities.

It is worthwhile to note that the early gang studies provided a rich source of information about white urban gangs. These early gangs were usually described according to nationality and/or ethnicity, not race. Researchers began to identify gang members by race in the 1950's. This change in gang composition is closely tied to the social disorganization of urban areas and the research focus on urban youth.

As research expands to more representative samples of the general population, a redefinition of the racial and ethnic composition of gang members is likely. Esbensen and Lynskey report that community-level demographics are reflected in the composition of youth gangs; that is, gang members are white in primarily white communities and are African American in predominantly African American communities.

Family characteristics of gang members, such as family structure and parental education and income, also have been revised, because the traditional stereotype of gang members as urban, minority males from single-parent families is too restrictive. In fact, gang youth are found in intact two-parent, single-parent, and recombined families. In addition, gang youth are not limited to homes in which parents have low educational achievement or low incomes.

Although it would be erroneous to conclude that demographic characteristics alone can explain gang affiliation, individual factors are nevertheless clearly associated with gang membership; that is, minority youth residing in single-parent households are at greater risk for joining gangs than are white youth from two-parent households.

Personal Attributes

Some researchers have found that, compared with nongang youth, gang members are more socially inept, have lower self-esteem, and, in general, have sociopathic characteristics. Moffitt (1993) stated that youth gang members are likely to be "life-course persistent offenders." To what extent are such depictions accurate? Are gang youth substantially different from nongang youth? Recent surveys in which gang and nongang youth's attitudes were compared found few consistent differences. This lack of consistent findings, however, may reflect differences in survey methods and question content. Comparisons between gang and nongang youth have been reported from Rochester, Seattle, and San Diego. These authors used different questions and different sampling methods and reported slightly different findings. In the Seattle study, Hill and colleagues (1999) found that gang youth held more antisocial beliefs, while Maxson, Whitlock, and Klein (1998), among others, found that gang members had more delinquent self-concepts (based on statements such as the following: "I'm the kind of person who gets into fights a lot, is a bad kid, gets into trouble, and does things against the law."), had greater tendencies to resolve conflicts by threats, and had experienced more critical stressful events. On a more generic level, both the Seattle and San Diego studies found significant differences between gang and nongang youth within multiple contexts; that is, individual, school, peer, family, and community characteristics.

Research shows that the notion of youth joining gangs for life is a myth. While some members make the gang a lifelong endeavor, findings from three longitudinal studies indicate that one-half to two-thirds are members for 1 year or less.

Peer Group, School, and Community Factors

One consistent finding from research on gangs, as is the case for research on delinquency in general, is the overarching influence of peers on adolescent behavior. In their comparison of stable and transient gang youth, Battin-Pearson and colleagues reported that the strongest predictors of sustained gang affiliation were a high level of interaction with antisocial peers and a low level of interaction with prosocial peers. Researchers have examined the influence of peers through a variety of measures, including exposure to delinquent peers, attachment to delinquent peers, and commitment to delinquent peers. Regardless of how this peer affiliation is measured, the results are the same: association with delinquent peers is one of the strongest predictors (that is, risk factors) of gang membership.

Gang researchers examine school factors less frequently than other factors. However, they have found that these issues are consistently associated with the risk of joining gangs. Research indicates that gang youth are less committed to school than nongang youth. Some gender differences have been reported in regard to this issue. In OJJDP's Rochester study, expectations for educational attainment were predictive of gang membership for girls but not for boys. In a similar vein, Esbensen and Deschenes (1998) found that commitment to school was lower among gang girls than nongang girls. No such differences were found for boys. Studies that examine juveniles' cultures and ethnic backgrounds also attest to the role of school factors in explaining gang membership.

The community is the domain examined most frequently in regard to both the emergence of gangs and the factors associated with joining gangs. Numerous studies indicate that poverty, unemployment, the absence of meaningful jobs, and social disorganization contribute to the presence of gangs. There is little debate that gangs are more prominent in urban areas and that they are more likely to emerge in economically distressed neighborhoods. However, as previously stated, surveys conducted during the 1990's identified the proliferation of youth gangs in rural and suburban communities. Except for law enforcement identification of this phenomenon, few systematic studies have explored these rural and suburban youth gangs.

The traditional image of American youth gangs is characterized by urban social disorganization and economic marginalization; the housing projects or barrios of Chicago, Los Angeles, and New York are viewed as the stereotypical homes of youth gang members. In addition to the pressures of marginal economics, these gang members experience the added burden of having marginal ethnic and personal identities. They look for identity and stability in the gang and adopt the cholo subculture—customs that are associated with an attachment to and identification with gangs—that includes alcohol and drug use, conflict, and violence.

Prevention Strategies

Given the risk factors associated with violent offending and gang affiliation, are specialized prevention and intervention programs necessary for gang members? This is a critical question that has been asked all too infrequently in research on gang behavior. The trend has been to study gangs as a phenomenon distinct from delinquency in general. Despite the recent emphasis on gangs as a separate topic in research literature, there is reason to believe that gangs and gang programs should also be studied within the overall context of juvenile delinquency. It has been suggested that while the gang environment facilitates delinquency, gang members are already delinquent prior to joining the gang. However, rates of delinquent activity increase dramatically during the period of gang membership. From a prevention and intervention perspective, three thoughts emerge. First, the finding that delinquency generally precedes gang membership suggests that gang programs should not be limited to gang intervention or suppression. General prevention efforts that target the entire adolescent population may also prove beneficial in reducing youth gang involvement. Second, certain risk factors associated with gang membership have been identified. As such, prevention and intervention strategies that specifically target at-risk youth are warranted. Third, given the level of delinquent activity that occurs within the gang environment, specific programs that seek to intervene in the lives of gang-affiliated youth should also be encouraged.

This section addresses the following types of prevention efforts:

- Primary prevention focuses on the entire population at risk and the identification of those conditions (personal, social, environmental) that promote criminal behavior.

- Secondary prevention targets those individuals who have been identified as being at greater risk of becoming delinquent.

- Tertiary prevention targets those individuals who are already involved in criminal activity or who are gang members.

The preceding discussion of risk factors emphasizes the necessity for all three strategies. In addition, law enforcement has tried a variety of suppression strategies designed to disrupt gang activity.

The past 60 years have seen a variety of gang prevention and intervention strategies. These strategies include efforts that focus on environmental factors and the provision of improved opportunities—for example, the Chicago Area Project developed by Shaw and McKay (1942), the Boston Midcity Project evaluated by Miller (1962), and the Mobilization for Youth program in New York (Bibb, 1967); programs with a distinct social work orientation; and the strategy of gang suppression by law enforcement. Most of these programs experienced short life spans because changes did not take place immediately or because of a change in administrative priorities.

As indicated previously, there is a general lack of consensus about why gangs emerge and why juveniles join gangs. Therefore, it is more difficult to develop gang prevention programs and assess their impact.

Prevention Programs

Primary, secondary, and tertiary prevention: The Chicago Area Project (CAP). CAP is representative of a community change approach and is perhaps the most widely known delinquency prevention program in American history. CAP was based on the theoretical perspective of Shaw and McKay and is summarized in their 1942 publication. Its intent was to prevent delinquency, including gang activity, through neighborhood and community development. CAP organized community residents through self-help committees based in preexisting community structures such as church groups and labor unions. Consistent with the research findings of Shaw and McKay, it was believed that the cause of maladaptive behavior was the social environment, not the individual. CAP and other similar programs are, at least in part, primary prevention efforts that target all adolescents in the neighborhood.

During the latter part of the 1940's, CAP introduced its detached worker program, which focused on either at-risk youth (secondary prevention) or, in some instances, current gang members (tertiary intervention). It recruited community members to help develop recreational activities and community improvement campaigns (e.g., health care, sanitation, education). These individuals worked with specific neighborhood gangs and served as advocates for gang members. This included advocating for gang members when they were confronted by the justice system and helping them find employment, health care, and educational assistance, among other services. The intent of the detached worker program was to transform the gang from an antisocial youth group to a prosocial group.

Primary prevention: school-based prevention programs. Schools provide one of the common grounds for American youth. Although growing numbers of children are being home schooled, the majority participate in the public education system. In recent years, schools have become a focal point for general delinquency prevention programs. The average middle school provides 14 different violence, drug, and other social problem prevention programs. One gang-specific prevention program that has received considerable attention is the Gang Resistance Education and Training (G.R.E.A.T.) program. The

Phoenix Police Department introduced this school-based program in 1991 to provide students with real tools to resist the attraction of gangs. Modeled after the Drug Abuse Resistance Education (D.A.R.E.) program, the 9-week G.R.E.A.T. program introduces students to conflict resolution skills, cultural sensitivity, and the negative aspects of gang life. G.R.E.A.T. has spread throughout the country; to date, it has been incorporated in school curriculums in all 50 States and several other countries.

The objectives of the G.R.E.A.T. program are to reduce gang activity and to educate young people about the negative consequences of gang life. The curriculum consists of nine lessons offered once a week to middle school students (primarily seventh graders). Law enforcement officers (who always teach the program) are given detailed lesson plans that clearly state the purposes and objectives of the curriculum. The program consists of the following nine lessons: introduction; crime, victims, and your rights; cultural sensitivity and prejudice; conflict resolution (two lessons: discussion and practical exercises); meeting basic needs; drugs and neighborhoods; responsibility; and goal setting. The curriculum includes a discussion about gangs and their effects on the quality of people's lives and addresses the topic of resisting peer pressure.

As evidenced by the curriculum, the intent of the G.R.E.A.T. program is to provide life skills that empower adolescents with the ability to resist peer pressure to join gangs. The strategy is a cognitive approach that seeks to produce a change in attitude and behavior through instruction, discussion, and role-playing. Another notable feature of the program is its target population. In contrast to suppression and intervention programs, which are directed at youth who already are gang members, G.R.E.A.T. is intended for all youth. This is the classic, broad-based primary prevention strategy found in medical immunization programs: They intervene broadly, with a simple and relatively unintrusive program, well before any problem is detectable and without any attempt to predict who is most likely to be affected by the problem.

Secondary prevention: Boys & Girls Clubs of America program and the Montreal program. The Boys & Girls Clubs of America (BGCA) has developed a program "to aggressively reach youth at risk of gang involvement and mainstream them into the quality programs the Club already offers" (Boys & Girls Clubs of America, 1993). This program, Gang Prevention through Targeted Outreach, is an example of secondary prevention and consists of structured recreational, educational, and life skills programs (in conjunction with training) that are geared to enhance communication skills, problem-solving techniques, and decision making abilities. This strategy targets youth who are at risk of becoming involved in gangs and seeks to alter their attitudes and perceptions and to improve their conflict resolution skills.

The BGCA outreach program also involves at-risk youth in conventional activities. Through its case management system, BGCA maintains detailed records on each youth, including participation in program activities, school attendance, contact with the justice system, and general achievements or problems. This information allows caseworkers to reward prosocial behavior or to take proactive measures in the event the youth engages in behaviors likely to lead to gang involvement (for example, skipping school, breaking curfew, and associating with delinquent friends).

The Montreal Preventive Treatment Program is another secondary prevention program. It addresses early childhood risk factors for gang involvement by targeting boys from low socioeconomic backgrounds who display disruptive behavior while in kindergarten. It offers parents training sessions on effective discipline techniques, crisis management, and other parenting skills while the boys participate in training sessions that emphasize development of prosocial skills and self-control. An evaluation of the program showed that, compared with the control group, significantly fewer boys in the treatment group were gang members at age 15.

Tertiary prevention. Tertiary prevention programs target individuals who are already involved with gangs. Although this approach includes detached worker programs such as those described above, a more common strategy implemented during the past decade has relied on law enforcement suppression tactics. Two such programs serve as examples. During the early 1990's, the Chicago Police Department experimented with the "Flying Squad," a special unit comprising young officers selected from the department's three gang units. Chicago's chronic gang problem had left residents feeling intimidated and harassed. In response, the Chicago Police Department decided to give the impression of an omnipresent police force by assigning an additional 100 officers (the Flying Squad) to the Gang Crime Section and saturating an area of approximately 5 square blocks every night. As with most gang prevention programs, this program was short lived and was disbanded by 1998.

The Los Angeles Police Department (LAPD), with its long history of dealing with gangs, organized a suppression unit in 1977. It was known as the Community Resources against Street Hoodlums (CRASH) unit, and its mission was to combat gang crime. This unit stressed high visibility, street surveillance, suppression activities, and arrests. At approximately the same time, LAPD began Operation Hammer, in which hundreds of officers saturated a predesignated area and arrested citizens for every possible legal violation and suspicious activity. Evaluations of these types of suppression efforts are lacking, but the consensus is that they are not likely to be an effective means of combating gang crime.

Law enforcement also has responded to juvenile violence and gangs with new ordinances, including curfew laws, antiloitering laws, and civil injunctions. These suppression tactics limit the ability of certain groups of people (based on age or group affiliation) to congregate in public places based on the belief that such restrictions will reduce gang activity. However, constitutional concerns (that is, violations of the 1st, 4th, 5th, 9th, and 14th amendments) have been raised, and a 1999 U.S. Supreme Court decision declared that a Chicago antiloitering law was unconstitutional. This law targeted gang members (that is, persons the police believed to be gang members) by prohibiting the gathering of two or more people in any public place. Other jurisdictions have implemented civil injunctions and statutes that restrict or prohibit gang members from gathering in particular places (for example, parks, specific street corners, playgrounds) or from engaging in specific acts or wearing certain paraphernalia (wearing pagers or bandannas, riding bicycles, flashing gang signs). Evaluations of these city ordinances are mixed, as is legal opinion assessing their constitutionality (American Civil Liberties Union, 1997).

Conclusion

In light of the risk factors discussed at the outset of this chapter, what conclusions can be made about gang prevention strategies? In regard to primary prevention, three facts are particularly salient. First, gang formation is not restricted to urban, underclass areas. Second, gang members come from a variety of backgrounds; they are not exclusively male, urban, poor, minority, or from single-parent households. Third, once juveniles join a gang, they engage in high levels of criminal activity. Therefore, it is appropriate to formulate primary gang prevention efforts that target the entire adolescent population.

In terms of secondary prevention approaches, some youth are at higher risk of joining gangs. Although social structural conditions associated with gang formation and demographic characteristics attributed to gang members are diverse (and despite the facts stated above), youth gangs are still more likely to be found in socially disorganized or marginalized communities. Secondary prevention strategies should, therefore, focus on communities and youth exposed to these greater risk factors. Community-level gang problem assessments may help guide prevention strategies by identifying areas and groups of youth that are most at risk for gang activity.

Tertiary prevention programs, such as CAP and a variety of gang suppression techniques, have shown little promise. Some detached worker programs produced the unintended consequence of increasing gang cohesion. Operation Hammer, CRASH, and similar law enforcement crackdowns have proven to be inefficient suppression approaches to gang activity and are not cost effective.

In conclusion, there is no clear solution to preventing or reducing gang activity, although some promising programs have been identified.

Recent findings from a Seattle study in which early predictors of gang affiliation were identified highlight the importance of early primary prevention strategies. Additionally, given results from relatively recent studies of girls in gangs and girls who associate with gang members but are not part of the gang, prevention programs may need to consider gender as part of their efforts.

Much of this chapter has focused on individual factors. However, prevention efforts that concentrate only on individual characteristics will fail to address the underlying problems.

This overview of gang prevention strategies has sought to highlight the complexity of the youth gang issue, dispel some common stereotypes about youth gangs, and provide a framework within which to develop prevention programs. Clearly, there is no one "magic bullet" program or "best practice" for preventing gang affiliation and gang-associated violence. The youth gang problem is one that will be best addressed through a comprehensive strategy that incorporates primary, secondary, and tertiary prevention approaches.

Chapter 59

Keeping Kids Safe on the Internet

Introduction

While on-line computer exploration opens a world of possibilities for children, expanding their horizons and exposing them to different cultures and ways of life, they can be exposed to dangers as they hit the road exploring the information highway. There are individuals who attempt to sexually exploit children through the use of on-line services and the Internet. Some of these individuals gradually seduce their targets through the use of attention, affection, kindness, and even gifts. These individuals are often willing to devote considerable amounts of time, money, and energy in this process. They listen to and empathize with the problems of children. They will be aware of the latest music, hobbies, and interests of children. These individuals attempt to gradually lower children's inhibitions by slowly introducing sexual context and content into their conversations.

There are other individuals, however, who immediately engage in sexually explicit conversation with children. Some offenders primarily collect and trade child-pornographic images, while others seek face-to-face meetings with children via on-line contacts. It is important for parents to understand that children can be indirectly victimized through conversation, i.e. chat, as well as the transfer of sexually

Excerpted from "A Parent's Guide to Internet Safety," an undated webpage produced by the Crimes Against Children Program, Federal Bureau of Investigation. U.S. Department of Justice, http://www.fbi.gov/publications/pguide/pguidee.htm, downloaded August 2002.

explicit information and material. Computer-sex offenders may also be evaluating children they come in contact with on-line for future face-to-face contact and direct victimization. Parents and children should remember that a computer-sex offender can be any age or sex—the person does not have to fit the caricature of a dirty, unkempt, older man wearing a raincoat to be someone who could harm a child.

Children, especially adolescents, are sometimes interested in and curious about sexuality and sexually explicit material. They may be moving away from the total control of parents and seeking to establish new relationships outside their family. Because they may be curious, children/adolescents sometimes use their on-line access to actively seek out such materials and individuals. Sex offenders targeting children will use and exploit these characteristics and needs. Some adolescent children may also be attracted to and lured by on-line offenders closer to their age who, although not technically child molesters, may be dangerous. Nevertheless, they have been seduced and manipulated by a clever offender and do not fully understand or recognize the potential danger of these contacts.

This chapter was prepared from actual investigations involving child victims, as well as investigations where law enforcement officers posed as children.

What Are Signs That Your Child Might Be at Risk On-Line?

Your child spends large amounts of time on-line, especially at night. Most children that fall victim to computer-sex offenders spend large amounts of time on-line, particularly in chat rooms. They may go on-line after dinner and on the weekends. They may be latchkey kids whose parents have told them to stay at home after school. They go on-line to chat with friends, make new friends, pass time, and sometimes look for sexually explicit information. While much of the knowledge and experience gained may be valuable, parents should consider monitoring the amount of time spent on-line.

Children on-line are at the greatest risk during the evening hours. While offenders are on-line around the clock, most work during the day and spend their evenings on-line trying to locate and lure children or seeking pornography.

You find pornography on your child's computer. Pornography is often used in the sexual victimization of children. Sex offenders often supply their potential victims with pornography as a means of opening sexual discussions and for seduction. Child pornography may be used to show the child victim that sex between children and adults is normal. Parents should be conscious of the fact that a child may hide the pornographic files on diskettes from them. This may be especially true if the computer is used by other family members.

Your child receives phone calls from men you don't know or is making calls, sometimes long distance, to numbers you don't recognize. While talking to a child victim on-line is a thrill for a computer-sex offender, it can be very cumbersome. Most want to talk to the children on the telephone. They often engage in phone sex with the children and often seek to set up an actual meeting for real sex.

While a child may be hesitant to give out his/her home phone number, the computer-sex offenders will give out theirs. With Caller ID, they can readily find out the child's phone number. Some computer-sex offenders have even obtained toll-free 800 numbers, so that their potential victims can call them without their parents finding out. Others will tell the child to call collect. Both of these methods result in the computer-sex offender being able to find out the child's phone number.

Your child receives mail, gifts, or packages from someone you don't know. As part of the seduction process, it is common for offenders to send letters, photographs, and all manner of gifts to their potential victims. Computer-sex offenders have even sent plane tickets in order for the child to travel across the country to meet them.

Your child turns the computer monitor off or quickly changes the screen on the monitor when you come into the room. A child looking at pornographic images or having sexually explicit conversations does not want you to see it on the screen.

Your child becomes withdrawn from the family. Computer-sex offenders will work very hard at driving a wedge between a child and their family or at exploiting their relationship. They will accentuate any minor problems at home that the child might have. Children may also become withdrawn after sexual victimization.

Your child is using an on-line account belonging to someone else. Even if you don't subscribe to an on-line service or Internet service, your child may meet an offender while on-line at a friend's house or the library. Most computers come preloaded with on-line and/

or Internet software. Computer-sex offenders will sometimes provide potential victims with a computer account for communications with them.

What Should You Do If You Suspect Your Child Is Communicating with a Sexual Predator On-Line?

- Consider talking openly with your child about your suspicions. Tell them about the dangers of computer-sex offenders.

- Review what is on your child's computer. If you don't know how, ask a friend, coworker, relative, or other knowledgeable person. Pornography or any kind of sexual communication can be a warning sign.

- Use the Caller ID service to determine who is calling your child. Most telephone companies that offer Caller ID also offer a service that allows you to block your number from appearing on someone else's Caller ID. Telephone companies also offer an additional service feature that rejects incoming calls that you block. This rejection feature prevents computer-sex offenders or anyone else from calling your home anonymously.

- Devices can be purchased that show telephone numbers that have been dialed from your home phone. Additionally, the last number called from your home phone can be retrieved provided that the telephone is equipped with a redial feature. You will also need a telephone pager to complete this retrieval. This is done using a numeric-display pager and another phone that is on the same line as the first phone with the redial feature. Using the two phones and the pager, a call is placed from the second phone to the pager. When the paging terminal beeps for you to enter a telephone number, you press the redial button on the first (or suspect) phone. The last number called from that phone will then be displayed on the pager.

- Monitor your child's access to all types of live electronic communications (i.e., chat rooms, instant messages, Internet Relay Chat, etc.), and monitor your child's e-mail. Computer-sex offenders almost always meet potential victims via chat rooms. After meeting a child on-line, they will continue to communicate electronically—often via e-mail.

Should any of the following situations arise in your household, via the Internet or on-line service, you should immediately contact your local or state law enforcement agency, the FBI (Federal Bureau of Investigation), and the National Center for Missing and Exploited Children:

- Your child or anyone in the household has received child pornography.

- Your child has been sexually solicited by someone who knows that your child is under 18 years of age.

- Your child has received sexually explicit images from someone that knows your child is under the age of 18.

If one of these scenarios occurs, keep the computer turned off in order to preserve any evidence for future law enforcement use. Unless directed to do so by the law enforcement agency, you should not attempt to copy any of the images and/or text found on the computer.

What Can You Do to Minimize the Chances of an On-Line Exploiter Victimizing Your Child?

- Communicate, and talk to your child about sexual victimization and potential on-line danger.

- Spend time with your children on-line. Have them teach you about their favorite on-line destinations.

- Keep the computer in a common room in the house, not in your child's bedroom. It is much more difficult for a computer-sex offender to communicate with a child when the computer screen is visible to a parent or another member of the household.

- Utilize parental controls provided by your service provider and/ or blocking software. While electronic chat can be a great place for children to make new friends and discuss various topics of interest, it is also prowled by computer-sex offenders. Use of chat rooms, in particular, should be heavily monitored. While parents should utilize these mechanisms, they should not totally rely on them.

- Always maintain access to your child's on-line account and randomly check his/her e-mail. Be aware that your child could be

515

contacted through the U.S. Mail. Be up front with your child about your access and reasons why.

- Teach your child the responsible use of the resources on-line. There is much more to the on-line experience than chat rooms.

- Find out what computer safeguards are utilized by your child's school, the public library, and at the homes of your child's friends. These are all places, outside your normal supervision, where your child could encounter an on-line predator.

- Understand, even if your child was a willing participant in any form of sexual exploitation, that he/she is not at fault and is the victim. The offender always bears the complete responsibility for his or her actions.

- Instruct your children:

  - to never arrange a face-to-face meeting with someone they met on-line;

  - to never upload (post) pictures of themselves onto the Internet or on-line service to people they do not personally know;

  - to never give out identifying information such as their name, home address, school name, or telephone number;

  - to never download pictures from an unknown source, as there is a good chance there could be sexually explicit images;

  - to never respond to messages or bulletin board postings that are suggestive, obscene, belligerent, or harassing;

  - that whatever they are told on-line may or may not be true.

Frequently Asked Questions

My child has received an e-mail advertising for a pornographic website, what should I do? Generally, advertising for an adult, pornographic website that is sent to an e-mail address does not violate federal law or the current laws of most states. In some states it may be a violation of law if the sender knows the recipient is under the age of 18. Such advertising can be reported to your service provider and, if known, the service provider of the originator. It can also be reported to your state and federal legislators, so they can be made aware of the extent of the problem.

Is any service safer than the others? Sex offenders have contacted children via most of the major on-line services and the Internet. The most important factors in keeping your child safe on-line are the utilization of appropriate blocking software and/or parental controls, along with open, honest discussions with your child, monitoring his/her on-line activity, and following the tips in this chapter.

Should I just forbid my child from going on-line? There are dangers in every part of our society. By educating your children to these dangers and taking appropriate steps to protect them, they can benefit from the wealth of information now available on-line.

Chapter 60

Effects of Media Violence on Children and Youth

Children and Media Violence

Did you know?

- By the time an average child (one who watches two to four hours of television daily) leaves elementary school, he or she will have witnessed 8,000 murders and over 100,000 other acts of violence.

- By the time a child is 18 years old, he or she will witness (with average viewing time) 200,000 acts of violence including 40,000 murders.

- On an individual day, there are about 5 to 6 violent acts per hour on prime-time television, and 20 to 25 acts of violence on Saturday morning children's television.

- Weekly, in the United States, this adds up to about 188 hours of violent programs or about 15% of the program time.

This chapter contains text reprinted with permission from "Children and Media Violence," a fact sheet published by the National Institute on Media and the Family, www.mediafamily.org. © 2000 National Institute on Media and the Family. Updated in 2000. And from "Children and TV Violence," a factsheet published by the American Academy of Child and Adolescent Psychiatry (AACAP). © 1999 AACAP, "Children and the News," a factsheet published by AACAP. © 2002 AACAP, "The Influence of Music and Music Videos," a factsheet published by AACAP. © 2000 AACAP. Reprinted with permission.

- Cable can add to the violence by rerunning old shows and the showing of more violent new ones.

- Many popular R-rated films available on video contain far more violence than seen on commercial television.

- Children with VCR or cable access have seen more R-rated films than their non-cable, non-VCR counterparts.

- Since 1955, reports, studies, and congressional testimonies by experts in the field have overwhelmingly concluded that "the mass media are significant contributors to the aggressive behavior and aggression related attitudes of many children, adolescents and adults."

- Two large meta analysis studies have been conducted on research linking media violence to aggression in children. One looked at 67 studies and over 30,000 subjects. The other looked at 230 studies and almost 100,000 subjects. Both supported a number of conclusions: "First, there is a positive association between televised violence exposure and behavior. Second, exposure to violent programming not only increases aggressive behavior, but is associated with lower levels of prosocial behavior."

Many factors in the portrayal of media violence contribute to its affect on teens:

- Is the aggressive behavior on screen rewarded or punished?

- Is the violence gratuitous, is it justified or does it lack consequences?

- Does the viewer identify with the aggressor or the victim?

- Does the viewer become engaged with or aroused by the violence on screen?

- What is the age of the child? Although violence affects children of all ages, middle childhood, ages 8 to 12, seem particularly sensitive.

- What is the total amount of television watched?

- Does the child see television violence as realistic?

Children and TV Violence

American children watch an average of three to fours hours of television daily. Television can be a powerful influence in developing value systems and shaping behavior. Unfortunately, much of today's television programming is violent. Hundreds of studies of the effects of TV violence on youth and teenagers have found that children may:

- become "immune" to the horror of violence

- gradually accept violence as a way to solve problems

- imitate the violence they observe on television

- identify with certain characters, victims, and/or victimizers

Extensive viewing of television violence by youth causes greater aggressiveness. Sometimes, watching a single violent program can increase aggressiveness. Children who view shows in which violence is very realistic, frequently repeated, or unpunished, are more likely to imitate what they see. Youth with emotional, behavioral, learning or impulse control problems may be more easily influenced by TV violence. The impact of TV violence may be immediately evident in the youth's behavior or may surface years later, and young people can even be affected when the family atmosphere shows no tendency toward violence.

While TV violence is not the only cause of aggressive or violent behavior, it is clearly a significant factor.

Parents can protect children from excessive TV violence in the following ways:

- pay attention to the programs their children are watching and watch some with them

- set limits on the amount of time they spend with the television; consider removing the TV set from their bedroom

- point out that although the actor has not actually been hurt or killed, such violence in real life results in pain or death

- refuse to let them see shows known to be violent, and change the channel or turn off the TV set when offensive material comes on, with an explanation of what is wrong with the program

- disapprove of the violent episodes in front of the children, stressing the belief that such behavior is not the best way to resolve a problem

- to offset peer pressure among friends and classmates, contact other parents and agree to enforce similar rules about the length of time and type of program the children may watch

Parents can also use these measures to prevent harmful effects from television in other areas such as racial or sexual stereotyping. The amount of time youth watch TV, regardless of content, should be moderated because it decreases time spent on more beneficial activities such as reading, playing with friends, and developing hobbies. If parents have serious difficulties setting limits, or have ongoing concerns about how their child is reacting to television, they should contact a child and adolescent psychiatrist for consultation and assistance.

Children and the News

Youth often see or hear the news many times a day through television, radio, newspapers, magazines, and the Internet. Seeing and hearing about local and world events, such as natural disasters, catastrophic events, and crime reports, may cause children to experience stress, anxiety, and fears.

There have also been several changes in how news is reported that have given rise to the increased potential for children to experience negative effects. These changes include the following:

- television channels and Internet services and sites which report the news 24 hours a day

- television channels broadcasting live events as they are unfolding, in "real time"

- increased reporting of the details of the private lives of public figures and role models

- pressure to get news to the public as part of the competitive nature of the entertainment industry

- detailed and repetitive visual coverage of natural disasters and violent acts

While there has been great public debate about providing television ratings to warn parents about violence and sex in programming, news shows have only recently been considered in these discussions. Research has shown, however, that children and adolescents are prone to imitate what they see and hear in the news, a kind of contagion effect described as "copy cat" events. Chronic and persistent exposure to such violence can lead to fear, desensitization (numbing), and in some children an increase in aggressive and violent behaviors. Studies also show that media broadcasts do not always choose to show things that accurately reflect local or national trends.

For example, statistics report a decrease in the incidence of crime, yet, the reporting of crime in the news has increased 240%. Local news shows often lead with or break into programming to announce crime reports and devote as much as 30% of the broadcast time to detailed crime reporting.

The possible negative effects of news can be lessened by parents, teachers, or other adults by watching the news with the youth and talking about what has been seen or heard. The child's age, maturity, developmental level, life experiences, and vulnerabilities should guide how much and what kind of news the child watches.

Guidelines for minimizing the negative effects of watching the news include:

- monitor the amount of time your child watches news shows

- make sure you have adequate time and a quiet place to talk if you anticipate that the news is going to be troubling or upsetting to the child

- watch the news with your child

- ask the child what he/she has heard and what questions he/she may have

- provide reassurance regarding his/her own safety in simple words emphasizing that you are going to be there to keep him/her safe

- look for signs that the news may have triggered fears or anxieties such as sleeplessness, fears, bedwetting, crying, or talking about being afraid

Parents should remember that it is important to talk to the child or adolescent about what he/she has seen or heard. This allows parents to lessen the potential negative effects of the news and to discuss their own ideas and values. While children cannot be completely protected from outside events, parents can help them feel safe and help them to better understand the world around them.

The Influence of Music and Music Videos

Singing and music have always played an important role in learning and the communication of culture. Youth learn from the role models what they see and hear. For the past 35 years, some children's television has very effectively used the combination of words, music, and fast-paced animation to achieve learning.

Most parents are concerned about what their young children see and hear, but as children grow older, parents pay less attention to the music and videos that hold their children's interest.

The sharing of musical tastes between generations in a family can be a pleasurable experience. Music also is often a major part of a teenager's separate world. It is quite common for teenagers to get pleasure from keeping adults out and causing adults some distress.

A concern to many interested in the development and growth of teenagers is the negative and destructive themes of some rock and other kinds of music, including best-selling albums promoted by major recording companies. The following troublesome themes are prominent:

- advocating and glamorizing abuse of drugs and alcohol

- pictures and explicit lyrics presenting suicide as an "alternative" or "solution"

- graphic violence

- rituals in concerts

- sex which focuses on control, sadism, masochism, incest, children devaluing women, and violence toward women

Parents can help their teenagers by paying attention to their teenager's purchasing, downloading, listening, and viewing patterns, and by helping them identify music that may be destructive. An open discussion without criticism may be helpful.

Music is not usually a danger for a teenager whose life is happy and healthy. But if a teenager is persistently preoccupied with music that has seriously destructive themes, and there are changes in behavior such as isolation, depression, alcohol or other drug abuse, a psychiatric evaluation should be considered.

Chapter 61

Helping Children and Adolescents Cope with Violence and Disasters

The National Institute of Mental Health (NIMH) has joined with other Federal agencies to address the issue of reducing school violence and assisting children who have been victims of or witnesses to violent events. Nationally reported school shootings such as those that occurred in Bethel, Alaska; Pearl, Mississippi; West Paducah, Kentucky; Jonesboro, Arkansas; Edinboro, Pennsylvania; Springfield, Oregon; and Littleton, Colorado have shocked the country. Many questions are being asked about how these tragedies could have been prevented, how those directly involved can be helped, and how we can avoid such events in the future.

Research has shown that both adults and children who experience catastrophic events show a wide range of reactions. Some suffer only worries and bad memories that fade with emotional support and the passage of time. Others are more deeply affected and experience long-term problems. Research on post-traumatic stress disorder (PTSD) shows that some soldiers, survivors of criminal victimization, torture, and other violence, and survivors of natural and man-made catastrophes suffer long-term effects from their experiences. Children who have witnessed violence in their families, schools, or communities are also vulnerable to serious long-term problems. Their emotional reactions,

Excerpted from "Helping Children and Adolescents Cope with Violence and Disasters," National Institute of Mental Health (NIMH), National Institutes of Health (NIH), NIH Pub. No. 99-3518, http://www.nimh.nih.gov/publicat/violence.cfm, page last updated January 13, 2000.

including fear, depression, withdrawal, or anger, can occur immediately or some time after the tragic event. Youngsters who have experienced a catastrophic event often need support from parents and teachers to avoid long-term emotional harm. Most will recover in a short time, but the minority who develop PTSD or other persistent problems need treatment.

The school shootings caught the Nation's attention, but these events are only a small fraction of the many tragic episodes that affect children's lives. Each year many children and adolescents sustain injuries from violence, lose friends or family members, or are adversely affected by witnessing a violent or catastrophic event. Each situation is unique, whether it centers upon a plane crash where many people are killed, automobile accidents involving friends or family members, or natural disasters such as Hurricane Andrew where deaths occur and homes are lost. But these events have similarities as well, and cause similar reactions in children. Helping young people avoid or overcome emotional problems in the wake of violence or disaster is one of the most important challenges a parent, teacher, or mental health professional can face. The purpose of this chapter is to tell what is known about the impact of violence and disasters on children and suggest steps to minimize long-term emotional harm.

Trauma—What Is It?

Trauma includes emotional as well as physical experiences and injuries. Emotional injury is essentially a normal response to an extreme event. It involves the creation of emotional memories, which arise through a long-lasting effect on structures deep within the brain. The more direct the exposure to the traumatic event, the higher the risk for emotional harm. Thus in a school shooting, the student who is injured probably will be most severely affected emotionally. And the student who sees a classmate shot, even killed, probably will be more emotionally affected than the student who was in another part of the school when the violence occurred. But even second-hand exposure to violence can be traumatic. For this reason, all children and adolescents exposed to violence or a disaster, even if only through graphic media reports, should be watched for signs of emotional distress. In addition to this psychiatric definition, trauma also has a medical definition, which refers to a serious or critical bodily injury, wound, or shock, often treated with trauma medicine practiced in emergency rooms.

How Adolescents React to Trauma

Reactions to trauma may appear immediately after the traumatic event or days and even weeks later. Loss of trust in adults and fear of the event occurring again are responses seen in many children and adolescents who have been exposed to traumatic events. Other reactions vary according to age:

Children 6 to 11 years old may show extreme withdrawal, disruptive behavior, and/or inability to pay attention. Regressive behaviors, nightmares, sleep problems, irrational fears, irritability, refusal to attend school, outbursts of anger and fighting are also common in traumatized children of this age. Also the child may complain of stomach aches or other bodily symptoms that have no medical basis. School work often suffers. Depression, anxiety, feelings of guilt and emotional numbing or "flatness" are often present as well.

Adolescents 12 to 17 years old may exhibit responses similar to those of adults, including flashbacks, nightmares, emotional numbing, avoidance of any reminders of the traumatic event, depression, substance abuse, problems with peers, and anti-social behavior. Also common are withdrawal and isolation, physical complaints, suicidal thoughts, school avoidance, academic decline, sleep disturbances, and confusion. The adolescent may feel extreme guilt over his or her failure to prevent injury or loss of life, and may harbor revenge fantasies that interfere with recovery from the trauma.

Some youngsters are more vulnerable to trauma than others, for reasons scientists don't fully understand. It has been shown that the impact of a traumatic event is likely to be greatest in the child or adolescent who previously has been the victim of child abuse or some other form of trauma, or who already had a mental health problem. And the youngster who lacks family support is more at risk for a poor recovery.

Helping the Child or Adolescent Trauma Victim

Early intervention to help children and adolescents who have suffered trauma from violence or a disaster is critical. Parents, teachers and mental health professionals can do a great deal to help these youngsters recover. Help should begin at the scene of the traumatic event. According to the National Center for Post-Traumatic Stress

Disorder of the Department of Veterans Affairs, workers in charge of a disaster scene should:

- Find ways to protect children from further harm and from further exposure to traumatic stimuli. If possible, create a safe haven for them. Protect children from onlookers and the media covering the story.

- When possible, direct children who are able to walk away from the site of violence or destruction, away from severely injured survivors, and away from continuing danger. Kind but firm direction is needed.

- Identify children in acute distress and stay with them until initial stabilization occurs. Acute distress includes panic (marked by trembling, agitation, rambling speech, becoming mute, or erratic behavior) and intense grief (signs include loud crying, rage, or immobility).

- Use a supportive and compassionate verbal or non-verbal exchange (such as a hug, if appropriate) with the child to help him or her feel safe. However brief the exchange, or however temporary, such reassurances are important to children.

After violence or a disaster occurs, the family is the first-line resource for helping. Among the things that parents and other caring adults can do are:

- Explain the episode of violence or disaster as well as you are able.

- Encourage the children to express their feelings and listen without passing judgment. Help younger children learn to use words that express their feelings. However, do not force discussion of the traumatic event.

- Let children and adolescents know that it is normal to feel upset after something bad happens.

- Allow time for the youngsters to experience and talk about their feelings. At home, however, a gradual return to routine can be reassuring to the child.

- If your children are fearful, reassure them that you love them and will take care of them. Stay together as a family as much as possible.

- If behavior at bedtime is a problem, give the child extra time and reassurance. Let him or her sleep with a light on or in your room for a limited time if necessary.

- Reassure children and adolescents that the traumatic event was not their fault.

- Do not criticize regressive behavior or shame the child with words like "babyish."

- Allow children to cry or be sad. Don't expect them to be brave or tough.

- Encourage children and adolescents to feel in control. Let them make some decisions about meals, what to wear, etc.

- Take care of yourself so you can take care of the children.

When violence or disaster affects a whole school or community, teachers and school administrators can play a major role in the healing process. Some of the things educators can do are:

- If possible, give yourself a bit of time to come to terms with the event before you attempt to reassure the children. This may not be possible in the case of a violent episode that occurs at school, but sometimes in a natural disaster there will be several days before schools reopen and teachers can take the time to prepare themselves emotionally.

- Don't try to rush back to ordinary school routines too soon. Give the children or adolescents time to talk over the traumatic event and express their feelings about it.

- Respect the preferences of children who do not want to participate in class discussions about the traumatic event. Do not force discussion or repeatedly bring up the catastrophic event; doing so may re-traumatize children.

- Hold in-school sessions with entire classes, with smaller groups of students, or with individual students. These sessions can be very useful in letting students know that their fears and concerns are normal reactions. Many counties and school districts have teams that will go into schools to hold such sessions after a disaster or episode of violence. Involve mental health professionals in these activities if possible.

- Offer art and play therapy for children in primary school.

- Be sensitive to cultural differences among the children. In some cultures, for example, it is not acceptable to express negative emotions. Also, the child who is reluctant to make eye contact with a teacher may not be depressed, but may simply be exhibiting behavior appropriate to his or her culture.

- Encourage children to develop coping and problem-solving skills and age-appropriate methods for managing anxiety.

- Hold meetings for parents to discuss the traumatic event, their children's response to it, and how they and you can help. Involve mental health professionals in these meetings if possible.

Most children and adolescents, if given support such as that described above, will recover almost completely from the fear and anxiety caused by a traumatic experience within a few weeks. However, some children and adolescents will need more help over a longer period of time in order to heal. Grief over the loss of a loved one, teacher, friend, or pet may take months to resolve, and may be reawakened by reminders such as media reports or the anniversary of the death.

In the immediate aftermath of a traumatic event, and in the weeks following, it is important to identify the youngsters who are in need of more intensive support and therapy because of profound grief or some other extreme emotion. Children who show avoidance and emotional numbing may need the help of a mental health professional, while more common reactions such as re-experiencing the event and hyperarousal (including sleep disturbances and a tendency to be easily startled) may respond to help from parents and teachers.

Post-Traumatic Stress Disorder

As stated earlier, some children and adolescents will have prolonged problems after a traumatic event. These potentially chronic conditions include depression and prolonged grief. Another serious and potentially long-lasting problem is post-traumatic stress disorder (PTSD). This condition is diagnosed when the following symptoms have been present for longer than one month:

- Re-experiencing the event through play or in trauma-specific nightmares or flashbacks, or distress over events that resemble or symbolize the trauma.

- Routine avoidance of reminders of the event or a general lack of responsiveness (e.g., diminished interests or a sense of having a foreshortened future).

- Increased sleep disturbances, irritability, poor concentration, startle reaction and regressive behavior.

Rates of PTSD identified in child and adult survivors of violence and disasters vary widely. For example, estimates range from 2% after a natural disaster (tornado), 28% after an episode of terrorism (mass shooting), and 29% after a plane crash. The disorder may arise weeks or months after the traumatic event. PTSD may resolve without treatment, but some form of therapy by a mental health professional is often required in order for healing to occur. Fortunately, it is more common for a traumatized child or adolescent to have some of the symptoms of PTSD than to develop the full-blown disorder. People differ in their vulnerability to PTSD, and the source of this difference is not known in its entirety.

Research has shown that PTSD clearly alters a number of fundamental brain mechanisms. Because of this, abnormalities have been detected in brain chemicals that affect coping behavior, learning, and memory among people with the disorder. Recent brain imaging studies have detected altered metabolism and blood flow as well as anatomical changes in people with PTSD. Resources providing more information on PTSD may be found in the "Additional Help and Information" section of this *Sourcebook*.

Treatment of PTSD

People with PTSD are treated with specialized forms of psychotherapy and sometimes with medications or a combination of the two. One of the forms of psychotherapy shown to be effective is cognitive/behavioral therapy, or CBT. In CBT, the patient is taught methods of overcoming anxiety or depression and modifying undesirable behaviors such as avoidance. The therapist helps the patient examine and re-evaluate beliefs that are interfering with healing, such as the belief that the traumatic event will happen again. Children who undergo CBT are taught to avoid "catastrophizing." For example, they are reassured that dark clouds do not necessarily mean another hurricane, that the fact that someone is angry doesn't necessarily mean that another shooting is imminent, etc. Play therapy and art therapy also can help younger children to remember the traumatic event safely and express their feelings about it. Other forms of psychotherapy that have been found to help persons with PTSD include group and exposure therapy. A reasonable period of time for treatment of PTSD is 6 to 12 weeks with occasional follow-up sessions, but treatment may be longer depending on a patient's particular circumstances. Research has shown that support from family and friends can be an important part of recovery and that involving people in group discussion very soon after a catastrophic event may reduce some of the symptoms of PTSD.

There has been a good deal of research on the use of medications for adults with PTSD, including research on the formation of emotionally charged memories and medications that may help to block the development of symptoms. Medications appear to be useful in reducing overwhelming symptoms of arousal (such as sleep disturbances and an exaggerated startle reflex), intrusive thoughts, and avoidance; reducing accompanying conditions such as depression and panic; and improving impulse control and related behavioral problems. Research is just beginning on the use of medications to treat PTSD in children and adolescents. There is preliminary evidence that psychotherapy focused on trauma and grief, in combination with selected medications, can be effective in alleviating PTSD symptoms and accompanying depression. More medication treatment research is needed to increase our knowledge of how best to treat children who have PTSD.

A mental health professional with special expertise in the area of child and adolescent trauma is the best person to help a youngster with PTSD.

Chapter 62

Effects of Witnessing Domestic Violence

Children who witness violence between adults in their homes have become more visible in the spotlight of public attention. The purpose of this document is to further an understanding of the current literature on the effects of witnessing adult domestic violence on the social and physical development of children. Out of 84 studies reporting on children's witnessing of domestic violence originally identified, 31 studies met criteria of rigorous research, with 18 of them comparing children who witnessed adult domestic violence to other groups of children, 12 others using multiple regression procedures to compare subjects along a continuum of violence exposure or by demographic characteristics, and one study applying qualitative research methods. The findings of these 31 studies can be divided into three major themes: (1) the childhood problems associated with witnessing domestic violence; (2) the moderating factors present in a child's life that appear to increase or decrease these problems; and (3) an evaluation of the research methods used in the studies reviewed.

Jeffrey L. Edleson, Ph.D. (1999). *Problems Associated With Children's Witnessing of Domestic Violence*. Harrisburg, PA: National Resource Center on Domestic Violence, VAWnet Applied Research Forum Paper, National Electronic Network on Violence Against Women, http://www.vawnet.org. The full version of this text, including references, can be found at the following website: http://www.vaw.umn.edu/vawnet/witness.htm.

Children's Problems Associated with Witnessing Violence

Reviewed studies report a series of childhood problems statistically associated with a child's witnessing domestic violence. These problems can be grouped into the three main categories presented in more detail below: (1) behavioral and emotional; (2) cognitive functioning and attitudes; and (3) longer-term.

Behavioral and Emotional Problems

The area in which there is probably the greatest amount of information on problems associated with witnessing violence is in the area of children's behavioral and emotional functioning. Generally, studies using the Child Behavior Checklist and similar measures have found child witnesses of domestic violence to exhibit more aggressive and antisocial (often called "externalized" behaviors) as well as fearful and inhibited behaviors ("internalized" behaviors), and to show lower social competence than other children. Children who witnessed violence were also found to show more anxiety, self-esteem, depression, anger, and temperament problems than children who did not witness violence at home. Children from homes where their mothers were being abused have shown less skill in understanding how others feel and examining situations from others' perspectives when compared to children from non-violent households. Peer relationships, autonomy, self-control, and overall competence were also reported significantly lower among boys who had experienced serious physical violence and been exposed to the use of weapons between adults living in their homes.

Overall, these studies indicate a consistent finding that child witnesses of domestic violence exhibit a host of behavioral and emotional problems. A few studies have reported finding no differences on some of these measures but these same studies found significant differences on other measures.

Another aspect of the effects on children is their own use of violence. Social learning theory would suggest that children who witness violence may also learn to use it. Several researchers have attempted to look at this link between exposure to violence and subsequent use of it. Some support for this hypothesis has been found. For example, for 2,245 children and teenagers, recent exposure to violence in the home was a significant factor in predicting a child's violent behavior.

Cognitive Functioning and Attitudes

A number of studies have measured the association between cognitive development problems and witnessing domestic violence. While academic abilities were not found to differ between witnesses and other children, another study found increased violence exposure associated with lower cognitive functioning. One of the most direct consequences of witnessing violence may be the attitudes a child develops concerning the use of violence and conflict resolution. Children's exposure to adult domestic violence may generate attitudes justifying their own use of violence. Adolescent boys incarcerated for violent crimes who had been exposed to family violence believed more than others that "acting aggressively enhances one's reputation or self-image." Believing that aggression would enhance their self-image significantly predicted violent offending. Boys and girls appear to differ in what they learn from these experiences. Boys who witnessed domestic abuse were significantly more likely to approve of violence than were girls who had also witnessed it.

Longer-Term Problems

Most studies reviewed above have examined child problems associated with recent witnessing of domestic violence. A number of studies have mentioned much longer-term problems reported retrospectively by adults or indicated in archival records. For example, a 1995 study of 550 undergraduate students found that witnessing violence as a child was associated with adult reports of depression, trauma-related symptoms, and low self-esteem among women and trauma-related symptoms alone among men. Witnessing violence appeared to be independent of the variance accounted for by the existence of parental alcohol abuse and divorce. In the same vein, among 123 adult women who had witnessed domestic violence as a child, greater distress and lower social adjustment existed when compared to 494 non-witnesses. These findings persisted even after accounting for the effects of witnessing parental verbal conflict, being abused as a child, and the level of reported parental caring.

Factors Influencing the Degree of Problems Associated with Witnessing Violence

Several factors appear to moderate the degree to which a child is affected by witnessing violence. As will be seen below, a number of these factors also seem to interact with each other creating unique outcomes for different children.

Abused and Witnessing Children

Some have suggested that both witnessing abuse and also being abused is a "double whammy" for children. A 1989 study compared children who were both abused and had witnessed violence to children who had only witnessed violence and to others who had been exposed to neither type of violence. They found that children who were both abused and witnesses exhibited the most problem behaviors, the witness-only group showed moderate problem symptoms, and the comparison group the least. This same pattern appears in series of other studies. One study indicated that the experience of being abused or both abused and a witness is more negative than witnessing adult domestic violence alone.

The combination of being abused and witnessing violence appears to be associated with more serious problems for children than witnessing violence alone. However, after accounting for the effects of being abused, adult reports of their childhood witnessing of interparental violence still accounted for a significant degree of their problems as children. Witnessing domestic violence may result in traumatic effects on children that are distinct from the effects of child abuse.

Child Characteristics

Some findings point to different factors for boys and girls that are associated with witnessing violence. In general, boys have been shown to exhibit more frequent problems and ones that are categorized as external, such as hostility and aggression, while girls generally show evidence of more internalized problems, such as depression and somatic complaints. There are also findings that dissent from this general trend by showing that girls, especially as they get older, also exhibit more aggressive behaviors.

Children of different ages also appear to exhibit differing responses associated with witnessing violence. Children in preschool were reported by mothers to exhibit more problems than other age groups.

Few studies have found differences based on race and ethnicity. A study of white, Latino, and African-American families of battered women found that all the children were viewed by their mothers as having serious emotional and behavioral problems. The only difference found between the groups was on social competence; African-American mothers rated their children more competent when compared to other mothers' ratings of their own children.

Time since Violent Event

The longer the period of time since exposure to a violent event, the fewer effects a child experiences. For example, more social problems were found among children residing in shelters than among children who had at one time in the past been resident in a shelter. The effect of the immediate turmoil may temporarily escalate child problems as observed in a shelter setting.

Parent-Child Relationship Factors

A number of authors have discussed a child's relationship to adult males in the home as a key factor. One suggests that children's relationships with their battering fathers were confusing, with children expressing both affection for their fathers and resentment, pain and disappointment over his violent behavior.

Children's relationships to their mothers have also been identified as a key factor in how children are affected by witnessing domestic violence. Some have conjectured that a mother's mental health would negatively affect a child's experience of violence but the data are conflicting. Maternal stress statistically accounted for a large amount of child behavior problems. Another study of child witnesses of violence, however, found that mothers' mental health did not affect a child's response to violence in the home.

Family support and children's perceptions of their parental relationships have also been identified as key parent-child variables. For example, home environments were important among the 225 urban black adolescents studied. Adolescents exposed to community and domestic violence appeared to cope better if they lived in more stable and socially connected households.

Implications

The studies reviewed for this document provide strong evidence that children who witness domestic violence at home also exhibit a variety of behavioral, emotional, cognitive and longer-term developmental problems. Each child will experience adult domestic violence in unique ways depending on a variety of factors that include direct physical abuse of the child, his or her gender and age, the time since exposure to violence, and his or her relationship with adults in the home. Significant percentages of children in the studies reviewed showed no negative developmental problems despite witnessing repeated violence. We must be careful to not assume that witnessing violence automatically leads to negative outcomes for children.

These data are primarily based on samples of children living in shelters for battered women. This has been used as a criticism of these studies on the grounds that shelter residence is a time of crisis and not representative of a child's on-going life. These data do, however, provide shelters with a much better understanding of the problems many of their resident children may be experiencing. And despite the limitations of some individual studies cited, the number and variety of studies so far reported provide a strong basis for accepting the overall findings.

There is a danger that these data may lead some child protection agencies to more frequently define child witnessing of violence as a form of child abuse or neglect. It is not uncommon to see battered women charged with "failure to protect" their children from a batterer. Many child protection agencies continue to hold battered mothers solely responsible for their children's safety. These actions are often based on the belief that separating from a batterer will always be the safest path for the battered woman and her child.

Yet these actions on the part of the child protection system ignore the reality that the majority of assaults and murders of battered women occur after they have been separated or divorced from their perpetrator. Such actions also ignore the reality that battered mothers often make decisions about their relationships with male partners based on their judgments of what will be best for their children.

The responsibility for creating a dangerous environment should be laid squarely on the shoulders of the adult who is using violent behavior, whether or not that adult is the legal guardian of the child. Responsibility and blame should not be placed on adult survivors in the home. Holding the violent abuser responsible for ending the use of violence is the path that leads to safety for these children and their abused mothers.

Part Eight

Protection from Youth Mental and Emotional Health Risks

Chapter 63

Conduct Disorder and Oppositional Defiant Disorder in Youth

Oppositional Defiant Disorder (ODD)

What Is It?

ODD is a psychiatric disorder that is characterized by two different sets of problems. These are aggressiveness and a tendency to purposefully bother and irritate others. It is often the reason that people seek treatment. When ODD is present with ADHD (attention deficit hyperactivity disorder), depression, Tourette syndrome, anxiety disorders, or other neuropsychiatric disorders, it makes life with that child far more difficult. For example, ADHD plus ODD is much worse than ADHD alone, often enough to make people seek treatment. The criteria for ODD are:

A pattern of negativistic, hostile, and defiant behavior lasting at least six months during which four or more of the following are present:

- often loses temper

- often argues with adults

Reprinted with permission from "Oppositional Defiant Disorder (ODD) and Conduct Disorder (CD) in Children and Adolescents: Diagnosis and Treatment," a pamphlet written by pediatric psychiatrist James Chandler, M.D., FRCPC. © 2002 James Chandler. Updated January 2002, downloaded August 2002. Full text of this article can be found at http://www.klis.com/chandler/pamphlet/oddcd/ oddcdpamphlet.htm.

- often actively defies or refuses to comply with adults' requests or rules
- often deliberately annoys people
- often blames others for his or her mistakes or misbehavior
- is often touchy or easily annoyed by others
- is often angry and resentful
- is often spiteful and vindictive

The disturbance in behavior causes clinically significant impairment in social, academic, or occupational functioning.

How Often Is Often?

All of the criteria above include the word often. But what exactly does that mean? Recent studies have shown that these behaviors occur to a varying degree in all children. These researchers have found that the often is best solved by the following criteria.

- Has occurred at all during the last three months
  - is spiteful and vindictive
  - blames others for his or her mistakes or misbehavior

- Occurs at least twice a week
  - is touchy or easily annoyed by others
  - loses temper
  - argues with adults
  - actively defies or refuses to comply with adults' requests or rules

- Occurs at least four times per week
  - is angry and resentful
  - deliberately annoys people

What Causes It?

No one knows for certain. The usual pattern is for problems to begin between ages 1–3. If you think about it, a lot of these behaviors are normal at age 2, but in this disorder they never go away. It does run in families. If a parent is alcoholic and has been in trouble with the law, their children are almost three times as likely to have ODD. That is, 18% of children will have ODD if the parents are alcoholic and the father has been in trouble with the law.

How Can You Tell If a Child Has It?

ODD is diagnosed in the same way as many other psychiatric disorders in children. You need to examine the child, talk with the child, talk to the parents, and review the medical history. Sometimes other medical tests are necessary to make sure it is not something else. You always need to check children out for other psychiatric disorders, as it is common the children with ODD will have other problems, too.

Who Gets It?

A lot of children! This is the most common psychiatric problem in children. Over 5% of children have this. In younger children it is more common in boys than girls, but as they grow older, the rate is the same in males and females.

ODD Rarely Travels Alone

It is exceptionally rare for a physician to see a child with only ODD. Usually the child has some other neuropsychiatric disorder along with ODD. The tendency for disorders in medicine to occur together is called comorbidity. Understanding comorbidity in pediatric psychiatry is one of the most important areas of research at this moment.

What Happens to Children Who Have This When They Grow Up?

There are three main paths that a child will take. First, there will be some lucky children who outgrow this. The exact number is not clear, but probably not the majority. The aggressiveness is very stable. That is, aggressive 2 year olds are likely to be aggressive 20 year olds. Only IQ is more stable over years than aggression.

Second, ODD may turn into something else. About 5–10% of preschoolers with ODD will eventually end up with ADHD and no signs of ODD at all. Other times ODD turns into conduct disorder (CD). This usually happens fairly early. That is, after 3–4 years of ODD, if it hasn't turned into CD, it won't ever. What predicts a child with ODD getting CD? A history of a biologic parent who was a career criminal, and very severe ODD.

Third, the child may continue to have ODD without any thing else. However, by the time preschoolers with ODD are 8 years old, only 5% have ODD and nothing else.

Fourth, they continue to have ODD but add on comorbid anxiety disorders, comorbid ADHD, or comorbid depressive disorders. By the time these children are in the end of elementary school, about 25% will have mood or anxiety problems which are disabling. That means that it is very important to watch for signs of mood disorders and anxiety as children with ODD grow older.

Will Children with ODD End up as Criminals?

Probably not unless they develop conduct disorder. Even then many will grow out of it. Life may not be easy. People with ODD who are grown up often do best if they can work for themselves and stay away from alcohol. However their tendency to irritate others often leads to a lonely life.

My Father-in-Law Says the Whole Problem Is My Husband and I. My Daughter Convinced Him That She Is a Victim of Uncaring Parents. How Often Does This Happen?

Too often! Children and adolescents with ODD produce strong feelings in people. They are trying to get a reaction out of people, and they are often successful. Common ones are: inciting spouses to fight with each other and not focus on the child, making outsiders believe that all the fault lies with the parents, making certain susceptible people believe that they can "save" the child by doing everything the child wants, setting parents against grandparents, setting teachers against parents, and inciting the parents to abuse the child. I frequently see children with ODD in which teachers and parents and sometimes others are all fighting amongst each other rather than with the child who is causing all the turmoil in the first place.

Conduct Disorder (CD)

In some ways, conduct disorder (CD) is just a worse version of ODD. However recent research suggests that there are some differences. Children with ODD seem to have worse social skills than those with CD. Children with ODD seem to do better in school. Conduct disorder is the most serious childhood psychiatric disorder. Approximately 6–10% of boys and 2–9% of girls have this disorder. Here is the definition:

A repetitive and persistent pattern of behavior in which the basic rights of others or major society rules are violated. At least three of the following criteria must be present in the last 12 months, and at least one criterion must have been present in the last 6 months. The problem causes significant impairment in social, academic, and occupational functioning.

Aggression to People and Animals

- often bullies, threatens, or intimidates others
- often initiates physical fights
- has used a weapon that can cause serious physical harm to others (a bat, brick, broken bottle, knife, gun)
- physically cruel to animals
- physically cruel to people
- has stolen while confronting a victim (mugging, purse snatching, extortion, armed robbery)

Destruction of Property

- has deliberately engaged in fire setting with the intention of causing serious damage
- has deliberately destroyed other's property other than by fire setting

Deceitfulness or Theft

- has broken into someone else's house, building, or car
- often lies to obtain goods or favors or to avoid work
- has stolen items of nontrivial value without confronting a victim (shoplifting, forgery)

Serious Violations of Rules

- often stays out at night despite parental prohibitions, beginning before 13 years of age
- has run away from home overnight at least twice without returning home for a lengthy period
- often skips school before age 13

Diagnosis

Conduct disorder is diagnosed like all things in pediatric psychiatry. The child and the caregivers will be interviewed together and separately to go over the history and check out all other possible comorbid conditions. Usually there are school reports, too. The child is examined to look for signs of many disorders. This usually includes some school work, some parts of the physical exam, and getting the child's perspective on things. Occasionally, there are lab tests and x-rays to do.

Prognosis and Course of Conduct Disorder

Perhaps about 30% of conduct disorder children continue with similar problems in adulthood. It is more common for males with CD to continue on into adulthood with these types of problems than females. Females with CD more often end up having mood and anxiety disorders as adults. Substance abuse is very high. About 50–70% of ten year olds with conduct disorder will be abusing substances four years later. Cigarette smoking is also very high. A recent study of girls with conduct disorder showed that they have much worse physical health. Girls with conduct disorder were almost 6 times more likely to abuse drugs or alcohol, eight times more likely to smoke cigarettes daily, where almost twice as likely to have sexually transmitted diseases, had twice the number of sexual partners, and were three times as likely to become pregnant when compared to girls without conduct disorder.

Looked at from the other direction, by the time they are adults, 70% of children no longer show signs of conduct disorder. Are they well? Some are, but what often happens is that the comorbid problems remain or get worse. A girl with CD and depression may end up as an adult with depression, but no conduct disorder. The same pattern can be true of CD plus bipolar disorder and other disorders.

Families and CD

It is not unusual to see signs of stress in the parents and other siblings when a child has CD. One of the hardest questions is figuring out whether or not difficulties in the family are causing CD or whether the stress of CD is causing family problems. Often it is impossible to determine this, or there are reasons to suggest both the CD is causing the family problems and the family is causing the CD to be worse. CD is a very difficult problem to live with. It would be very unusual to see a family where it was not causing grave distress. This obviously needs to be addressed in any treatment plan.

What Can Be Done?

Treat Comorbid Disorders

CD plus ADHD. Recent studies have shown that treating CD plus ADHD with stimulants helps the conduct disorder and the ADHD symptoms. This effect appears independent of how bad the ADHD is. Since 60–70% of children who go to a clinic for help with CD also have ADHD, this is extremely important. Serious consideration should be given to medically treating all children with CD plus ADHD. Although this type of medical intervention does not make the children "normal," it can make a big difference. It often means that the non-medical interventions will work much better.

CD plus depression. Recent work also suggests that treating depression in the context of CD is effective. While Prozac was used in this study, most likely other drugs in that same family would be effective.

CD plus substance abuse, movement disorders, bipolar disorder, psychosis, pervasive developmental disorders. Although there is not as much data on these areas, it is a good idea to always vigorously treat any disorder which is comorbid with CD. The importance of treating comorbid conditions cannot be overstated.

Non-Medical Strategies for ODD and CD

Containment. The essence of this group of interventions is to make it impossible for ODD or CD to "work." That is, it is a way of making sure all these attempts to irritate and annoy others and to cause fighting between others are not successful. There are three elements to this.

1. Come together. The most common thing I see in children with ODD (except for aggressiveness) is that a lot of the suffering that the child inflicts on others is blamed on others. Children and adolescents with ODD convince mothers that fathers have mistreated them. They convince parents that the teachers are treating their child unfairly. They convince teachers that the parents are bad, etc. You have to come together and never believe anything the child with ODD tells you about how others treat them. Instead, all parties need to talk directly with each other without the child as an intermediary.

Sometimes parole officers, parents, teachers and others have to all sit down together for the purpose of making it impossible for the child to play one person or group off against another.

2. Have a plan. That is, a plan to deal with all of this oppositional and defiant behavior. If you react on the spur of the moment, your emotions will guide you wrongly in dealing with children and adolescents with ODD. They will work to provoke intense feelings in everyone. Everyone needs to agree on what happens when the child with ODD does certain things. What do we do if she disrupts class, annoys others incessantly, fights, has a major temper tantrum, states she is going to kill herself or run away? You need a behavior modification or management plan. For behavior modification to work, the program must target a few important clear cut behaviors, and it must be consistent. There is no bending of rules in this sort of thing: no difference between the baby-sitter, mom, or dad.

3. Decide what you are going to ignore. Most children and adolescents with ODD are doing too many things you dislike to include every one of them in a behavior management plan. The main caregivers have to decide ahead of time what sort of thing will just be ignored.

4. Try very hard not to show any emotion when reacting to the behaviors of children and adolescents with ODD. The worst thing to do with a kid with ODD is to react strongly and emotionally. This will just make the child push you that same way again. You do not want the child to figure out what really bugs you. You want to try to remain as cool as possible while the child is trying to drive you over the edge. This is not easy. Once you know what you are going to ignore and what will be addressed through behavior modification, it should be far easier not to let your feelings get the best of you.

Make sure that you are as healthy and strong as you can be. Children and adolescents with ODD will find the weakness in the family system and exploit it. Is there tension between father and mother? They will aim to worsen this. Trouble with the in-laws? These children and adolescents will try to exploit this. Are you out of shape and exhausted after work? That's when they will be most trying. Are you worried or depressed about something? They will try to figure it out and torment you. Dealing with a child with ODD is very exhausting and trying. It will take about 1/3 to 1/4 of all your emotional, mental, and physical resources. If you knew that you would be chopping wood for four hours every day, you would make sure you got enough rest, a good diet, and had plenty of time to relax. The same is true for dealing with ODD in the long term. You have to take care of yourself in ways you would not have to if your child did not have ODD.

Limit television. Television is a major force in our lives. Study after study have shown that television is filled with violence, drug and alcohol use, and sexuality. The average child spends at least 2–3 hours a day watching this stuff. Many children spend 4–6 hours a day watching this. It should not be any wonder then that children who watch a lot of TV are more violent, are more likely to do drugs, and are preoccupied with sex. In a child with a problem like ADHD or ODD, this is clearly something that needs to be done.

Eliminate or reduce video and computer games. Anyone who has ever seen a child play Nintendo can see that there is a very potent force at work here. Unfortunately, the vast majority of computer and video games are violent and are becoming more graphic, not less, in their depiction of violence. As mentioned above, large amounts of television viewing can cause increased psychiatric problems for children. Although there is a less research on games, the same trend is there.

Enlist others to help you. Caring for a child with ODD can take a lot out of anyone, especially if you are one of the main people the child is trying to aggravate. Some children with ODD and more children with ODD plus other psychiatric problems can require an incredible amount of patience, energy, and determination. Often this is more than any one or two human beings can provide. There is no natural law that states that all children can be managed by one or two reasonable parents. Many children are born who require three to five full-time parents. You may have one!

First think who in your family can take care of this child reasonably well for an hour? a day? a weekend? a week? Try what is available publicly. Daycare for little kids? After school programs for older children and adolescents? Big brother and big sisters?

Hospitalize the child. Some children with ODD plus a few other psychiatric diagnoses or CD are just totally out of control. They have everyone fighting with each other, are controlling the family, and are causing so much chaos that caregivers can only concentrate on surviving each minute. Sometimes putting the child in the child psychiatric ward can do wonders. You get some rest, and most importantly have some time to figure out what to do next with the assistance of the child psychiatric ward staff.

Full time parenting. If you are the full time parent with a child like this, it is a full time job. That means that either both parents/caregivers work part time or one works and the other doesn't. Don't expect to both work full time outside the home. It won't work. You won't spend every minute with the child, but by the time you address all the needs of the child and yourself and your family, there will be no time for work, too.

Someone to talk to. Whether it is your spouse, relative, friend, pastor, or a counselor, you need to be able to talk to someone with total frankness, especially if things go wrong. You cannot do it yourself.

Medical Interventions

When do you consider medications? There are three reasons to consider this:

1. if medically treatable CO-morbid conditions are present (ADHD, depression, tic disorders, seizure disorders, psychosis)

2. if non-medical interventions are not successful

3. when the symptoms are very severe

In choosing drugs for ODD, I look for drugs that have been proven safe in children, have no long term side effects, and have been found in research studies to be effective in extremely aggressive children and adolescents or in co-morbid conditions which children with CD often have. Each drug has certain problems that need to be watched for.

Clonidine

This drug was originally developed for treating blood pressure and it is very safe. It turns out to be useful for a lot of things. Tics, severe ADHD, detoxifying heroin addicts, menopausal flushing, and sometimes autism with hyperactivity or severe aggression are the usual indications. The good thing about this is that it never aggravates tics, works when autism is present, and works in very aggressive children and adolescents who never sleep. It is safe for pre-schoolers and comes in a pill called Dixarit that is sweet tasting and looks exactly like smarties. As a result, children and adolescents will easily take it. It also comes in a larger size. It is my first choice when tics are present. It is also used in autism, preschoolers, and very aggressive children and adolescents with ADHD and insomnia.

And the bad side? About one out of every 10 to 20 people who take this will become depressed. It comes on within about 3–4 days and after the drug is stopped, it can take 3–4 days to clear.

This drug also has an effect on the heart. It can lower the pulse and blood pressure. To be cautious, I check an EKG before I start the drug and once the child is on it. I also check their blood pressure and pulse at every visit.

It will make some children sedated, but usually by cutting back the dose you can avoid this.

Risperidone

This drug was initially developed to be a safer drug for adult schizophrenia. It was then found to be effective in children with schizophrenia and other psychoses. Then it was found to be helpful in some children with tic disorders. Based on those findings it has been used in conduct disorder. There are some promising studies that show that this drug can help some of the core conduct disorder symptoms. When a group of hospitalized aggressive children with conduct disorder and borderline mental retardation were given an average of 2 mg of Risperidal a day about half of the children were a lot better and another quarter were somewhat better. Violence against others, verbal abuse, and property damage all significantly decreased. Another recent study found that risperidone was very helpful to children with conduct disorder when compared to placebo. These drugs were very well tolerated. These studies are probably the most exciting news for the medical treatment of CD in 20 years.

Weight gain is the biggest problem with this drug. Most studies show that some children gain from 10–35 lbs taking it. Stiffness, restlessness, and tremor—these occasionally happen with this drug, too, but to a much less extent than with the others. Tardive dyskinesia (a movement disorder) can still occur. A recent study with many children who had mild or borderline mental retardation showed that after a year on atypical antipsychotics at a dose of about 3–4 mg a day, 4 out of 46 (8.5%) had tardive dyskinesia.

This drug can also cause something called neuroleptic malignant syndrome. This is a rare reaction to antipsychotic medication where people are very ill and have a fever, stiffness, and they are not thinking clearly. It can be very serious and has even caused deaths.

Anti-Convulsants

It has been known for some time that children and adults with brain damage can have severe temper problems. The drugs Tegretol (carbamazepine) and Epival (divalproex [trade name in the U.S. is Depakote]) have successfully been used to treat the temper problems in people with brain damage. These drugs are usually used for seizures and bipolar disorder. Recently, there have been some studies of these drugs in children and adults with severe problems with aggression and temper who do not have any brain damage. Most of these are in adults and show some of the same difficult personality characteristics that children with ODD show. Although there is not a lot of data, so far it does look promising.

While both Epival and Tegretol are safe to use in children, they are not without side effects.

Conclusion

ODD and CD are bad problems. There is no one thing that will probably fix them. Make sure you are not prematurely ruling out any of the possible interventions above. If you are not careful, it can destroy you long before it ruins the kid. If nothing is done, the outcome can be dismal. It is absolutely key to keep working to do everything you can to keep this problem from devastating your life and your child's.

Chapter 64

Attention Deficit/Hyperactivity Disorder

Attention deficit hyperactivity disorder (ADHD), once called hyper-kinesis or minimal brain dysfunction, is one of the most common mental disorders among children. It affects 3 to 5 percent of all children, perhaps as many as 2 million American children. Two to three times more boys than girls are affected. On the average, at least one child in every classroom in the United States needs help for the disorder. ADHD often continues into adolescence and adulthood, and can cause a lifetime of frustrated dreams and emotional pain.

But there is help...and hope. In the last decade, scientists have learned much about the course of the disorder and are now able to identify and treat children, adolescents, and adults who have it. A variety of medications, behavior-changing therapies, and educational options are already available to help people with ADHD focus their attention, build self-esteem, and function in new ways.

The individuals referred to in this chapter are not real, but their stories are representative of people who show symptoms of ADHD.

Excerpted from "Attention Deficit Hyperactivity Disorder," National Institute of Mental Health (NIMH), National Institutes of Health (NIH), U.S. Department of Health and Human Services, NIH Publication No. 96-3572, http://www.nimh.nih.gov/publicat/adhd.cfm, printed 1994, reprinted 1996, last updated March 10, 2000.

Understanding the Problem

What Are the Symptoms of ADHD?

At present, ADHD is a diagnosis applied to children and adults who consistently display certain characteristic behaviors over a period of time. The most common behaviors fall into three categories: inattention, hyperactivity, and impulsivity.

Inattention. People who are inattentive have a hard time keeping their mind on any one thing and may get bored with a task after only a few minutes. They may give effortless, automatic attention to activities and things they enjoy. But focusing deliberate, conscious attention to organizing and completing a task or learning something new is difficult.

Hyperactivity. People who are hyperactive always seem to be in motion. They can't sit still. They may dash around or talk incessantly. Sitting still through a lesson can be an impossible task. Hyperactive children squirm in their seat or roam around the room. They might wiggle their feet, touch everything, or noisily tap their pencil. Hyperactive teens and adults may feel intensely restless. They may be fidgety or they may try to do several things at once, bouncing around from one activity to the next.

Impulsivity. People who are overly impulsive seem unable to curb their immediate reactions or think before they act. As a result they may blurt out inappropriate comments. They may run into the street without looking. Their impulsivity may make it hard for them to wait for things they want or to take their turn in games. They may grab a toy from another child or hit when they're upset.

To assess whether a person has ADHD, specialists consider several critical questions: Are these behaviors excessive, long-term, and pervasive? That is, do they occur more often than in other people the same age? Are they a continuous problem, not just a response to a temporary situation? Do the behaviors occur in several settings or only in one specific place like the playground or the office? The person's pattern of behavior is compared against a set of criteria and characteristics of the disorder. These criteria appear in a diagnostic reference book called the *DSM* (short for the *Diagnostic and Statistical Manual of Mental Disorders*).

According to the diagnostic manual, there are three patterns of behavior that indicate ADHD. People with ADHD may show several signs of being consistently inattentive. They may have a pattern of being hyperactive and impulsive. Or they may show all three types of behavior.

According to the *DSM*, signs of inattention include:

- becoming easily distracted by irrelevant sights and sounds

- failing to pay attention to details and making careless mistakes

- rarely following instructions carefully and completely

- losing or forgetting things like toys, or pencils, books, and tools needed for a task

Some signs of hyperactivity and impulsivity are:

- feeling restless, often fidgeting with hands or feet, or squirming

- running, climbing, or leaving a seat, in situations where sitting or quiet behavior is expected

- blurting out answers before hearing the whole question

- having difficulty waiting in line or for a turn

Because everyone shows some of these behaviors at times, the *DSM* contains very specific guidelines for determining when they indicate ADHD. The behaviors must appear early in life, before age 7, and continue for at least 6 months. In children, they must be more frequent or severe than in others the same age. Above all, the behaviors must create a real handicap in at least two areas of a person's life, such as school, home, work, or social settings. So someone whose work or friendships are not impaired by these behaviors would not be diagnosed with ADHD. Nor would a child who seems overly active at school but functions well elsewhere.

ADHD is a serious diagnosis that may require long-term treatment with counseling and medication. So it's important that a doctor first look for and treat any other causes for these behaviors.

What Causes ADHD?

Understandably, one of the first questions parents ask when they learn their child has an attention disorder is "Why? What went wrong?"

Health professionals stress that since no one knows what causes ADHD, it doesn't help parents to look backward to search for possible reasons. There are too many possibilities to pin down the cause with certainty. It is far more important for the family to move forward in finding ways to get the right help.

Scientists, however, do need to study causes in an effort to identify better ways to treat, and perhaps some day, prevent ADHD. They are finding more and more evidence that ADHD does not stem from home environment, but from biological causes. When you think about it, there is no clear relationship between home life and ADHD. Not all children from unstable or dysfunctional homes have ADHD. And not all children with ADHD come from dysfunctional families. Knowing this can remove a huge burden of guilt from parents who might blame themselves for their child's behavior.

ADHD is not usually caused by:

- too much TV
- food allergies
- excess sugar
- poor home life
- poor schools

Getting Help

How Is ADHD Identified and Diagnosed?

Many parents see signs of an attention deficit in toddlers long before the child enters school. But in many cases the teacher is the first to recognize that a child is hyperactive or inattentive and may consult with the school psychologist. Because teachers work with many children, they come to know how "average" children behave in learning situations that require attention and self control. However, teachers sometimes fail to notice the needs of children who are quiet and cooperative.

Types of Professionals Who Make the Diagnosis

School-age and preschool children are often evaluated by a school psychologist or a team made up of the school psychologist and other specialists. But if the school doesn't believe the student has a problem, or if the family wants another opinion, a family may need to see a specialist in private practice. In such cases, who can the family turn to? What kinds of specialists do they need?

Table 64.1. Types of professionals.

Speciality	Can diagnose ADHD	Can prescribe medications, if needed	Provides counseling or training
Psychiatrists	yes	yes	yes
Psychologists	yes	no	yes
Pediatricians or family physicians	yes	yes	no
Neurologists	yes	yes	no

The family can start by talking with the child's pediatrician or their family doctor. Some pediatricians may do the assessment themselves, but more often they refer the family to an appropriate specialist they know and trust. In addition, state and local agencies that serve families and children, as well as some of the volunteer organizations listed in the back of this *Sourcebook*, can help identify an appropriate specialist.

What Are the Educational Options?

Children with ADHD have a variety of needs. Some children are too hyperactive or inattentive to function in a regular classroom, even with medication and a behavior management plan. Such children may be placed in a special education class for all or part of the day. In some schools, the special education teacher teams with the classroom teacher to meet each child's unique needs. However, most children are able to stay in the regular classroom. Whenever possible, educators prefer to not to segregate children, but to let them learn along with their peers.

Children with ADHD often need some special accommodations to help them learn. For example, the teacher may seat the child in an area with few distractions, provide an area where the child can move around and release excess energy, or establish a clearly posted system of rules and reward appropriate behavior. Sometimes just keeping a card or a picture on the desk can serve as a visual reminder to use the right school behavior, like raising a hand instead of shouting out, or staying in a seat instead of wandering around the room. Giving a child extra time on tests can make the difference between passing and failing, and gives her a fairer chance to show what she's learned. Reviewing instructions or writing assignments on the board, and even listing the books and materials they will need for the task, may make it possible for disorganized, inattentive children to complete the work.

Many of the strategies of special education are simply good teaching methods. Telling students in advance what they will learn, providing visual aids, and giving written as well as oral instructions are all ways to help students focus and remember the key parts of the lesson.

Students with ADHD often need to learn techniques for monitoring and controlling their own attention and behavior. The process of finding alternatives to interrupting the teacher makes them more self-sufficient and cooperative.

Because schools demand that children sit still, wait for a turn, pay attention, and stick with a task, it's no surprise that many children with ADHD have problems in class. Their minds are fully capable of learning, but their hyperactivity and inattention make learning difficult. As a result, many students with ADHD repeat a grade or drop out of school early. Fortunately, with the right combination of appropriate educational practices, medication, and counseling, these outcomes can be avoided.

Some Coping Strategies for Teens and Adults with ADHD

- When necessary, ask the teacher or boss to repeat instructions rather than guess.

- Break large assignments or job tasks into small, simple tasks. Set a deadline for each task and reward yourself as you complete each one.

- Each day, make a list of what you need to do. Plan the best order for doing each task. Then make a schedule for doing them. Use a calendar or daily planner to keep yourself on track.

- Work in a quiet area. Do one thing at a time. Give yourself short breaks.

- Write things you need to remember in a notebook with dividers. Write different kinds of information like assignments, appointments, and phone numbers in different sections. Keep the book with you all of the time.

- Post notes to yourself to help remind yourself of things you need to do. Tape notes on the bathroom mirror, on the refrigerator, in your school locker, or dashboard of your car—wherever you're likely to need the remainder.

- Store similar things together. For example, keep all your Nintendo disks in one place, and tape cassettes in another. Keep canceled checks in one place, and bills in another.

- Create a routine. Get yourself ready for school or work at the same time, in the same way, every day.

- Exercise, eat a balanced diet and get enough sleep.

What Treatments Are Available?

For decades, medications have been used to treat the symptoms of ADHD. Three medications in the class of drugs known as stimulants seem to be the most effective in both children and adults. These are methylphenidate (Ritalin), dextroamphetamine (Dexedrine or Dextrostat), and pemoline (Cylert). For many people, these medicines dramatically reduce their hyperactivity and improve their ability to focus, work, and learn.

Unfortunately, when people see such immediate improvement, they often think medication is all that's needed. But these medicines don't cure the disorder, they only temporarily control the symptoms. Although the drugs help people pay better attention and complete their work, they can't increase knowledge or improve academic skills. The drugs alone can't help people feel better about themselves or cope with problems. These require other kinds of treatment and support.

For lasting improvement, numerous clinicians recommend that medications should be used along with treatments that aid in these other areas. There are no quick cures. Many experts believe that the most significant, long-lasting gains appear when medication is combined with behavioral therapy, emotional counseling, and practical support. Some studies suggest that the combination of medicine and therapy may be more effective than drugs alone. NIMH is conducting a large study to check this.

Use of Stimulant Drugs

Stimulant drugs, such as Ritalin, Cylert, and Dexedrine, when used with medical supervision, are usually considered quite safe. Although they can be addictive to teenagers and adults if misused, these medications are not addictive in children.

Other types of medication may be used if stimulants don't work or if the ADHD occurs with another disorder. Antidepressants and other medications may be used to help control accompanying depression or anxiety. In some cases, antihistamines may be tried. Clonidine, a drug normally used to treat hypertension, may be helpful in people with both ADHD and Tourette syndrome. Although stimulants tend to be more effective, clonidine may be tried when stimulants don't work or can't be used. Clonidine can be administered either by pill or by skin patch and has different side effects than stimulants. The doctor works closely with each patient to find the most appropriate medication.

The Medication Debate

As useful as these drugs are, Ritalin and the other stimulants have sparked a great deal of controversy. Most doctors feel the potential side effects should be carefully weighed against the benefits before prescribing the drugs. While on these medications, some children may lose weight, have less appetite, and temporarily grow more slowly. Others may have problems falling asleep. Some doctors believe that stimulants may also make the symptoms of Tourette syndrome worse, although recent research suggests this may not be true. Other doctors say if they carefully watch the child's height, weight, and overall development, the benefits of medication far outweigh the potential side effects. Side effects that do occur can often be handled by reducing the dosage.

Treatments to Help People with ADHD and Their Families Learn to Cope

Medication can help to control some of the behavior problems that may have lead to family turmoil. But more often, there are other aspects of the problem that medication can't touch. Even though ADHD primarily affects a person's behavior, having the disorder has broad emotional repercussions. For some children, being scolded is the only attention they ever get. They have few experiences that build their sense of worth and competence. If they're hyperactive, they're often told they're bad and punished for being disruptive. If they are too disorganized and unfocused to complete tasks, others may call them lazy. If they impulsively grab toys, butt in, or shove classmates, they may lose friends. And if they have a related conduct disorder, they may get in trouble at school or with the law. Facing the daily frustrations that can come with having ADHD can make people fear that they are strange, abnormal, or stupid.

Often, the cycle of frustration, blame, and anger has gone on so long that it will take some time to undo. Both parents and their children may need special help to develop techniques for managing the patterns of behavior. In such cases, mental health professionals can counsel the child and the family, helping them to develop new skills, attitudes, and ways of relating to each other. In individual counseling, the therapist helps children or adults with ADHD learn to feel better about themselves. They learn to recognize that having a disability does not reflect who they are as a person. The therapist can also help people with ADHD identify and build on their strengths, cope with daily problems, and control their attention and aggression. In group counseling, people learn that they are not alone in their frustration and that others want to help. Sometimes only the individual with ADHD needs counseling support. But in many cases, because the problem affects the family as well as the person with ADHD, the entire family may need help. The therapist assists the family in finding better ways to handle the disruptive behaviors and promote change. If the child is young, most of the therapist's work is with the parents, teaching them techniques for coping with and improving their child's behavior.

Controversial Treatments

Understandably, parents who are eager to help their children want to explore every possible option. Many newly touted treatments sound reasonable. Many even come with glowing reports. A few are pure quackery. Some are even developed by reputable doctors or specialists—but when tested scientifically, cannot be proven to help.

Here are a few types of treatment that have not been scientifically shown to be effective in treating the majority of children or adults with ADHD:

- biofeedback
- restricted diets
- allergy treatments

- medicines to correct problems in the inner ear
- megavitamins
- chiropractic adjustment and bone re-alignment
- treatment for yeast infection
- eye training
- special colored glasses

A few success stories can't substitute for scientific evidence. Until sound, scientific testing shows a treatment to be effective, families risk spending time, money, and hope on fads and false promises.

Sustaining Hope

Can ADHD Be Outgrown or Cured?

Even though most people don't outgrow ADHD, people do learn to adapt and live fulfilling lives. With effective combinations of medicine, new skills, and emotional support, people with ADHD can develop ways to control their attention and minimize their disruptive behaviors. They may find that by structuring tasks and controlling their environment, they can achieve personal goals. They may learn to channel their excess energy into sports and other high energy activities. They can identify career options that build on their strengths and abilities.

As they grow up, with appropriate help from parents and clinicians, children with ADHD become better able to suppress their hyperactivity and to channel it into more socially acceptable behaviors, like physical exercise or fidgeting. And although we know that half of all children with ADHD will still show signs of the problem into adulthood, we also know that the medications and therapy that help children also work for adults.

All people with ADHD have natural talents and abilities that they can draw on to create fine lives and careers for themselves. In fact, many people with ADHD even feel that their patterns of behavior give them unique, often unrecognized, advantages. People with ADHD tend to be outgoing and ready for action. Because of their drive for excitement and stimulation, many become successful in business, sports, construction, and public speaking. Because of their ability to think about many things at once, many have won acclaim as artists and inventors. Many choose work that gives them freedom to move around and release excess energy. But some find ways to be effective in quieter, more sedentary careers. Sally, a computer programmer, found that she thinks best when she wears headphones to reduce distracting noises. Some people strive to increase their organizational skills. Others who own their own business find it useful to hire support staff to provide day-to-day management.

What Are Sources of Information and Support?

Publications, organizations, and support groups exist to help individuals, teachers, and families to understand and cope with attention disorders. Other resources are outpatient clinics of children's hospitals, university medical centers, and community mental health centers. Please see the Additional Help and Information section of this *Sourcebook* for contact information and further resources.

Chapter 65

Anxiety Disorders in Youth

Introduction

Up to 12% of ninth graders have had a panic attack. About 1–2% of all adults have multiple panic attacks. If you look at adults with panic disorder, 20% had their first panic attack before age 10. The first question is, what is a panic attack? Here are the official criteria:

Panic Attack

A discrete period of intense fear or discomfort, in which four (or more) of the following symptoms develop abruptly and reach a peak within 10 minutes:

1. palpitations, pounding heart, or accelerated heart rate
2. sweating
3. trembling or shaking
4. sensations of shortness of breath or smothering
5. feeling of choking

Reprinted with permission from "Panic disorder, Separation Anxiety disorder, and Agoraphobia in Children and Adolescents," a pamphlet written by pediatric psychiatrist James Chandler, M.D., FRCPC. © 2002 James Chandler. Updated June 2002, downloaded August 2002. The full text of this document can be found at http://www.klis.com/chandler/pamphlet/panic/panicpamphlet.htm.

6.   chest pain or discomfort

7.   nausea or abdominal distress

8.   feeling dizzy, unsteady, lightheaded, or faint

9.   derealization (feelings of unreality) or depersonalization (being detached from oneself)

10. fear of losing control or going crazy

11. fear of dying

12. parasthesia (numbness or tingling sensation)

13. chills or hot flushes

What Causes Panic Attacks?

Most researchers have found that they are caused by an abnormality in the part of the brain which tells the brain how much carbon dioxide (CO_2) is in the blood. If your brain finds there is too much CO_2, it usually means that you are not breathing fast enough, or there is too much CO_2 in the air (for example, in a room with no ventilation or a cave). So your body sends all sorts of signals to increase breathing and a rush of adrenaline to help you get out of wherever you are in a hurry. This is a great thing if you are in a fire, for example.

It is thought that in panic attacks this carbon dioxide sensor is too sensitive, and tells the brain there is not enough oxygen when there is just plenty. So a person could be just sitting quietly and then *boom*, this rush of adrenaline and fast breathing appears out of nowhere. Since there is no reason outside the body to be worried, most people will start thinking there is something horribly wrong with their own body.

Beyond this brain problem, panic attacks are inherited. If a parent has an anxiety disorder, their children are much more likely to have an anxiety disorder, too. Part of this heredity is expressed through something called behavioral inhibition.

Behavioral inhibition is a tendency to react negatively to new situations or things. Some infants and children will be very happy and curious about new people and things. However, roughly 15% of children will be shy, withdrawn, and irritable when they are in a new situation or with new people or things. Often these children are irritable as infants, shy and fearful as toddlers, and cautious, quiet, and introverted at school age. Children who are consistently this way are much more likely to have biological parents with anxiety disorders. The children themselves are much more likely to develop anxiety disorders.

On the other hand 5–10 percent of children with behavioral inhibition will never develop anxiety disorders. At the moment it is thought that the majority of the genetic predisposition to anxiety disorders is expressed through behavioral inhibition. Often there is a combination of an inherited predisposition plus stress in the environment. Deaths in the family, divorce, and abuse will make panic attacks much more likely.

How Can You Be Sure That What Happened Was a Panic Attack and Not Some Other Medical Problem?

Panic attacks in children can be confused with many things. Common imitators are ulcers, irritable bowel syndrome, thyroid disease, some prescription drugs, migraines, epilepsy, diabetes, drug abuse, and other psychiatric disorders. There are some research tests which look at the brain which will show certain abnormalities in panic attacks. However, for a variety of reasons these are not in regular clinical use. The main principle is to rule out other problems using a careful medical history, a physical exam, and often certain lab or x-ray examinations. If the history and exam looks like panic attacks and no other cause is found, then a physician assumes it is a panic attack.

In females, stomach aches and headaches together are very, very common. In fact, recent studies have shown that when these two are found together in the same child, 69% had an anxiety disorder.

Panic Disorder

One panic attack is bad enough, but recurrent panic attacks can be devastating. If a child or adolescent has recurrent panic attacks and the following, it is called panic disorder.

1. recurrent unexpected panic attacks

2. at least one of the attacks has been followed by 1 month (or more) of one (or more) of the following:

   a. persistent concern about having additional attacks

   b. worry about the implications of the attack or its consequences (e.g., losing control, having a heart attack, "going crazy")

   c. a significant change in behavior related to the attacks.

Panic disorder in children is a very disabling condition. It will often affect a child's school performance. It almost always impairs them socially, and can lead to a lot of other problems. It is not a common illness in children. While perhaps 10% of children will have a panic attack, about 1–2% will develop panic disorder. Of those that do develop panic disorder, 10–35% will recover and remain well the rest of their lives. At least 50% will be mildly affected years later, and the rest will have chronic panic disorder for years. If you follow-up children with panic disorder, about 25% will still have it years later. Of those who continue to have panic disorder as they go into adulthood, many will develop other psychiatric difficulties. About 50% will develop agoraphobia, 20% will make suicide attempts, 27% will develop alcohol abuse, 60% will develop depression, 35% will believe they are unhealthy, 27% will not be financially independent, 28% will make frequent outpatients visits, and 50% will show significant social impairment.

Comorbidity

"My daughter has panic attacks, but it is her other nervous problems which are causing her the most trouble. What is going on?"

Panic disorder with agoraphobia often does not exist alone. Many children will also have another disorder. Here is a list of the other common childhood disorders.

- separation anxiety disorder
- obsessive-compulsive disorder
- generalized anxiety disorder
- social phobia
- selective mutism
- post-traumatic stress disorder
- tic disorders
- specific phobias
- attention deficit hyperactivity disorder (ADHD)
- depression

What Can Be Done?

If panic disorder with or without agoraphobia persists into adolescence, often the teenager will have become depressed, become involved with drugs and alcohol, fail or drop out of school, become socially isolated and almost house bound, or all of the above. The same is true for separation anxiety disorder.

The treatment of these conditions revolves around two things, medications and psychological treatments. I will start with psychological treatments. There are three elements to the psychological treatment of anxiety disorders.

Behavioral Treatments

Graduated exposure. It has been found that children, like adults, will be able to overcome phobias with this technique. What you do is gradually expose yourself to the thing that makes you so panicky.

Response prevention. The key to this technique is to keep yourself from doing the thing you want to when you get panicky. For example, if a child is in class and wants desperately to raise his hand so that he can go home and call his mother to come and get him, teach the child to wait 5 minutes before calling.

Relaxation techniques. When people start having panic symptoms, or if they are having to tolerate separation in separation anxiety disorder, if they have learned some specific techniques they can often ride out the panic much easier. These involve 1) slow, regulated breathing 2) saying a little memorized phrase like, "Everyone's stomachs gurgle. My stomach gurgles many times a day. I do not need to leave and go to the bathroom."

Cognitive therapy. This consists of learning about how certain thought patterns are leading to worsening of the anxiety disorder.

Medical Treatments

Often the idea of taking medicines for anxiety disorders makes either the parents or the child very nervous. Before discussing the individual drugs, I will discuss the general approach to pediatric psychopharmacology that I use.

Why Would Anyone Want to Give Drugs That Affect the Brain to Children?

The main reason would be if the non-medical interventions are not working. No one would suggest trying medical treatments before the non-medical interventions are used. It is similar to diabetes in that way. If you have diabetes which is not severe, your doctor will first suggest you try diet control. If that doesn't work, only then will the doctor consider medical treatment. In some situations, a child is very ill, has numerous disorders or there is some urgency. For example, a child has multiple anxiety disorders and depression and is either in the hospital or unable to go to school. Then I consider medications as a first line approach along with other interventions.

If the Drug Works, How Will My Child Be Different?

In cases where the drugs work very well, a child will be able to face situations in which they usually panic with little or no anxiety. Panic attacks should be basically eliminated. Children are usually more carefree, enthusiastic, and less depressed. Each drug works in a different way on the chemical transmitters in the brain.

What If It Doesn't Work?

Sometimes a medication won't work because the dose is too high or too low. Some people will not respond to one medication for the treatment of this problem but they will respond to another. If the drug doesn't work, of course, it is discontinued, and then you and your child's doctor decide what do next. Try something else? Abandon medical treatment? Both are sometimes reasonable options.

I Have Heard That These Drugs Can Do a Lot of Bad Things. Is This True?

Yes, it is. Like all medical treatments, there are side effects and sometimes people can have pretty bad side effects. There are two types of side effects. One type are the kind that disappear when you stop the drug. The other kind can last long after the drug is discontinued. I do not use any of the drugs which can cause permanent side effects after the drug is stopped.

Are They That Dangerous?

Yes, when used improperly they can be quite dangerous. However, when used carefully they can be almost 100% safe.

Here Are the Specific Drugs

Serotonin reuptake inhibitors (SRIs). In most cases, these are the first choice drugs for anxiety disorders in pediatrics. They are well tolerated, cause few side effects, and have been found to be quite effective in multiple studies. While there are fewer studies involving their use in separation anxiety disorder, researchers have found these drugs to work as well as in panic disorder. Common brands are Prozac, Paxil, Celexa, Zoloft, and Luvox.

Benzodiazepines. This is a group of drugs which are commonly called "minor tranquilizers." They work on a certain chemical in the brain called GABA and basically slow down many brain functions. The primary use in children is anxiety disorders or to help with anesthesia. Two are used for seizures. Commonly used ones are Xanax, Ativan, Serax, Valium, Dalmane, Librium, and Rivotril.

Other drugs. Venlafaxine (Effexor XR) has been found to be very useful for the treatment of anxiety disorders in adults. It is mostly used for depression in adults. There have been recent studies of this drug for anxiety disorders in children. Nevertheless, if a child, especially a teenager, had failed two trials of an SRI, it is the next choice.

In summary, anxiety disorders can be very disabling in children and should be treated. You need to make sure it is not some other medical problem and also see if other psychiatric problems are present, too. Most studies have found the best results when medical and non-medical treatments are combined. Most children with anxiety disorders should benefit significantly from treatment.

Agoraphobia

The most common fear or phobia in the context of panic disorder is agoraphobia. Here is the official definition of agoraphobia.

1. Anxiety about being in places or situations from which escape might be difficult (or embarrassing) or in which help might not be available in the event of having an unexpected panic attack or panic-like symptoms. Agoraphobic fears typically involve characteristic clusters of situations that include being outside the home alone, being in a crowd or standing in line, being on a bridge, and traveling in a bus, train, automobile, or plane.

2. The situations are avoided (e.g., travel is restricted) or else are endured with marked distress or with anxiety about having a panic attack or panic-like symptoms, or require the presence of a companion.

571

3. This is not due to social phobia, obsessive-compulsive disorder, post traumatic stress disorder, or separation anxiety disorder.

The usual pattern I find with children is not that different than with adults. Panic attacks will set in process a slow restricting of peoples lives. Slowly they stop doing all sorts of things they used to and stop going all sorts of places. Lots of times, especially with children, they have some excuse (other than fear of panic) for not going which seems fairly reasonable at first. Often they play at their home without problems, but if they have to go there is always a reason they aren't going. Sometimes it is because the child says he doesn't want to (even though you know he would love to do this before) other times it is because all of a sudden her stomach is hurting, she feels weak and tired, her eyes hurt, or she needs to go use the bathroom.

Agoraphobia and School

This is of only minor concern compared with agoraphobia that revolves around school. There are many parts of school which are the cause of problems in agoraphobics. I have never seen an agoraphobic child or adolescent who did not have problems with school. I will start from the beginning.

Wake up — Many children with agoraphobia will awaken on school days with horrible abdominal pain, diarrhea, nausea, headache, or many other signs of physical illness which all disappear as soon as there is no chance they are going to school. This is real, not made up. The anxiety is making their body react this way.

Bus rides — It is common that children with agoraphobia will be afraid that something horrible or embarrassing will happen on the bus such as diarrhea, vomiting, going crazy, and getting sick with no one to help. Often this results in parents driving the child to school.

Going in the school — Other children are fine until they see the school and they know they have to go in. The idea of going and sitting in their classrooms leads to all sorts of anxiety about what could go wrong (as in the bus ride). Some children will just refuse to go to school.

Leaving class — For some agoraphobic children, they get into school, but they can not stay the whole day. Their physical signs of anxiety are enough to get most teachers to call home and have a parent come and get the child. As a result, the parent is basically "on-call" throughout the school day.

Special events—Some agoraphobic children can handle the usual school day but not field trips (without their mother), performances, and changes in teachers.

All of these can lead to school refusal. There are other reasons besides agoraphobia that children will refuse to go to school. However, it is usually what will bring a child to my attention. Any of the other anxiety disorders of children can lead to school refusal. The most important thing is to get them back in school as soon as possible and find out what the problem(s) is.

My Son Says He Is Fine As Long As We Don't Do Anything to Make Him Worse

Many children with agoraphobia and panic disorder will have come up with their own "treatment." This consists of getting everyone else on the planet to live their lives such that it minimizes the anxiety for this child. When people (usually family members) forget or refuse to follow one of these many rules, then the child with the anxiety disorder blames the family member for his or her anxiety. Common rules are:

- I don't ride in other people's cars.
- I don't go to birthday parties.
- I don't go to the mall.
- I am driven to school.
- I don't wait in lines.
- I don't go on the 101 or 103.

This "treatment" drives caregivers nuts. Any worsening of anxiety is now the parents fault. Obviously, this is not the way to go. However, most children prefer this as they have no responsibility, and the focus is not on them.

Separation Anxiety Disorder

Agoraphobia and panic attacks often go together. More recently it has been discovered that panic attacks and agoraphobia are much more common in children who currently have separation anxiety disorder or had it in the past.

What Is Separation Anxiety Disorder?

It is a worry about being away from home or about being away from parents which is way out of line for that child's age, culture, and life.

Signs of Separation Anxiety Disorder

* getting nervous if the parent is going to leave, even if they haven't left yet
* worrying that something bad is going to happen to a parent
* worrying that a they will be lost or kidnaped
* being afraid to go places without parents
* can't be alone at home without parents
* can't sleep alone
* nightmares about being separated
* all the signs of panic attacks occurring when parent is leaving or child is forced to leave

Separation anxiety disorder can persist into adulthood. As mentioned above, it is very common for a child to start with this and later develop panic disorder or agoraphobia or all three! As far as causes go, the same things cause separation anxiety disorder that cause panic disorder and agoraphobia. However, some research now suggests that having a parent with alcoholism significantly increases a child's risk of having separation anxiety disorder. About 14% of children of alcoholic parents will have separation anxiety disorder.

Chapter 66

Depression in Youth

Introduction

You know that the school years can be complicated and demanding. Deep down, you are not quite sure of who you are, what you want to be, or whether the choices you make from day to day are the best decisions. Sometimes the many changes and pressures you are facing threaten to overwhelm you. So, it isn't surprising that from time to time you feel "down" or discouraged.

But what about those times when activity and outlook on life stay "down" for weeks? If you know someone like this, they might be suffering from depression. As a friend or care giver, you can help.

Find out More about Depression

What Is Depression?

Depression is more than the blues or the blahs; it is more than the normal, everyday ups and downs.

When that "down" mood, along with other symptoms, lasts for more than a couple of weeks, the condition may be clinical depression. Clinical depression is a serious health problem that affects the total person. In addition to feelings, it can change behavior, physical health

---

Excerpted from "What to Do When a Friend Is Depressed," National Institutes of Mental Health (NIMH), National Institutes of Health (NIH), NIH Pub. No. 00-3824, http://www.nimh.nih.gov/publicat/friend.cfm, April 2000.

and appearance, academic performance, social activity, and the ability to handle everyday decisions and pressures.

What Causes Clinical Depression?

We do not yet know all the causes of depression, but there seem to be biological and emotional factors that may increase the likelihood that an individual will develop a depressive disorder.

Research over the past decade strongly suggests a genetic link to depressive disorders; depression can run in families. Difficult life experiences and certain personal patterns such as difficulty handling stress, low self-esteem, or extreme pessimism about the future can increase the chances of becoming depressed.

How Common Is It?

Clinical depression is a lot more common than most people think. It will affect more than 19 million Americans this year.

One-fourth of all women and one-eighth of all men will suffer at least one episode or occurrence of depression during their lifetimes. Depression affects people of all ages but is less common for teenagers than for adults. Approximately 3 to 5 percent of the teen population experiences clinical depression every year. That means among 25 friends, 1 could be clinically depressed.

Is It Serious?

Depression can be very serious.

It has been linked to poor school performance, truancy, alcohol and drug abuse, running away, and feelings of worthlessness and hopelessness. In the past 25 years, the rate of suicide among teenagers and young adults has increased dramatically. Suicide is often linked to depression.

Are All Depressive Disorders Alike?

There are various forms or types of depression.

Some people experience only one episode of depression in their whole life, but many have several recurrences. Some depressive episodes begin suddenly for no apparent reason, while others can be associated with a life situation or stress. Sometimes people who are depressed cannot perform even the simplest daily activities—like getting out of bed or getting dressed; others go through the motions, but it is clear they are not acting or thinking as usual. Some people suffer from bipolar depression in which their moods cycle between two extremes—from the depths of desperation to frenzied talking or activity or grandiose ideas about their own competence.

Can It Be Treated?

Yes, depression is treatable. Between 80 and 90 percent of people with depression—even the most serious forms—can be helped.

There are a variety of antidepressant medications and psychotherapies that can be used to treat depressive disorders. Some people with milder forms may do well with psychotherapy alone. People with moderate to severe depression most often benefit from antidepressants. Most do best with combined treatment: medication to gain relatively quick symptom relief and psychotherapy to learn more effective ways to deal with life's problems, including depression.

The most important step toward overcoming depression—and sometimes the most difficult—is asking for help.

Why Don't People Get the Help they Need?

Often people don't know they are depressed, so they don't ask for or get the right help. Teenagers and adults share a problem—they often fail to recognize the symptoms of depression in themselves or in other people.

Be Able to Tell Fact from Fiction

Myths about depression often separate people from the effective treatments now available. Friends need to know the facts. Some of the most common myths are these:

Myth: Young people who claim to be depressed are weak and just need to pull themselves together. There's nothing anyone else can do to help.

Fact: Depression is not a weakness, but a serious health disorder. Both young people and adults who are depressed need professional treatment. A trained therapist or counselor can help them learn more positive ways to think about themselves, change behavior, cope with problems, or handle relationships. A physician can prescribe medications to help relieve the symptoms of depression. For many people, a combination of psychotherapy and medication is beneficial.

577

Myth: Talking about depression only makes it worse.

Fact: Talking through feelings may help someone recognize the need for professional help. By showing friendship and concern and giving uncritical support, you can encourage someone to get treatment.

Myth: Telling an adult that a friend might be depressed is betraying a trust. If someone wants help, he or she will get it.

Fact: Depression, which saps energy and self-esteem, interferes with a person's ability or wish to get help. And many parents may not understand the seriousness of depression or of thoughts of death or suicide. It is an act of true friendship to share your concerns with a school guidance counselor, a favorite teacher, your own parents, or another trusted adult.

Know the Symptoms

The first step toward defeating depression is to define it. But people who are depressed often have a hard time thinking clearly or recognizing their own symptoms. They may need help. Check the following to see if the person has had any of these symptoms persisting longer than two weeks.

Do they express feelings of

- sadness or "emptiness"?
- hopelessness, pessimism, or guilt?
- helplessness or worthlessness?

Do they seem

- unable to make decisions?
- unable to concentrate and remember?
- to have lost interest or pleasure in ordinary activities—like sports or band or talking on the phone?
- to have more problems with school and family?

Do they complain of

- loss of energy and drive—so they seem "slowed down"?
- trouble falling asleep, staying asleep, or getting up?

- appetite problems; are they losing or gaining weight?
- headaches, stomach aches, or backaches?
- chronic aches and pains in joints and muscles?

Has their behavior changed suddenly so that

- they are restless or more irritable?
- they want to be alone most of the time?
- they've started cutting classes or dropped hobbies and activities?
- you think they may be drinking heavily or taking drugs?

Have they talked about

- death?
- suicide—or have they attempted suicide?

Find Someone Who Can Help

If you answered yes to several of the items, this young person may need help. Don't assume that someone else is taking care of the problem. Negative thinking, inappropriate behavior or physical changes need to be reversed as quickly as possible. Not only does treatment lessen the severity of depression, treatment also may reduce the length of time (duration) the young person is depressed and may prevent additional bouts of depression.

If a young person shows many symptoms of depression, you can listen and encourage him or her to ask a parent or teacher about treatments.

There are many places in the community where people with depressive disorders can be diagnosed and treated. Help is available from family doctors, mental health specialists in community mental health centers or private clinics, and from other health professionals.

Chapter 67

Managing Childhood Aggression

Children aren't born aggressive, they learn it. However, children, parents, and caregivers also can learn how to cope with aggression. This chapter answers some questions about aggression and how to teach social coping skills to children.

Where Does Aggression Come from?

Do humans just have a fighting instinct? Is aggression the outcome of frustration? Most recent studies view aggressive acts not as the sole fault of the individual, but also as related to a set of cultural and social circumstances.

What Factors Lead to Aggression?

The Child

A child's temperament and his/her learned coping skills are critical to the youngster's being able to manage aggression. Statements such as "boys are supposed to act out their anger" or "she is wild" are common expressions that parents and others use to refer to a child's temperament. Temperament is that part of the personality that seems

---

Excerpted from "Childhood Aggression: Where Does it Come From? How Can it be Managed?," by Karen DeBord, Ph.D., Associate Professor and Extension Child Development Specialist, North Carolina State University. © 2000. Reprinted with permission.

to be controlled by genetics. There are basically three types of temperament—easy or flexible (60 percent of children), fearful and sensitive (25 percent of children), and feisty or difficult (15 percent of children).

The Family

The level of family stress and the positive and negative interactions of the family influence children learning aggression. Children model their behavior after adults around them, observing and imitating how others handle their anger and frustration.

The Community

Communities that understand and support children's rights are communities that support children and all their developmental stages. Places where there are supportive adults and healthy alternatives for recreation can protect children while they are learning to deal with many situations, including those that give rise to aggression.

The Environment

Some studies have found that housing, schools, and neighborhoods can contribute to aggression. For example, extreme heat or overcrowding has been shown to increase aggression.

The Culture

What sorts of models are children exposed to on television and in the community? When people try to solve problems with physical violence, children mistakenly learn that this is an appropriate behavior.

Why Are Children Aggressive?

Sometimes children do not have the social skills or self-control to manage their behavior. These must be taught. When children can't find the words to deal with aggressive feelings or are not encouraged to express themselves, they become frustrated. At other times, children cannot cope with growing levels of anger in themselves or in others. In both cases, children need to learn acceptable ways to assert themselves and to learn coping skills.

What Does Aggression Look Like in Children of Different Ages?

Infants

The most common complaint with infants is their crying or biting, both signs of aggression. Crying is one way children talk. They let you know when they are happy (coo and babble) or when they need something (cry). We should find out what they need and provide it, whether it be a dry diaper, food, or warm touches.

Toddlers

In toddlers, the most aggressive acts occur over toys. To adults it looks like fighting, but to children it's learning how to get along. They have not learned how to say, "Let's play." The overuse of a "time-out" or a "thinking chair" can cause children to act more aggressively the next time. However, turning the incident into a punishment or control by force will only cause the child to think of ways to strike back. It may help to ask the child to rest from the activity that creates aggression.

Preschoolers

With loving guidance, parents will see children from 2 to 5 years of age decrease their physical aggression as they begin to use words to communicate needs. Knowing what to expect from normally developing children is critical. Here are some tips that can help parents understand what is typical in children:

- Preschoolers are self-centered and have not developed all the brain connections needed to see another's point of view.

- Young children see all or nothing. They do not understand that someone is not all good or not all bad.

- Children have a hard time thinking about the future or planning for it.

- They need concrete guides like picture lists to remember what to do and how to act.

- Young children cannot sort out fantasy from reality and get mixed up about what is real on TV.

- Children with difficult temperaments have difficulty reading the small cues that other children send out in social situations. A 5-year-old may want to join another who is building with blocks. The aggressive child (the one with the blocks) may misread the other's attempt to join his play and view it as a hostile intrusion. He may protect his territory by striking the uninvited child. Even when a teacher points out to the aggressive child that the intentions of the other were not hostile, the aggressive child may have difficulty understanding the situation for what it really is.

Schoolagers

Between 1st and 3rd grade, most children lose the impulse and need to attack others aggressively. An aggressive child may strike a sibling, but seldom would he or she hit a friend at school or on the playground. Door slamming and foot stomping may occur at home, but most 3rd graders have enough control to contain themselves at school.

Some children continue to act aggressively between 4th and 9th grade. Boys display aggression in the form of direct confrontations and physical attacks. Girls seldom display physical aggression in this same age range, but they act aggressively by shunning, ostracizing, and defaming others.

Researchers have found that children who are the most aggressive in 4th grade tend to continue to be aggressive thereafter. However, even older children can learn coping strategies and self-control.

Older Children

Even a child who seems to have grown out of his aggressive ways can be provoked when placed in an oppressive environment, for instance, poverty, social disorganization, crowding, neighborhood tensions, or a threatening situation. Children who have been handled harshly, inconsistently, and with little consideration may have built up anger from lack of love and nurturing. This can lead to mean, hateful, hurtful, and violent behavior in an attempt to strike back.

As children age, they tend to take their lead from peers. Peers, however, can reinforce an aggressor's actions. If peers also show aggression or do not correct aggressive acts, the aggressive behavior is encouraged. Many aggressive children have a network of aggressive friends. Although these clusters may encourage and strengthen antisocial behavior, they also appear to provide friendships and social support.

Even if parents hold off their child's aggressive behavior with firm but not harsh control, other things influence aggression. Neighborhoods, schools, and the media may provide aggressive environments where children witness aggression and violence in a variety of forms daily.

Biting as Aggression

Biting usually occurs in young children who are either teething or showing love. During teething, make sure infants have firm surfaces on which to bite, such as a soft toy, plastic ring, clean washcloth, or clean sock. Often babies want to show affection and kiss, but they get so involved in what little they know about affection that they bite instead of kiss.

When biting occurs, look at the child and say firmly, "No biting! That hurts!" This shows you are not pleased. To prevent the biting, gently steer the child away and say, "I will help you stop biting, Jerome."

Never bite children back! Young children have not developed empathy and do not know how you feel. If you raise your voice because it hurt, they may cry simply because you were loud or had an angry expression. But they didn't realize how you felt. They also do not know how to feel sorry yet.

What Can You Do?

For young children to outgrow their aggressive ways, they need positive, consistent, nurturing discipline. They need to learn positive problem-solving techniques. Parents and teachers need to place children in environments that offer a setting and support for learning positive social behavior rather than aggressive, hostile, antisocial acts.

In extreme cases, try some of these options:

- Observe to get the facts. Keep a log to find the theme of what triggers the acts of aggression; then help the child steer clear of these activities.

- Share your notes or journal with the parent or caregiver. Compare to see if similar behaviors are triggered at home and at school.

- Take a look at the environment. Is some activity or room arrangement causing anxiety or frustration? Does the child feel crowded, or is he or she made to sit too long? Does the child have enough personal space?

- For school-age children, write a plan of action for what the child will do when the negative behavior occurs.

- Make a list of activities to do instead (play with Play-Doh, run around the house, vacuum, draw, take a bath, etc.). Use a picture graph if the child can't read.

- Recognize success. "Even though I could tell you were mad, that was a great way you controlled your anger!"

- Teach the child deep breathing and visualization relaxation exercises.

- During a calm time, talk with the child so he or she understands the consequences of actions. Bedtimes are often quiet times for talking.

- If all of your strategies have been used to no avail, seek counseling or assistance in developing a child/family plan to learn aggression management.

Teaching caring behaviors in groups:

- In child care, plan a group time to allow each child to share and build a sense of community with his or her peers.

- Plan group rules that include sticking together, no hurts, and having fun.

- Say something positive about each child every day.

- Midday circle time can help children to regroup and will allow children to tell what they have been doing during the morning.

- Children who help plan their learning and choose their own activities will feel more in control, and they will feel more competent.

- Plan transitions. Music, finger play, and poems are all signals to change activities smoothly.

- Really listen when children speak. Seek to understand the message behind their words.

Summary

Behaviors are learned, and aggression is a learned behavior. When children are young, the foundation is set for the ways they will shape their personality and behaviors. Parents and caregivers who use patient, consistent, firm, and loving guidance can learn to shape a child's ability to cope with his or her anger and aggression.

Table 67.1. Ways to Help Children Control Aggression (continued on pages 588-590)

Strategy	Pre-schoolers	School-agers	Teens
Use reasoning with children to explain things.	X	X	X
Accept your child and understand his or her unique temperament. While his/ her behavior will be challenging at times, remain patient and supportive.	X	X	X
Tell your child how you expect him or her to behave. You will need to keep telling the child. Be specific and positive. Rather than saying to your toddler, "Don't hit." Say, "Hitting hurts. Please use your words."	X		
Be consistent so children know what to expect.	X	X	X
Organize the home environment, set limits on what the child may use.	X		
Limit access to aggressive toys (swords, toy guns).	X		
Monitor television for aggressive shows.	X	X	
Watch television with your child and comment on the content.	X	X	

Table 67.1. Ways to Help Children Control Aggression (continued from p. 587; continued on pages 589-590)

Strategy	Pre-schoolers	School-agers	Teens
Provide the child with play things that give him or her some choices, like dress-up and puppets.	X	X	
Sing songs and tell stories about feelings & frustrations. Talk about what anger may feel like.	X	X	
Allow some independence by providing a help-yourself shelf with blocks, art supplies, puzzles or other things. Define where children may use these materials.	X	X	
Provide enough materials so children don't have to wait to use them and become frustrated.	X		
Allow transition time between activities; give a five-minute warning that activity will change or it is "time to come in from play."	X	X	X
Be a model for controlled behavior and avoid angry outbursts and violence.	X	X	X
Monitor out-of-home activity for older children. Know where they are and whom they are with.		X	X
Avoid extreme permissiveness, laxness and tolerance OR too much structure and too many demands.	X	X	X
Figure out what the child needs—attention, security, control or to feel valued. Try to fill the need so he or she won't continue to act undesirably.	X	X	X

Table 67.1. Ways to Help Children Control Aggression (continued from p. 587-588; continued on page 590)

Strategy	Pre-schoolers	School-agers	Teens
Use closeness for control. When you sense your child is about to lose control, quietly and gently move close. Often your calm presence is enough to settle your child.	X	X	
Help children talk to each other to solve problems. Ask open-ended questions to help them think about options to solve their own problems.		X	X
Give children choices so they feel empowered. Pick two acceptable choices to offer.	X	X	X
Redirect your child. If your child is pushing, hitting or grabbing, move him or her in another direction and another activity. Stay by his or her side until he or she is positively engaged.	X	X	
Remove the object. If your child is misusing a toy—destroying it in an aggressive manner, remove it. Get out play dough, arrange an interlude of water play, or put your child in his or her sand box. These tactile experiences magically quiet aggression.	X	X	
Remove your out-of-control child from the scene. Hold the child, go for a walk, go to another room, stay with him or her until all is calm.	X	X	

Table 67.1. Ways to Help Children Control Aggression (continued from pages 587-589)

Strategy	Pre-schoolers	School-agers	Teens
Be your child's control. If your child is hitting another, your words may not be enough to stop the aggression. You must move in and gently but firmly stop the behavior. You provide the control your child lacks. In time your control transfers to your child. Say, "I'll keep you from hitting your sister."	X		
Note improved behaviors..."I like the way you used words to solve that problem."	X	X	X
Avoid difficult situations. If you know going to the park where there are lots of kids sends your child into an aggressive tirade, avoid going. Find a less stimulating setting where your youngster can meet with more social success.	X	X	X
Seek support yourself when you need a break	X	X	X
Be right there. If you have a toddler and preschooler in your home, watch and guide their play to assure interaction stays non-aggressive.	X		
Banish punching bags. If you have a child who is aggressive, realize that the effect of "Hit the punching bag, not Jo," hasn't proven effective for reducing aggressive attacks.	X	X	X
Prepare the child. Before your child meets new friends, tell him or her what behavior you expect. With young children, remind them that people don't like to be hit or pushed.	X	X	

Chapter 68

Warning Signs of Suicidal Youth

When a teen commits suicide, everyone is affected. Family members, friends, teammates, neighbors, and sometimes even those who didn't know the person well are united by feelings of grief, confusion, guilt—and the sense that if only they had done something differently, the suicide could have been prevented. The reasons behind a teen's suicide or attempted suicide are often complex. Read this article to learn about risk factors and warning signs and how to cope with such a devastating loss.

Suicide Statistics

Unfortunately, teen suicide is not a rare event. According to the U.S. Centers for Disease Control and Prevention (CDC), suicide is the third leading cause of death for those ages 15 to 24, surpassed only by car accidents and homicide. Suicide rates are on the rise for younger adolescents as well, with dramatic increases noted in this age group from 1980 to 1996. Suicide attempts are even more prevalent, though it is difficult to track the exact rates.

"Understanding and Preventing Teen Suicide," http://kidshealth.org/parent/emotions/behavior/suicide.html, reviewed September 2001. This information was provided by KidsHealth, one of the largest resources online for medically reviewed health information written for parents, kids, and teens. For more articles like this one, visit http://www.KidsHealth.org or http://www.TeensHealth.org. © 2001 The Nemours Foundation. Reprinted with permission.

591

"Suicide rates jump precipitously in the teen years for a number of reasons," says David Sheslow, PhD, a pediatric psychologist. These reasons might include greater access to lethal weapons such as firearms and greater access to drugs and alcohol.

Gender differences affect the means teens use to commit suicide. Girls, who are about twice as likely to attempt suicide as boys, tend to overdose on drugs or cut themselves. Boys, who complete suicide more often than girls, use firearms, hanging, or jumping more frequently. Because they tend to choose more sudden, lethal methods, boys are three or four times more likely to succeed in their attempts than girls.

The risk of suicide increases dramatically when kids and teens have access to firearms at home, and nearly 60% of all successful suicides in the United States are committed with a gun. That's why it's imperative that any gun in your home be unloaded, locked, and kept out of the reach of children and adolescents. Ammunition must be stored and locked apart from the gun, and the keys for both should be kept in a different area from where you store your household keys. Always keep the keys to any firearms out of the reach of children and adolescents.

Risk Factors

Now that you're a parent, you might not remember how it felt to be a teen, caught in that gray area between childhood and adulthood. Sure, it's a time of great possibility, but it can also be a period of great confusion and anxiety. There's pressure to fit in socially, to perform academically, and to act responsibly. There's the awakening of sexual feelings, a growing self-identity, and a need for autonomy that often conflicts with the rules and expectations set by others. A teen with an adequate support network of friends, family, religious affiliations, peer groups, or extracurricular activities may have an outlet to deal with his everyday frustrations. A teen without an adequate support network, however, may feel disconnected and isolated from his family and peer group. It's these teens who are at increased risk for suicide.

Teens who are at increased risk for suicide include those who:

- Face problems that are out of their control, such as divorce, alcoholism of a family member, or exposure to domestic violence.

- Have suffered physical or sexual abuse.

- Have poor relationships with their parents, lack a support network, are socially isolated, devalued, or rejected.

- Have a family history of depression or suicide. Because depressive illnesses may have a genetic component, some teens may be predisposed to suffer major depression.

- Experience the feelings of helplessness and worthlessness that often accompany depression. A teen, for example, who experiences repeated failures at school, who is overwhelmed by violence at home, or who is isolated from peers, is likely to experience such feelings. "If a teen sees himself as inadequate and worthless and he believes the future is unchangeable, these are clear warning signs of possible trouble," says Dr. Sheslow.

- Are dealing with homosexual feelings in an unsupportive family or community or hostile school environment. Several studies have reported greater rates of suicide attempts among gay, lesbian, and bisexual youth than among their heterosexual peers.

- Use alcohol or drugs in an attempt to numb their pain. Substance abuse is a major risk factor for suicide.

- Express their feelings violently.

- Have had a previous suicide attempt.

Warning Signs

Teens are most likely to consider suicide at certain times in their lives, particularly if they have suffered a loss or rejection. Failures at school, breaking up with a boyfriend or girlfriend, the death of a loved one, their parents' divorce—all of these risk factors can be triggers for dangerous behavior.

Seek professional help if your child experiences serious mood changes that last more than a couple of weeks. Don't wait. The American Psychiatric Association recommends seeking help if your teen:

- Withdraws from friends and family.

- Shows an inability to concentrate.

- Sleeps too much or too little.

- Talks of suicide.

- Has dramatic changes in personal appearance.

- Loses interest in favorite activities.

- Expresses hopelessness, helplessness, or excessive guilt.

- Exhibits self-destructive behavior (such as reckless driving, drug abuse, or promiscuity).

- Seems preoccupied with death.

- Bequeaths his favorite possessions.

Seek professional help as soon as possible if your teen says he is thinking about suicide. Contrary to popular belief, people who talk about suicide are likely to follow through. Pay attention to phrases such as, "It's no use, I'd be better off dead." Also be suspicious if a child who has been very depressed suddenly becomes extremely cheerful or hopeful. This intense mood swing may indicate that he believes suicide will be a solution to all his problems.

What Can Parents Do?

If your child seems depressed and withdrawn, the experts suggest that you watch him carefully. Poor grades, for example, may signal that your teen is withdrawing at school. It is important that you keep the lines of communication open by expressing your concern, support, and love.

It's also important to seek outside help and support for your teen. Make an appointment with a mental health professional and go with your teen to the appointment. Share your concerns and fears about suicide openly with the professional so that any problems, such as major depression, can be evaluated and treated.

Remember that any ongoing conflicts between a parent and child can fuel the fire for a teen who is feeling isolated, misunderstood, devalued, or suicidal. Get help to air family problems and resolve them in a constructive way. Also let the mental health professional know if there is a history of depression, substance abuse, family violence, or other stresses at home, such as an ongoing environment of criticism.

Providing Help

Although you may feel powerless, there are a number of things you can do to help a teen who is going through a difficult time. If you are concerned about your teen's behavior:

- Make sure your child has someone he can confide in. If your teen feels you don't understand, suggest a more neutral person—a grandparent, a clergy member, a coach, a school counselor, or your child's doctor.

- Don't minimize or discount what your child is going through. This will only reinforce his sense of hopelessness.

- Take your child's behavior seriously. Three quarters of all people who attempt suicide have given some type of warning to loved ones.

- Always express your love, concern, and support.

- Don't postpone seeing a doctor. Your child should be evaluated for depression so that treatment can begin immediately.

- Express to your child that with help he will begin to feel better and that his problems can be overcome.

If you think your child is suicidal, get help immediately. Your child's doctor can refer you to a psychologist or psychiatrist, or call your local hospital's department of psychiatry and ask for a list of doctors in your area. Your local mental health association or county medical society can also provide references. In an emergency, you can call the National Suicide Hotline at (800) SUICIDE.

Coping with Loss

What should you do if someone your child knows, perhaps a friend or a classmate, has attempted or committed suicide? First, acknowledge your child's many emotions. Some teens say they feel guilty—especially those who felt they could have interpreted their friend's actions and words better. Others say they feel angry with the person who committed or attempted suicide for having done something so selfish. Still others say they feel nothing at all—they are too overwhelmed with confusion and grief. All of these emotions are appropriate; stress to your child that there is no right or wrong way to feel.

When someone attempts suicide and survives, the people around him may be afraid or uncomfortable about talking with him about it. Tell your child to resist this urge; this is a time when a person absolutely needs to feel connected to others.

When a teen commits suicide, the people around him may become depressed and suicidal themselves. It's important to let your child know that he should never blame himself for someone's death; questioning whether he could have done something differently won't bring his friend or classmate back and it won't help him heal.

Many schools address a student's suicide by calling in special counselors to talk with the students and help them deal with their feelings. If your child is having difficulty dealing with a friend or classmate's suicide, it's best for him to make use of these resources or to talk to you or another trusted adult.

If You've Lost a Child to Suicide

For parents, the death of a child is probably the most painful loss imaginable. For parents who've lost a child to suicide, the pain and grief may be intensified. Although these feelings may never completely go away, there are some things that survivors of suicide can do to begin the healing process.

- Maintain contact with others. Suicide can be a very isolating experience for surviving family members because friends often don't know what to say and how to help. Seek out supportive people with whom you can talk about your child and your feelings. If you find that those around you are uncomfortable talking about your child, initiate the conversation and ask for their help.

- Remember that your other family members are grieving, too, and that everyone expresses grief in their own way. Your other children, in particular, may try to deal with their pain alone so as not to burden you with additional worries. Be there for each other through the tears, anger, and silences, and, if necessary, seek help and support together.

- Expect that anniversaries, birthdays, and holidays may be difficult. Important days and holidays often reawaken a sense of loss and anxiety. On those days, do what's best for your emotional needs, whether that means surrounding yourself with family and friends or planning a quiet day of reflection.

- Understand that it's normal to feel guilty and to question how this could have happened, but it's also important to realize that you may never get the answers you are looking for. The healing that takes place over time comes from reaching a point of forgiveness—for both your child and yourself.

Counseling and support groups can play a tremendous role in helping you to realize you are not alone.

Part Nine

Additional Help and Information

Chapter 69

Glossary of Related Terms

active listening: A communication method where the listener uses both nonverbal body language, such as eye contact and gestures, and verbal behavior, including tone of voice, open-ended questions, restatements, and summaries to demonstrate to the speaker that he or she is being heard.

aggravated assault: Attack or attempted attack with a weapon, regardless of whether or not an injury occurs, and attack without a weapon when serious injury results.

bad touch: A term used by primary child abuse prevention programs for children to describe hitting, punching, biting, erotic touch, and other acts that hurt children.

bias: A preconceived opinion or attitude about something or someone. A bias may be favorable or unfavorable.

Excerpted from "Peace under Pressure," U.S. Department of Justice, http://www.usdoj.gov/kidspage/getinvolved/2_3.htm, 1998, and "Indicators of School Crime and Safety," U.S. Department of Justice and U.S. Department of Education, http://www.ojp.usdoj.gov/bjs/pub/pdf/iscs00.pdf, 2000, and "A Parent's Guide to Internet Safety," Federal Bureau of Investigation, http://www.fbi.gov/publications/pguide/pguidee.htm, undated, and "The Role of Educators in the Prevention and Treatment of Child Abuse and Neglect," National Clearinghouse on Child Abuse and Neglect Information, http://www.calib.com/nccanch/pubs/usermanuals/educator/glossary.cfm, 1992.

brainstorming: A storm of ideas. A group thinking technique for helping disputants create multiple options for consideration in solving a problem. Brainstorming separates the creative act from the critical one—all criticism and evaluation of ideas are postponed until later.

bulletin board systems (BBSs): Electronic networks of computers that are connected by a central computer setup and operated by a system administrator or operator and are distinguishable from the Internet by their dial-up accessibility. BBS users link their individual computers to the central BBS computer by a modem which allows them to post messages, read messages left by others, trade information, or hold direct conversations. Access to a BBS can, and often is, privileged and limited to those users who have access privileges granted by the systems operator.

chat: Real-time text conversation between users in a chat room with no expectation of privacy. All chat conversation is accessible by all individuals in the chat room while the conversation is taking place.

Child Protective Services (CPS): The designated social service agency in most states to receive, investigate, and provide rehabilitation services to children and families with problems of child maltreatment. Frequently, this agency is located within larger public social services agencies, such as Departments of Social Services or Human Services.

collaboration: A way of working with another person to seek solutions that completely satisfy both people. This involves accepting both people's concerns as valid and digging into an issue in an attempt to find innovative possibilities. It also means being open and exploring many ideas to help resolve a dispute.

commercial on-line service (COS): Examples of COSs are America Online, Prodigy, and Microsoft Network, which provide access to their service for a fee. COSs generally offer limited access to the Internet as part of their total service package.

confidentiality: A provision in all state child abuse and neglect reporting laws that protects the privacy of children and families by not permitting information about the finding of the child maltreatment report to be released to other agencies without permission of the family. In some states, members of multidisciplinary teams may receive information without a release of information.

conflict: An expressed struggle between at least two interdependent people who perceive themselves as having incompatible goals, view their resources as being scarce, and regard each other as interfering with the achievement of their own goals; a controversy or disagreement; coming into opposition with another individual or group.

conflict resolution: A spectrum of processes that all use communication skills and creative thinking to develop voluntary solutions that are acceptable to those concerned in a dispute. Conflict resolution processes include negotiation (between two people), mediation (involving a third person who can help resolve the conflict), and consensus decision making (encouraging group problem solving).

confusing touch: A term used by primary child abuse prevention programs for children to describe any type of contact that "does not feel right."

consensus: An agreement reached by identifying the interests of all concerned people and then building a balanced solution that satisfies as many of the disputants' interests as possible; a combining and blending of solutions.

crime: Any violation of a statute or regulation or any act that the government has determined is injurious to the public, including felonies and misdemeanors. Such violation may or may not involve violence, and it may affect individuals or property.

disputant: One who is engaged in a disagreement or conflict.

electronic mail (e-mail): A function of BBSs, COSs, and internet service providers which provides for the transmission of messages and files between computers over a communications network similar to mailing a letter via the postal service. E-mail is stored on a server, where it will remain until the addressee retrieves it.

good touch: A term used by primary prevention programs for children to describe hugs, encouraging pats, and other gestures that are not erotic.

ground rule: A basic rule of behavior that is spelled out and agreed upon at the beginning of a conflict resolution procedure.

immunity: Established in all child abuse laws to protect reporters from civil lawsuits and criminal prosecution resulting from filing a report of child abuse and neglect. This immunity is provided as long as the report is made in good faith.

incident: A specific criminal act or offense involving one or more victims and one or more offenders.

instant messages: Private, real-time text conversation between two users in a chat room.

Internet: An immense, global network that connects computers via telephone lines and/or fiber networks to storehouses of electronic information. With only a computer, a modem, a telephone line and a service provider, people from all over the world can communicate and share information with little more than a few keystrokes.

Internet relay chat (IRC): Real-time text conversation similar to public and/or private chat rooms on COS.

Internet service provider (ISP): Examples of ISPs are Erols, Concentric, and Netcom. These services offer direct, full access to the Internet at a flat, monthly rate and often provide electronic-mail service for their customers. ISPs often provide space on their servers for their customers to maintain World Wide Web (WWW) sites. Not all ISPs are commercial enterprises. Educational, governmental, and nonprofit organizations also provide Internet access to their members.

juvenile and family courts: Established in most states to resolve conflict and to otherwise intervene in the lives of families in a manner that promotes the best interests of children. These courts specialize in areas such as child maltreatment, domestic violence, juvenile delinquency, divorce, child custody, and child support.

mandated reporter: One who in his/her professional capacity is required by state law to report suspected cases of child maltreatment to the designated state agency. Some states clearly define that teachers, principals, nurses, and counselors are included, while other states designate all school personnel.

mediation: Intervention in a dispute by an impartial third person who can assist the disputants in negotiating an acceptable settlement.

mediator: An invited intervener in a dispute whose expertise and experience in conflict resolution techniques and processes are used to help disputants create a satisfactory solution. The mediator is a process guide whose presence is acceptable to both disputants and who has no decision making power concerning the issues in the dispute.

multidisciplinary team: Established between agencies and professionals within the child protection system to mutually discuss cases of child abuse and neglect and to aid decisions at various stages of the child protection system case process. These teams may also be designated by different names, including child protection teams or case consultation teams.

negotiation: An interaction between two or more people who have an actual or perceived conflict of interest. In a negotiation, the participants join voluntarily in a dialog to educate each other about their needs and interests, to exchange information, and to create a solution that meets the needs of both parties.

out-of-home care: Child care, foster care, or residential care provided by persons, organizations, and institutions to children who are placed outside of their families, usually under the jurisdiction of the juvenile and family court.

parent/caretaker: Person responsible for the care of the child.

prevalence: The percentage of the population directly affected by crime in a given period. This rate is based upon specific information elicited directly from the respondent regarding crimes committed against his or her person, against his or her property, or against an individual bearing a unique relationship to him or her. It is not based upon perceptions and beliefs about, or reactions to, criminal acts.

property victimization: Theft of property from a student's desk, locker, or other locations at school.

public chat rooms: Created, maintained, listed and monitored by the commercial on-line service (COS) and other public domain systems such as Internet Relay Chat. A number of customers can be in the public chat rooms at any given time, which are monitored for illegal activity and even appropriate language by systems operators (SYSOP). Some public chat rooms are monitored more frequently than others, depending on the COS and the type of chat room. Violators can be reported to the administrators of the system (at America On-line they are referred to as terms of service [TOS]) which can revoke user privileges. The public chat rooms usually cover a broad range of topics such as entertainment, sports, game rooms, children only, etc.

Public Law 94-142: This special education law protects the right of every child to individualized education.

rape: Forced sexual intercourse including both psychological coercion as well as physical force. Forced sexual intercourse means vaginal, anal, or oral penetration by the offender(s). This category also includes incidents where the penetration is from a foreign object such as a bottle.

reporting laws: All states have child abuse and neglect reporting laws that mandate who must report suspected child abuse and neglect cases, which agencies are charged with investigating alleged instances, and the responsibility of state and local agencies in responding to these children and families.

reporting policies/procedures: Written referral procedures established by schools and other professional agencies that have a mandated responsibility to report suspected child abuse and neglect cases and that delineate how to initiate a suspected child maltreatment report and to whom it should be made.

resolution: A course of action agreed upon to solve a problem.

robbery: Completed or attempted theft, directly from a person, of property or cash by force or threat of force, with or without a weapon, and with or without injury.

rural: A place not located inside a metropolitan statistical area (MSA). This category includes a variety of localities, ranging from sparsely populated rural areas to cities with populations of less than 50,000.

serious violent crime: Rape, sexual assault, robbery, or aggravated assault.

sexual assault: A wide range of victimizations, separate from rape or attempted rape. These crimes include attacks or attempted attacks generally involving unwanted sexual contact between the victim and offender. Sexual assault may or may not involve force and includes such things as grabbing or fondling. Sexual assault also includes verbal threats.

simple assault: Attack without a weapon resulting either in no injury, minor injury, or in undetermined injury requiring less than 2 days of hospitalization. Also includes attempted assault without a weapon.

substantiated: A finding made by Child Protective Services after investigating a child abuse or neglect report indicating that credible evidence exists to support that child maltreatment did occur. The criteria used to substantiate a report are different in each state. Another term used by some states is *founded* or *supported.*

suburban: A county or counties containing a central city, plus any contiguous counties that are linked socially and economically to the central city. On the data tables, suburban areas are categorized as those portions of metropolitan areas situated outside central cities.

survivors: A term used frequently to refer to adults who were abused or neglected as children.

unsubstantiated: A finding made by Child Protective Services after investigating a child abuse or neglect report indicating that there was insufficient evidence to support that child maltreatment occurred. In some states, the term *unfounded* is used.

urban: the largest city (or grouping of cities) in an metropolitan statistical area.

usenet (newsgroups): Like a giant, cork bulletin board where users post messages and information. Each posting is like an open letter and is capable of having attachments, such as graphic image files (GIFs). Anyone accessing the newsgroup can read the postings, take copies of posted items, or post responses. Each newsgroup can hold thousands of postings. Currently, there are over 29,000 public newsgroups and that number is growing daily. Newsgroups are both public and/or private. There is no listing of private newsgroups. A user of private newsgroups has to be invited into the newsgroup and be provided with the newsgroup's address.

victimization: A crime as it affects one individual person or household. For personal crimes, the number of victimizations is equal to the number of victims involved. The number of victimizations may be greater than the number of incidents because more than one person may be victimized during an incident.

victimization rate: A measure of the occurrence of victimizations among a specific population group.

violent crime: Rape, sexual assault, robbery, or assault.

violent victimization: Physical attacks or taking property from the student directly by force, weapons, or threats.

Chapter 70

Resources and Recovery Programs for Young Victims of Violence

This chapter lists resources and recovery programs for young victims of violence. Information is listed in alphabetical order.

American Academy of Child and Adolescent Psychiatry
3615 Wisconsin Avenue, NW
Washington, DC 20016-3007
Phone: 202-966-7300
Fax: 202-966-2891
Website: www.aacap.org

American Psychiatric Association
1400 K Street, NW
Washington, DC 20005
Toll Free: 888-357-7924
Phone: 202-682-6000
Fax: 202-682-6850
Website: www.psych.org
E-Mail: apa@psych.org

The resources listed in this section were compiled from a wide variety of sources deemed accurate. Contact information was updated and verified in September 2002. Inclusion does not constitute endorsement.

American Psychological Association
750 First Street, NE
Washington, DC 20002-4242
Toll Free: 800-374-2721
Phone: 202-336-5510
TDD/TTY: 202-336-6123
Website: www.apa.org

Anxiety Disorders Association of America
8730 Georgia Ave, Suite 600
Silver Spring, MD 20910
Phone: 240-485-1001
Fax: 240-485-1035
Website: www.adaa.org

Caught in the Crossfire
Youth Alive
3300 Elm Street
Oakland, CA 94609
Phone: 510-594-2588
Fax: 510-594-0667
Website: www.youthalive.org
E-Mail: mail@youthalive.org

The Caught in the Crossfire (CC) program in Oakland has been hailed as a model program. It maintains a hotline for the Alameda County Medical Center to call when a youth between the ages of 12 and 19 is admitted to the emergency room with a gunshot wound. CC crisis intervention specialists visit the patient at bedside and review the violent incident, explore alternative strategies for conflict resolution, provide information on risk factors for violence, explore coping skills and safety plans, and arrange for followup contacts. The recovery period in a hospital and rehabilitation center offers victims an opportunity to be exposed to supportive services. After victims have been discharged, followup visits are scheduled for a minimum of 12 months. The CC program uses trained peer counselors, many in wheelchairs because they too were victims of gun violence.

Center for Mental Health Services (CMHS)
Emergency Services and Disaster Relief Branch
5600 Fishers Lane, Room 17C-20
Rockville, MD 20857
Toll Free: 800-789-2647
Phone: 301-443-4735
E-Mail: ken@mentalhealth.org
Website: www.mentalhealth.org/cmhs/emergencyservices/index.htm

Family Bereavement Center
213 St. Paul Place, 4th Floor
Baltimore, MD 21201
Phone: 410-396-7351

The Family Bereavement Center in Baltimore, Maryland, is administered by the state's attorney's office. The center reaches out to every homicide victim's family by sending a letter encouraging them to call for services. Center staff provide liaison services with the police department, the medical examiner, and the state's attorney's office. They offer crime scene cleanup services, court support and escort services, notification of case status and victims' rights, assistance in applying for victim compensation, and individual and group grief counseling sessions. They also sponsor educational and support activities such as memorial services, weekend camps for adolescents and younger children who have lost family and friends to violence, and a quarterly newsletter.

Federal Emergency Management Agency
(Information for children and adolescents)
P.O. Box 2012
Jessup, MD 20794-2012
Toll Free: 800-480-2520
Website: www.fema.gov/kids

International Society for Traumatic Stress Studies (ISTSS)
60 Revere Drive, Suite 500
Northbrook, IL 60062
Phone: 847-480-9028
Fax; 847-480-9282
E-Mail: istss@istss.org
Website: www.istss.org

Juvenile Justice Clearinghouse (JJC)
P.O. Box 6000
Rockville, MD 20849-6000
Toll Free: 800-638-8736
Fax: 301-519-5212
E-Mail: askjj@ncjrs.org
Website: www.ojjdp.ncjrs.org

National Center for Juvenile Justice
(the research arm of the National Council of Juvenile and Family
Court Judges)
710 Fifth Avenue, Suite 3000
Pittsburgh, PA 15219
Phone: 412-227-6950
Fax: 412-227-6955
Website: www.ncjj.org

National Center for Missing and Exploited Children
699 Prince Street
Alexandria, VA 22314
Toll Free: 800-843-5678
TDD: 800-826-7653
Website: www.missingkids.com

National Center for Post Traumatic Stress Disorder (PTSD)
215 N. Main Street
White River Junction, VT 05009
Phone: 802-296-5132
E-Mail: ncptsd@ncptsd.org
Website: www.ncptsd.org

National Center for Victims of Crime
2000 M Street, NW, Suite 480
Washington, DC 20036
Toll Free: 800-FYI-CALL
Phone: 202-467-8700
TTY/TDD: 800-211-7996
Fax: 202-467-8701
E-Mail: webmaster@ncvc.org
Website: www.ncvc.org

National Center on Child Abuse Prevention Research
(the research arm of Prevent Child Abuse America)
200 South Michigan Avenue, 17th Floor
Chicago, IL 60604
Phone: 312-663-3520
Fax: 312-939-8962
E-Mail: mailbox@preventchildabuse.org
Website: www.preventchildabuse.org

National Clearinghouse on Child Abuse and Neglect Information
330 C Street SW
Washington, DC 20447
Phone: 703-385-7565
Fax: 703-385-3206
Website: www.calib.com/nccanch

National Institute of Mental Health (NIMH)
Information Resources and Inquiries Branch
6001 Executive Boulevard, Rm. 8184, MSC 9663
Bethesda, MD 20892-9663
Phone: 301-443-4513
TTY: 301-443-8431
Fax: 301-443-4279
E-Mail: nimhinfo@nih.gov
Website: www.nimh.nih.gov

National Organization for Victim Assistance (NOVA)
1730 Park Road, NW
Washington, DC 20010
Toll Free: 800-879-6682
Phone: 202-232-6682
Fax: 202-462-2255
E-Mail: nova@try-nova.org
Website: www.try-nova.org

National Resource Center for Safe Schools
Northeast Regional Educational Laboratory
101 Southwest Main Street, Suite 500
Portland, OR 97204
Toll Free: 800-268-2275
Fax: 503-275-0444
E-Mail: safeschools@nwrel.org
Website: www.nwrel.org/safe

National Resource Center on Domestic Violence
6400 Flank Drive, Suite 1200
Harrisburg, PA 17112-2778
Toll Free: 800-537-2238
Phone: 717-545-6400
TDD: 800-553-2508

Office for Victims of Crime Resource Center
National Criminal Justice Reference Service
P.O. Box 6000
Rockville, MD 20849-6000
Toll Free: 800-851-3420
Phone: 301-519-5500
TTY: 877-712-9279
Fax: 301-519-5212
E-Mail: askncjrs@ncjrs.org
Website: www.ojp.usdoj.gov/ovc/ovcres

Recover
730 11th Street, NW, Third Floor
Washington, DC 20001-4510
Phone: 202-624-0010
Fax: 202-624-0062
E-Mail: info@lossandhealing.org
Website: www.lossandhealing.org

The Recover program in Washington, D.C., has a professional grief counselor in the Office of the Chief Medical Examiner to offer emotional support before, during, and after the process of identification of a loved one. Recover staff do an early assessment of needs, including inquiring about children who may be affected, and set up case management services. Staff or trained volunteers are available for practical and emotional support, including planning a funeral, explaining the grieving process, talking to children about death, driving the family to the store, helping with paperwork, or simply listening. Recover also makes referrals to mental health counseling and other services but recognizes that these may be premature and/or insufficient for victims having trouble getting out of the house, getting food on the table, and dealing with funeral homes and police investigators.

Resource Center on Domestic Violence: Child Protection and Custody
P.O. Box 8970
Reno, NV 89507
Toll Free: 800-527 3223
Website: www.dvlawsearch.com/res_center

Rise Above It
Kessler Anti-Violence Program
Kessler Institute for Rehabilitation
1199 Pleasant Valley Way
West Orange, NJ 07052
Toll Free: 888-KESSLER or 888-721-3214
Website: www.kessler-rehab.com

The power of peer counseling, evident in the hospital-based programs, also is an important component of school-based violence prevention programs. The Rise Above It program was launched in 1995 in direct response to an increasing number of gunshot wounds in young people in the Newark, New Jersey, area. Program presenters, like Hashim Garrett, the Violence Prevention Coordinator for Rise Above It, are individuals who were paralyzed as a result of violent acts. They are teamed with able-bodied peer educators to let the students see the long-lasting effects of gunshot wounds and to teach them skills to deal with anger and prevent fights. The classes are part of the public school health sciences curriculum and have reached more than 10,000 students. The program has been post-tested, meaning that the program surveyed students before and after they participated in the program, asking questions about their behavior and their beliefs about the consequences of fighting and shows positive results as both students and teachers report a decrease in arguments and violent incidents.

U.S. Department of Education
400 Maryland Avenue, SW
Washington, DC 20202
Toll Free: 800-USA-LEARN
TTY: 800-437-0833
E-Mail: customerservice@inet.ed.gov
Website: www.ed.gov

U.S. Department of Justice
950 Pennsylvania Avenue, NW
Washington, DC 20530-0001
E-Mail: askdoj@usdoj.gov
Website: www.usdoj.gov

Chapter 71

Child and Youth Security-Related Resources

This chapter lists contact information for child and youth security-related government agencies, professional organizations, websites, and publications. Information is listed according to the organization of the sections in this *Sourcebook*.

Protection from School Crime and Violence

National Crime Prevention Council
1000 Connecticut Avenue, NW, 13th Floor
Washington, DC 20036
Phone: 202-466-6272
Fax: 202-296-1356
Website: www.ncpc.org
E-Mail: webmaster@ncpc.org

Protection from Child Abuse and Neglect

Childhelp USA/Forrester National Child Abuse Hotline
15757 N. 78th Street
Scottsdale, AZ 85260
Toll Free: 800-4-CHILD
Phone: 480-922-8212
TDD: 800-2-A-CHILD
Fax: 480-922-7061
Website: www.childhelpusa.org

The resources listed in this section were compiled from a wide variety of sources deemed accurate. Contact information was updated and verified in September 2002. Inclusion does not constitute endorsement.

Family Violence Prevention Fund/Health Resource Center
383 Rhode Island St., Suite #304
San Francisco, CA 94103-5233
Phone: 415-252-8900
Fax: 415-252-8991
TTY: 800-595-4889
E-Mail: fvpf@netcampaign.com
Website: http://endabuse.org

Justice Statistics Clearinghouse
810 Seventh Street, NW
Washington, DC 20531
Toll Free: 800-732-3277
Phone: 202-307-0765
Website: www.ojp.usdoj.gov/bjs
E-Mail: askbjs@ojp.usdoj.gov

National Clearinghouse on Child Abuse and Neglect Information
330 C Street, SW
Washington, DC 20047
Toll Free: 800-394-3366
Phone: 703-385-7565
Fax: 703-385-3206
Website: www.calib.com/nccanch
E-Mail: nccanch@calib.com

National Resource Center on Domestic Violence
6400 Flank Drive, Suite 1200
Harrisburg, PA 17112-2778
Toll Free: 800-537-2238
Phone: 717-545-6400
TDD: 800-553-2508

Parents of Murdered Children
100 East Eighth Street
Suite B-41
Cincinnati, OH 45202
Toll Free: 888-818-7662
Phone: 513-721-5683
Fax: 513-345-4489
E-Mail: natlpomc@aol.com
Website: www.pmoc.com

Resource Center on Domestic Violence: Child Protection and Custody
P.O. Box 8970
Reno, NV 89507
Toll Free: 800-527-3223
Website: www.dvlawsearch.com/res_center

Protection from Sexual Abuse

Rape, Abuse, and Incest National Network (RAINN)
635-B Pennsylvania Ave., SE
Washington, DC 20003
Toll Free: 800-656-4673
Phone: 202-544-1034
E-Mail: RAINNmail@aol.com
Website: www.feminist.com/rain.htm

Missing and Abducted Children

Consular Assistance, U. S. Department of State
The Office of Children's Issues
2201 C Street, NW
SA-22, Room 2100
Washington, DC 20520-4818
Phone: 202-736-7000
Fax: 202-312-9743
Website: http://travel.state.gov/
children's_issues.html

Federal Parent Locator Service (FPLS)
Department of Health and Human Services
Office of Child Support Enforcement
370 L'Enfant Promenade, SW
Washington, DC 20447
Phone: 202-401-9267
Website: www.acf.dhhs.gov/programs/cse

International Social Services/American Branch
700 Light Street
Baltimore, MD 21230
Phone: 410-230-2734
Fax: 410-230-2741
E-Mail: issusa@lirs.org
Website: www.iss-usa.org

National Center for Missing and Exploited Children (NCMEC)
699 Prince Street
Alexandria, VA 22314-3175
Toll Free: 800-THE-LOST
Phone: 703-274-3900
Fax: 703-235-4067
Website: www.missingkids.org

Office of Victims of Crime (OVC)
United States Department of Justice
633 Indiana Ave., NW
Washington, D.C. 20531
Toll Free: 800-627-6872
TTY: 877-712-9279
E-Mail: askovc@ojp.usdoj.gov
Website: www.ojp.usdoj.gov/ovc

Protection from Youth Substance Abuse

African American Parents for Drug Prevention
311 Martin Luther King Drive
Cincinnati, OH 45219
Phone: 513-475-5359

American Council for Drug Education
164 W. 74th Street
New York, NY 10023
Toll Free: 800-488-3784
E-Mail: acde@phoenixhouse.org
Website: www.acde.org

American Society of Addiction Medicine
4601 North Park Ave., Arcade Suite 101
Chevy Chase, MD 20815
Phone: 301-656-3920
Fax: 301-656-3815
E-Mail: Email@asam.org
Website: www.asam.org

Association for Medical Education and Research in Substance Abuse
125 Whipple Street, Third Floor
Providence, RI 02908
Phone: 401-349-0000
Fax: 877-418-8769
Website: www.amersa.org

Community Anti-Drug Coalitions of America (CADCA)
901 North Pitt St., Suite 300
Alexandria, VA 22314
Toll Free: 800-54-CADCA
Phone: 703-706-0560
Fax: 703-706-0565
E-Mail: info@cadca.org
Website: www.cadca.org

Mothers against Drunk Driving (MADD)
511 E. John Carpenter Freeway, Suite 700
Irving, TX 75062
Toll Free: 800-GET-MADD
Phone: 214-744-6233
Website: www.madd.org

National Asian Pacific American Families against Substance Abuse
340 East Second Street, Suite 409
Los Angeles, CA 90012
Phone: 213-625-5795
Fax: 213-625-5796
Website: www.napafasa.org

National Association for Native American Children of Alcoholics
P.O. Box 2708
Seattle, WA 98111-2708
Phone: 206-903-6574
Fax: 206-624-4452
E-Mail: nanacoa@nanacoa.org

National Clearinghouse for Alcohol and Drug Information
P.O. Box 2345
Rockville, MD 20847
Toll Free: 800-729-6686
Phone: 301-468-2600
TDD: 800-487-4889
Fax: 301-468-6433
E-Mail: info@health.org
Website: www.health.org

National Council on Alcoholism and Drug Dependence
20 Exchange Place, Suite 2902
New York, NY 10005
Toll Free: 800-NCA-CALL
Phone: 212-269-7797
Fax: 212-269-7510
E-Mail: national@ncadd.org
Website: www.ncadd.org

National Families in Action
Century Plaza II
2957 Clairmont Road, Suite 150
Atlanta, GA 30329
Phone: 404-248-9676
Fax: 404-248-1312
Website: www.emory.edu/NFIA

National Hispanic/Latino Community Prevention Network
P.O. Box 2215
Espanola, NM 87532
Phone: 505-747-1889
Fax: 505-747-1623
E-Mail: hmontoya@aol.com

National Institute on Alcohol Abuse and Alcoholism
Publication Distribution Center
6000 Executive Boulevard
Willco Building
Rockville, MD 20849-7003
Website: www.niaaa.nih.gov

National Institute on Drug Abuse
6001 Executive Blvd., Room 5213
Bethesda, MD 20892-9561
Toll Free: 888-NIH-NIDA
E-Mail:
information@lists.nida.nih.gov
Website: www.nida.nih.gov/
NIDAHome1.html

Parents' Resource Institute for Drug Education, Inc. (PRIDE)
3610 DeKalb Technology Pkwy,
Suite 105
Atlanta, GA 30340
Toll Free: 800-853-7867
Website: www.prideusa.org

Protection from Social Harm

American Arbitration Association
335 Madison Avenue, Floor 10
New York, NY 10017-4605
Toll Free: 800-778-7879
Phone: 212-716-5800
Fax: 212-716-5905
E-Mail: websitemail@adr.org
Website: www.adr.org

America's Promise—The Alliance for Youth
909 North Washington Street,
Suite 400
Alexandria, VA 22314 1556
Toll Free: 888-55-YOUTH
Phone: 703-684-4500
Fax: 703-535-3900
E-Mail:
commit@americaspromise.org
Website:
www.americaspromise.org

Association for Conflict Resolution
1527 New Hampshire Ave., NW
Washington, DC 20036
Phone: 202-667-9700
E-Mail: acr@acresolution.org
Website: www.acresolution.org

Big Brothers Big Sisters of America (BBBSA)
National Headquarters
230 North 13th Street
Philadelphia, PA 19107-1510
Phone: 215-567-7000
Fax: 215-567-0394
E-Mail: national@bbbsa.org
Website: www.bbbsa.org

Boys and Girls Clubs of America
1230 West Peachtree Street NW
Atlanta, GA 30309
Phone: 404-815-5700
Fax: 404-815-5789
Website: www.bgca.org

National Association for Community Mediation
1527 New Hampshire Ave., NW
Washington, DC 20036-1206
Phone: 202-667-9700
www.nafcm.org

National Center for Conflict Resolution Education
Illinois Bar Center
424 S. Second Street
Springfield, IL 62701
Phone: 217-523-7056
Fax: 217-523-7066
E-Mail: info@nccre.org
Website: www.nccre.org

The National Mentoring Partnership
1600 Duke Street, Suite 300
Alexandria, VA 22314
Phone: 703-224-2200
Website: www.mentoring.org

YMCA of the USA
101 North Wacker Drive
Chicago, IL 60606
Phone: 312-280-3400
Website: www.ymca.net

Protection from Youth Mental and Emotional Health Risks

ADD Warehouse
300 NW 70th Avenue, Suite 102
Plantation, FL 33317
Toll Free: 800-233-9273
Phone: 954-792-8100
Fax: 954-792-8545
E-Mail: sales@addwarehouse.com
Website: http://addwarehouse.com

Anxiety Disorders Association of America
8730 Georgia Ave, Suite 600
Silver Spring, MD 20910
Phone: 240-485-1001
Fax: 240-485-1035
Website: www.adaa.org

Attention Deficit Information Network (Ad-IN)
58 Prince Street
Needham, MA 02492
Phone: 781-455-9895
E-Mail: adin@gis.net
Website: www.addinfonetwork.com

Center for Mental Health Services (CMHS)
Emergency Services and Disaster Relief Branch
5600 Fishers Lane, Room 17C-20
Rockville, MD 20857
Toll Free: 800-789-2647
Phone: 301-443-4735
E-mail: ken@mentalhealth.org
Website: www.mentalhealth.org/cmhs/emergencyservices/index.htm

Center for Mental Health Services
Office of Consumer, Family, and Public Information
5600 Fishers Lane, Room 15-105
Rockville, MD 20857
Phone: 301-443-2792
Website: www.mentalhealth.org/cmhs

Children and Adults with Attention Deficit Disorders (CH.A.D.D.)
8181 Professional Place, Suite 201
Landover, MD 20785
Toll Free: 800-233-4050
Phone: 301-306-7070
Fax: 301-306-7090
Website: www.chadd.org
E-Mail: national@chadd.org

Chapter 72

References for
Additional Reading

This chapter lists book titles, brochures, pamphlets, and articles that contain useful information on some of the topics in this *Sourcebook*. For easy reference, the listings are organized in alphabetical order. Contact information is included when available.

A New Understanding of Parent Involvement: Family-Work-School Conference Proceedings (1996). Washington, D.C. and New York: U.S. Department of Education and Teachers College, Columbia University.

Blomquist, M. 1998. "Studying risk factors for family abduction." In *Prevention of Parent or Family Abduction through Early Identification of Risk Factors*, edited by J.R. Johnston, I. Sagatun-Edwards, M. Blomquist, and L.K. Girdner. Washington, DC: American Bar Association, Center on Children and the Law.

Coburn, *Runaway Father: One Man's Odyssey from Revenge to Love*. Red Fox Publishing. Bellevue, WA. (1998).

De Hart, *International Child Abduction: A Guide to Applying the 1988 Hague Convention, with Forms* (A publication of the Section of Family Law, American Bar Association) (1993).

Family Abduction Guide, National Center for Missing and Exploited Children. Written in both English and Spanish, this guide describes the actions that parents and family members can take and the laws that can help when their child is abducted. Single copies are available free of charge from the National Center for Missing and Exploited Children (800-THE-LOST or 800-843-5678).

Hoff, *Parental Kidnaping: How to Prevent an Abduction and What to Do If Your Child Is Abducted*, National Center for Missing and Exploited Children. Single copies are available free of charge from the National Center for Missing and Exploited Children (800-THE-LOST or 800-843-5678).

Johnston, J. 1998a. "Descriptive study of preventive interventions in families at-risk for abduction." In *Prevention of Parent or Family Abduction through Early Identification of Risk Factors*, edited by J.R. Johnston, I. Sagatun-Edwards, M. Blomquist, and L.K. Girdner. Washington, DC: American Bar Association, Center on Children and the Law.

Johnston, J. 1998b. "Empirical study of two counseling interventions in families at-risk for abduction." In *Prevention of Parent or Family Abduction through Early Identification of Risk Factors*, edited by J.R. Johnston, I. Sagatun-Edwards, M. Blomquist, and L.K. Girdner. Washington, DC: American Bar Association, Center on Children and the Law.

Johnston, J. 1998c. "Interview study of risk factors for family abduction." In *Prevention of Parent or Family Abduction through Early Identification of Risk Factors*, edited by J.R. Johnston, I. Sagatun-Edwards, M. Blomquist, and L.K. Girdner. Washington, DC: American Bar Association, Center on Children and the Law.

Johnston, J. 2000. "Building multidisciplinary professional partnerships with the court on behalf of high conflict divorcing families and their children: Who needs what kind of help." *University of Arkansas at Little Rock Law Review* 22(3):453 479.

Johnston, J., and Roseby, V. 1997. *In the Name of the Child: A Developmental Approach to Understanding and Helping Children of Conflicted and Violent Divorce*. New York, NY: Free Press.

Johnston, J.R., Sagatun-Edwards, I., Blomquist, M., and Girdner, L.K. 1998. *Prevention of Parent or Family Abduction through Early Identification of Risk Factors. Final Report*. Washington, DC: American Bar Association, Center on Children and the Law.

Joshi, P., Carre, F., Place, A. & Rayman, P. (1996). *The New Economic Equation*. Cambridge: Radcliffe College/ Radcliffe Public Policy Institute.

Keeping Youth Drug-Free: A Guide for Parents, Grandparents, Elders, Mentors, and Other Caregivers. 1996. U.S. Dept. of Health and Human Services.

Missing and Abducted Children: A Law Enforcement Guide to Case Investigation and Program Management, National Center for Missing and Exploited Children. Single copies are available free of charge from the National Center for Missing and Exploited Children (800-THE-LOST or 800-843-5678). This document provides law enforcement with a step-by-step guide on how to respond to and investigate missing children cases.

Recovery and Reunification of Missing Children: A Team Approach, National Center for Missing and Exploited Children. Single copies are available free of charge from the National Center for Missing and Exploited Children (800-THE-LOST or 800-843-5678). This report discusses the recovery and reunification of children with their families, with emphasis on a multi-agency, multidisciplinary approach.

Sagatun-Edwards, I. 1998. "Documentary study of risk factors for family abduction." In *Prevention of Parent or Family Abduction through Early Identification of Risk Factors*, edited by J.R. Johnston, I. Sagatun-Edwards, M. Blomquist, and L.K. Girdner. Washington, DC: American Bar Association, Center on Children and the Law.

Steinberg, L., Brown, B.B. & Dornbusch S.M. (1996). *Beyond the Classroom: Why School Reform Has Failed and What Parents Need to Do*. New York: Simon & Schuster.

Turner, Johanna. 1996. *Grief at School*. Washington, DC: American Hospice Foundation. This booklet for educators and counselors provides suggestions for helping children to cope with crisis and grief in the school setting. The booklet is available from the American Hospice Foundation, http://www.americanhospice.org, (202-223-0204).

Walsh, John. 1997. *Tears of Rage*. New York, NY: Pocket Books. This book recounts the powerful and emotional story of John Walsh and his wife Revé following the 1981 abduction and murder of their 6-year-old son Adam. The book also chronicles John Walsh's 16-year exhaustive efforts on behalf of missing and exploited children.

Wilmes, David J. *Parenting for Prevention*. 1995. The Johnson Institute-QVS, Inc.

Index

Index

Page numbers followed by 'n' indicate a footnote. Page numbers in *italics* indicate a table or illustration.

631

CMHS *see* Center for Mental Health Services
cocaine 432–33
code of silence, threat assessment 156
code words, child abduction checklist 346
coercion, described 288
coffin nail (slang) *see* tobacco use
coke (slang) *see* cocaine
collaboration, defined 600
collaborative action steps, described 22–24
"Combating Fear and Restoring Safety in Schools" (DOJ) 123n
commercial on-line service (COS), defined 600
Community Anti-Drug Coalitions of America (CADCA), contact information 618
community involvement
  after-school programs 89, 91–92
  child abuse issues 253–54
  child care 73–74
  drug use prevention 401–2
  gang membership 503–4
  mediation programs 471
  school safety 97
  youth tobacco use 425
community violence, fear-based truancy 132–36
computer access
  Internet safety 511–17
  threat assessment 156
conduct disorder (CD) 544–52
confidentiality, defined 600
conflict, defined 601
conflict resolution
  defined 601
  overview 457–60
confusing touch, defined 601
consensus, defined 601
Consular Assistance, US Department of State, contact information 617
Consumer Product Safety Commission (CPSC), child care safety publication 243n
copilots (slang) *see* amphetamine
coping skills, threat assessment 149
copycat behavior, alcohol use 157

COS *see* commercial online service
cousin sexual abuse, described 295–96
  see also incest; siblings
CPIAP *see* Children's Passport Issuance Alert Program
CPS *see* Child Protective Services
CPSC *see* Consumer Product Safety Commission
crack cocaine 433
crank (slang) *see* methamphetamine
crib safety 246
crime
  defined 601
  reporting likelihood 8–9
criminal background investigations, school personnel 135
Criminal Code (Canada) 263
criminal justice system, child witnesses of crime 18–21
croak (slang) *see* methamphetamine
crypto (slang) *see* methamphetamine
crystal ice (slang) *see* methamphetamine
curtain cord safety 247
custody decrees 351–52
cycle of violence, described 17

D

Dalmane 571
"'Date Rape' Drug (Rohypnol)" (DHHS) 313n
date rape drugs *see* flunitrazepam; gamma hydroxybutyric acid
dating violence
  myths *304–5*
  overview 303–12
  warning signs 307–8
"Dating Violence" (Health Canada) 303n
day care centers, touching *versus* child abuse 257–59
DCAP *see* Dependent Care Assistance Plans
"Dealing with Bullies" (Kraizer) 117n
DeBord, Karen 221n, 581n

gamma hydroxybutyric acid (GHB)
315–16, 432, 447–48
gangs
fear-based truance 127–29
firearm injuries 45–46
overview 497–510
school violence warning signs 105
gangster (slang) *see* marijuana
ganja (slang) *see* marijuana
gender factor
attention deficit hyperactivity disorder 553
bullying 118
child sexual abuse 267
emotional abuse 306
firearm homicides 32–33
homicide statistics 5, 42
maltreatment statistics 10, 13–14
sexual abuse 280, 288, 290–91
suicides 37
Georgia home boy (slang) *see* gamma
hydroxybutyric acid
GHB *see* gamma hydroxybutyric acid
Ginott, Hiam 488
glass (slang) *see* methamphetamine
good touch, defined 601
goodfella (slang) *see* fentanyl
grandparents, childhood drug use
prevention 386–87
grass (slang) *see* marijuana
grievous bodily harm (slang) *see*
gamma hydroxybutyric acid
ground rule, defined 601
"Growing Up Drug-Free" (DOE) 381n,
395n, 427n
"Guidelines to Help Children Who
Have Been Reported for Suspected
Child Abuse and Neglect" (AHA)
199n
guns *see* firearms; weapons
"Guns and Other Weapons" (NCPC)
39n

H

Hague Convention on the Civil Aspects of International Child Abduction 354–61

hallucinogens 435–36, 448
handguns *see* firearms
harassment
coping mechanisms 177–78
described 173, 175–76
hash (slang) *see* marijuana
hashish *see* marijuana
hate crime prevention 479–88
"Hate Hurts: Tips for Teachers/
Parents" (ADL) 479n
hazing, described 176
Health Canada, publications
adolescent sex offenders 287n
child sexual abuse 263n
dating violence 303n
emotional abuse 191n
hearts (slang) *see* amphetamine
"Help Your Kids Get Back to School
Safely" (NHTSA) 159n
"Helping Children and Adolescents
Cope with Violence and Disasters"
(NIMH) 525n
herb (slang) *see* marijuana
herbal ecstasy 431
heroin 433–34
HIPPY *see* Home Instruction Program for Preschool Youngsters
HIV *see* human immunodeficiency virus
home alone time 237–42
Home Instruction Program for Preschool Youngsters (HIPPY), described 75
homework, increased quality 88
homicides
child witnesses 16–17
firearms 29–38
secondary victims 43–44
statistics 124
see also murders
horse (slang) *see* heroin
household chemicals safety 389
"How Does Alcohol Affect the World of
a Child?" (NIAAA) 405n
human immunodeficiency virus (HIV)
dating violence 306
marijuana use 443
hyperactivity, described 554

lady (slang) *see* cocaine
Laney, Ronald 363n
laughing gas (nitrous oxide) 436–37
leakage, described 148–49
legislation
  child abuse issues 254–55
  gun-free school zones 130, 134
  Public Law 94-142 (Education for
    All Handicapped Children Act
    (1975)) 604
Leshner, Alan I. 447n
Librium 571
liquid ecstasy *see* gamma hydroxybutyric acid
love relationships, threat assessment
  149
LSD *see* lysergic acid diethylamide
Luvox 571
lysergic acid diethylamide (LSD)
  435–36, 448

M

MADD *see* Mothers against Drunk
  Driving
magic mushrooms (slang) *see* psilocy-
  bin
"Make a Difference, Talk to Your
  Child about Alcohol" (NIAAA) 405n
"Make a Friend - Be a Peer Mentor"
  (DOJ) 461n
"Making Peace: Tips on Managing
  Conflict" (NCPC) 457n
maltreatment, statistics 9–12, 169–71
mandated reporter, defined 602
manipulative behavior, threat assess-
  ment 152
marijuana
  described 437–38
  overview 439–46
  parental example 391
  statistics 58–59
"Marijuana: Facts Parents Need to
  Know" (NIDA) 439n
Marks, Julie 277n
Martin, Sally S. 207n
Mary Jane (slang) *see* marijuana
Maui wowie (slang) *see* marijuana

MDMA *see* methylenedioxy amphetamine
media violence
  effects 519–24
  threat assessment 157
mediation
  defined 602
  described 469–78
mediator, defined 602–3
medical marijuana 393
  see also marijuana
medical neglect
  described 188
  statistics 170
mental disorders, parental abduction
  369–70
mentoring programs
  described 462–68
  youth delinquency prevention 79
meth (slang) *see* methamphetamine
methamphetamine
  described 448
  overview 429
methylenedioxy amphetamine (Ecstasy) 430, 447–49
methylphenidate 430–31
microdot (slang) *see* lysergic acid diethylamide
Miller, A. K. 57n
mind-erasers (slang) *see*
  flunitrazepam
misbehavior *see* behavior change
missing children
  law enforcement 340–43
  overview 319–29
  parental checklist 331–39
  see also abduction; kidnaping; run-
    aways
mixed-culture marriages 370–73
Mothers against Drunk Driving
  (MADD), contact information 618
movement disorders, conduct disorder 547
mud (slang) *see* heroin
multidisciplinary team, defined 603
murders, juveniles 4–5
  see also homicide
mushrooms *see* psilocybin
music videos, influence 524